India: Monetary Policy, Financial Stability and Other Essays

Dr. Chakravarthi Rangarajan, a distinguished economist, has been a cerebral policy maker of India who brought to bear not only deep scholarship but lateral thinking on the formulation of public policy. He is presently a member of the Rajya Sabha, the upper house of Indian parliament.

Dr. Rangarajan has held several important positions in the Government. He was Chairman-Economic Advisory Council to the Prime Minister (2004-2008) and headed the Twelfth Finance Commission (2003-04) which paved the way for fiscal consoli-dation. He was Governor, Andhra Pradesh (1997-2003) and Governor, Reserve Bank of India (1992-1997).

As Governor RBI, Dr. Rangarajan gave a major thrust to financial sector reforms. The institutional environment was altered to make monetary policy a more effective instrument of economic policy. The exchange rate regime underwent a fundamental change.

He was member of the Planning Commission during 1991-92. Prior to that, he held the position of Deputy Governor, Reserve Bank of India, for almost a decade. During this period, he was instrumental in bringing about a number of changes in the credit and financial system, both in terms of induction of new instru-ments and new institutions. Dr. Rangarajan has taught at the Wharton School of Finance and Commerce, University of Pennsylvania and the Graduate School of Business Administration, New York University. In India, he has taught at Loyola College, Madras; Indian Statistical Institute, New Delhi and for well over a decade and a half at the Indian Institute of Management, Ahmedabad.

He is the author or co-author of the following books: *Short-term Investment Forecasting* (1974); *Principles of Macroeconomics* (1979); *Strategy for Industrial Development in the '80s* (1981); *Innovations in Banking* (1982); *Indian Economy: Essays on Money and Finance* (1998); *Perspectives on Indian Economy* (2000); *Structural Reforms in Industry, Banking and Finance* (2000) and *Select Essays on Indian Economy* (2 vols., 2004).

Among the several awards received by him are: Business Man of the Year 1997 (Madras Management Association); Honorary Fellow, Indian Institute of Management, Ahmedabad 1997; Award of Excellence in Finance (Bank of India) 1998; Finance Man of the Decade (Bombay Management Association) 1998; Financial Express Award for Economics 1998; Wharton-Indian Alumni Award for Outstanding Leadership (2002).

Dr. Rangarajan was awarded the Padma Vibhushan, the second highest civilian honour, by the President of India in January 2002.

India: Monetary Policy, Financial Stability and Other Essays

C. Rangarajan

ACADEMIC FOUNDATION

NEW DELHI

First published in 2009
by

ACADEMIC FOUNDATION
4772-73 / 23 Bharat Ram Road, (23 Ansari Road),
Darya Ganj, New Delhi - 110 002 (India).
Phones : 23245001 / 02 / 03 / 04.
Fax : +91-11-23245005.
E-mail : books@academicfoundation.com
www. academicfoundation.com

© 2009 Copyright: Academic Foundation

ALL RIGHTS RESERVED.
No part of this book shall be reproduced, stored in a retrieval system, or transmitted by any means, electronic, mechanical, photocopying, recording, or otherwise, without the prior written permission of the publishers.

Cataloging in Publication Data--DK
 Courtesy: D.K. Agencies (P) Ltd. <docinfo@dkagencies.com>

Rangarajan, C. (Chakravarthy), 1932-
 India : monetary policy, financial stability and other essays /
C. Rangarajan.
   p.   cm.
   ISBN 13: 9788171887354
   ISBN 10: 817188735X

 1. Monetary policy--India. 2. Finance--India. 3. Fiscal policy--India. 4. Economic stabilization--India. 5. Economic development--India. 6. Globalization--Economic aspects--India. 7. India--Economic policy--1991-   I. Title.

DDC 332.4954   22

Typeset by Italics India, New Delhi.
Printed and bound in India.

Contents

Introduction 11

Part I: Monetary Policy and Fiscal Issues

1. Challenges for Monetary Policy 31
    Historical Evolution
    Issue of Concern
       *Objective; Transmission Mechanism; Intermediate Target;
       Level of Interest Rate; Exchange Rate Management;
       Financial Stability; Autonomy of Central Banks*
    Conclusion

2. Financial Stability: Some Analytical Issues 61
    Defining Financial Stability
    Instability Bias
    Regulating Institutions and Markets
    Components of Regulation
    Regulating Payment and Settlement Systems
    Macroeconomic Stability
    Crisis Prevention and Crisis Management
    Monetary Policy and Financial Stability

3. The Importance of being Earnest about Fiscal Responsibility ... 85
    Fiscal Responsibility—The Debate
    Post-Reform Trends in Deficits
    Impact of Deficits on Economic Prospects
    Fiscal Adjustment—The Contrarian View
    In Defence of Fiscal Adjustment
    Targeting Deficits—Some Issues
    Conclusion

4. Dynamics of Debt Accumulation in India:
   Impact of Primary Deficit, Growth and Interest Rate 99
   Introduction
   Decomposing Accumulation of Debt
   Some Data Preliminaries
   Accumulation of Central Debt
   Profiles of Growth and Interest Rates
   Accumulation of Primary Deficit
   Summary and Medium-Term Prospects

5. Fiscal Federalism: Some Current Concerns 123
   Federalism—As a Form of Government
   Fiscal Federalism
   Fiscal Transfers
   Competitive and Cooperative Federalism

6. Issues Before the Twelfth Finance Commission 133
   Fiscal Trends
   Sustainability Issues
   Design of Fiscal Transfers
   Vertical Dimension
   Horizontal Dimension
   Restructuring Issues

7. Twelfth Finance Commission Report:
   Approach and Recommendations 155
   Vertical Transfers
   Horizontal Transfers
   Role of Grants
   Debt Restructuring
   Institutional Changes
   Restructuring Public Finance

Part II: Growth and Development

8. Indian Economy: Challenges and Opportunities 163
   Challenges Ahead
   1991 Reforms—Genesis
   Economic Reforms—Break with the Past
   Rationale Underlying Reforms
   Stabilisation and Structural Adjustment
   Uniqueness of India's Reforms

Post-Reform Growth Performance
Six Challenges on the Way Forward
Technology
Sustaining the High Growth
Conclusion

9. Economic Growth and Social Development 175
   Evolution of Thinking on Growth
   Performance of the Indian Economy
   Interaction between Growth and Human Development
   Efficiency in Expenditures
   Conclusion

10. Economic Growth and Issues of Governance 185
    What is Good Governance?
    Nexus between Good Governance and Economic Development
    State and Market
    Role of the Government
    Good Governance—Characteristics
    Conclusion

11. Employment and Growth 197
    Employment and Unemployment Scenario
    Sectoral Distribution of Employment
    Occupational Status of Workforce
    Elasticity of Employment
    Employment Projections
    Conclusion

12. Rural Employment Guarantee Scheme: Physical
    and Financial Planning 215
    Physical and Financial Planning
    Delivery Systems and Capacity Building
    Asset Creation
    Monitoring and Experience Sharing
    Conclusion

13. State, Market and the Economy: The Shifting Frontiers 225
    Developments in the Literature
    Government Intervention and Planning
    Historical Experiences: East Asia, Russia and India
    Conclusion

14. National Statistical Commission: An Overview
of the Recommendations 241
    Approach of the Report
    Administration of Indian Statistical System
    Agricultural Statistics
    Industrial Statistics
    Services Sector Statistics
    Infrastructure Statistics
    Socio-Economic Statistics
    Financial and External Sector Statistics
    Price Statistics
    Corporate Sector Statistics
    National Accounts Statistics
    Conclusion

Part III: Sectoral Issues: Industry, Power, Banking and Agriculture

15. Paradigm Shifts in Industrial Policy 273
    Introduction
    Pre-Reform Industrialisation Paradigm
    New Economic Policy
    Trends in Industrial Production
    New Challenges
    Technology Intensity
    Road Map for Indian Industry

16. Banking Sector Reforms in India 295
    Banking in the Pre-Reform Period
    Contours of Reforms
    Processes of Reform
    Way Ahead

17. Financial Inclusion: Some Key Issues 307
    Nature of Inclusion
    Extent of Exclusion
    Institutional Changes
    Commercial Banks
    Regional Rural Banks
    Role of Technology
    Micro Financial Institutions
    National Rural Financial Inclusion Plan

18. Agricultural Credit: Reaching the Marginalised Farmers 317
    Banking Reforms and their Impact
    Credit to Agriculture
    Credit to Marginal Farmers
    Strategy for Enhanced Credit to Marginal Farmers

19. Regulation of Tariffs in the Power Sector 327
    Elements in the Power Reform Process
    Role of Regulatory Commissions
    Tariff Fixation
    Price Discrimination
    Tariffs and Competition
    Other Issues
    Conclusion

20. The Widening Scope of Insurance 333
    What is Insurance?
    Insurance and Growth
    Assessment of Risks
    Regulatory Framework
    Conclusion

21. Reforming the Pension System 339
    Demographic Changes
    Existing Coverage of Pensions
    Issues in Pension Reform

Part IV: External Sector and Globalisation

22. Globalisation and its Impact 345
    Introduction
    Historical Development
    Gains and Losses from Globalisation
    Concerns and Fears
    India and the External Sector
    Framework of Policy
    Conclusion

23. Global Imbalances and Policy Responses 367
    Introduction
    Is it a Cause for Concern?
    Status of Global Imbalances
    Factors behind the Current Account Deficit of the US

      Redressing Global Imbalances
      Fiscal Policy
      Monetary Policy
      Expanding Domestic Demand Outside the US
      Exchange Rate Policies
      Indian Response
      Conclusion

24. **Nature and Impact of Capital Flows** 385
      Capital Flows: Magnitude and Composition
      East Asian Crisis
      Forms of Capital Controls
      The Indian Experience

25. **The Financial Crisis and its Fallout** 405
      Evolution of the Crisis
      Regulatory Failure
      Immediate Tasks
      Medium Term Concerns
      Impact on India
      Monetary and Fiscal Actions

Index *411*

Introduction

This is a collection of essays written over different points in time during the last five years. These essays do not focus on a single theme; they cover a wide range. Nevertheless, it is hoped that each essay has sufficient meat to hold the interest of the readers. In this introduction, I pick up a few select essays and make some comments on them.

The opening essay which is on monetary policy touches on issues such as objectives, intermediate targets, role of interest rate, links with exchange rate management and financial stability. Among the objectives of monetary policy, price stability has to remain the dominant one. The 'assignment rule' in policy analysis favours monetary policy as the most appropriate instrument to achieve the objective of price stability. At the same time, concerns relating to growth cannot be ignored. Thus, the relative emphasis as between the two objectives changes depending on the conditions prevailing in a particular year. This is a version of Taylor's rule in a loose form. One way of reconciling the twin objectives of price stability and economic growth in the short run is by estimating the threshold level of inflation. If the actual inflation runs above the threshold level, price stability becomes the more dominant objective. Below and around this threshold, there is greater manoeuverability for the policy makers to take into account other considerations. The issue of 'inflation targeting' is not directly alluded to in the essay. Whether or not a target rate for inflation is specified, it goes without saying that the dominant objective of monetary policy has to be the control of inflation and maintenance of price stability.

In India, until recently, money supply has been the intermediate target variable. An objective such as price stability was sought to be achieved by bringing about changes in money supply. The institutional environment in which the Indian monetary policy operates has undergone significant changes since the early 1990s. With the dismantling of the administered interest rate structure, induction of new instruments and the creation of new financial markets, interest rate is also becoming an appropriate intermediate variable. Perhaps, one lesson that can be drawn from our experiences is that while money supply may be an appropriate intermediate target when inflation rate remains high, interest rate may be a more appropriate target when inflation is moderate and fluctuates within a narrow range.

With the deepening of the financial structure, financial stability has also become a major concern of all central banks including the Reserve Bank of India. Normally price stability should provide an environment favourable for financial stability. However, there can be occasions—as the recent global experience has shown—when dealing directly with financial stability becomes necessary. While maintenance of financial stability is in the long-run interest of economic stability, it should not lead to excessive compromise with the objective of price stability.

The second essay deals with various aspects of 'financial stability'.

Serious financial crises that have gripped several countries in the last two decades have brought to the fore the issue of financial stability. The key element of a financial crisis is the disruption that is caused to the financial system and the consequent loss in real output. Stability applies to both institutions and markets. A question that is being increasingly asked is whether the financial sector today is inherently more volatile and vulnerable than before. Close inter-dependencies among markets and market participants have increased the potential for contagion. The approach to regulating financial markets as distinct from institutions has been somewhat unclear and ambiguous.

Regulations are aimed at ensuring the "soundness and safety" of the financial system. The oversight over financial institutions has three components: (i) setting standards, (ii) assessing risk and internal controls, and (iii) supervision. Each of these elements has several sub-components. The capital adequacy ratio has emerged as a major instrument of financial regulation. Despite its widespread adoption, this indicator is not without its shortcomings. There is now a greater emphasis on the assessment of risk and Basel-II seeks to encourage banks to go for a balanced portfolio and reduce the overall risk exposure. An important development in the supervisory system is the move from an inspection which is transaction based to a framework that emphasises the implementation of effective risk management systems. An "incentive-compatible" financial regulation is also being contemplated to use market forces to supplement the regulatory system. Another improvement in the supervisory process has been the introduction of macro prudential indicators to assess the vulnerability of the financial system.

With the emergence of financial institutions providing multiple services, the issue of single *versus* multiple regulators has assumed importance. The disadvantage of a single authority is that it becomes unwieldy because of the enormity of the work involved. Effective supervision of the various components may become difficult. Such a system can function efficiently only in countries where the various individual regulatory authorities had already achieved certain levels of maturity in terms of supervision. As recent experience has shown, neither a single authority nor multiple regulators is proof against failure of individual institutions.

The paper "Importance of Being Earnest about Fiscal Responsibility" (ch.3) emphasises the need for staying within the discipline imposed by the Fiscal Responsibility and Budget Management Act. High fiscal deficits disempower the government's fiscal stance by pre-empting a larger share of the public resources for debt servicing thereby leaving with much less for desirable developmental expenditures. This also leads to a decline in the ratio of capital expenditures to total expenditures. The paper also provides a rationale for prescribing a fiscal deficit target of 3 per cent for the Centre and 3 per cent for all the States taken together. The combined fiscal deficit of 6 per cent of GDP will be consistent with the existing ratio of savings of the household sector in financial assets relative to GDP and with prudent levels of current account deficit and the demand on those financial savings by the private corporate sector and public enterprises. Remaining committed to fiscal responsibility will only go to strengthen the growth momentum.

The essay on "Dynamics of Debt Accumulation in India" (ch. 4) looks at the factors contributing to the accumulation of debt. Accumulation of debt can be seen as the resultant of two factors, accumulated primary deficits and accumulated weighted excess of growth rate over interest rate. Decomposing the changes in the Central government's liabilities relative to GDP since 1951-52, it is seen that except for some recent years, the accretion to debt relative to GDP was principally due to the accumulated primary deficits. A significant part of the effect of the accumulated primary deficits was offset in the sixties, seventies and nineties by the excess of growth rate over interest rate. The excess of growth rate over interest rate is a cushion that may not be available always. For the stabilisation of the debt-GDP ratio at current or reduced levels, the focus on primary balance becomes necessary.

There are three essays that deal with fiscal federalism. Chapter 5 "Fiscal Federalism: Some Current Concerns" discusses the concerns that have arisen in the context of the two contrary pulls of globalisation and decentralisation. Recognising the existence of imbalance between resources and responsibilities at various levels of government, many countries have a system of intergovernmental transfers. In fact, intergovernmental transfers constitute a distinct economic policy instrument in fiscal federalism. Correcting the vertical and horizontal imbalances has been a major concern in fiscal federalism. While the mainstream literature on federalism assumes different units of the government have essentially a cooperative relationship, a key feature of the literature on competitive federalism is the existence of a competitive relationship among sub-national units. It is being argued that jurisdictional competition can lead to increase in efficiency. The extent and areas in which various levels of government in a country function in a competitive manner will largely be determined by the nature of the government structures. "Voting by feet" which means migration of people from one jurisdiction to another in search of a better mix of policies may not necessarily happen in all countries.

The other two papers on fiscal federalism (ch. 6 and ch. 7) deal with the issues which came up before the Twelfth Finance Commission and the conclusions and the recommendations made by that Commission. The main function of a Finance Commission is to correct the vertical and horizontal imbalances. Determination of the vertical imbalance is partly a matter of judgement. However, it should be always possible to move from a historical base and assess whether or not the vertical imbalance has increased or decreased. The considerations that should go in determining the distribution among the states of the resources to be transferred from the Centre have been examined in great length by various Finance Commissions. Equity issues have dominated the discussions, as they should. In designing a suitable scheme of fiscal transfers, three considerations are seen to be relevant—needs, cost disability and fiscal efficiency. A good transfer system must establish an appropriate balance between equity and efficiency—a system in which fiscal disadvantage is taken care of but fiscal imprudence is effectively discouraged. The Twelfth Finance Commission recommended a scheme of fiscal transfers that could serve the objectives of equity and efficiency within a framework of fiscal consolidation. The Twelfth Finance Commission made a departure from the previous Commissions in two or three aspects. First, it increased the proportion of grants to tax devolution in the scheme of transfers. The recommended grants constituted around 19 per cent of the total transfers. Second, the Commission applied the equalisation principle to the expenditure side and recommended special grants for health and education to states whose per capita expenditures under these heads were below the national average. Third, the Commission proposed a scheme of debt restructuring which imposed a hard budget constraint on the states while, at the same time, providing them relief both with respect to interest and repayment of debt.

The first essay in Part II (ch. 8) critically examines the challenges before the Indian economy. 1991 is an important landmark in the post-Independence economic history. This was the year in which the economy was faced with a severe economic crisis triggered in part by an acute balance of payments problem. Fortunately, the crisis was converted into an opportunity to bring about some fundamental changes in the approach and content of our economic policies. We do the reform process a disservice by treating it as a continuation of the earlier period. There was a break with the past in three important directions. The first was to dismantle the complex regime of licences, permits and controls that dictated almost every facet of production and distribution. The second change in direction was to reverse the strong bias towards State ownership particularly in the production of marketable goods and services. The third change in direction was to abandon the inward looking trade policies. By embracing international trade, India was getting more closely integrated with the global economy.

There is a common thread running through the various measures introduced since 1990-91. It was to improve the productivity and efficiency of the system by injecting a greater element of competition. The New Economic Policy has not necessarily diminished the role of the government. In some areas it has widened the role of the government and in some others it has diminished its role. As has been paradoxically remarked, "more market does not mean less government but different governments". That the content and process of our economic reforms are on the right track is indicated by the performance of the economy since the launch of the reforms. While recognising the good performance of the Indian economy in the recent years, the paper mentions six important challenges warranting priority attention. These are: (1) stepping up agricultural growth, (2) infrastructure development, (3) fiscal consolidation, (4) building social infrastructure, (5) managing globalisation, and (6) good governance. The article discusses the implications of these challenges and what needs to be done to meet the challenges. In terms of sustaining high growth over the medium term, the essay recognises that some of the macro-economic parameters are in the right direction. In terms of savings and investment rates the conditions for achieving a growth rate of 9 per cent are already there.

The Indian economy has undergone some rapid changes in the last 15 months. Towards the end of 2006 and in the early months of 2007, a frequently asked question was "Is the Indian economy overheating?" Inflation was on the rise and the trade deficit was widening. These were interpreted as the signs of overheating. However, these signs abated and the inflation situation remained benign throughout the rest of 2007. At one point, inflation had touched as low a level as 3 per cent. There has, however, been a reversal of the situation since the beginning of 2008. Since the first quarter of 2008 inflation has been rising steadily. With the recent hike in domestic oil prices, inflation has crossed 12.0 per cent. In this context, the questions currently being asked are "When will this inflation abate? Will the continuance of inflation affect economic growth?" The rise in inflation is due both to domestic and international factors. Globally, prices in general and more particularly oil and food prices have been rising. Domestically, there has been a significant expansion of money supply in recent years. For the past three years and more, money supply has been growing at an annual rate exceeding 20 per cent and this has injected significant liquidity into the system. At the same time, there have been supply side bottlenecks in relation to certain commodities. There are, however, some favourable factors in sight. The procurement of wheat this year has been good. It has touched a record figure of 22 million tonnes. There are indications that the monsoon will be a normal one this year. These factors should contribute to moderating inflationary expectations. As mentioned earlier, prices rose modestly during April-December 2007. Therefore, the base effect will be to highten the inflation in the current year. If the monsoon is good, it will dampen inflationary expectations. It is also hoped that oil prices internationally will stabilise around the current level. Under these circumstances, we can hope to see inflation come down to around 10 per cent by the end of December 2008. Thereafter, however, because of the base effect inflation could go down further. The Economic Advisory Council had originally projected a growth of 8.5 per cent for 2008-2009 in January. Given the domestic and international factors it may be reasonable to expect the growth rate to remain around 7.5 per cent in 2008-09. This will be as a consequence of a moderation in the growth rates of agriculture, manufacturing and services as compared to the previous year. All in all, growth in the current year will show distinct signs of moderation.

The second essay in Part II (ch. 9) discusses the interrelationship between economic growth and social development. At a fundamental level, there is no conflict between economic growth and social or human development. Economic growth implies improvement in the material wellbeing of the people which necessarily includes better health, education and sanitation. While it is true that nutrition, health and education can and should be treated as ends in themselves, there is no assurance that improved health and education will automatically result in higher economic growth. They only create conditions under which growth in the sense of rise in national income can be accelerated. However, enhanced human development expenditures cannot be sustained over a long period unless supported by accelerated economic growth. When there is a dichotomy between human development indicators and economic development, it can be a source of social tension. For example, as education spreads, the economy must have the ability to productively absorb the growing number of educated. Economic growth and social development must move in tandem so as to reap the synergic effects of the two moving together. We need, therefore, to stress simultaneously on economic development in the conventional sense of accelerating growth rate and social development in the sense of securing for everyone the basic needs. The two have a mutually interacting beneficial impact and the two must be pursued together. These are the two legs on which the country must walk. Any strategy of development which ignores any one of the two legs will only make the country limp along.

The paper "Economic Growth and Issues of Governance" (ch. 10) deals with different dimensions of good governance and the steps required to be taken to achieve a system of administration, that is, clean, transparent and accountable. That good governance is the very heart of economic growth and poverty reduction, and even political legitimacy is now a part of conventional wisdom. In the ultimate analysis it is the quality of governance that separates success and failures in economic development. The three essential components of good governance are: (1) rule of law, (2) accountability for action and results, and (3) elimination of corruption. There is a close link between rule of law and economic development. A clean law and order situation, free of extortion and violence is a basic requirement of economic growth. The government is the trustee of public resources and is responsible for using them for maximising collective welfare. This requires that there are institutional mechanisms not only for determining how the resources are allocated but also for demanding accountability for results. Increasingly the trend is towards accountability in terms of standards of performance and service delivery of public agencies to citizens. Concern about corruption is as old as the history of government. Corruption, broadly defined, is an abuse of public office for private gains. The negative consequences of corruption are well known. Corruption impedes growth, inhibits potential investment, increases inefficiency and breeds vested interests. A two-fold strategy is needed to contain corruption. First, opportunities for corruption must be reduced. This can happen as the economic reforms are carried forward and all forms of controls which result in rent-seeking opportunities are reduced. Second, the government agencies charged with combating corruption must show determination in identifying corrupt officials and public personalities and getting them convicted. Above all the public must show in a decisive way their disapproval and displeasure of people who are corrupt.

The paper "Employment and Growth" (ch. 11) contrasts the findings of the 55th and 61st Rounds of NSS on the employment scene. The results of the 55th Round led to major concerns about the slow growth in employment and the phenomenon came to be widely described as "jobless growth". There was scepticism on the ability of economic growth to tackle the problem of employment. As per the 61st Round, the employment scenario has undergone big changes. Employment in the period 1999-2000 to 2004-05 has increased at an annual rate of 2.89 per cent. This is in sharp contrast to the annual growth rate of 0.98 per cent in the period 1993-94 to 1999-2000. Along with the sharp increase in employment during the later period, the labour force has also increased dramatically. The employment elasticity with respect to growth for the later period is 0.48. A simple projection shows that even after adjusting the sectoral elasticities to low figures, with a GDP growth rate of 9 per cent, very soon the workforce will become equal to labour force. Growth, it appears, is a major driving force in achieving higher levels of employment. Available data also show that bulk of the increase in employment has happened in the informal sector and agriculture. This trend is a cause for concern, as relatively low wages and lack of social security characterise these sectors. In other words, the congruence of the labour force and workforce by itself does not guarantee elimination of poverty. The new challenge is one of improving the total factor productivity in the informal sector and in agriculture so that there is a significant improvement in emoluments of those who are employed, that is, in the quality of employment.

Among the issues of pubic policies, the one that has attracted the widest attention has been the issue of State *versus* market in economic development. The issue has once again assumed importance in the context of economic reforms and structural adjustment that are currently underway in many countries. The paper "State, Market and Economy" (ch. 13) addresses the evolution of thinking in the economic literature on the respective roles of State and market. It also provides the historical experience. In any economic system State can play three important roles. They are: (1) as a producer of marketable goods and services, (2) a regulator of the system, and (3) as a supplier of 'public goods' or 'merit goods'. Countries, in general, are moving away from the role of State as a producer of marketable goods and services. The decreasing role of State in this area and the simultaneous increasing role of market have enhanced the role of State as a 'regulator'. It is said that "State should not row but steer." Even while recognising the role of State in the provision of 'public goods' the exact modality of intervention in discharging this function can vary from country to country. The serious question which policy makers should address is not one of either State or market, but one of how much State intervention, what kind and by what means. "Mixed economy" is a reality. The crucial factor for determining the mix is that of comparative efficiency. It is necessary to create a matrix of activities and interventions and determine for each activity what form of intervention is best. With limited resources government should reallocate resources more to areas where it has a comparative advantage over the market and vacate those where it has less advantage. The ultimate test is not ideology but what works best under a given set of circumstances.

Part II also includes a paper on recommendations of the National Statistical Commission of which the author was the Chairman (ch. 14). The Indian statistical system has over the years built an elaborate statistical infrastructure to capture a wide variety of data generated by a very large and decentralised economy. However, due to over dependence on the administrative set up and traditional records, the system has not been able to keep pace with the demands of statistical requirements of a fast growing economy. The process of development has also brought out significant structural changes in the economy which need to be captured by the statistical system. While the scientific basis for the generation of data and methodologies adopted may not be in question, in many cases what has brought out a decline in the quality and reliability of the statistics generated by the system is the inability of the present system or procedure of collecting data to meet the quality standards. Adequacy, credibility and timeliness of the data are the hallmarks of a good statistical system. The National Statistical Commission after analysing the deficiencies of the Indian statistical system made several recommendations to revamp the statistical system. Specific recommendations have been made with respect to each type of statistics. The Commission also proposed setting up of a National Commission on Statistics as a nodal policy-making and supervisory non-official body which could oversee the collection of statistics in our country. Such a body would help not only in ensuring coordination but also in improving the quality standards. This recommendation has been implemented with the appointment of a National Statistical Commission in 2007.

The first essay in Part III, "Paradigm Shifts in Industrial Policy" (ch. 15) traces the evolution of industrial policy in India. The process of industrialisation in India in the first four decades after Independence was governed by two considerations—import substitution and industrial licensing. With the advent of the New Economic Policy, the industrial policy paradigm underwent a fundamental change. As mentioned earlier, the thrust of the new economic policy has been towards creating a more competitive environment in the economy as a means to improving the productivity and efficiency in the system. While the changes in the industrial policy sought to bring about a greater competitive environment domestically, changes in foreign trade policy sought to improve the international competitiveness subject to the degree of protection offered by the tariffs. The paper outlines the changes in the industrial production since the introduction of reforms. Looking ahead, the three areas which will need attention will be: (1) globalisation and competition, (2) productivity growth, and (3) technology intensity. The primary focus has to be on the strategy and quality of microeconomic business management and the goal must be to reach higher levels of efficiency and productivity. In addition, technology is the life blood of industry. Future progress will be propelled by technology, as it has been so in the past. What is needed today is a road map for Indian industries. It must delineate the path different industries must take to achieve productivity and efficiency levels comparable to the best in the world. The goal must be how through a combination of technology modernisation and changes in organisational structure which promote productivity, Indian industry can compete effectively in the world market.

The second essay in Part III (ch. 16) touches on banking reform. After describing the banking scenario in the pre-reform period, it points out the various steps taken to modernise the Indian banking system and to ensure its soundness and safety. On the way ahead, the paper deals with four issues: (1) consolidation, (2) capital adequacy, (3) risk management, and (4) customer service. The process of consolidation must come out of the felt need for merger rather than as an imposition from outside. The synergic benefits must be felt by the entities themselves. With the rapid growth of the economy, there is need for injection of equity in the state owned banks to enable them to meet better the growing needs for credit. In this situation the government will have to make up its mind either to bring in additional capital or move towards reducing its share from 51 per cent through appropriate statutory changes. The third alternative could however, be to include in the definition of government such entities as the Life Insurance Corporation which are quasi-government in nature and are likely to remain an integral part of the government system. However, even for this, a statutory amendment is needed.

The paper on "Financial Inclusion" (ch. 17) elaborates on the role that the various institutions which provide micro finance can play in bringing about greater inclusion. Financial inclusion denotes delivery of credit and other financial services at an affordable cost to the disadvantaged and low income groups. Financial inclusion represents a process of bringing within the ambit of institutional finance the vulnerable groups. The data provided by NSSO on financial exclusion are very telling. Nearly 51.4 per cent of the former households in the country do not have access to credit either from institutional or non-institutional sources. Further despite the vast network of bank branches only 27 per cent of the farmer households have access to formal sources. In order that financial inclusion becomes effective, we need to address the issues on the supply side as well as demand side. Even as the credit delivery system is improved, the absorbing capacity of the borrowers has also to be increased. The suggestions made in the paper regarding commercial banks include a change in the attitude of rural bank officers, opening of more branches in inadequately banked areas, simplification of the procedures in relation to granting of loans and provision of advice by branches to the borrowers on various aspects of agriculture. The paper speaks on the need to take further SHG-bank linkage scheme which has proved to be extremely successful. The paper also recommends formation of federations of SHGs but points out that these federations should act as facilitators rather than as financial intermediates. One other recommendation is the promotion of joint liability groups to help marginal farmers and tenant farmers. Most importantly, the paper suggests effective implementation of the scheme of business facilitators and correspondents. Recognising the important role that RRBs play in the rural and suburban areas the paper argues for the strengthening of RRBs. The paper also recommends that RBI may recognise a separate category of micro finance—non-banking finance companies. Following the recommendation of the Committee on Financial Inclusion, the paper emphasises the need for launching a National Rural Financial Inclusion Plan which would mandate a minimum target of covering of 250 new households per branch per annum. This would bring at least 50 per cent of financial excluded households within the ambit of the banking system by 2012. The paper concludes: "The goal of making a significant progress towards financial inclusion seems to be attainable. Financial inclusion is no longer an option but a compulsion."

The paper "Agriculture Credit—Reaching the Marginalised Farmers" (ch. 18) focuses on how far the organised financial system has been able to meet the credit needs and requirements of small and marginal farmers. Contrary to the general impression, even in relation to agricultural credit a number of initiatives were taken in the post-liberalisation period. The period since 1991-92 has also seen a fairly rapid expansion of credit to agriculture. The flow of credit to agriculture by commercial banks and the regional rural banks taken together during the period 1991-92 to 2003-04 increased at a compound annual growth rate of 22.2 per cent. Despite this, it has fallen short of expectations. The recent NSS data clearly point to several deficiencies in the flow of credit to agriculture. The deficiencies are even more striking in relation to the availability of credit to small and marginal farmers. In evolving a strategy for an enhanced flow of credit to marginal farmers, the paper emphasises that rural branches must go beyond providing credit and extend a helping hand in terms of advice on a wide variety of matters relating to agriculture. The paper also stresses on the need to strengthen the SHG-bank linkage schemes as an effective means of providing micro finance. The paper concludes: "Credit has to be an integral part of an overall programme aiming at improving the productivity and income of such farmers. Putting in place an appropriate credit delivery system to meet the needs of marginal and sub-marginal farmers must go hand-in-hand with others to improve the productivity of such farm households. It is this integrated approach which would provide the solution to the problems of these farm households."

The term "globalisation" is generally used to describe a wide range of things and, in the process, there is no consensus on what it specifically means, even though it has, over time, become an expression of common usage. The first essay in Part IV, "Globalisation and its Impact" (ch. 22) examines the various concerns raised in the context of globalisation.

Broadly put, globalisation means the integration of economies and societies through cross country flows of information, ideas, technologies, goods, services, capital, finance and people. The essence is connectivity and cross-border integration and goes beyond the economic dimension to include the cultural, social and political. In this article, however, the term has been restricted to denote economic integration which can happen through the channels of trade in goods and services, movement of capital and flow of finance. Besides, there is also the channel through the movement of people. Historically, globalisation has been a process with highs and lows and during 1870 to 1914, there was a rapid integration of the economies in terms of trade flows, movement of capital and migration of people. Empirical evidence shows that capital markets are no more globalised today than they were at the end of the nineteenth century.

Today, the concerns are primarily regarding the nature and speed of transformation and the enormous impact of new information technologies on market integration, efficiency and industrial organisation. These go together with two major concerns: one, that globalisation leads to a more iniquitous distribution of income among countries and within countries; and two, that globalisation leads to loss of national sovereignty and imposes constraints on the pursuit of independent domestic policies. Empirical evidence on the impact of globalisation on inequality is not clear. In aggregate world exports, the share of developing countries increased from 20.6 per cent in 1988-1990 to 29.9 per cent in 2000. Similarly, the share of developing countries in aggregate world output has increased from 17.9 per cent in 1988-1990 to 40.4 per cent in 2000. However, what is essentially required is a balancing mechanism to ensure that the handicaps of the developing countries are overcome. And, while globalisation may accelerate the process of technology substitution in developing economies, these countries, even without globalisation will face the problem associated with moving from lower to higher technology. If the growth rate of the economy accelerates sufficiently, part of the resources can be directed by the state to re-equip people who may have been affected adversely by the process of technology upgradation. On the second concern, as nations come together whether it be in the political, social or economic arena, some sacrifice of sovereignty is inevitable, but it need not necessarily result in the abdication of domestic objectives.

What should be India's attitude in this ambience of growing globalisation? Opting out of the process of globalisation is not a viable choice. What is needed is to evolve a framework to wrest maximum benefits out of international trade and investment. This should include (a) making a list of explicit demands that India would like to make on the multilateral trade system; (b) measures that the developed countries should undertake to enable developing countries to gain more from international trade; and (c) steps that India should take to realise the full potential from globalisation. We must voice our concerns and in cooperation with other developing countries modify the international trading arrangements to take care of the special needs of developing countries. At the same time, we must identify and strengthen our comparative advantages. It is this two-fold approach which will enable us to meet the challenges of globalisation which may be the defining characteristic of the new millennium.

The paper "Global Imbalances and Policy Responses" (ch. 23) focuses on the need for an orderly unwinding of the global imbalances. The current account deficit of the USA has risen to unprecedented levels matched by the surpluses of some of its trading partners. Is the large global imbalance a cause for concern? The persistence of the global imbalance over so many years is seen by some as a natural corollary of a world economy that has been running on a single engine, namely the US economy. Some have speculated that even if the US current account deficit reaches 8-10 per cent of GDP, the situation will nevertheless be sustainable. On the other hand, a weighty body of opinion has taken the view that the current account imbalance is indeed very large and not sustainable over any significant length of time. Policy options to encourage gradual unwinding is infinitely preferable to the disorderly unwinding that is perhaps inevitable in the medium term. The consequences of the disorderly unwinding—on exchange rates and interest rates—that would follow would be unpleasant not only for the US but also for most of developing Asia.

This paper argues for the need to adopt policies that can create conditions for the imbalance to reduce over time and the need for global coordination. But the patterns of current account are not homogeneous across nations and hence, the incentive for common action is not strong. Even if there is a broad agreement on the strategy for an orderly unwinding, the response by different countries is likely to be uneven in view of domestic considerations. Thus though the process of orderly unwinding may be necessarily slow, a greater recognition of the need for such coordination will be helpful.

The 1990s, which is the focus of the paper "Nature and Impact of Capital Flows" (ch. 24), witnessed large private capital flows to emerging markets. Some countries have gained immensely by capital inflows which have helped them to grow faster. It should not be forgotten that the five countries caught in the East Asian crisis had benefited greatly for almost a decade by large capital inflows. At the peak, net private capital inflows accounted for as much as 17.4 per cent of the GDP in Malaysia in 1993 and 12.5 per cent of the GDP in Thailand in 1995. While foreign direct investment has remained steady, portfolio investment and banking inflows have fluctuated. In the East Asian situation, even after the advent of the crisis, direct investment and portfolio investment remained positive. It was only banking flows which turned negative.

Opening up of capital account need not preclude the imposition of moderate controls, either price-based or regulatory, on capital flows. Controls should be selective, designed to achieve the specific objective of containing speculative flows. Controls should not be disruptive or dislocate genuine trade related activities. The Asian crisis is not an argument against capital account liberalisation. Capital account liberalisation is not a discrete event and it is a process which should be done in stages. The scope for raising resources abroad and investing can be steadily expanded. An important lesson to draw from the events in Asia and elsewhere is that capital account liberalisation and reform of the financial system should move in tandem. The Indian system already operates with a number of capital controls. If anything, we should move towards a more liberalised regime, even as the regulatory system of the financial sector keeps improving. India as a country must take full advantage of the global changes in capital flows and attract not only more but also high quality investment which has strong links to the domestic economy, export orientation and advanced technology.

The last essay included in this volume deals with the international financial crisis and its fallout. The New Year has opened on a sombre mood with the world passing through a difficult time. The developed world is hit the hardest. The industrially advanced countries are now officially in recession having had two consecutive quarters of negative growth. The impact of the financial crisis is now being felt by the developing economies as well. Growth is slowing down in these countries including India. Globalisation spreads both prosperity and distress.

What stands out glaringly in the current episode is the regulatory failure. Regulation was soft and unfocussed on segments of the market which should have been closely regulated. This also led to "regulatory arbitrage" with funds moving more towards unregulated segments. The other failure is the imperfect understanding of the implications of the various derivative products. Quite clearly, there was a mismatch between financial innovation and the ability of the regulators to monitor them.

The immediate tasks before the authorities in the developed world are two-fold: one is to fix the financial system and the other is to maintain the aggregate demand at a high enough level to stimulate the real sector. Even as these immediate tasks are addressed, there are medium term concerns. the US has been incurring heavy current account deficit year after year for a decade or so. The US must address these imbalances. Closely related to this is the issue of leverage. Almost every segment of the US society including its households is a net borrower. The extent of leverage is an issue which regulators and policy makers must pay attention, if financial stability is to be achieved.

The Indian financial system is not directly exposed to the 'toxic' or 'distressed' assets of the developed world. However, the indirect impact on the economy because of the recession abroad is very much there. "Decoupling theory" does not hold good. The role of monetary policy under these circumstances is to ensure that the financial system is provided with adequate liquidity. Fiscal actions aimed to stimulate the economy comprise of reduction in taxes and enlargement of government expenditure. That public spending should remain at a high level in a situation like the present one is not a matter of dispute. Exceeding the FRBM targets of fiscal and revenue deficits is understandable in the current situation. However, keeping the targets as cyclical averages is a good guidance in the medium term.

Part I

Monetary Policy and Fiscal Issues

1 | Challenges for Monetary Policy

The challenges for monetary policy in general and in particular for India have been changing over time, even though some basic issues have remained of perennial concern. As the institutional environment both domestic and global changes, the tasks of monetary policy also undergo a change. The monetary and financial system is far more complex today than it has been in the past. Financial intermediation has reached a high level of sophistication. The menu of financial products available has expanded enormously. Derivative products which were unknown till a few decades ago, have become common. All these changes have an important role to play in relation to the transmission mechanism. The impact of monetary policy action can be felt through a variety of channels some of which though recognised in the past have become more important. The speed with which funds can move across borders has raised issues regarding coordination of monetary policies among countries. Prices and interest rates are no longer determined by domestic factors. While the traditional issues such as the objectives of monetary policy, the possible trade-off among them and appropriate intermediate targets remain relevant, they need to be related to the changing institutional environment at home and abroad.

At a theoretical level, in the classical tradition, strict neutrality of money ruled out monetary influence on real output. The formal enunciation of money and price relationship was made in the form of the famous Quantity Theory of Money under which money influenced only price. The neutrality proposition underwent a change in the Keynesian analysis. The neutrality view was abandoned and money was seen to have an influence on output through a variety of channels. The Phillip's Curve depicting the inverse relationship between unemployment and wage inflation provided the empirical basis for the non-neutrality proposition. While several economists (Friedman, 1968; 1975; Phelps, 1967) have challenged the basic micro economic under-pinning of the wage and price mechanism that leads to the possibility of a trade-off between price stability and growth, the theoretical debate is far from settled. However, the general consensus is that while, in the short run, money can have an impact on output, in the long run it may not. In other words, in the long run repeated monetary shocks to bring about a sustained improvement in growth may result in accelerating levels of inflation.

There has also been continuing debate on the transmission mechanism both at theoretical and empirical levels. This discussion has implications for appropriate intermediate targets. A crucial behavioural relationship in this context is the demand function for money. There have been many theoretical refinements to the original demand function for money as outlined by Keynes. A key concern has been in relation to the stability of the demand function for money. Against the background of growing number of financial assets which are becoming close substitutes to money, the identification of a suitable monetary aggregate has become an issue.

HISTORICAL EVOLUTION

Monetary policy has had its ups and downs in the post-Second World War period. In industrially advanced countries, after decades of eclipse, monetary policy re-emerged as a potent instrument of economic policy, in the fight against inflation in the 1980s. Issues relating to the conduct of monetary policy came to the forefront of policy debates at that time. The relative importance of growth and price stability as the objective of monetary policy as well as the appropriate intermediate target of monetary policy became the focus of attention. Over the years, a consensus has emerged among the industrially advanced countries that the dominant objective of monetary policy should be price stability. Differences, however, exist among central banks even in these countries as regards the appropriate intermediate target. While some central banks consider monetary aggregates and, therefore, monetary targeting as operationally meaningful, some others focus on the interest rate. There is also the more recent practice to ignore intermediate targets and focus on the final goal such as inflation targeting.

A similar trend regarding monetary policy is discernible in developing economies as well. Much of the early literature on development economics focused on real factors such as savings, investment and technology as mainsprings of growth. Very little attention was paid to the financial system as a contributory factor to economic growth even though attention was paid to develop financial institutions which provide short term and long term credit. In fact, many writers felt that inflation was endemic in the process of economic growth and it was accordingly treated more as a consequence of structural imbalance than as a monetary phenomenon. However, with the accumulated evidence, it became clear that any process of economic growth in which monetary expansion was disregarded led to inflationary pressures with a consequent impact on economic growth. Accordingly, the importance of price stability and, therefore, the need to use monetary policy for that purpose also assumed importance in developing economies. Nonetheless, the debate on the extent to which price stability should be deemed to be the overriding objective of monetary policy in such economies continues.

The Reserve Bank of India was set up in 1935. Like all central banks in developing countries, the Reserve Bank has been playing a developmental and a regulatory role. In its developmental role, the Reserve Bank focused attention on deepening and widening the financial system. It played a major part in building up appropriate financial institutions to promote savings and investment. In the realm of agricultural credit, term finance to industries and credit to export, the apex institutions that are now operating were essentially spun off from the Reserve Bank. Strengthening and establishing new institutions to meet the country's requirements is a continuing process. The promotional role had taken the Reserve Bank into the area of credit allocation as well. Pre-emption of credit for certain sectors and that too at concessional rates of interest became part of the overall policy. Commercial banks over time had been required to provide a certain percentage of their total credit to certain sectors which were regarded as 'priority sector'.

An active role by the Reserve Bank of India in terms of regulating the growth in money and credit became evident only after 1950s (Rangarajan, 1988). During the 1950s the average annual increase in the wholesale price was only 1.8 per cent. However, during the 1960s, the average annual increase was 6.2 per cent and in the 1970s, it was around 10.3 per cent. In the early years of planning, there was considerable discussion on the role of deficit financing in fostering economic growth. The First Plan said: "Judicious credit creation somewhat in anticipation of the increase in production and availability of genuine savings has also a part to play". Thus, deficit financing, which in the Indian context meant Reserve Bank credit to the Government, was assigned a place in the financing of the plan, though its quantum was to be limited to the extent it was non-inflationary. Monetary growth, particularly in the 1950s, was extremely moderate. However, as each successive plan came under a resource crunch, there was an increasing dependence on market borrowing and deficit financing. These became pronounced in the 1970s and thereafter. The single most important factor influencing the conduct of monetary policy after 1970 had been the phenomenal increase in reserve money contributed primarily by the Reserve Bank credit to the Government.

To summarise, the system as it existed at the end of 1970s was characterised by the following features. The Reserve Bank of India as the central monetary authority prescribed all the interest rates on deposits and lending. The commercial banks were required to allocate a certain percentage of credit to what were designated as 'priority sector'. Credit to parties above a stipulated amount required prior authorisation from the central bank. After the nationalisation of major commercial banks in 1969, nearly 85 per cent of the total bank assets came under public sector. Apart from small private banks, foreign banks were allowed to operate with limited branches.

The increase in the scale of borrowing by the Government resulted in: (a) the steady rise in statutory liquidity ratio (SLR) requiring banks to invest higher and higher proportion of their deposits in government securities which carried less than 'market rates' and (b) the Reserve Bank of India becoming a residual subscriber to securities and Treasury Bills leading to monetisation of the deficit. The Reserve Bank had, therefore, to address itself to the difficult task of neutralising to the extent possible the expansionary impact of deficits. The increasing liquidity of the banking sector resulting from rising levels of reserve money had to be continually mopped up. The instrument of open market operations was not available for this task since the interest rates on government securities were well below 'market rates'. The task of absorbing excess liquidity in the system had to be undertaken mainly through increasing the cash reserve ratio (CRR). In fact, in mid-1991, the CRR was 25 per cent on incremental deposits. In addition, the SLR was 38.5 per cent. Thus, nearly 63.5 per cent of incremental deposits was pre-empted in one form or another.

In 1983, the Reserve Bank of India appointed a Committee under the Chairmanship of the distinguished economist Prof. Sukhamoy Chakravarty to review the working of the Indian Monetary System. I was a member of the Committee. The Committee's Report (Reserve Bank of India, 1985) covered a wide range. One of its major recommendations was to regulate money supply consistent with the expected growth rate in real income and a tolerable level of inflation. Recognising the fact that government borrowing from the Reserve Bank had been a major factor contributing to the increase in reserve money and therefore, money supply, the Committee wanted an agreement between the Central Government and the Reserve Bank on the level of monetary expansion and the extent of monetisation of the fiscal deficit. Without such a coordination, the Committee felt that Reserve Bank's efforts to contain monetary expansion within the limits set by expected increase in output could become impossible. While this recommendation of the Committee was accepted in principle, it could take a concrete shape only in the Nineties.

In the wake of the economic crisis in 1991 triggered by a difficult balance of payments situation, the Government introduced far reaching changes in India's economic policy. Monetary policy was used effectively to overcome the balance of payments crisis and promptly restore stability. An extremely tight monetary policy was put in place to reap the full benefits of the devaluation of the rupee that was announced. However, it did not stop with that. Financial sector reforms became an integral part of the new reform programme. Reform of the banking sector and capital market was intended to help and accelerate the growth of the real sector. Banking sector reforms covered a wide gamut. The most important of the reforms was the prescription of prudential norms including capital-adequacy ratio. In addition, certain key changes were made with respect to monetary policy environment which gave commercial banks greater autonomy in relation to the management of their liabilities and assets. First and foremost, the administered structure of interest rates was dismantled step by step. Banks in India today enjoy full freedom to prescribe the deposit rates and interest rates on loans except in the case of very small loans and export credit. Second, the government began borrowing at market rates of interest. The auction system was introduced both in relation to Treasury Bills and dated securities. Third, with the economic reforms emphasising a reduction in fiscal deficit, pre-emptions in the form of CRR and SLR were steadily brought down. Fourth, while the allocation of credit for the priority sector credit continued, the extent of cross subsidisation in terms of interest rates was considerably brought down because of the reform of the interest rate structure.

Monetary policy in the 1990s in India had to deal with several issues, some of which were traditional but some totally new in the context of the increasingly open economy in which the country had to operate. In the first few years, monetary policy had to contend with the consequences of devaluation and the need to quickly restore price stability to obtain the full benefits of devaluation. While the fiscal deficit was being brought down, the question of monetisation of the deficit continued to remain an issue and a solution had to be found. This eventually led to a new agreement between Government and RBI on financing deficit. The system of ad hoc Treasury Bills under which Government of India could replenish its cash balances by issuing Treasury Bills in favour of the Reserve Bank and which had the effect of monetising deficit was phased out. It was replaced by a system of Ways and Means Advances which had a fixed ceiling. The Reserve Bank of India continued to subscribe to the dated securities at its discretion. During 1993 and 1994, for the first time monetary policy had to deal with the monetary impact of capital inflows with the foreign exchange reserves increasing sharply from $ 9.2 billion in March 1992 to $ 25.1 billion in March 1995. In fact we face today a similar situation. The problem is of a larger magnitude. Our capability in those days to stabilise was limited as the available government securities at market or near market rates was limited. The RBI also today faces a similar situation even though all government securities at the disposal of the

RBI are at market related interest rate. The issue is one of adequacy. In 1995-96, the change in perception with reference to exchange rate after a prolonged period of nominal exchange rate stability *vis-a-vis* the US dollar brought into play the use of monetary policy to stabilise the rupee—an entirely new experience for the central bank. Similar situations arose later on also at the time of the East Asian crisis.

Monetary policy has begun to operate within a changed institutional framework brought about by the financial sector reforms. It is this change in the institutional framework that has given a new dimension to monetary policy. New transmission channels have opened up. Indirect monetary controls have gradually assumed importance. With the progressive dismantling of the administered interest rate structure and the evolution of a regime of market determined interest rate on government securities, open market operations including 'repo' and 'reverse repo' operations emerged for the first time as an instrument of monetary control. The Liquidity Adjustment Facility introduced first in 1999 and refined later is emerging as a principal operative instrument to manage market liquidity on a daily basis. Bank Rate acquired a new role in the changed context. So too the repo and reverse repo rates. The Nineties have paved the way for the emergence of monetary policy as an independent instrument of economic policy (Rangarajan, 2002).

ISSUE OF CONCERN

Monetary policy acts through influencing the cost and availability of credit and money. As an instrument of economic policy, it has certain advantages. "Inside Lag" which refers to the lag between the time when action is needed and when action is actually taken is shorter in the case of monetary policy than fiscal policy. Monetary policy has thus the ability to respond quickly to changes in the short-term.

Let me now turn to some of the issues relating to monetary policy which have come to be debated extensively in the last few decades. These issues are not specific to India or developing economies. They have been debated in the context of the developed countries also. Nevertheless, these issues which I want to highlight have a special significance for developing countries like India.

Objective

The first question that needs to be addressed relates to the objective or objectives of monetary policy. A recurring question is whether monetary policy should be concerned with all the goals of economic policy. The issue of 'objective' has become important because of the need to provide a clear guidance to monetary policy makers. Indeed, this aspect has assumed added significance in the context of the increasing stress on the autonomy of Central Banks. Autonomy goes with accountability and accountability in turn requires a clear enunciation of the goals (Tarapore, 2000).

The various enactments setting up the central banks normally specify the goals of central banks. The Federal Reserve Act in the United States requires the central bank to pursue both "maximum employment" and "stable prices". In fact the Act specifies a third goal—"moderate long term interest rates". The Reserve Bank of India Act requires the Reserve Bank to conduct its operations "with a view to securing monetary stability in India and generally to operate the currency and credit system of the country to its advantage." Most central bank legislations are not helpful in clearly charting out the path that a central bank should pursue as multiplicity of objectives mentioned in the legislations tends to obfuscate the issue. In the last few decades, most central banks in the industrially advanced countries have accepted price stability as the most important objective of monetary policy. According to George, Governor of Bank of England (1996), "It is true that most central banks at least would traditionally have regarded controlling inflation as a core responsibility. In some cases—most famously in the case of Bundesbank—the duty of preserving the value of the currency has long been written into the central bank's statutes. But what is remarkable today is the extent of the international consensus on effective price stability—in the sense of eliminating inflation as a factor in economic decisions—as the immediate aim of monetary policy; and this is increasingly reflected in more or less explicit targets for low rates of inflation against which monetary policy performance can be measured." This is clearly built into the mandate of the European Central Bank (Duisenberg, 2003). The inflation picture has changed dramatically over the last 20 years in the industrial countries.

Gone are the days of high and variable inflation rates. Since the early 1990s, these countries have entered a period of relatively low or stable inflation. However, currently the high level of unemployment prevailing in many of these countries has raised certain questions as to how to balance the objectives of growth and stability. It may also be noted that central banks think of price stability more in terms of stabilising inflation, that is the rate of increase, rather than the price index at a certain level.

In talking of the objectives of monetary policy in India, I had said on an earlier occasion "In a broad sense the objectives of monetary policy can be no different from the overall objectives of economic policy. The broad objectives of monetary policy in India have been: (1) to maintain a reasonable degree of price stability and (2) to help accelerate the rate of economic growth. The emphasis as between the two objectives has changed from year to year, depending upon the conditions prevailing in that year and in the previous year" (Rangarajan, 1997). In fact what I had said is a version of the Taylor's rule (Taylor, 1993) in its most discretionary form.

The choice of a dominant objective arises essentially because of the multiplicity of objectives and the inherent conflict among such objectives. Faced with multiple objectives that are equally relevant and desirable, there is always the problem of assigning to each instrument the most appropriate objective. This "assignment rule" favours monetary policy as the most appropriate instrument to achieve the objective of price stability (Chakravarty, 1986).

The crucial issue that is being debated in India as elsewhere is whether the pursuit of the objective of price stability by monetary authorities undermines the ability of the economy to attain and sustain high growth. A considerable part of the relevant research effort has been devoted to the trade-off between economic growth and price stability. Empirical evidence on the relationship between growth and inflation in a cross country framework is somewhat inconclusive because such studies include countries with an inflation rate as low as one to two per cent to those with inflation rates going beyond 200 to 300 per cent. These studies (Barro, 1995; Sarel, 1996; Khan and Senhadji, 2000), however, clearly establish that growth rates become increasingly negative at higher rates of inflation.

The case of price stability as the objective of monetary policy rests on the assumption that volatility in prices creates uncertainty in decision-making. Rising prices adversely affect savings while they make speculative investments more attractive. The most important contribution of the financial system to an economy is its ability to augment savings and allocate resources more efficiently. A regime of rising prices vitiates the atmosphere for promotion of savings and allocation of investment. Apart from all these, there is a social dimension particularly in developing countries. Inflation adversely affects those who have no hedges against it and that includes all the poorer sections of the community. The fiscal consolidation also becomes easier in an environment of reasonable degree of price stability. In a period of rising prices, the gap between revenues and expenditures widens (Rangarajan and Arif, 1990). Expenditures tend to grow at a faster rate than revenues because many components of expenditures such as employees' compensation are closely linked to variations in prices.

The question that recurs very often in the minds of the policy makers is whether in the short run, there is a trade-off between inflation and growth which can be exploited. In the industrial countries, a solution is sought through the adoption of Taylor's rule which prescribes that the signal interest rate be fixed taking into account the deviations of inflation rate from the target and actual output from its potential. The Taylor's rule is written as:

$$i_t = i_t^* + \lambda_1(Y_t - Y^*) + \lambda_2(\pi_t - \pi^*)$$

where,

i_t = the signal interest rate,

i_t^* = the equilibrium nominal interest rate,

Y_t = logarithm of level of actual output

Y^* = logarithm of level of trend output

π_t = actual inflation rate

π^* = target inflation rate, and

λ_1 and λ_2 are the respective coefficients.

The rule requires the federal funds rate to be raised, if inflation increases above the target or if real GDP rises above trend GDP. In the original version, the weights of deviation from target inflation and potential output were assumed to be the same at 0.5. However, it was subsequently felt that the coefficient of inflation deviation term must be higher than one. Taylor himself did not want the rule to be applied in a mechanical way. While the rule is intuitively appealing, there are serious problems in determining the value of the coefficients. There is also a lot of judgement involved in determining the potential output and target inflation rate. However, the rule offers a convenient way of determining when the Central Bank should act.

Another way of reconciling the conflicting objectives of price stability and economic growth in the short run is through estimating the "threshold level of inflation". It is this inflation threshold which will provide some guidance to the policy makers. Below and around this threshold level of inflation, there is greater maneuverability for the policy makers to take into account other considerations. Interestingly, the Chakravarty Committee regarded the acceptable rise in prices as 4 per cent. This, according to the Committee, will reflect changes in relative prices necessary to attract resources to growth sectors. I have myself indicated that in the Indian context, inflation rate around 6 per cent may be acceptable (Rangarajan, 1998). Some studies have estimated the level of threshold inflation in India to be in the range of 5 to 7 per cent (Vasudevan et al., 1998; Samantaraya and Prasad, 2001 and Reserve Bank of India, 2002). There is some amount of judgement involved in this, as econometric models are not in a position to capture all the costs of inflation. This approach provides some guidance as to when policy has to become tight or to be loosened. It is also necessary for the policy makers to note that this order of inflation is higher than what the industrial countries are aiming at. This will have some implications for the exchange rate of the currency. While the open economy helps to overcome domestic supply shocks, it also imposes the burden to keep the inflation rate in alignment with other countries. Price stability thus remains a major objective of monetary policy.

Transmission Mechanism

An understanding of the transmission mechanism is critical to the conduct of monetary policy. The transmission mechanism explains how the actions taken by the monetary authorities influence the key macro economic variables in the economy. The literature on monetary economics talks of four transmission channels. They are: (i) quantum channel, especially through money supply and credit, (ii) interest rate channel (iii) the exchange rate channel, and (iv) the asset price channel (Mishkin, 1996; Kamin et al., 1998). The quantum channel focuses on changes in money supply and credit brought about by monetary authorities while tracing the impact on output and price. The difference between the classical approach and the Keynesian approach on how money supply works through the system is well known. The interest rate channel traces the impact of changes in interest rate initiated by monetary authorities on output and price through changes in aggregate demand. The exchange rate channel emphasises the impact on the outflow or inflow of funds from abroad resulting from monetary actions. The asset price channel traces the impact of interest rate changes on aggregate demand through the changes in the prices of assets principally those of bonds, equities and real estate.

While several distinct channels are identified, in the real world all the channels work simultaneously. Which of the channels is more effective in a particular country depends on the institutional environment. With the development of financial markets and closer integration of such markets, domestically and globally, the balance sheet effects as well as the exchange rate effects assume as much importance as the direct interest rate effect. The transmission channel has important implications for monetary authorities in terms of determining what the appropriate intermediate target should be for the central bank.

Intermediate Target

The next issue relates to the intermediate target. In India since the mid-eighties the target chosen has been broad money. The Chakravarty Committee recommended a system of flexible monetary targeting. It is true that central banks in several countries in the industrial world have abandoned intermediate targets and have focused on the final target such as inflation control. While this has the advantage of specifying the ultimate objective in clear and precise terms, it must be admitted that there is not enough clarity regarding the channel through which this will be achieved. One of the reasons for the abandonment of intermediate targets in these countries has been the breakdown of the relationship between monetary aggregates and inflation rate. The demand function for money has been found to be unstable. However, in India, studies (Nag and Upadhyay, 1993; Joshi and Saggar, 1995 and Arif, 1996) show that the money demand function is a stable function of select variables and it can be used to reasonably predict inflation. Several statistical functions of the demand for money estimated by using equilibrium and disequilibrium analysis provide strong evidence on the long-run stability of the money demand function. Perhaps some of the factors that have contributed to the instability of the demand function for money in the industrially advanced countries such as financial innovations and large movements of funds across the border are yet to have the same impact in India. In the demand function for money in India, income emerges as the most dominant variable. This is partly due to the reason that interest rate which is the other relevant variable had been until recently an administered rate, with changes occurring in discreet steps. Such a function enables the authorities to estimate the appropriate growth in money supply, given the expected increase in real output and the acceptable level in price increase. The inverse money demand function, in which price is related to money supply and income shows that the average of price changes over a period of three years are predicted with reasonable accuracy by such an equation.[1] Even, a simple correlation between money supply growth and inflation rate is high.[2] However, without bringing in output, the relationship is not complete. As we move into an era of openness, the impact of money supply on price can diminish, as supply bottlenecks are eased. So far, money supply has proved to be an appropriate target. Such a target is relatively well understood by the public and signals unambiguously the stance of monetary policy. However, with the freeing of the interest rate structure, interest rate can also become an appropriate intermediate variable. It is already happening. This has also been facilitated by the reduced direct monetisation of fiscal deficit. It appears from our experience that while money supply may be an appropriate intermediate target while inflation rate remains high, interest rate may be more appropriate when inflation remains low and fluctuates within a narrow range. It must, however, be noted that at the equilibrium both quantity and price are determined. Changes in interest rates cannot be ordained. The appropriate quantitative changes in money will have to be brought about even though the signal for change may be given by the price variable like interest rate.

Level of Interest Rate

Another question of importance that has arisen relates to the appropriate level of interest rate. The nominal interest rate comprises of three elements: (i) the real rate of interest, (ii) inflation expectations and (iii) a discount factor for uncertainties. The effectiveness of monetary policy to bring down the nominal interest rate will depend on the impact that this policy will have on inflation expectations and on the perception of uncertainty in the economy. A monetary policy that is geared to maintain reasonable price stability, if it is successful, can help to bring down the interest rate in sympathy with the downward drift in inflation. Inflationary expectations can be broken, if the monetary authority enjoys high credibility. However, this leaves the real rate of interest to be determined.

The real interest rate is not an observed variable. The real interest rate is influenced by several long-term factors such as saving and investment balance in the economy and the rate of return on capital. Theory tells us that in a closed economy, this rate should equal the real rate of growth.[3] This is the well known Phelps' golden rule. An economy in which this equality is not met is treated as 'dynamically inefficient'. However, allowance has to be made for the impact of capital flows and in an open economy, this equality does not strictly hold. Only in a completely open system with no frictions, there will be a convergence of growth rates and real interest rates among countries. This will also take a long time to reach. In the meanwhile, in fast growing economies the real rate of interest will have to be higher. In South Korea during the years of very rapid economic growth the real rate of interest was around 6 to 7 per cent in several years. The real rate of interest is thus related to the rate of growth of the economy. In the famous Taylor's rule, the constant term refers to the 'equilibrium' real rate which is assumed to be equal to the steady state growth rate. For the US, he assumed this rate to be 2.2 per cent. The real rate of interest will have to be substantially higher in developing economies which seek to maintain a high savings rate and which aim at growing at more than 6 to 7 per cent per annum. This is typically the situation in India.

A situation of high real rate of interest accompanied by high growth rate must be distinguished from other situations when real rates of lending may remain high because of market imperfections. In this context, it is worth noting that the high level of nominal lending rates in developing economies may also be due to high intermediation costs. Improved efficiency can reduce the spread between the deposit rate and lending rate and bring the lending rate in closer alignment with fundamental factors. While the interest rate may be adjusted upwards or downwards depending on the nature and extent of output gap and inflation gap, the level also requires to be maintained at an appropriate level consistent with real rate of growth of the economy. Most importantly, real interest rate should be kept at a level necessary to generate savings and investment that are needed to support rapid economic growth.

Exchange Rate Management

The role of monetary authority in exchange rate management in India came into focus in the 1990s. Since 1975, the exchange rate of the rupee was determined with reference to the daily exchange rate movements of a selected number of currencies of the countries which were India's major trading partners. The Reserve Bank of India was required to maintain the exchange rate within a band on either side of a base 'basket' value. This allowed the achievement of a medium-term real effective exchange rate (REER) objective through changes in the NEER. Such a regime could be maintained only with the support of extensive exchange controls and import controls. The reform measures introduced in 1991 included significant changes in the foreign trade regime and exchange rate management. The devaluation of the rupee in mid 1991 was followed by a system of dual exchange rate system in March 1992. A year later, the dual system was abolished and the country moved towards a unified market determined exchange rate system. The monetary authority does not intervene in the market process of rate determination as long as orderly conditions prevail in the exchange market and the exchange rate reflects macroeconomic fundamentals.

The approach to exchange rate by the monetary authorities in the developed world generally has been to let the market determine the rate. However, there have been several exceptions. There have been occasions when central banks in these countries have intervened, some times in a concerted way, when exchange markets became volatile. The Indian experience with market determined exchange rate system is that there have been several occasions when the RBI had to intervene strongly to prevent volatility. This happened in 1995 and 1996 and later in 1997 and 1998 at the time of the East Asian crisis. The impact of the East Asian crisis on the Indian market was minimal. This was partly due to the reason that while India subscribed to current account convertibility under Clause VIII of the IMF agreement, the capital account liberalisation was undertaken cautiously. Besides, India's current account deficit during this period was low. In fact, in 1993, a High Level Committee on Balance of Payments (Government of India, 1993) had made specific recommendations regarding the level of current account deficit, the size and composition of capital flows, the management of external debt including short-term debt and the quantum of foreign exchange reserves. Implementation of these recommendations stood India in good stead at the time of the East Asian crisis. The management of the exchange rate in 1998 was clearly a success story.

In narrow underdeveloped markets like in India, there is a tendency for the herd instinct which amplifies the fluctuations. This can cause volatile and destabilising movements in the exchange rate which may go beyond any correction, required by the fundamentals. Even in developed markets there is a tendency for the market to "overshoot", when a critical mass in terms of the perception of overvaluation in the exchange rate is reached. With narrow markets, the danger is greater. On such occasions, the monetary authority has to step in to ensure orderly market conditions (Jalan, 2000). The monetary authority must, however, recognise that integration of markets is inevitable and therefore action must be spread across the markets to achieve results.

In countries like India, trade flows both visible and invisible, dominate the balance of payments. That is why for the exchange rate regime in India, continuous monitoring of the real exchange rate with an appropriate base becomes important. It provides valuable information to the authorities on the behaviour of the current account to which it is intrinsically linked. A monetary policy geared to domestic price stability in this situation helps to avoid disruptive adjustments in the exchange rate. In that sense monetary policy and exchange rate management become intertwined. However, on occasions, there can be conflicts between domestic considerations and external stability. The doctrine of "Impossible Trinity" holds that monetary independence, exchange rate stability and full financial integration cannot be achieved simultaneously. One of the three will have to be sacrificed. Even in the current situation in India, one can observe the opposite pulls. If the interest rate goes down because of capital flows well below what is considered desirable from the domestic point of view such as augmenting savings, a choice becomes inevitable. Even now, there is a divergence between real rate of interest and real rate of growth. In times of conflict, the Central Bank will have to decide which should be the dominant concern and give priority to it.

Financial Stability

Increasingly macroeconomic stability as an objective of central banking is closely linked to financial stability. It is easy to see how the two are interlinked. Financial stability broadly implies the stability of the important institutions and markets forming part of the financial system. Financial stability requires that the key institutions in the financial system are stable, in that, there is a high degree of confidence about meeting contractual obligations without interruption or outside assistance (Crockett, 1997). While the complementarity between the objectives of macro stability and financial stability is easily recognised, the one question that needs to be addressed is whether there can be a conflict between the two objectives. It is not inconceivable to have situations in which the price stability objective might call for a restrictive policy, while the financial market conditions may demand a somewhat liberal policy to provide relief (Goodhart, 2001). The Reserve Bank of India was extremely conscious of this dilemma. Banking sector reforms were in full swing in the 1990s which necessarily put the banking system under strain. While facilitating the smooth transition,

RBI took care that there was no dilution of the basic objectives of monetary policy. However, viewed as part of overall economic stability, financial stability need not run at cross-purpose with other dimensions of macroeconomic stability. Normally, price stability should provide an environment favourable to financial stability. If on occasions dealing directly with financial stability becomes necessary, it must be done as in the case of intervention in the foreign exchange markets. Actions to maintain financial stability in those circumstances may be in the long-run interest of economic stability.

Autonomy of Central Banks

Autonomy of central banks has become an article of faith in the industrial countries. It has been written into the constitution setting up the European Central Bank. The literature on this subject is growing. A distinction has to be made between operational and target independence. Buiter (2000) advocates usefulness of operational independence while leaving the target to be set by the government. There is a general consensus to give operational or instrument independence to central banks among countries that have decided that the key objective of monetary policy is inflation control. Autonomy implies discretion to central banks to decide on the timing and nature of monetary policy intervention. It also calls for transparency in relation to both objectives and strategies. The increased use of explicit targets by central banks is part of the broader move to build credibility through transparency. It is quite true that in India, monetary policy has been very much conditioned by the stance of fiscal policy. The system of the scheme of ad hoc Treasury Bills facilitated monetisation of the fiscal deficit without limit and without prior approval (Rangarajan, 1993). The 1990s saw the phasing out of the system and the introduction of the scheme of Ways and Means Advance. This was a major step towards the achievement of greater discretion. The Fiscal Responsibility and Budget Management Act takes this to its logical conclusion. Two associated comments may be made in this context. First, an autonomous central bank does not mean lack of coordination with the Government. Nor does it imply lack of harmony. In fact, harmony in the sense in which it is used in classical symphonic music will be achieved. In a symphony, different artistes play different notes simultaneously but in effect create a blend that produces the best of music. However, the stances of monetary policy and fiscal policy cannot run at cross-purposes. For example, a lax fiscal policy accompanied by a tight monetary policy can lead to a sharp increase in interest rate. On the other hand, an accommodative monetary policy in a period of lax fiscal policy can lead to explosive increase in prices. While monetary and fiscal coordination is desirable, it is important at the same time that the monetary authority which has its own specific agenda must have the institutional autonomy and should not be burdened with functions which may come in conflict with its own special objective. It is in this context that the issue of delinking the management of public debt from RBI becomes relevant. Second, the emergence of an autonomous central bank does not mean that the 'state of bliss' has arrived (Rangarajan, 1993). It only enables the central bank to pursue a consistent monetary policy over a long time. Then the onus of responsibility for the conduct of monetary policy will rest on the shoulders of the Reserve Bank, where it should logically rest. In an open economy, the task of the central bank will be rendered more difficult if it does not have the autonomy and discretion to make changes quickly in response to external shocks.

There was a time when it was said that central banking was neither a science nor an art but a craft. This is at best a half-truth. Central banking has never been a case of applying well known remedies to well known problems. 'Rules *versus* discretion' has been a subject of long-standing debate in monetary policy. Rigid rules such as those implicit in gold standard will give central banks no room for maneuverability. On the other hand, total discretion with respect to objectives and instruments will make monetary policy indeterminate. That is why the new phrase 'constrained discretion'. This will require the central banks to be transparent and explicit with respect to objectives and strategies, while leaving the freedom to them to choose the timing and nature of their actions. This is the type of autonomy towards which every central bank should move.

CONCLUSION

The institutional environment in which the Indian monetary policy operates underwent a significant change in 1990s. The administered structure of interest rate was dismantled. Governments at the Centre and in States borrow at market rates. Reserve requirements have been drastically reduced. The relationship between Government and Reserve Bank of India is changing with the latter acquiring a greater maneuverability. All these changes have provided the Reserve Bank with enhanced ability to influence the economic variables. Direct instruments of control are getting substituted by indirect controls. Bank Rate and repo rates send appropriate signals to the market.

Among the objectives of monetary policy, price stability has to remain the dominant one. The "Assignment Rule" in policy analysis favours monetary policy as the most appropriate instrument to achieve the objective of price stability. At the same time, concerns relating to growth have to be kept in view. One way of reconciling the twin objectives of price stability and economic growth in the short run is through estimating the threshold level of inflation. If the actual inflation runs above the threshold level, price stability becomes the more dominant objective. Below and around this threshold, there is greater maneuverability for the policy makers to take into account other considerations. In an increasingly open economy, it also becomes necessary to keep the domestic inflation rate in alignment with the level in other countries.

In India so far, money supply has been the target variable. An objective such as price stability was sought to be achieved by bringing about changes in money supply. However with the dismantling of the administered interest rate structure, the induction of new instruments and the creation of new financial markets, interest rate is also becoming an appropriate intermediate variable. Perhaps the lesson that can be drawn from our experience is that while money supply may be an appropriate immediate target when inflation rate remains high, interest rate may be the more appropriate target when inflation remains low and fluctuates within a narrow range.

Monetary authorities also need to pay attention to the level of interest rate. While interest rate may be adjusted upwards and downwards depending on the nature and extent of output gap and inflation gap, the rate requires to be maintained at an appropriate level consistent with real rate of growth of the economy. The real rate of interest will have to be substantially higher in developing economies like India which seek to maintain a high savings rate and which aim at growing at more than 6 to 7 per cent per annum. Lending rates must be brought down through improved efficiency and reducing the spread between the deposit rate and lending rate.

Changes in the exchange rate and foreign trade regimes have added an additional dimension to India's monetary policy. External considerations have now to be taken into account in the conduct of monetary policy. There have been years in which the Reserve Bank had to fight the impact of capital outflows and there have also been years in which the major concern is how to deal with the large capital inflows. The current year is a good example of this latter phenomenon. When a conflict arises between domestic considerations and external stability, central bank will have to decide which should be the dominant concern.

Financial stability has also become a major concern of central banks including Reserve Bank of India. Normally price stability should provide an environment favourable to financial stability. However, there could be occasions when dealing directly with financial stability becomes necessary. Maintenance of financial stability is in the long run interest of economic stability.

Phasing out the ad hoc Treasury Bills system was an important step towards the autonomy of the Reserve Bank. The Fiscal Responsibility and Budget Management Act, if implemented in its true spirit, will be a great step forward not only in fiscal but monetary management. While monetary and fiscal coordination is desirable, it is important that the monetary authority which has its own specific agenda must have the institutional autonomy to decide on the timing and nature of monetary policy intervention.

I am grateful to Dr. D.K. Srivastava for helpful discussions on deriving the relationship between real rate of interest and real rate of growth. I am thankful to Dr. Amaresh Samantaraya for his help in the preparation of this lecture.

Notes

1. Using the data for the period 1970-71 to 2002-03, the price equation, i.e. the inverted money demand function for India correcting for the serial correlation was estimated in double log form as

$$P_t = 4.83 + 0.38\ M_t - 0.57\ Y_t + 0.57\ P_{t-1} \qquad \ldots(i)$$

   (1.58) (1.97)   (-1.70)   (2.08)

   Adjusted $R^2 = 0.99$

   where,

   P_t = Log of Wholesale Price Index (average of weeks)

   M_t = Log of Broad Money i.e. M3 (outstanding as on 31st March)

   Y_t = Log of GDP at factor cost at constant prices (1993-94=100)

   In the above equation, all the variables are found to be non-stationary of order 1 but co-integrated. It is observed that, the percentage variation of actual WPI and that of estimated values from the inverted money demand function show very close fit, particularly, when 3-year moving averages are taken (Table 1.1, Figure 1.1). However, one can notice contrary movements between the actual and fitted in the four years following 1997-98. Even in these years, the differences, particularly, in the case of 3-year moving averages is small. The rate of interest should be a relevant variable in the equation. However, the impact of interest rate has not so far been significant because of the system of administered structure of interest rate. However, its relevance will assume importance now.

Table 1.1

Percentage Variation of Actual and Fitted WPI

Year	Year to Year			3-Year Moving Averages		
	Actual WPI	Fitted WPI	Error=2-3	Actual WPI	Fitted WPI	Error=5-6
1981-82	9.5	14.5	-5.0			
1982-83	4.7	8.8	-4.1	7.3	8.6	-1.3
1983-84	7.6	2.4	5.2	6.3	7.1	-0.8
1984-85	6.6	10.1	-3.5	6.2	6.2	0.0
1985-86	4.3	6.0	-1.6	5.6	7.1	-1.5
1986-87	5.9	5.3	0.6	6.1	6.0	0.1
1987-88	8.0	6.6	1.4	7.1	5.8	1.3
1988-89	7.4	5.6	1.9	7.7	6.9	0.8
1989-90	7.6	8.6	-1.0	8.4	6.9	1.4
1990-91	10.2	6.7	3.5	10.5	9.8	0.8
1991-92	13.8	14.0	-0.2	11.3	10.6	0.7

contd. ...

...contd. ...

	Year to Year			3-Year Moving Averages		
Year	Actual WPI	Fitted WPI	Error=2-3	Actual WPI	Fitted WPI	Error=5-6
1992-93	10.0	11.1	-1.1	10.7	11.3	-0.6
1993-94	8.3	8.8	-0.5	10.3	9.4	0.9
1994-95	12.5	8.3	4.2	9.6	8.9	0.7
1995-96	8.1	9.7	-1.6	8.4	8.0	0.4
1996-97	4.6	6.1	-1.5	5.7	7.2	-1.5
1997-98	4.4	5.7	-1.3	5.0	5.5	-0.5
1998-99	5.9	4.8	1.2	4.5	5.3	-0.7
1999-2000	3.3	5.3	-2.1	5.5	4.8	0.6
2000-01	7.2	4.4	2.7	4.7	5.6	-0.9
2001-02	3.6	6.9	-3.3	4.7	4.8	-0.1
2002-03	3.4	3.1	0.3			

From the estimated price equation as given above, the short-run elasticity of price with respect to money and output are 0.38 and 0.57, respectively. The long-run elasticity of price with respect to money and output can be estimated to be 0.88 and 1.32, respectively. The implicit income elasticity of demand for money is worked out to be 1.50.

Figure 1.1

3-Year Moving Averages of Percentage Variation of Actual and Fitted WPI

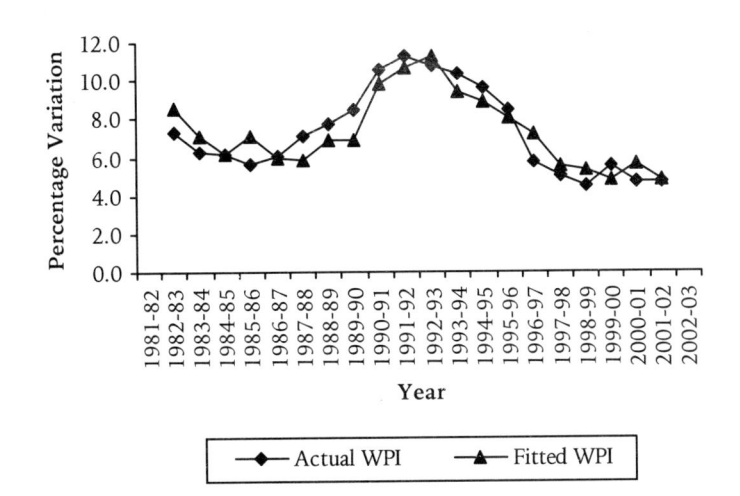

2. RBI in its *Annual Report 1998-99* points out: "While M3 growth closely tracked the movement in inflation up to 1996-97, it deviated in the subsequent period, providing an indication of certain degree of overprediction of inflation rate by the M3 growth. This deviation has been particularly significant in 1998-99 and during the current financial year up to June 1999." This relationship is further examined in the light of the data available till 2002-03.

Table 1.2 provides the growth rates of M3 and inflation rate based on WPI. M3 series refers to outstanding figures as on March 31. Being a stock, it is appropriate to use outstanding figures. WPI inflation rate is based on weekly averages. Average figures are preferred over the point-to-point because they are more inclusive. The growth rates of M3 and WPI are also shown in Figure 1.2. From this figure, it can be observed that, since 1991-92 money supply growth rate and inflation move in tandem. Since 1991-92, in 9 out of 12 years, money supply and inflation move in the same direction. Since 1998-99 they are consistently moving together.

From Table 1.2, it can also be observed that, during the period 1992-93 to 1998-99, the average growth rates of M3 and WPI were 17.5 per cent and 7.7 per cent, respectively. In the next four years (1999-2000 to 2002-03) average inflation has come down to 4.4 per cent. This is consistent with lower average M3 growth rate at 14.7 per cent during the period 1999-2000 to 2002-03.

Table 1.2

Growth Rate of M3 and WPI

Year	WPI	M3
1971-72	5.6	15.2
1972-73	10.0	18.3
1973-74 *	20.2	17.4
1974-75	25.2	10.9
1975-76	-1.1	15.0
1976-77	2.1	23.6
1977-78	5.2	18.4
1978-79	0.0	21.9
1979-80	17.1	17.7*
1980-81	18.2	18.1
1981-82	9.3	12.5
1982-83	4.9	16.6
1983-84	7.5	18.2
1984-85	6.5	19.0
1985-86	4.4	16.0
1986-87	5.8	18.6
1987-88	8.1	16.0

contd. ...

Challenges for Monetary Policy

...contd. ...

Year	WPI	M3
1988-89	7.5	17.8
1989-90	7.5	19.4
1990-91	10.3	15.1
1991-92	13.7	19.3
1992-93	10.1	14.8
1993-94	8.4	18.4
1994-95	12.5	22.4
1995-96	8.1	13.6
1996-97	4.6	16.2
1997-98	4.4	18.0
1998-99	5.9	19.4
1999-2000	3.3	14.6
2000-01	7.2	16.8
2001-02	3.6	14.2
2002-03	3.4	13.0

Note: 1. M3 referes to outstanding as on 31st March.
2. WPI refers to average of weeks.
Source: Handbook of Statistics on Indian Economy, 2002-03. RBI.

Figure 1.2

Annual Growth Rate of M3 and WPI

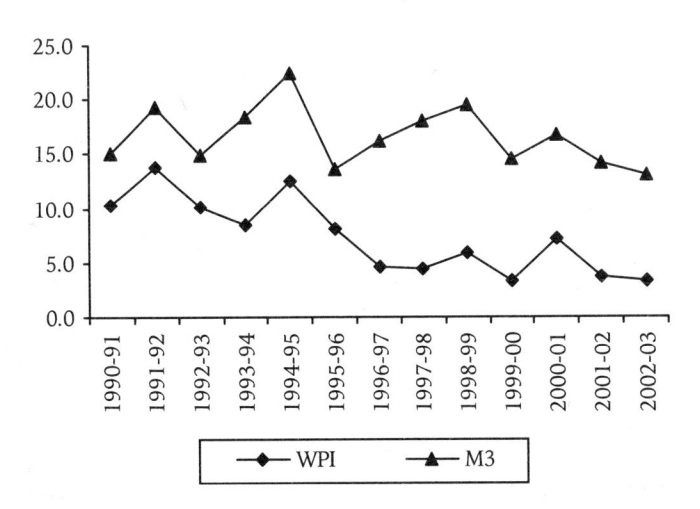

3. In the literature, many writers have examined the relationship between real interest rate and growth rate. For example, Phelps' golden rule (Phelps, 1961) establishes the equality between real interest rate and the growth rate of the economy. The rule can be derived as follows.

Let us denote, $\alpha = K/Y$ (Capital-Output Ratio)

$\Rightarrow K = \alpha.Y$

$\Rightarrow dK = \alpha.dY$ ...(1)

Let $S = s.Y$ (Saving Function)

In equilibrium, $S = s.Y = I = dK$

$\Rightarrow dK = s.Y$ ...(2)

From Equations (1) and (2), $\alpha.dY = s.Y$

$\Rightarrow dY/Y = s/\alpha$ ...(3)

Also, from Equation (1) $dY/dK = 1/\alpha$ ...(4)

From Equations (3) and (4), $dY/Y = s.(dY/dK)$ ...(5)

Phelps (1961) has shown,

$s = F_k(K_0, N_0).\{K_0/Y_0\}$

where, $F_k(K_0, N_0)$ = marginal productivity of capital which can be denoted as 'r'

Thus,

$dY/Y = r.(K_0/Y_0).(dY/dK)$
$= r.[(dY/dK)/(Y_0/K_0)]$ ...(6)

Now, $[(dY/dK)/(Y_0/K_0)]$ is output elasticity w.r.t capital which can be denoted as 'e'. Further, dY/Y can be denoted as 'g'.

Thus, Equation (6) can be rewritten as

$g = r.e$

In a steady state equilibrium e = 1 i.e., the ratio of output growth rate and growth rate of investment is unity.

Thus, g = r i.e., the rate of growth of output is equal to rate of return on capital or real rate of interest.

There are others who have analysed the relationship between real interest rate and growth rate with different types of growth models. Koyck and Hooft-Walvaars (1966) write, "An optimum rate of investment can be found which maximises per capita consumption at every point of time on the equilibrium path. The optimum rate of interest corresponding with this optimum rate of investment appears to be equal to the rate of growth of gross output." Robin Matthews (1960) using typical Harrod-Domar growth model says, "It may seem paradoxical that a high r is associated with high g. But this is as it should be: a high r means a low K/Y, and a low K/Y means a given rate of saving is able to support a high rate of growth of output." Sen (1970) has argued that in the framework of neo-classical growth theories, a rise in the real interest rate seems to induce a higher rate of growth because in such models there is no investment function and investment is assumed simply to be determined by savings behaviour. Khan and Villanueva (1991) support the positive association between high interest rate and high growth rate based on the argument that the real interest rate is a good proxy for the efficiency (productivity) of capital accumulation. However, if high real interest rate does not reflect efficiency of investment and is caused by market imperfections, there may not be a positive association with growth rate. Thus, a situation of high real rate of interest accompanied by high growth rate must be distinguished from other situations.

References

Arif, R.R. (1996). "Money Demand Stability: Myth or Reality—An Econometric Analysis", *Development Research Group Study* No. 13. Reserve Bank of India.

Barro, Robert (1995). "Inflation and Economic Growth", *Bank of England Quarterly Bulletin* 35(2), May.

Bergo, Jarle (2003). "The Role of the Interest Rate in the Economy", Speech at AON Grieg Investors. Zurich. October 19.

Buiter, Willem H. (2000). "Targets, Instruments and Institutional Arrangements for an Effective Monetary Authority", 7th L.K. Jha Memorial Lecture. Oct. 16. Mumbai: RBI.

Chakravarty, Sukhamoy (1986). "Report of the Committee to Review the Working of the Monetary System—A Re-examination" *Sir Purushotamdas Thakurdas Memorial Lecture*. Mumbai: The Indian Institute of Bankers.

———. (1986). "Analytical Base", in *Monetary Policy: Review of the Sukhamoy Chakravarty Report. IIC Monograph Series* No. 10. New Delhi: India International Centre.

Crockett, Andrew (1997). "Why is Financial Stability a Goal of Public Policy", Paper presented at the Federal Reserve Bank of Kansas City's 1997 Symposium, *Maintaining Financial Stability in a Global Economy*. Jackson Hole. Wyoming. August 28-30.

Duisenberg, Willem F. (2003). "Maastricht and the Future of Europe", At the presentation of a stamp commemorating the 10-year anniversary of the Maastricht Treaty. Bundesfinanz- ministerium. Berlin. October 22.

Fischer, Stanley (1994). "Modern Central Banking", in Forrest Capie, Charles Goodhart, Stanley Fischer and Nobert Schnadt (eds.), *The Future of Central Banking, The Tercentenary Symposium of the Bank of England*. Cambridge: Cambridge University Press.

Friedman, Milton (1968). "The Role of Monetary Policy", *American Economic Review* LVII: 1-17.

———. (1975). "Unemployment *versus* Inflation? An Evaluation of the Phillips Curve", *Occasional Paper 44*. London: The Institute of Economic Affairs.

George, Edward (1996). "Economic Policy Approaches: Some Reflections", 9th C.D. Deshmukh Memorial Lecture. Mumbai, 14 October and included in *C.D. Deshmukh Memorial Lecture Series—Centenary Commemorative Volume*. Mumbai: RBI.

Goodhart, Charles A.E. (2001). "Whither Central Banking?", *RBI Bulletin*, January.

Government of India (1993). *Report of the High Level Committee on Balance of Payments* (Chairman: C. Rangarajan). New Delhi.

Jadav, Narendra (2003). "Central Banking Strategies, Credibility and Independence: Global Evolution and the Indian Experience", *RBI Occasional Papers* 24(1&2): 1-104.

Jalan, Bimal (2000). "Monetary Policy: Is a Single Target Relevant?", in Bimal Jalan, *India's Economy in the New Millennium: Selected Essays*. New Delhi: UBSPD.

Joshi, Himansu and Mridul Saggar (1995). "The Demand for Money in India: Stability Revisited" *RBI Occasional Papers* 16(2), June.

Kamin, Steven, Philip Turner and Jozef Van 't dack (1998). "The Transmission Mechanism of Monetary Policy in Emerging Market Economies: An Overview", *BIS Policy Papers* No. 3. January. Basel: BIS.

Khan Mohsin S. and Delano Villanueva (1991). "Macroeconomic Policies and Long-term Growth: A Conceptual and Empirical Review", *IMF Working Paper* WP/91/28. Washington DC: IMF.

Khan Mohsin S. and A.S. Senhadji (2000). "Threshold Effects in the Relationship between Inflation and Growth", *IMF Working Paper* WP/00/110. Washington DC: IMF.

King, Mervyn (1999). "Challenges for Monetary Policy: New and Old", Paper prepared for the Symposium on *New Challenges for Monetary Policy* sponsored by the Federal Reserve Bank of Kansas City. Jackson Hole. Wyoming. August 27.

Koyck, L.M. and Maria J. 't Hooft-Welvaars (1966). "Economic Growth, Marginal Productivity of Capital and the Rate of Interest", in F.H. Hahn and F.P.R. Brechling (eds.), *The Theory of Interest Rates*. New York: MacMillian.

Krugman, Paul (1996). "Stable Prices and fast Growth: Just Say No", *Economist*, August 31, pp.15-18.

Matthews, R.C.O. (1960). "The Rate of Interest in Growth Models", *Oxford Economic Papers* 12.

McCallum, Bennett T. (2000). "Alternative Monetary Policy Rules: A Comparision with Historical settings for the United States, the United Kingdom and Japan", *Economic Quarterly*, Federal Reserve Bank of Richmond.

Mishkin, Frederic S. (1996). "The Channels of Monetary Transmission: Lessons for Monetary Policy", *NBER Working Paper* No. 5464, February.

———. (1999). "International Experience with Different Monetary Policy Regimes", *Journal of Monetary Economics* 43: 579-605.

Nag, Ashok K. and G. Upadhyay (1993). "Estimating Money Demand Function: A Co-integration Approach" *RBI Occasional Papers* 14(1), March.

Phelps, Edmund S. (1961). "The Golden Rule of Accumulation", in A.K. Sen (1970) (ed.), *Growth Economics: Penguin Modern Economic Readings*.

Phelps, Edmund S. (1967). "Phillips Curves, Expectation of Inflation and Optimal Unemployment Over Time", *Economica* 34: 254-81, August.

Poole, William (1999). "Monetary Policy Rules?", *Review*, March/April. Federal Reserve Bank of St. Louis.

Rangarajan, C. (1988). "Issues in Monetary Management", in C. Rangarajan, *Indian Economy: Essays on Money and Finance*. New Delhi: UBSPD.

Rangarajan, C. and R.R. Arif (1990). "Money, Output and Prices: A Macro Econometric Model", *Economic and Political Weekly*: 837-852, April 21.

Rangarajan, C. (1993). "Autonomy of Central Banks", in C. Rangarajan (1998). *Indian Economy: Essays on Money and Finance*. New Delhi: UBSPD.

———. (1997). "Dimensions of Monetary Policy", in C. Rangarajan (1998). *Indian Economy: Essays on Money and Finance*. New Delhi: UBSPD.

———. (1998). "Development, Inflation and Monetary Policy", in I.J. Ahluwalia and I.M.D. Little (eds.), *India's Economic Reforms and Development: Essays for Manmohan Singh*. Delhi: OUP.

———. (2002). *Leading Issues in Monetary Policy*. New Delhi: Sukhamoy Chakravarty Memorial Trust and Bookwell.

Rangarajan, C. and M.S. Mohanty (1997). "Fiscal Deficit, External Balance and Monetary Growth—A Study of the Indian Economy", *RBI Occasional Papers* 18(4): 583-653.

Reddy, Y.V. (2000). "Monetary Policy in India: Objectives, Instruments, Operating Procedure and Dilemmas" in *Monetary and Financial Sector Reforms in India: A Central Banker's Perspective*. New Delhi: UBSPD.

———. (2002). "Parameters of Monetary Policy in India", *RBI Bulletin*: 95-109, February.

Reserve Bank of India (1985). *Report of the Committee to Review the Working of the Monetary System* (Chairman: Sukhamoy Chakravarty). Mumbai.

———. (1999). *Annual Report 1998-99*. Mumbai.

———. (2002). *Report on Currency and Finance, 2000-01*. Mumbai.

Samantaraya, A. and A. Prasad (2001). "Growth and Inflation in India: Detecting the Threshold Level", *Asian Economic Review* 43(3): 414-28.

Sarel, Michael (1996). "Nonlinear Effects of Inflation on Economic Growth", *IMF Staff Papers* 43(1): 199-215, March.

Sen, A.K. (1970). "Interest, Investment and Growth", in A.K. Sen (Ed.), *Growth Economics: Penguin Modern Economic Readings*.

Sterne, Gabriel (1999). "The Use of Explicit Targets for Monetary Policy: Practical Experiences of 91 Economies in the 1990s", *Bank of England Quarterly Bulletin*, August.

Tarapore, S. (2000). "Monetary Policy: Today, Tomorrow and the Day After", in S. Tarapore (2003), *Capital Account Convertibility: Monetary Policy and Reforms*. New Delhi: UBSPD.

Taylor, John B. (1993). "Discretion *versus* Policy Rules in Practice", *Carnegie-Rochester Conference Series on Public Policy* 39: 195-214, North-Holland.

Vasudevan, A., B.K. Bhoi and S.C. Dhal (1998). "Inflation Rate and Optimal Growth—Is there a Gateway to 'Nirvana'?" in A. Vasudevan *et al.* (eds.), *Fifty Years of Development Economics: Essays in Honour of Prof. Brahmananda*. Mumbai: Himalaya Publishing House.

White, William (2002). "Changing Views on How Best to Conduct Monetary Policy", Speech at the *Central Bank Governors' Club Meeting*. Nafplio. Greece. October 18.

Kale Memorial Lecture–2004. Pune, January 18, 2004.

2 Financial Stability
Some Analytical Issues

Serious financial crises that have rocked several countries particularly in the last two decades have brought to the fore the issues of financial stability. These bouts of financial instability within individual countries and across countries have compelled policy makers and analysts to pay attention to the problem of predicting, avoiding and managing financial crises. Fundamental to all these prescriptions is a clear understanding of the causes of the crises.

In the sixties and seventies of the last century, the major concern in relation to the financial sector was how to avoid financial repression. It was felt that the administered structure of interest rates combined with various other direct controls by the central banks had inhibited the growth of financial sector in many countries. These controls, it has been argued, had the effect of diluting the operational and allocative efficiency of the financial institutions. By and large the emphasis was on the developmental role of the financial sector. Deepening and widening of the financial system was a major concern of public policy. However, attention has recently shifted to stability because of the frequency of financial crises and the costs they have imposed. Besides causing a significant loss to private wealth, they have imposed a substantial burden on the public finance because of the need to re-capitalise financial institutions and restore public confidence. "Resolution Costs" in several countries have been estimated to exceed 10 per cent of gross domestic product (GDP). One estimate puts the average fiscal costs of banking resolution alone across countries at 16 per cent of GDP (Hoggarth and Saporta, 2001).

Defining Financial Stability

It is difficult to define the term "financial stability". There is no universally accepted definition. The term 'stability' or 'instability' refers to the behaviour of the system rather than to individual institutions. However, one cannot rule out that failure of a single financial institution can trigger significant financial turmoil. Nevertheless, the key element of a financial crisis is the disruption that is caused to the financial system and the resultant cost to real output. Stability applies to both institutions and markets. Crockett (1997) writes "Stability requires (i) the key institutions in the financial system are stable, in that there is a high degree of confidence that they can continue to meet their contractual obligations without interruption or outside assistance, and (ii) that the key markets are stable in that participants can confidently transact in them at prices that reflect fundamental forces and that do not vary substantially over short periods when there have been no changes in fundamentals." Alternatively instability implies inability of institutions to meet their obligations on their own. Markets are said to be unstable when prices in financial markets are volatile and moved by amounts not justified by changes in fundamentals. Like unstable equilibrium, instability implies inability to correct itself on its own. Instability, if it persists, turns into a crisis. It is this potential for full blown crisis involving bankruptcy of institutions and loss of wealth by individuals that compels regulators and other policy makers to take action to contain instability. In the past, financial crises tended to occur in two areas, (i) banking, and (ii) foreign exchange market. While over extended loan portfolio and imprudent lending were usually the major causes of banking crises, exchange rate crises were the outcome of the pressures developing in foreign exchange markets supplemented by actions of speculators to force a depreciation of the currency. However, crisis in one market can lead to a crisis in another. For example, the currency crisis can lead to a banking crisis which in turn can lead to a financial sector crisis with damaging effects on the real sector. The East Asian crisis of 1997 is a typical example of this sequence. However, in the East Asian episode, given the fragility of the financial sector, the crisis could very well have originated in the banking arena and later spread to the currency market. With increasing interdependence of markets, instability in one market can lead to instability in another.

Instability Bias

Anyone can recognise the very fast growth of the financial sector in almost all countries, both developed and developing. A question that is being asked increasingly is whether the financial sector today is inherently more fragile and vulnerable than before. The very factors that have contributed to the growth of the financial sector may well have contributed to the increased fragility. Financial institutions have become more sophisticated; the volume of transactions has increased phenomenally and competitive pressures have grown. As a result of very rapid increase in telecommunications and computer-based technologies, a dramatic expansion in financial flows both cross-border and within countries has emerged. Along with these changes, consolidation, increased geographic spread of banks and other financial service providers, and the blurring of the distinctions between various financial institutions have also occurred. Developments in technology and in the pricing of assets have enabled innovations and financial instruments that allowed risks to be separated and allocated to parties most willing and able to bear them. Thus the menu of financial products has expanded enormously. For example, in the case of debt instruments, investors can now choose among structured notes, syndicated loans, coupon strips and bonds secured by pool of other debt instruments. Another dramatic development is the growing use of financial derivatives. All these changes have undoubtedly created new opportunities, but they have also magnified risks. In fact, it has been remarked that the increased complexity of new instruments makes it harder to understand the risks to which the institutions concerned are exposed. Close inter-dependencies among markets and market participants have increased the potential for adverse events to spread quickly. They have increased significantly the scope for and speed of contagion.

Apart from these factors, sometimes a fear is expressed that the financial system may be prone to instability because of its inherently pro-cyclical character (Berger and Udell, 2003; Borio, 2004). Asset prices move pro-cyclically. So too is the ratio of credit to GDP. However, if these normal behavioural patterns reach abnormal proportions, they become the cause of financial distress. For example, asset price booms in property markets when they come to an end cause serious distortions since they constitute the collateral for various loans. Hence, the old adage "Bad loans are sown in good times." The financial system may not always be able to build sufficient cushions in good times which can act as effective shock absorbers in bad times. Therefore, the search for early warning signals of financial imbalances. The critical thing to identify is the timing of when "exuberance" turns into "irrational exuberance", so that imbalances do not build up.

Regulating Institutions and Markets

It is well understood that if financial stability is to be achieved, it must relate to both institutions and markets. However, much of the discussions and regulatory measures focus primarily on institutions. The case for public intervention in relation to financial institutions is well understood and, has indeed, a long history. Financial institutions and, more particularly, banks have been subjected to a number of regulatory measures for a long time even though in recent years, there has seen a significant tightening. Vulnerability and contagion have been the major reasons for advocating public intervention. Vulnerability of financial institutions to pressures comes from the maturity mismatch between liabilities and assets. This mismatch particularly is stark in the case of banks. A good part of the liabilities of banks is redeemable on demand while their assets have a much longer maturity. While this mismatch may not cause any problem in the normal circumstances, any loss of confidence can lead to destabilisation. The vulnerability of banks to 'runs' has always been recognised. The other major reason is contagion. The failure of a financial institution, such as a bank, causes losses not only to its depositors and owners but also to all the institutions with which it is interlinked. This exposure to other institutions and individuals is extremely high in the case of banks because of the role they play in the payments system. It is this possibility of negative externality that has resulted in financial institutions to be brought under regulatory regimes (Stiglitz, 1994). The multiplicity of financial products and more particularly derivative products has tended to heighten the contagion factor. To take care of the changing environment in which financial institutions operate and the new types of pressures that they are subjected to, the regulatory mechanism relating to financial institution has undergone a change. These issues are discussed at a later stage.

The approach to regulating financial markets as distinct from institutions has, however, been somewhat unclear and ambiguous. Regulation of asset price runs into problems because there is no easy way of determining what the appropriate or equilibrium price is. However, one can perceive certain differences in approach with respect to various markets. In the foreign exchange markets, central banks do intervene to offset tendencies that are not considered desirable. Even in countries where currencies are not pegged, central banks make a distinction between interfering with fundamental factors and correcting volatile or disorderly conditions in the market and are willing to intervene to maintain orderly conditions. That foreign exchange markets tend to overshoot is well known. With technology facilitating speedy transfer of funds and with the free movement of funds across countries, exchange rates no longer reflect the behaviour of the current account of balance of payments.

Thus, intervention is resorted to in one way or the other by several central banks in the foreign exchange markets. However, most central banks, at least in the developed countries, would in normal times, prefer to let the markets determine the price. But the need to watch over the foreign exchange markets is accepted and intervention is not ruled out.

However, in relation to equity markets, bond markets or real estate markets, there is much less emphasis on direct public intervention to alter the asset prices. Instability in stock markets can have serious consequences not only for the investors in these markets, but also for the rest of the financial system as well as the real economy. However, there is no direct attempt at influencing prices in these markets. The regulatory approach has been to ensure investor protection, prevention of manipulation and establishing transparency. Nevertheless, the question of assessing, when these markets are 'overpriced' and when they are misaligned with fundamentals, is critically important both for monetary authorities and regulators of financial markets. In fact, an issue that is being debated now is how central banks should take into account factors relating to financial stability in the conduct of monetary policy. This has implications both for the timing and specifics of monetary policy.

Components of Regulation

The need to regulate financial institutions, particularly banks, from the point of view of system stability, has been long understood. In fact, it has even been argued that there exist some forms of government intervention that will not only make the institutions function better but also improve the performance of the economy (Stiglitz, 1994).

The early regulations in banking is related to licensing. But, countries like the U.S. initially had adopted a liberal policy, with different authorities entrusted with the power of licensing. However, in the U.S. there were certain preventive measures such as activity restraints as under the Glass-Steagel Act and restrictions on branch banking, mergers and acquisitions. Nowadays, regulations are aimed at ensuring, to use a cliché, the 'soundness and safety' of the financial system. The broad oversight over financial institutions can be viewed from several angles. For example, one can classify the elements of oversight into three components:

(i) setting standards

(ii) assessing risk and internal controls, and

(iii) supervision.

Each of these elements has several sub-components. These have been discussed at length in international fora. In fact, the regulations have become more complex, raising questions of compliance costs. The "dense regulatory style", to borrow an expression from Greenspan, has come in for some criticism.

Setting Standards

Standards can be interpreted in a number of ways. Narrowly interpreted, they refer to norms with respect to some performance or activity indicator. Capital adequacy ratio is a classic example of this. Broadly viewed, standards can be applied to diverse areas such as accounting, transparency and legal framework including bankruptcy legislations. Much work has been done at both levels in recent years. Starting with the Core Principles for Effective Banking Supervision initiated by the Basel Committee on Banking Supervision in 1988, the move to establish standards has extended to other areas such as securities trading and insurance. The internationalisation of standards has become necessary to avoid "regulatory arbitrage", i.e., an attempt by multinational financial corporations from moving the centres of activities to less and loosely regulated areas.

The evolution of prudential norms was a major development in the 1990s. While capital adequacy ratio has emerged as a primary instrument of financial regulation, the prudential norms cover other important areas such as income recognition, provisioning for bad and doubtful debts and the classification of assets into performing and non-performing. Capital adequacy ratio tries to ensure that the banks maintain a minimum amount of own funds in relation to the credit risks they face. The availability of adequate equity capital is a basic requirement for stability in a market economy. This is all the more so in the case of banks, given their high degree of leverage. Risk weighted capital adequacy requirement which was the result of the 1998 Basel Capital Accord is one of the main pillars of the present regulatory regime in banks. The risk weighted capital adequacy framework (Basel-I) required banks to hold different categories of capital against both on-balance sheet asset and off-balance sheet asset items with different risk weights assigned to counterparties. There is no doubt that the capital held by banks should be appropriately related to the size and nature of the risk they run. The adequacy ratio was originally related only to credit risk. However, an expanded system of capital adequacy ratio incorporating market risks was introduced in 1996.

While the capital adequacy ratio has been adopted by more than 100 countries including India, it is not without shortcomings (Nachane *et al.*, 2000). One can think in terms of three sets of issues which need to be resolved. The first concerns how much capital banks should be required to hold. The second concerns the relationship between the level of capital and the economic cycle. And the third concerns the specific question of how to measure the risks against which capital is to be held and fix the weights.

The very simplicity of the formula relating to capital adequacy ratio carries with it many problems. Though what the Accord prescribed was a minimum capital ratio, very often it was assumed to be the most appropriate, leading on occasions to regulatory forbearance. This may have also led to depositors taking less interest in monitoring banks' activities. Minimum capital ratio has to be distinguished from 'maximum insolvency probability'. If the regulators had to adopt the latter criterion, the required capital would be much higher. This may, however, impose undue burden. There were two other drawbacks. First, the capital adequacy ratio did not take into account explicitly the risks other than market and credit risks. Increasingly, there is greater stress on 'operational risk'. Second, the Accord treated all assets falling into a certain risk category as carrying the same weight. It ignored the fact that assets in the same risk class can have widely varying quality. The degree of concentration or diversification of a portfolio, which is an important determinant of risk, was ignored.

While the prescription of a minimum capital linked to riskiness of assets was an important first step, the changing financial scenario comprising of advancement in technology and telecommunications, innovations in financial products and services and the increasing globalisation of the markets calls for more sophisticated systems of assessment of risk (Caruana, 2004). Banks have evolved, on their own, various techniques to measure and manage risk. The Basel Accord-II, which is under discussion and which is to be adopted by 2006, takes note of the need to link capital adequacy to risk management.

It may be pointed out at this stage that capital adequacy ratio as a regulatory measure suffers from some analytical shortcomings (Stiglitz, 2003). It may pose a 'moral hazard' problem. The maintenance of the soundness of the system cannot be achieved by continuously raising the ratio. This may make the banks to go in for more risky assets within a certain risk bracket in order to earn a higher return. The regulatory system must encourage the banks to go for a balanced portfolio and reduce the overall risk exposure. Forward-looking provisioning for Non Performing Assets (NPAs) should be encouraged in good times. The capital-adequacy ratio can also cut the other way. In an effort to maintain the ratio consistent with the available capital, banks may cut down their asset portfolios. While on occasions, this may be welcome, this may not be desirable, if resorted to by a large number of banks at a time when credit expansion is needed.

Assessing Risk and Internal Controls

Financial institutions face a wide range of risks. These include credit, interest rate, foreign exchange, liquidity and operational risks. While these risks could analytically be separated, they are highly interdependent and events that affect one area of risk can have implications for other risk categories. As a consequence, various types of risk evaluation tools including value at risk models and stress tests are being increasingly used to assess risks. These models provide continuous information for the management and Basel-II seeks to build on these developments. With the move towards Basel II, banks would be encouraged to go for a balanced portfolio, reduce the overall risk exposure and enable maintenance of adequate capital. The new Basel Accord rests on the assumption that an internal assessment of risk by a financial institution will be a better measure than an externally imposed formula. However, much will depend on the model used by individual institutions and this will require external validation.

There are three pillars to Accord-II (BIS, 2003 and Nachane, 2003). These are: (i) minimum capital requirement, (ii) supervisory review, and (iii) market discipline.

Basel II—Pillar I: Minimum Capital Requirements

With respect to minimum capital requirement, the new Accord has made substantial changes to the treatment of credit risk relative to the current Accord. It has also introduced an explicit treatment of operational risk. Deviating from the earlier one-size-fits-all approach, the new Accord allows banks a certain latitude in determining their own capital requirements based on internal models. With respect to the assessment of credit risk, there are two approaches. One is a Standardised Approach and the other is the Internal Rating Based approach (IRB). The standardised approach is very similar to the present Accord except that the risk weights are revised depending upon the rating of the counterparties by external credit rating agencies. There is also greater differentiation across risk categories. In the IRB approach, banks calculate their own risk exposures through internal models and these exposures are converted into a single numerical component of risk-weighted assets in a prescribed manner.

Regarding the first pillar, several reservations have been expressed. With respect to the standard approach to credit risk, a major objection has been to the involvement of external rating agencies in the regulatory process. Many developing countries including India have taken objections to this. This shows a certain lack of faith in the rating agencies. Besides, in a country like India, only a small fraction of even the large borrowers is rated. In fact some of the rating agencies themselves are not in favour of their ratings to become part of the regulatory regime. This could be from the fear that such an involvement could lead to the ratings of the raters. On the other hand, the implementation of the IRB approach will involve substantial upgradation of the management information systems and risk management systems within the banks. A bank would need several core inputs for each credit facility such as the probability of default and the expected loss rate given a default. Apart from the complexity of the models that would be required to assess and measure risk, the possibility of manipulating the internal models by the banks to their own advantage cannot also be ruled out. Perhaps in the Indian situation, the best option would be to adopt a modification of the standard approach with the exclusion of the intervention of external agencies in determining risk weights. This is basically Basel I plus capital for operational risk. However, this should not preclude or underestimate the need for banks and other financial institutions to evolve and put in place appropriate risk assessment models. Supervisors should encourage banks and possibly even lay down a time table for at least the significant banks to adopt the internal ratings based approach.

Basel II—Pillar II: Supervisory Review Process

The supervisory review, as envisaged under the Basel-II, points to the need for banks to assess their capital adequacy positions relative to their overall risks including those for which no capital is maintained and for supervisors to review and take appropriate action in response to those assessments. Supervisors are required to take a comprehensive view on how banks handle the risk management and internal capital allocation process. On such a review, supervisors could require banks to hold higher than the minimum regulatory capital. The supervisory review process in the Indian context is critical given the longer transition required to move to more sophisticated risk management approaches under Pillar I. This review will enable supervisors to assess banks' economic capital and not just the regulatory capital.

Basel II—Pillar III: Market Discipline

The potential of market discipline to complement capital regulation depends on the disclosure of reliable and timely information that would allow market participants to access key information about a bank's risk profile and level of capitalisation. Underpinning meaningful disclosures is use of sound accounting and valuation standards. The information which should be disclosed has been classified under six categories. The disclosures envisaged are to be made available on a semi annual basis. In India, the disclosures are mostly quantitative and it is now opportune to introduce more qualitative disclosures such as risk management policies.

Supervision

The supervisory system is an integral part of the oversight over financial institutions. It is as part of the effort to strengthen the supervisory system, the prudential norms evolved. They formed part of what the Basel Committee called "Core Principles for Effective Banking Supervision". Supervision over the different segments of the financial system has always existed. Central banks the world over had regarded supervision of banks as a key function, even though there is some shift in thinking in recent times. In the case of banks, the main objectives of supervision are enshrined in the acronym CAMELS. For maintaining the safety and soundness of banks, supervision looks at six important dimensions of the functioning of banks. These are: capital adequacy, asset quality, management soundness, earnings and profitability, liquidity and sensitivity to market risk. In relation to each of these dimensions, there are several prescribed norms and bank supervisors try to see how far banks conform to these standards.

Process and Mechanism

The mechanism of supervision varies from country to country. In India, as in many other countries, on-site inspection is an important part of the supervisory process. However, it is based on historical data and is in a sense backward looking. It is also transaction based. While these are important and need to be pursued, if not as elaborately as before, on-site inspection has to be supplemented by off-site surveillance which has the advantage that it helps to continuously monitor the functioning of the institutions. The results of on-site analysis can be fine-tuned with the latest off-site data. By helping to monitor continuously the behaviour of several ratios, off-site surveillance becomes a better check on the efficiency and adequacy of management practices in banks.

An important development in the supervisory process is the move from an inspection which is transaction based and directed towards verifying compliance with prudential norms to supervisory framework that puts a greater emphasis on the accountability of bank boards and top management to formulate and implement effective risk management system. Such a shift in approach pre-supposes that banks have established the required risk management practices and controls. The Reserve Bank of India (RBI) in line with many other central banks had also issued risk management guidelines to banks. A full-fledged risk management system besides assessing and measuring risk must also include effective internal controls for prompt housekeeping and preventive measures against frauds. In countries which have moved to risk based supervision, the supervisory imposition and punishments are severe even for small violations. In the present stage, in the evolution of the banking system in developing countries like India, risk based supervision can only supplement on-site inspection and off-site surveillance, both of which are required to ensure compliance with prudential norms and to prevent individual transgressions. Needless to say, the implementation of risk based supervision would also require upgrading the technology support as well as skills of the supervisory staff in the central banks.

Increasingly another issue that is being debated is how far market forces can be used to supplement the regulatory system. The third pillar of Basel-II talks of market discipline as aiding regulation of banks. This is sought to be achieved by making available to all information relating to the functioning of banks. The BIS had identified six sets of information that should be made available to all. Such a transparency is expected to compel individual institutions to manage their affairs prudently and their counterparties to exercise appropriate discipline. This has sometimes been described as "incentive-compatible financial regulation". However, there are very few countries which depend exclusively on market forces to achieve the supervisory ends. Perhaps New Zealand is the only country which has gone the farthest in using the market discipline. Self-regulatory organisations which have a long history in relation to capital markets have not been of much success in regulating the capital market. At best the availability of information can play only a supplementary role. An interesting issue that arises in this context is how much of the information that comes into the possession of central banks should be revealed to the public. The central banks through inspection reports and direct contacts have access to a wide variety of information about individual banks. So too other regulators with respect to their respective institutions over which they have control. Sometimes, regulators also send certain warning signals to individual institutions. A complete silence on all of these will be inappropriate. At the same time, the central banks or any other regulator should not precipitate the very crisis they want to avoid. The timing of the release of the information is critically important. There is as yet no consensus on this. But the RBI has to take a lead to determine how far it will go.

Macro Prudential Indicators

Another improvement in the supervisory process has been the introduction of macro prudential indicators to assess the soundness and vulnerability of the financial system. The emphasis here is on assessing the system rather than the individual institutions. These macro prudential indicators comprise of (a) aggregated micro prudential indicators on the health of individual financial institutions, and (b) macroeconomic variables associated with the financial system soundness (Evans *et al.*, 2000). The indicators of financial soundness developed in relation to individual financial institutions have been referred to earlier. These indicators relate to six dimensions of supervisory oversight. While some of the financial soundness indicators measure the capacity of the system to absorb loss, others monitor vulnerability. A question that is relevant is whether an aggregation of financial soundness indicators is needed, if in relation to each individual institution, these indicators are at appropriate levels. Is there any additional information that comes out of aggregation? It is quite possible to envisage situations when the aggregated picture reveals vulnerability which may not be thrown up by looking at the ratios of individual institutions separately. For example, when we aggregate capital adequacy ratios, the aggregated picture includes not only the average of the ratios but also their dispersion. The frequency distribution of the ratio will throw additional light. While examining sectoral credit concentration under asset quality, the aggregated picture alone will reveal the vulnerability. Once again, it is the aggregation of the credit provided by all banks which will reveal how far the credit system is stretched. Thus, the supervisors gain by looking at the aggregated picture.

The operation of financial system depends on the overall economic activity and, therefore, the behaviour of certain macroeconomic variables need to be watched as part of the supervisory process. Macro prudential indicators, therefore, include several macroeconomic variables such as those relating to economic growth, balance of payments, inflation, interest and exchange rates and lending and asset price behaviour. Macro prudential analysis should therefore include stress tests and scenario analysis to determine the sensitivity of the financial sector to macroeconomic shocks. Some of the macroeconomic indicators can signal imbalance that may affect the financial system and, therefore, serve as lead indicators. Many research studies have been undertaken to understand the relationship between macroeconomic variables and financial crisis.

An analysis of the key relationships among financial soundness indicators is necessary to assess the impact of the shocks to financial soundness. A change in one indicator can affect another. For example, an increase in non-performing loans could lead to additional provisioning and thereby reducing the available capital. It is also necessary to monitor risks to financial system stability on account of developments in the corporate and household sector or exposure to non-banking financial intermediaries and real estate markets.

Single versus Multiple Regulators

Another issue in the system of supervision relates to the regulation of financial institutions such as banks whose activities are no longer confined to the provision of a single financial service. In recent years, market forces have led to the formation of financial groups that provide a range of financial services—banking, securities and insurance—across jurisdictions. Diversified financial groups are thus becoming the dominant institutional structure in the financial services industry, including in India. Diversification through ownership linkages, raises additional supervisory concerns, the principal of which are contagion, transparency, regulatory arbitrage and conflicts of interest. In response, financial sector supervisors have supplemented their traditional approach of supervising individual group entities on a "solo-basis" with "consolidated supervision". Consolidated supervision may be broadly defined as a quantitative and qualitative evaluation of the strength of a financial group. It allows financial sector supervisors to better understand the relationship among the different group entities and assess the potential for adverse developments in one part of the group affecting the operation of others. Prudential regulations such as capital adequacy, large exposures and risk concentration are assessed on group basis. However, so long as there are different regulators overseeing different financial services, a single institution or group offering more than one service will come under the supervisory review of several authorities. It is in this context, the concept of a 'lead regulator' has emerged. Under such circumstances, coordination among the authorities is required both at the policy and operational levels. There has to be an extensive exchange of information including inspection reports among the authorities.

Given the emergence of conglomerates, some countries are moving towards a single regulatory authority for all financial services. The creation of the Financial Supervisory Authority (FSA) in the United Kingdom, announced in May 1997, provided an enormous impetus for the establishment of single regulators in many other countries, given the role of London as one of the leading financial centers around the globe. There were several teething problems in setting up the single authority in the UK. However, it is understood that the system is functioning more smoothly now. Under a single regulatory authority regime, the focus of supervision may get blurred, since the supervisory objective varies from one type of institution to another. It has been argued that in the case of banks, there are some special advantages in vesting the supervision of banks in the central bank (Goodhart, 2000). The disadvantage of a single authority is that it becomes unwieldy. Because of the enormity of the work involved, effective supervision of the various components may become difficult. Such a system can function efficiently only in countries where the various individual regulatory authorities had already achieved certain levels of maturity in terms of supervision. In India, we have at the present moment, a coordinating mechanism among the regulators which operate primarily at the policy level and through technical committees at the operational level. While for the present, this arrangement of independent authorities may be the most workable scheme, eventually, we would also have to move towards a single authority supervising over the various financial service providers. Also in the meanwhile, the coordinating mechanism has to be further strengthened at the operational level through exchange of information.

Regulating Payment and Settlement Systems

Payment and settlement mechanism is a crucial component of any financial system and ensuring the integrity of the payment systems is a key central banking function. The efficiency with which the finance flows and the security and stability of these flows ultimately determine the impact of intermediation process on economic performance. They also affect the liquidity in the system and in the process impinge upon the transmission mechanism of monetary policy. The objective of an efficient payment and settlement system is to secure final settlement of all transactions in order to remove an important source of uncertainty in the financial system.

Payment systems may propagate disturbances because problems with one member are likely to have direct and rapid effects on other members. It can lead to unexpected financial exposures for members. Payment obligations generated in a particular market, if not honoured on time, will affect not only the financial entities in that market but also the liquidity and stability of other markets. Thus, the robustness of the payment system is critical for financial stability.

Macroeconomic Stability

As already indicated, the functioning of the financial system rests on the functioning of the real sector. Therefore, financial stability can be achieved only if they operate in a suitable environment. Every economy needs to grow. However, this must happen without causing serious upheavals. Growth with stability is not a contradiction in terms. Stability here refers to modest rates of inflation, acceptable level of fiscal deficit and orderly conditions in the foreign exchange market. Many of the problems faced by the financial system in the 1970s and 1980s were due to high and fluctuating rate of inflation. The need for hedges against inflation became necessary. Again, disorderly conditions in the foreign exchange market can lead to disturbing changes in the balance sheets of financial institutions. While markets have evolved products to provide cover for foreign exchange rate and interest rate fluctuations, for the system, as a whole, there is no escape. Thus, a policy framework relating to inflation and exchange rate management has a key role to play in ensuring financial stability.

As indicated earlier, the two sectors with which the financial system is closely associated are the household and corporate sectors. In developing countries like India, the household sector is a surplus sector. The corporate sector is the main borrower and, therefore, what affects the corporate sector has an immediate affect on the financial system. The standards maintained by the corporate sectors are, therefore, of relevance to the financial system. While lending institutions themselves compel the corporate sector entities to conform to certain standards, the recent revelations in several countries of the manipulation of accounts by well known corporates have brought to the fore issues of corporate governance. The need for accountability on the part of the management to various stakeholders including the shareholders, the public and the financial institutions has assumed importance. The accounting profession has also come in for severe criticism. Market discipline requires that the market is supplied with information that is credible and can be depended upon. This has become all the more important in the context of the changing structure of financial system with capital markets and traded securities playing a greater role in the allocation of capital. Thus, stability in the financial sector requires not only norms and standards to be maintained by the financial institutions but also corporate entities who borrow heavily from the financial system and the general public.

Crisis Prevention and Crisis Management

The purpose of regulation is to keep the volatility in check. Nevertheless, the authorities must know how to act when a crisis is brewing and when it actually hits the system. There has been a considerable discussion on crisis prevention and crisis management measures at home and abroad in recent times. In a broad sense, all the standards that are prescribed and the supervisory mechanism that is in place are intended to prevent crisis. In fact, recognising the fact that financial soundness indicators may show deterioration in individual institutions, several regulatory authorities have initiated what is known as 'prompt corrective action' programme. Under such a system when norms fall below a level, action is triggered and the central banks intervene through a set of mandatory actions to stem further deterioration in the health of the banks showing signs of weakness. In India, the RBI instead of placing reliance on a single trigger point such as capital adequacy, have set two more trigger points which serve as early warning signals. However, certain specific issues need to be tackled when signs of a crisis make their appearance. It is here that the roles of 'safety nets' and 'lender of last resort' (LOLR) come into picture. The most classic example of a 'safety net' is deposit insurance which protects depositors upto a limit in case of failure by a bank. The existence of a safety net ensures continued confidence in a bank. However, there is a 'moral hazard' problem. The potential for imprudent behaviour increases when such a cover exists. Several proposals have been made to limit the 'moral hazard' problem. Similarly 'the lender of last resort' function which has always been recognised as an integral part of the functions of a central bank since the days of Bagetrot is meant to provide support to banks in times of need. The 'need' in normal times is different from 'need' in extraordinary circumstances. In the former situation, central banks have less difficulty in providing support. In the latter situation, support may be needed by several banks at the same time. As these safety nets provide liquidity, an imminent crisis can be averted only if the problem is one of liquidity.

Timely action through the use of 'safety nets' can prevent contagion and limit the spread of a difficulty faced by a single institution from becoming a systemic problem. Although in the case of LOLR a distinction is made between illiquidity and insolvency, it is not easy to determine the problem in practical terms. There is also a moral hazard problem of too big to fail syndrome. Nevertheless every regulatory authority should have a policy towards safety nets which should include a well designed set of procedures to deal with demands of liquidity.

The same set of issues is faced more intensely, when a crisis actually hits. The first concern of authorities must be to prevent the contagion spreading. This, however, poses a dilemma. If a central bank or a regulatory authority takes extraordinary steps to bail out a single institution to avert contagion, it can invite criticism. The criticism will be louder, if the effort ultimately fails. The protection of the integrity of the payment system can become a dominant objective at times of crisis. Public sector intervention should be kept to the minimum compatible with addressing the crisis. Not all situations of crisis arise purely out of liquidity needs. Disturbances in foreign exchange market can occur for a variety of reasons, some of which can be due to inappropriate policy stances. Therefore, some policy corrections may be called for. Also at the policy level, some conflicts can arise between other objectives and financial stability objective. A balance will have to be struck by policy makers. This takes us to an important issue relating to monetary policy.

Monetary Policy and Financial Stability

In a broad sense, financial stability is very much an objective of monetary policy. Monetary authorities influence the economy through changes in the cost and availability of credit and money. The effectiveness of monetary policy actions depends upon the financial infrastructure in the country. Imperfections in the financial system can defeat or dilute the intentions of monetary authorities. A network of well functioning banks and other financial institutions is a necessary prerequisite for the efficient conduct of monetary policy. A stable financial system is, therefore, an important concern of monetary authorities. The objective of price stability which has become a dominant concern of most central banks facilitates financial stability.

Financial institutions grow faster in a stable price environment which promotes savings and investment. As already noted, financial instability if it leads to a real crisis involves heavy cost both in terms of fiscal burden and output loss. There is, therefore, a strong ground to treat financial stability as part of the objectives of monetary policy. This raises two questions. How can a central bank identify the situation when it has to intervene from the point of view of financial stability? Second, can any action that is called for from the angle of financial instability come into conflict with other objectives? (Laker, 1999). As for the identification of the appropriate time to intervene, the Central Bank faces the same dilemmas as it does in relation to other objectives. For example, the timing of the change in interest rate or money supply to correct the 'overheating' of the economy has always been a difficult decision. Monetary authorities have often been criticised for having acted 'too late' or 'too early'. However, Central Banks do decide when to intervene taking into account a wide variety of factors. With respect to financial stability what the Central Banks need to prevent is the excessive build up and the subsequent unwinding of imbalances. The authorities must be willing to tighten policy, when they perceive excessive build up of financial imbalances. Much effort is called for to identify the nature of imbalances and to determine when they are excessive. Judging asset price behavior particularly in the stock market is a difficult task. Nevertheless, regulators including the Central Bank need to evolve appropriate indicators which can reveal persistent deviation from the fundamentals.

The second issue of conflict with other objectives may arise not because of fundamental concerns but because of indicators showing contradictory signals. For example, a serious imbalance may be building up in the stock market. Stock prices may be booming. However, at the same time, the inflation situation may be benign. The question is whether monetary authorities should tighten policy, even though near term inflation pressures are not apparent. For one thing, such a contradiction arises because the price indices normally used do not include asset prices such as those of stock and real estate. A situation where conventional price index is subdued but asset prices are rising has been aptly described as 'disguised overheating'. Of course, a Central Bank tightening monetary policy when near-term inflation prospects are low, can be accused of aborting real growth. However, this will be true only by taking a very short term view. If the financial imbalances have to be wound up later, it can cause a much greater output loss. All these are difficult judgment calls. At an analytical level what can be said is that anticipations regarding financial instability need to be taken into account while deciding monetary action.

Many Central Banks bring out an 'Inflation Report' at periodic intervals. Some Central Banks in recent years also bring out semi-annually financial stability reports. The Norwegian Central Bank in its Financial Stability Report focuses on three aspects: (a) macroeconomic developments of particular importance for financial stability such as developments in debt, assets prices and the debt servicing capacity of borrowers, (b) banks' earning and financial strength and the risk picture banks face, and (c) developments in financial institutions other than banks. At the end, an overall qualitative assessment of risk magnitude is made. It also indicates the direction risk has moved since the previous Report. The inflation report should not be confined to a discussion of the sectoral trends. It must deal with aggregate demand pressures in relation to aggregate supply and point to the possibility of achieving any goal set. The Financial Stability Report besides analysing the trends in different markets must make some assessment of the risk profile and pressures faced by the different segments of the financial system.

The RBI brings out several publications at periodic intervals. Apart from the *Annual Report*, there is the *Report on Currency and Finance* which now focuses on a specific theme each time and the *Report on Trend and Progress of Banking in India*. Besides, there are bi-annual monetary and credit policy statements. While in a sense, these Reports in totality do bring out substantial set of information and perceptions on the financial system, there is some advantage in RBI brining out separately every quarter an Inflation Report and at least initially semi-annually a Financial Stability Report.

The purpose of this paper is to highlight some of the analytical issues relating to financial stability. The objective of banking sector reform in this country has been to improve the productivity of the system. The paper has, however, not addressed the international dimensions of the problem. The need for the creation of an appropriate international financial architecture to deal with the problem of contagion has been discussed extensively in the literature. Returning to banking reform in this country, the focus was on efficiency, as stability was not perceived as an issue or concern. In the period since 1991, there have been a number of disruptions to the financial system in India. These episodes of financial distress point to the need for (a) enlarging the legal framework of regulation to include all segments of the financial system, (b) moving towards internationally accepted prudential norms and other standards of transparency and disclosure, and (c) strengthening the supervisory system to take effective preventive actions. A number of significant steps have been taken in all these areas. Worldwide also, these have been the trends. While the regulatory system lays down the rules, it is the supervisory system that ensures their implementation. A regulatory system is only as good as its implementation. What is needed is to evolve a system that will improve the ability to detect sources of vulnerability and to take timely corrective measures. That will pave the way for financial stability.

References

Bank for International Settlements (2003). *Consultative Document—The New Basel Capital Accord*, April.

Bean, Charles (2004). "Asset Prices, Monetary Policy and Financial Stability: A Central Banker's View", Paper presented at the AEA Conference. San Diego.

Berger, Allen N. and Gregory F. Udell (2003). "The Institutional Memory Hypothesis and the Procyclicality of Bank Lending Behaviour", *BIS Working Papers* No. 125, January.

Borio, Claudio (2004). "The Elusive Search for Monetary and Financial Stability", Inaugural keynote address of the *6th Money and Finance Conference* organised by IGIDR, Mumbai, March 25-27.

Caruana, Jaime (2004). "Basel II—A New Approach to Banking Supervision", *BIS Review* 33: 1-9.

Craig, Sean and V. Sundararajan (2003). "Using Financial Soundness Indicators to Assess Risks to Financial Stability". *(mimeo)*.

Crockett, Andrew (1997). "Why is Financial Stability a Goal of Public Policy?", Paper presented at the Federal Reserve Bank of Kansas City's 1997 Symposium, *Maintaining Financial Stability in a Global Economy*. Jackson Hole, Wyoming, August 28-30.

———. (2002). "Strengthening the International Financial Architecture", Lecture delivered at ASCII, Hyderabad, January 28.

Das, Udaibir S. *et al.* (2004). "Does Regulatory Governance Matter for Financial System Stability? An Empirical Analysis", *IMF Working Paper* No. 04/89, May.

Evans, Owen *et al.* (2000). "Macroprudential Indicators of Financial System Soundness", *IMF Occasional Paper* No. 192. Washington DC: International Monetary Fund.

Goodhart, Charles A.E. (2000). "Whither Central Banking?", *Eleventh C.D. Deshmukh Memorial Lecture*, Organised by Reserve Bank of India, Mumbai, December 7.

Hemming, Richard *et al.* (2003). "Fiscal Vulnerability and Financial Crises in Emerging Market Economies", *IMF Occasional Paper* No. 218. Washington DC: International Monetary Fund.

Hoggarth, Glenn and Victoria Saporta (2001). "Costs of Banking System Instability: Some Empirical Evidence", *Financial Stability Review:* 148-165, June. Bank of England.

Laker, J.F. (1999). "Monitoring Financial System Stability", *Reserve Bank of Australia Bulletin:* 1-13, October. Reserve Bank of Australia.

Nachane, D.M. *et al.* (2000). "Capital Adequacy Requirements and the Behaviour of Commercial Banks in India: An Analytical and Empirical Study", *RBI Development Research Group Study* No. 22. Mumbai: Reserve Bank of India.

Nachane, D.M. (2003). "Basel Accord II: Implications for the Indian Banking System", *Bank Quest:* 47-54, October-December.

Norges Bank (2003). *Financial Stability,* 2/2003, November.

Rangarajan, C. (2001). "Financial Reforms and Stability: Systemic Issues", Speech at the Asian Regional Seminar on *Financial Sector Reforms and Stability.* Hyderabad: ASCII. March 29.

Reddy, Y.V. (2002). "Choice between Single and Multiple Regulators of the Financial System", in *Lectures on Economic and Financial Sector Reforms in India.* New Delhi: OUP.

Stiglitz, Joseph E. (1994). "The Role of the State in Financial Markets", Proceedings of the *World Bank Annual Conference on Development Economics 1993.* IBRD/World bank.

Stiglitz, Joseph and Bruce Greenwald (2003). *Towards a New Paradigm in Monetary Economics.* Cambridge University Press.

An earlier version of this paper was presented as the R.S. Bhatt Memorial Lecture delivered in Mumbai, June 2004. I am grateful to Ms. Shyamala Gopinath and Ms. Usha Thorat for their help in writing this paper. I am thankful to Mr. S.S. Tarapore for his suggestions for improving the text. I must also thank Dr. A. Prasad and Dr. A. Samantaraya for the assistance provided by them.

3 | The Importance of being Earnest about Fiscal Responsibility

Fiscal Responsibility—The Debate

There is, by definition, a tension between fiscal restraint and finding resources for all the expenditure needs of the government. Where this line is drawn and how this tension is managed is the stuff of much economic analysis as well as ideological debate. The Fiscal Responsibility and Budget Management (FRBM) Act mandates the Centre to reduce fiscal deficit to 3 per cent of GDP and to completely eliminate revenue deficit by 2008-09. Similarly, acting in response to the debt relief package recommended by the Twelfth Finance Commission (TFC) in return for fiscal correction, 24 of the 29 states too have enacted fiscal responsibility acts accepting similar obligations—fiscal deficit of 3 per cent of Gross State Domestic Product (GSDP) and zero revenue deficit by 2008-09. The case for fiscal responsibility, both at the Centre and in the states, was made on the argument that fiscal consolidation is an essential condition for accelerating growth.

Some economists and critics have called into question the advisability of fiscal restraint when the public sector investment needs are so large and pressing, and have contended that in the Indian context, it is not fiscal contraction, but fiscal expansion that is growth enhancing. The Approach Paper to the Eleventh Plan too has made out a case for relaxing the FRBM targets in order to find sufficient resources for the 'gross budgetary support' (GBS) that the Plan demands.

Co-author Duvvuri Subbarao.

This chapter will argue that staying the course and delivering on the FRBM targets is critical to sustaining the current growth momentum. The bedrock of sustainable growth is macroeconomic stability. Maintaining macroeconomic stability, as characterised by low inflation, stable interest rates and comfortable balance of payments, is critically dependent on redressing fiscal imbalances.

Three important qualifications on the way forward to fiscal responsibility are in order. First, there needs to be fiscal correction not just at the Centre but also in the states. Second, for sustaining and accelerating growth, achieving the FRBM targets is necessary, but not sufficient. We need to pay attention not only to achieving the targets in quantitative terms but also to the quality of adjustment. In particular, this will mean improving both the allocative and technical efficiencies of public expenditures. Third, a stand-alone deficit target is incomplete unless the level of revenue or expenditure is specified too. Given that fiscal deficit is the gap between the government's revenue and its expenditure, a given level of deficit can be achieved at different levels of revenue and expenditure. It is important that these levels are maintained sufficiently high even as we target a specified fiscal deficit.

Post-Reform Trends in Deficits

To put the fiscal responsibility debate in perspective, it is important to take stock of the trends in fiscal and revenue deficits in the post-reform period.

Public finances, both at the Centre and in the states, had deteriorated progressively since the mid-90s. The combined fiscal deficit of the Centre and the states which was 9.3 per cent of GDP in the crisis year of 1990-91 dropped to 6.3 per cent in 1996-97 (Figure 3.1 and Table 3.1) before creeping back up to 9.0 per cent in 1998-99 largely on account of the impact of the Fifth Pay Commission award. The fiscal deficit had remained at over 9.0 per cent until 2002-03 and has since been on a downward shift declining to 7.5 per cent in 2005-06 (RE). Similarly, the combined revenue deficit of the Centre and the states which was 4.2 per cent in the crisis year of 1990-91 and had declined to 3.2 per cent by 1992-93, grew to an alarming level of 6.9 per cent by

2001-02. Like fiscal deficit, revenue deficit too has shown a welcome downward shift since 2002-03 declining to 3.1 per cent for 2005-06 (RE).

Figure 3.1

Deficit Indicators—Centre and States Combined

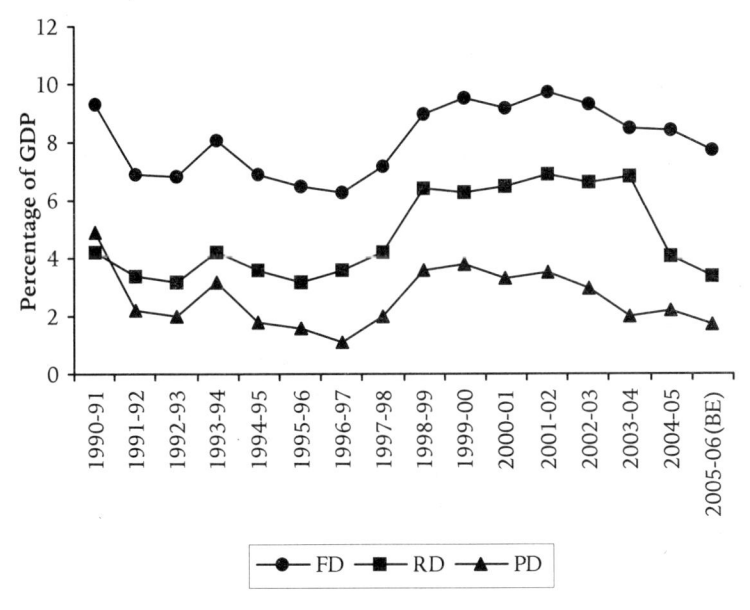

●— FD ■— RD ▲— PD

Table 3.1

Fiscal Indicators—Centre and States Combined

Year	Fiscal Deficit (FD)	Revenue Deficit (RD)	Primary Deficit (PD)	RD/FD	Debt	Interest Payments
	Per Cent of GDP			Per Cent	Per Cent of GDP	
	Combined for Centre and States					
1990-91	9.4	4.2	5.0	44.6	64.9	4.4
1995-96	6.5	3.2	1.6	48.8	61.3	5.0
2004-05	7.5	3.7	1.4	48.9	82.5	6.2
2005-06 (RE)	7.5	3.1	1.6	41.5	79.5	5.8
2006-07 (BE)	6.5	2.2	0.8	33.6	78.6	5.7

Source: Reserve Bank of India, *Handbook of Statistics on Indian Economy*, 2005-06.

The net picture that emerges is of a short-lived improvement in the deficit indicators in the immediate post-reform period followed by a steep deterioration from around the mid-90s until 2002-03 and gradual improvement since then.

The impact of year-on-year deficits shows up in the stock of debt and interest payment indicators (Table 3.1). The debt-GDP ratio of the Centre and states combined had increased from 64.9 per cent in 1990-91 to 79.5 per cent in 2005-06. Correspondingly, the ratio of interest payments to GDP had increased from 4.4 per cent to 5.8 per cent reflecting both higher debt stock as well as higher average interest rate.

What is even more worrisome in our situation is that we have not just fiscal deficits, but we have fiscal deficits together with revenue deficits. What this means is that governments, both at the Centre and in the states, are using up a significant proportion of the borrowed funds not for capital investment that will yield future incomes but for current consumption like payment of salaries, pensions and subsidies. A measure of this profligacy is the share of revenue deficit in fiscal deficit which increased from 45 per cent in 1990-91 to over 71 per cent in 2001-02—an increase of 25 percentage points. This ratio has since come down to 41.5 per cent by 2005-06 but even this is just too high. If the FRBM target on revenue deficit is achieved, this ratio should come down to zero by 2008-09.

Another cause for concern is that our fiscal deficits are actually higher than acknowledged. They are understated because some of the liabilities of the government are not treated as debt in the budget numbers. Notably, the oil bonds which have become a regular feature are not accounted for above the line. This year alone the oil bonds are of the order of Rs. 28,000 crore, and if acknowledged, will add to the fiscal deficit by a not insignificant 0.7 percentage points of GDP. Regardless of accounting practices, it is important to keep this in mind for its macroeconomic implications.

Impact of Deficits on Economic Prospects

It must be acknowledged upfront that fiscal deficits are not bad *per se*. In fact, they may be necessary, even desirable in some situations. The issue therefore is not whether or not there should be a fiscal deficit, but its appropriate level. The answer depends on a number of variables, particularly the level of savings and the ratio of revenues to GDP. It is also a function of the existing stock of debt and debt servicing burden, the rate of interest, the external payments situation, the degree of capital controls, and importantly the use to which the borrowed resources are put. The advisable fiscal deficit level therefore is very contextual and varies from country to country.

In general, continued high fiscal deficits are a concern for several reasons. First, they disempower the government's fiscal stance by pre-empting a larger share of public resources for debt servicing thereby leaving that much less for desirable expenditures such as physical infrastructure (e.g. roads, power) and social infrastructure (e.g. education, health). This leads to a declining ratio of capital expenditure to total expenditure as seen over the period 1990-91 to 2005-06 (Figure 3.2).

Figure 3.2

Direction of Fiscal Adjustment

(i) *Capital Expenditure as a Ratio of Total Expenditure*
(ii) *Interest Payments as a Ratio of Revenue Receipts*

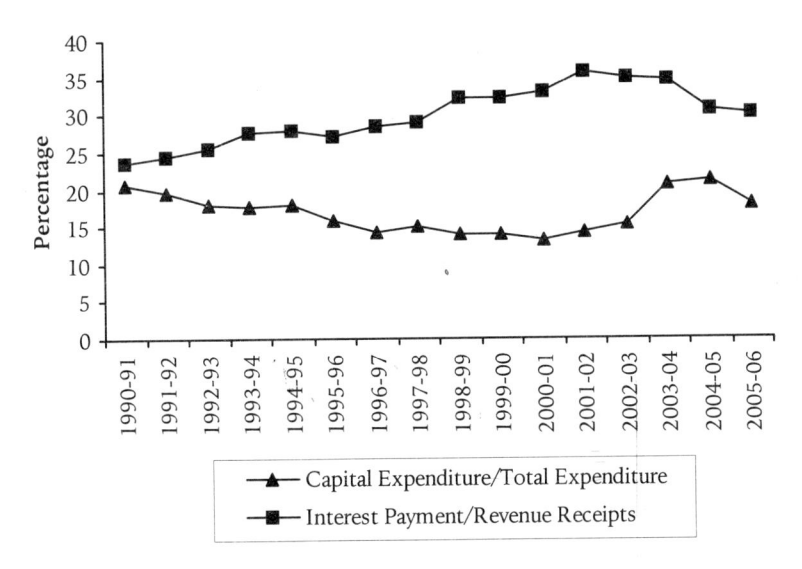

Source: Reserve Bank of India (2006). *Handbook of Statistics on Indian Economy, 2005-06.* September.

Second, if we incur fiscal deficits together with revenue deficits, it means we are using up borrowed resources for current consumption which may raise growth in the short-term, but of the spurious variety. For sustainable growth, we need to balance our books on the revenue account and use borrowed funds only for investment.

Third, to the extent the government pre-empts the available investible resources, it crowds out the private sector. A balance needs to be struck in apportioning the investible resources between the government and the private sector. The crowding out argument has even greater force in an economy with capital controls.

Fourth, continued fiscal deficits impact on interest and inflation rates depending on how the deficits are financed. If the government borrows in the domestic market, it puts pressure on the interest rate. If the government finances the deficit by creating high power money, it fuels inflation. In our case, since deficits are financed by open market borrowing, albeit through a preferential SLR window, the risk is largely of government borrowing leading to higher interest rates.

Finally, fiscal deficits are also bad for another little realised, but powerful reason. Fiscal deficits, especially in the face of revenue deficits, exacerbate inter-temporal equity concerns as they give the pleasure of spending to the current generation while passing on the pain of debt servicing to the later generation.

Fiscal Adjustment—The Contrarian View

While the mainstream view on fiscal adjustment accords with textbook economics, the contrarian view that an expansionary fiscal policy is the key to economic development has some distinguished academic credentials as well. Much of this debate between fiscal restraint and fiscal expansion has played out in the Indian context in recent months. It is important to visit this debate in order to make an informed appreciation of the quantum and quality of fiscal responsibility required of our economy.

The argument for fiscal expansion runs on two strands—an analytical one and an empirical one. The analytical argument is that the government should relax the FRBM targets, borrow aggressively and invest in physical and social infrastructure. This will accelerate growth and raise the tax buoyancy, and the higher revenues so generated will be more than sufficient to meet the additional debt service obligations. In other words, through a 'borrow and invest' fiscal stance, the economy can get on to a virtuous circle of higher growth and higher revenues, and in a manner of speaking the government can borrow its way out of a debt crisis!

The empirical argument for fiscal expansion draws from recent Indian experience. It goes as follows: The conventional wisdom that fiscal deficits put pressure on interest and exchange rates and fuel inflation is not borne out by the Indian experience of the recent period. On the contrary, during the period 1996-97–2001-02 when fiscal deficits were on the rise, inflation had remained subdued and interest rates were restrained. What this shows is that India was not affected by the maladies traditionally associated with high fiscal deficits because our economic dynamics are different from those underlying the mainstream theory. Fiscal deficits hurt growth only when the imbalances are way off track. In India we are still very much within the limits of safety. Too drastic an adjustment in pursuit of some pre-determined target for fiscal deficit (set by FRBM) will threaten the growth momentum. What we need is not fiscal contraction, but fiscal expansion.

In Defence of Fiscal Adjustment

The above expansionary fiscal stance argument is quite persuasive, but is contestable from both analytical and empirical perspectives.

From an analytical perspective, the fiscal expansion argument works only in a very limited case—there is no revenue deficit and the investments made out of the borrowing generate returns sufficient to service the debt. Neither of these conditions is met in the Indian case. Even if we achieve zero revenue deficit, and use borrowings only for investment expenditure *a la* the golden rule, we still need to restrain fiscal deficits because the budgetary returns on investment are typically lower than the cost of borrowing. We will need to dip into the revenue pool to service the debt. After all, today's fiscal deficits incurred to support capital expenditures can all too easily become tomorrow's revenue deficits. We need to operate the golden rule together with a ceiling on fiscal deficit. It is worth noting that even the UK's golden rule is subject to a debt ceiling.

From an empirical perspective, it is true that our high fiscal deficits have not, over an extended period, had an adverse economic impact by way of higher inflation or interest rates. Admittedly, this is contrary to received wisdom. But this apparent paradox is the result of a fortuitous combination of circumstances. The economic reforms launched in 1991—notably, the abolition of industrial licencing, dereservation of industries and trade liberalisation—had unleashed competitive forces resulting in higher investment as well as higher efficiency in production leading to an increase in production capacity which ran ahead of demand. This excess capacity led to a slackening of corporate investment demand which declined from 9.6 per cent of GDP in 1995-1996 to 5.6 per cent in 2001-02. The slackening of corporate investment demand coincided with the period when fiscal deficits, after the compression of the immediate post-reform period, started to expand once again (Figure 3.3). It was because of this sluggish private investment demand that we escaped higher interest rates despite higher fiscal deficits. These domestic dynamics were aided by some exogenous factors as well such as the softening of global interest rates which helped to restrain domestic interest rates.

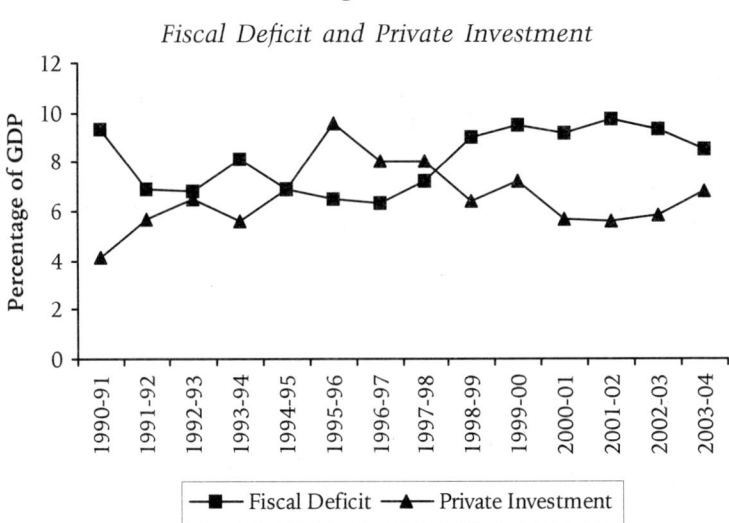

Figure 3.3

Fiscal Deficit and Private Investment

Some of these one-off circumstances are beginning to reverse. Globally, the era of cheap money has come to an end. For the first time in 15 years, the three big central banks, the US Federal Reserve, the European Central Bank and the Bank of Japan have all tightened monetary policy. More importantly, the slack in the economy has been fully absorbed and the 'output gap' has been fully bridged. In fact, the concern today is the precise opposite—that the economy is performing at its full capacity and demand is running ahead of potential output. Interest rates are inching back up and year-on-year inflation had crossed 6.5 per cent in January 2007. Two inferences follow from this. First, the temporary reprieve that the economy had in the later half of the 90s cannot be taken for granted; fiscal deficits do take their toll. Second, we are heading into a situation of increasing competition for the limited pool of investable resources, and this will intensify the crowding out impact of fiscal deficits and compromise the growth momentum.

A variant of the fiscal expansion argument, drawing from the Keynesian world view, is that the government needs to borrow and spend in order to stimulate aggregate demand, thereby, spurring employment and growth through the multiplier effect. But it is important to remember that the Keynesian logic works only if the economy is demand constrained and is operating below full employment as, for example, the US economy during the Great Depression of the 1930s.

The Keynesian effect does not materialise if the economy is not demand constrained. This is evidenced by our own experience over the last decade. The burgeoning fiscal deficits during the period 1998-99–2002-2003 were accompanied by economic slow down (Figure 3.4). This was because our debt was largely relative to GDP and the borrowings went not to finance productive expenditure but to service the debt. On the contrary, the fiscal correction starting 2002-03 saw a healthy rebound in growth. This cannot simply be a coincidence. It is important to remember that even Keynes recommended his approach only for 'pump priming', but not to keep the pump running on a long-term basis.

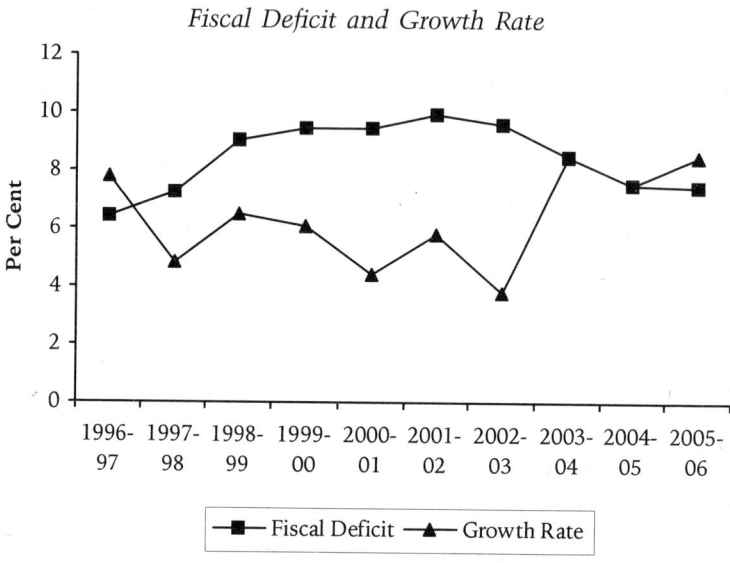

Figure 3.4

Fiscal Deficit and Growth Rate

Targeting Deficits—Some Issues

Even those who admit to fiscal responsibility at the big picture level question some of the details. The following paragraphs address the more contentious issues in this debate.

Is there Sanctity to a Three per cent Fiscal Deficit Target?

Among the most contentious issues is the sanctity of a three per cent target of fiscal deficit each for the Centre and the states. Is there a rationale for this or is it just a number pulled out of thin air?

First of all, it must be acknowledged that determining an appropriate level of fiscal deficit is a complex problem. There is an enormous amount of public finance literature on fiscal deficits but virtually no paper that gives a template for determining the appropriate fiscal deficit. It is this backdrop which has triggered the criticism that the three per cent target has no justification and that it has simply been copied from the Mastricht Treaty which mandates the members of the EU to maintain a three per cent fiscal deficit over an economic cycle.

Even though the FRBM Act has not been explicit about it, the targets for both fiscal and revenue deficits are based on the recommendations of a Finance Ministry Committee which determined these numbers on the basis of some simulations of the debt dynamics. The simulations themselves though are not in the public domain.

Quite independently, the Twelfth Finance Commission provided a detailed rationale for the fiscal deficit target of 6 per cent for the Centre and states combined. The Commission argued as follows. The Mastricht Treaty allows its members a 3 per cent fiscal deficit. Undoubtedly, the higher savings rate in India will allow a higher level of fiscal deficit relative of GDP to be maintained. Time-series data on savings show that the household sector in India has excess savings over its investments of the order of 10-11 per cent of GDP. Add to this foreign savings by way of current account deficit of the order of 1.5-2 per cent of GDP yielding savings of the order of 13 per cent of GDP available to be appropriated by the other two sectors of the economy—public sector and the corporate sector—for investment. Up to 5 per cent of this will go to the corporate sector and 8 per cent to the combined public sector. Of the latter, about 2 per cent will go to the non-departmental undertakings leaving 6 per cent for the government to be apportioned equally between the Centre and the states. Thus, a combined fiscal deficit of 6 per cent of GDP is consistent with the existing ratio of the savings of the household sector in financial assets relative to GDP and prudent levels of current account deficit, and the demand on these by the private corporate sector and non-departmental public enterprises.

Apart from the savings dimension, the target for fiscal deficit also needs to be informed by the debt dynamics such as the ratios of debt to GDP and interest payments to revenue. The debt dynamics are such that unrestrained fiscal deficits will put us on a vicious cycle of higher debt relative to GDP and a larger portion of the revenues being pre-empted for interest payments. It is important to restrain fiscal deficit in order to first bring down and then stabilise the debt-GDP and interest payments to revenues at reasonable levels.

Should Revenue Deficit be a Target?

Another contentious issue in the debate has been the need to target revenue deficit as part of fiscal responsibility. It is argued that internationally fiscal rules do not target revenue deficits; they focus instead on the fiscal deficit and on the primary deficit (i.e. fiscal deficit excluding interest payments) as the relevant control variables. The case for focusing on the primary deficit is simply that interest costs on accumulated debt are outside the scope of government control and while they may vary with interest rate changes, this variation does not reflect the quality of fiscal control.

This is debatable. First, it is not correct to say that the revenue deficit target is not internationally recognised. The UK, for example, has the 'golden rule' which mandates the government to restrict borrowing to the extent of capital expenditure. Accordingly, under the golden rule, capital expenditure equals borrowing plus any plough back from surplus on the revenue account. The golden rule is, therefore, similar to our zero revenue deficit target. Several other countries too have mandated discipline on maintaining a balance on the current account of the budget. If we do not hear much of a debate on revenue deficits, it is not because restraining them is considered unimportant for macro management, but because not many countries have revenue deficits as we know them. It may be recalled that even in India, revenue deficits were a phenomenon that started life only in the early 80s.

Second, in a conceptual sense, of the three variables, fiscal deficit, primary deficit and revenue deficit, it does not matter which two variables we target. As long as we target any two variables, the third variable is determined too. Illustratively, it is possible to calibrate a primary deficit target corresponding to a zero revenue deficit and shift targeting from revenue deficit to primary deficit. In that sense what matters is the quantum of adjustment we want to make and not which two variables we target.

Is a Cyclically Adjusted Fiscal Deficit Target Better than a Fixed Annual Target?

Reflecting the efficacy of a counter-cyclical fiscal policy, both the EU and the UK have cyclically adjusted fiscal deficit targets. This means that during an upturn the economy builds up credit by running a surplus, and encashes the credit by incurring a deficit during a downturn so that over the economic cycle the target deficit is maintained. It is argued that India too must adopt a similar cyclically adjusted fiscal management.

Notwithstanding the appeal of this argument, we would be better off with a fixed target. A cyclically adjusted policy works only when the debt-GDP ratio is already at a sustainable level. Debt sustainability and fiscal deficit are interlinked and should not be viewed on a stand-alone basis. A fiscal deficit of 8 per cent when the debt-GDP ratio is 100 per cent has sustainability implications quite different from an 8 per cent deficit when the debt-GDP ratio is 50 per cent. In our case the debt-GDP ratio is above the sustainability level. We need to first bring it down and then stabilise it at that low level. This cannot be achieved unless we maintain a low fiscal deficit over a period. A cyclically adjusted policy can certainly be an option after the adjustment phase is complete. Cyclical adjustment, of course, presupposes that the economy is subject to economic cycles.

Conclusion

After several years of discussion, the Centre and states have enacted fiscal responsibility legislations. It is important to remain committed to the FRBM targets. These targets need not necessarily come in the way of meeting necessary and desirable expenditures. Indeed recent experience shows that strong growth will make it possible to meet the deficit targets and still leave enough resources for meeting the expenditure needs. Remaining committed to fiscal responsibility will strengthen the present growth momentum.

Unabridged version of the paper published in the *Economic Times*, February 19 and 20, 2007.

4 Dynamics of Debt Accumulation in India

Impact of Primary Deficit, Growth and Interest Rate

Introduction

In the analysis of accumulation of the debt, two factors are identified as contributing to the debt-GDP ratio. One is the cumulated primary deficits and the other, the cumulated effect of the difference between growth rate and interest rate. This chapter looks at the relative contribution of cumulated primary deficits and the cumulated effect of the excess of growth rate over interest rate on the accumulation of outstanding liabilities[1] of the central government in India over the period 1951-52 to 2001-02. Interest rate in this discussion refers to the effective interest rate of the central government, calculated as the ratio of interest payments in a year to the outstanding liabilities at the beginning of the year. This chapter particularly highlights the implications of the sign reversal in the difference between real growth and interest rates, evidenced during the past three years. Throughout the stretch of 45 years from 1955-56 to 1999-2000, the real growth rate was in excess of the real interest rate. Since 2000-01, for three consecutive years, the real growth rate has been less than the real

---

1. Outstanding liabilities include all the three major components of debt, *viz.*, domestic non-monetised debt, monetised debt, and external debt. External debt is in terms of historical exchange rates, i.e., the rates that prevailed at the time of contracting the debt. Alternative series of external debt evaluated at current exchange rates, i.e., rates prevalent at the end of the financial year for which figures are given in both *Indian Public Finance Statistics* (since 1974-75) and CAG's Report on Union Finances (since 1991-92). The difference between the two series which was a little more than 11 per cent of GDP in 1991-92 has come down to about 5.6 per cent of GDP in 2001-02. The difference has been coming down in magnitude in recent years.

Co-author D.K. Srivastava.

interest rate. During the nineties, even when the GDP growth rate remained in excess of the interest rate, the gap between the two has been narrowing. If the days of large positive differences between growth and interest rates are all but over, there are serious implications for strategies aimed at containing the growth of debt relative to GDP. We are entering into an era, where corrections in the primary balance profile of the central government have become imperative.

This chapter is organised as follows: Section II proposes a methodology for decomposing the accumulation of debt into cumulated primary deficits and cumulated weighted excess of growth over interest rates. Section III sets out some data preliminaries, particularly in relation to data pertaining to the outstanding liabilities of the centre and the related fiscal deficits. Section IV provides a decade-wise examination of the growth of central debt and assesses the relative importance of cumulated primary deficits and cumulated impact of the differential between growth and interest rates in explaining the dynamics of debt accumulation. Section V looks at time profiles of growth and interest rates. Section VI looks at the pattern of growth of primary deficit relative to GDP. Section VII looks at the medium-term prospects in regard to central government's outstanding liabilities relative to GDP.

Decomposing Accumulation of Debt

The standard specification of the equation describing debt dynamics with discrete time periods[2] is given by

---

2. Let D = end-period outstanding debt, Y = GDP at market prices, g = growth rate, i = effective interest rate, P = primary deficit, F = fiscal deficit, and I = interest payment. The relevant period is indicated by the subscript t. The debt-GDP ratio is given by b and the primary deficit to GDP ratio is given by p. Thus, $b_t = D_t/Y_t$, and $p_t = P_t/Y_t$.

By definition,

$D_t - D_{t-1} = F_t$

or, $D_t - D_{t-1} = P_t + I_t$ ...(a)

We can write, $I_t = i\, D_{t-1}$, and $Y_t = Y_{t-1}(1+g_t)$

Dividing (a) by Y_t, we have

$b_t - b_{t-1}[1/(1+g_t)] = p_t + i_t\, b_{t-1}[1/(1+g_t)]$

or, $b_t = p_t + b_{t-1}\,[(1+i_t)/(1+g_t)]$ ...(b)

or, $b_t - b_{t-1} = p_t - b_{t-1}[1-(1+i_t)/(1+g_t)]$

or, $b_t - b_{t-1} = p_t - b_{t-1}[(g_t-i_t)/(1+g_t)]$ ...(c)

Dynamics of Debt Accumulation in India

$$b_t = p_t + b_{t-1}[(1+i_t)/(1+g_t)] \qquad \ldots(1)$$

Where

b_t = debt-GDP ratio in period t
p_t = ratio of primary-deficit to GDP in period t
g_t = growth rate of GDP in period t
i_t = effective nominal interest in period t

Writing

$z_t = b_t - b_{t-1}$, equation (1) can also be written as

$$z_t = p_t - b_{t-1}\left[\frac{(g_t - i_t)}{(1+g_t)}\right] \qquad \ldots(2)$$

The increment in debt can be cumulated over any relevant period t = 1 to T. Thus

$$\sum_{t=1}^{T} z_t = \sum_{t=1}^{T} p_t - \sum_{t=1}^{T} b_{t-1}[(g_t - i_t)/(1+g_t)] \qquad \ldots(3)$$

Equation 3 helps in decomposing the change in the debt-GDP ratio between any two benchmark years [$\sum_{t=1}^{T} z_t = (b_T - b_0)$] into the contribution of cumulated primary deficit relative to GDP and that of the cumulated effect of the weighted excess of growth over the interest rate. In the Indian case Sp_t has been much larger than Sz_t for long stretches of time, and the role of the growth/interest rate differential has been to absorb the impact of the cumulated primary deficits from getting translated into accretion to the debt-GDP ratio. It is, therefore, useful to write equation (3) as

$$\sum_{t=1}^{T} p_t = \sum_{t=1}^{T} z_t + \sum_{t=1}^{T} b_{t-1}[(g_t - i_t)/(1+g_t)] \qquad \ldots(4)$$

Of the cumulated primary deficit relative to GDP, that part which was absorbed by the differential of growth rate and interest rate is given by, say A1, where

$$A1 = \sum_{i=1}^{T} b_{t-1}[(g_t - i_t)/(1+g_t)] / \sum_{t=1}^{T} p_t \qquad \ldots(5)$$

Correspondingly, the share of the cumulated primary deficit which results in the accretion to the debt-GDP ratio (say A2) is given by

$$A2 = \sum_{t=1}^{T} z_t / \sum_{t=1}^{T} p_t \qquad \ldots(6)$$

Thus, A1 + A2 = 1

It might be useful to further decompose the term containing the effect of growth-interest rate differential between the effect of real growth-real interest rate differential and inflation. Writing g^* and i^* for real growth and real interest rates and π for the inflation rate, we have $(g_t - i_t = g_t^* - i_t^*)$ and $1 + g_t = 1 + g_t^* + \pi_t$. We can then write, using the expansion of the term and ignoring second order terms, with the assumption that $g_t << 1$:

$$(1+g_t)^{-1} = (1+g_t^* + \pi_t)^{-1} = 1 - g_t^* - \pi_t \qquad \ldots(7)$$

Thus,

$$\sum_{i=1}^{T} b_{t-1}(g_t - i_t)(1+g_t)^{-1} = \sum_{i=1}^{T} b_{t-1}(g_t^* - i_t^*)(1 - g_t^*) - \sum_{i=1}^{T} b_{t-1}(g_t^* - i_t^*)\pi_t \qquad \ldots(8)$$

The relative shares of the two terms on the right hand side in the factor giving the impact of the growth-interest rate differential can provide the relative contributions of the differential between real growth and interest rates and the inflation rate. It may be noted that the effect of inflation is in a direction opposite to that of the influence of the differential between real growth and real interest rate. Thus, when real growth rate exceeds the real interest rate, its beneficial effect in containing the process of debt accumulation is partly offset by the influence of the inflation rate, and *vice versa*.

Some Data Preliminaries

In theory, change in outstanding debt should be equal to the fiscal deficit. Estimating fiscal deficit in this manner and juxtaposing these to the official fiscal deficit figures show discrepancies. A comparison is made between the fiscal deficit as reported in the Receipts Budget of the central government and the fiscal deficit obtained by taking the change in the year-end outstanding liabilities as shown once again in the Receipts Budget. These figures for the period 1987-88 to 2001-02 RE are shown in the first three columns of Table 4.1. It is clear that the discrepancies between the two series are quite large after 1999-2000. The primary reason for this is the way in which liabilities on account of the National Small Savings Fund (NSFF) are shown in the Receipts Budget since 1999-2000.

Table 4.1
Adjusted Outstanding Liabilities and Derived Fiscal Deficit

(Rs. Crore)

	Out-standing Liabilities (Rec. Bud.)	Derived Fiscal Deficit (1)	Official Fiscal Deficit (OFD)	Difference with OFD	Out-standing Liabilities (CAG)	Derived Fiscal Deficit (2)	Difference with OFD
	1	2	3	4	5	6	7
1987-88	193651	27105	27044	61	195562	27105	61
1988-89	229771	36120	30923	5197	229771	34209	5197
1989-90	268193	38422	35630	2792	268193	38422	2792
1990-91	314558	46365	44650	1715	314558	46365	1715
1991-92	354662	40104	36325	3779	354662	40104	3779
1992-93	401924	47262	40173	7089	401923	47261	7088
1993-94	477968	76044	60257	15787	477968	76045	15788
1994-95	538610	60642	57703	2939	538610	60642	2940
1995-96	606232	67622	60243	7379	606233	67623	7379
1996-97	675676	69444	66733	2711	675676	69443	2710
1997-98	778294	102618	88937	13681	778294	102618	13681
1998-99	891806	113512	113348	164	891806	113512	166
1999-2000	1021029	129223	104716	24507	992411	100605	-4113
2000-01	1168541	147512	118816	28696	1114770	122359	3543
2001-02	1366409	197868	140955	56913	1271189	156419	15463
As Per cent of GDP at market prices							
1987-88	54.65	7.65	7.63	0.02	55.19	7.65	0.02
1988-89	54.50	8.57	7.34	1.23	54.50	8.11	1.23
1989-90	55.16	7.90	7.33	0.57	55.16	7.90	0.57
1990-91	55.31	8.15	7.85	0.30	55.31	8.15	0.30
1991-92	54.30	6.14	5.56	0.58	54.30	6.14	0.58
1992-93	53.71	6.32	5.37	0.95	53.71	6.32	0.95
1993-94	55.63	8.85	7.01	1.84	55.63	8.85	1.84
1994-95	53.18	5.99	5.70	0.29	53.18	5.99	0.29
1995-96	51.03	5.69	5.07	0.62	51.03	5.69	0.62
1996-97	49.38	5.08	4.88	0.20	49.38	5.08	0.20
1997-98	51.12	6.74	5.84	0.90	51.12	6.74	0.90
1998-99	51.22	6.52	6.51	0.01	51.22	6.52	0.01
1999-2000	52.71	6.67	5.41	1.27	51.24	5.19	-0.21
2000-01	55.53	7.01	5.65	1.36	52.98	5.81	0.17
2001-02	59.51	8.62	6.14	2.48	55.36	6.81	0.67

Source: Columns 1 and 3: Central Government Receipts Budget (2003-04 and earlier years).
Col 5: CAG's Report on Union Finances (No 1 of 2003).
GDP figures from NAS, CSO.

The NSSF was established with effect from April 1, 1999 and is maintained in the Public Account of India. The balance of collections into the NSSF over withdrawals is invested in special government securities issued by the central as well as the state governments, i.e., the central and the state governments borrow from the NSSF on the basis of these special securities. Prior to 1998-99, small savings were shown as part of 'other liabilities' of India, where all net borrowings from the public account were shown, whether ultimately lent to the central or the state governments. Since 1999-2000, the central borrowings from the NSSF constitute part of centre's 'internal debt'. However, one component of it continues to be shown as 'other liabilities' which primarily represents the borrowing from the NSSF by the state governments. This component needs to be taken out while showing centre's outstanding liabilities.

While the outstanding liabilities as shown in the Receipts Budget are overstated because of the 'double counting' on account of the small savings, the fiscal deficit is understated because certain securities issued by the central government are kept off budget. Important among these are securities issued to oil companies after the winding up of the Oil Pool Account as also securities issued to UTI, Industrial Investments Bank of India and the Kudremukh Iron Ore Project. The amount of these securities in some years is quite large. While it may be debated as to whether or not these liabilities should form part of the fiscal deficit, clearly these are accretions to central liabilities and would become a budgetary burden, whenever these are redeemed. Therefore, these securities need to be included as part of the outstanding liabilities and must form part of the fiscal deficit. However, the budget documents do not take these securities into account while calculating the fiscal deficit. It may be noted that the outstanding liabilities as reported by the CAG avoid the overstatement of outstanding liabilities on account of the NSSF and at the same time include the other securities issued by the central government kept off the budget in estimating fiscal deficit. We have, therefore, taken the figures of outstanding liabilities given by the CAG Report on Union Government (No. 1 of 2003, p.109) since 1976-77 as the basis for calculating the fiscal deficit. For the earlier years the figures used are drawn from the series of Indian Public Finance Statistics. The new series of fiscal deficit derived from taking the change in the outstanding liabilities may be referred to as

Dynamics of Debt Accumulation in India

the 'Derived Fiscal Deficit'. The revised outstanding liabilities and the 'Derived Fiscal Deficit' are shown in columns 1 and 2 of Table 4.2 since 1950-51 and 1951-52 respectively.[3]

Table 4.2
Central Debt and Derived Fiscal and Primary Deficits

	Total Central Debt (End-Year)	Derived Fiscal Deficit (Rs Crore)	Interest Payments	Derived Primary Deficit	Rate of Growth of Debt (Per Cent)
	1	2	3	4	5
1950-51	2865		37.5		
1951-52	2912	47	39.0	8	1.6
1952-53	2940	28	36.5	-8	1.0
1953-54	3013	72	40.8	32	2.5
1954-55	3282	269	39.7	229	8.9
1955-56	3511	229	41.2	188	7.0
1956-57	3869	358	36.7	321	10.2
1957-58	4509	640	42.4	597	16.5
1958-59	5394	885	48.6	836	19.6
1959-60	6060	667	69.4	597	12.4
1960-61	6544	484	193.5	290	8.0
1961-62	6966	422	214.4	207	6.4
1962-63	7683	717	245.4	472	10.3
1963-64	8706	1023	278.4	745	13.3
1964-65	10124	1418	316.4	1101	16.3
1965-66	11329	1206	370.6	835	11.9
1966-67	14355	3026	463.5	2563	26.7
1967-68	15859	1504	501.4	1002	10.5
1968-69	16849	990	528.0	462	6.2
1969-70	17845	996	564.9	431	5.9
1970-71	18836	991	605.5	385	5.6
1971-72	21440	2604	670.1	1934	13.8
1972-73	23924	2484	772.4	1712	11.6
1973-74	24267	343	881.6	-539	1.4
1974-75	26314	2047	1000.8	1046	8.4

contd...

---

3. It is somewhat surprising that there are large differences in the fiscal deficit figures between the Receipts Budget and the Economic Survey for 1997-98 and 1998-99. For 1997-98, the Economic Survey and the Receipts Budget report the fiscal deficit at Rs 73,205 crore and Rs 88,937 crore respectively. For 1998-99, the figures are Rs 89,560 crore in Economic Survey and Rs 1,13,348 crore in the Receipts Budget.

contd...

	1	2	3	4	5
1975-76	27393	1079	1228.2	-149	4.1
1976-77	33608	6215	1374.4	4841	22.7
1977-78	40173	6565	1521.4	5044	19.5
1978-79	43482	3309	1829.0	1480	8.2
1979-80	50214	6732	2209.9	4522	15.5
1980-81	59748	9534	2604.3	6930	19.0
1981-82	68185	8437	3194.7	5242	14.1
1982-83	84872	16687	3937.6	12749	24.5
1983-84	95261	10389	4795.5	5594	12.2
1984-85	113441	18180	5974.5	12206	19.1
1985-86	137484	24043	7512.0	16531	21.2
1986-87	166546	29062	9245.9	19816	21.1
1987-88	195562	29016	11251.4	17765	17.4
1988-89	229771	34209	14278.5	19931	17.5
1989-90	268193	38422	17756.9	20665	16.7
1990-91	314558	46365	21498.3	24867	17.3
1991-92	354662	40104	26595.6	13508	12.7
1992-93	401923	47261	31075.5	16186	13.3
1993-94	477968	76045	36740.6	39304	18.9
1994-95	538610	60642	44060.0	16582	12.7
1995-96	606233	67623	50045.0	17578	12.6
1996-97	675676	69443	59478.4	9965	11.5
1997-98	778294	102618	65637.3	36981	15.2
1998-99	891806	113512	77882.4	35630	14.6
1999-2000	992411	100605	94593.0	6012	11.3
2000-01	1114770	122359	103224.0	19135	12.3
2001-02	1271189	156419	114173.0	42246	14.0

Source: (Basic Data): *Indian Public Finance Statistics* (various issues) and Report of the CAG on *Union Finances* (No 1 of 2003) (for 1976-77 to 2001-02).

Thus, two modifications are being used in this exercise as compared to the published figures on the outstanding liability and fiscal deficit given in the Receipts Budget. First, the figures for outstanding liabilities are adjusted since 1999-2000 in respect of the NSSF as contained in CAG's Report on Union Finances (No. 1 of 2003). Secondly, the figures for fiscal deficit are adjusted to obtain the Derived Fiscal Deficit to take into account some of the liabilities kept off the budget. During 1987-88 to 2001-02 the differences between the official fiscal deficit and the derived fiscal deficit have ranged from -0.21 to 1.84 percentage points of GDP. These differences are reflected in the derived primary deficit figures also. These adjustments imply that the figures for outstanding liabilities of the central government are lower (since 1999-2000) than those given in the Receipts Budget, and the fiscal deficit and primary deficit figures are higher.[4]

Accumulation of Central Debt

The debt-GDP ratio at the end of 1950-51 was 28.84 per cent. During 1951-52 to 1959-60 a little less than 10 percentage points were added to the debt-GDP ratio. An additional accretion of about 3 percentage points took place in the sixties. In the seventies, and later in the nineties there was hardly any change in the debt-GDP ratio. It was only in the eighties that there was an increase of 13.6 percentage points in the debt-GDP ratio. We examine below how the cumulated primary deficit resulted in large cumulated increases in the debt-GDP ratio over some stretches of time and not in others. Table 4.3 and Figure 4.1 show the relative effects of the cumulated primary deficits and the factor reflecting the effect of growth-interest rate differential [called (g-i) differential, hereafter] in the process of accumulation of debt of the central government since 1951-52. The Indian experience shows that throughout the period from 1955-56 to 1999-2000, it was the primary deficit that caused the increase in the debt-GDP ratio. Often a significant part of the pressure of primary deficit could be absorbed by the excess of growth over interest rates. Had this cushion been not available, cumulated primary deficits through 1950-51 to 2001-02 would have resulted in a central debt to GDP ratio of about 146 percentage points (Table 4.6).

The decade-wise picture indicates that in the fifties, 52.2 per cent of the impact of cumulative primary deficit was absorbed by the growth-interest rate differential. Thus, only 47.8 per cent of the cumulated primary deficit of 20.5 percentage points resulted in an increase in the debt-GDP ratio of 9.8 percentage points. In the sixties, the pressure put by the cumulated primary deficit was relatively larger (29 percentage points). However, 89 per cent of this was absorbed by the differential of growth over interest rate, resulting in only a small increase of 3.1 percentage points in the debt-GDP ratio. During the seventies and again during the nineties, nearly 100 per cent of the impact of primary deficit was absorbed by the

---

4. There is a small difference between the derived fiscal deficit figures and the CAG's fiscal deficit figures. In the latter case, net borrowing is fiscal deficit minus net drawal from cash balances.

growth/interest rate differential leading to a negligible increase in the debt-GDP ratio during these two decades considered as a whole. In the eighties, only 72 per cent of the pressure of cumulated primary deficit could be absorbed by the (g-i) differential.

Table 4.3

Decade-wise Decomposition of Debt Accumulation Relative to GDP

	Cumulated Changes in			Impact of Cumulated Primary Deficit	
	Debt-GDP Ratio	Primary Def-GDP Ratio	Growth and Interest Rate Differential	Increase in Debt-GDP Ratio	Absorption by Gr/Int Differential
1951-52 to 1959-60	9.82	20.54	10.72	47.80	52.20
1960-61 to 1969-70	3.08	28.89	25.81	10.66	89.34
1970-71 to 1979-80	-0.19	23.76	23.95	-0.79	100.79
1980-81 to 1989-90	13.61	48.53	34.92	28.05	71.95
1990-91 to 2001-02	0.20	24.56	24.36	0.82	99.18
1951-52 to 2001-02	26.52	146.28	119.76	18.13	81.87
Memo:					
Debt-GDP Ratio at the end of-					
1950-51	28.84				
2001-02	55.36				

Source: (Basic data): As in Table 4.2.

Figure 4.1

Growth of Central Debt Relative to GDP: Relative Roles of Cumulated Primary Deficit and Excess of Growth over Interest Rates

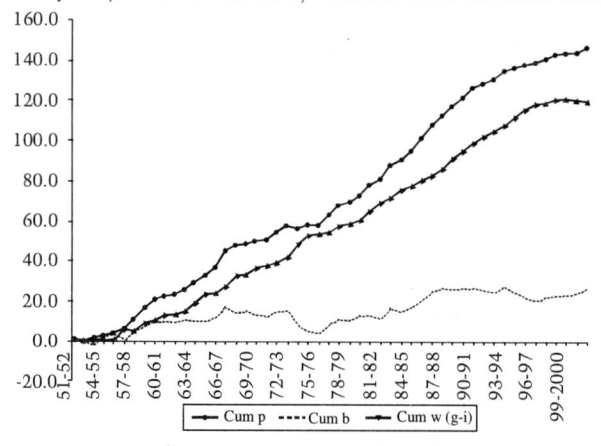

Key: Cum p: Cumulated primary deficit to GDP ratio
Cum b: Cumulated debt to GDP ratio
Cumw(g-i): Cumulated effect deffecit of weighted excess of growth over interest rate

Using a similar decomposition for the OECD countries, in a recent contribution, Shigehara (1995) observes that "for the two decades 1974 to 1994, the ratio of net debt to GDP for the OECD area as a whole rose by about 23 percentage points, of which about 18 percentage points can be accounted for by cumulated primary deficits, and 5 percentage points can be attributed to the differential between interest rates and growth rates. However, since 1980 when the debt dynamics became unfavourable for the OECD area, the debt-GDP ratio has risen by about 18 percentage points of which only 8 percentage points can be attributed to primary deficits and 10 percentage points are accounted for by the effect of the interest rate/growth rate differential."

The long-term Indian experience is different in as much as for a stretch of 48 years, the single cause of the rise in debt was the cumulated primary deficit. The excess of growth rate over interest rate helped to mitigate the situation. In the case of the OECD countries, while both factors contributed to rise in the debt-GDP ratio, the growth-interest differential had become more important in recent years. In India over the period from 1951-52 to 2001-02, the central debt-GDP ratio rose by 26.5 percentage points. The increase occurred mainly in the fifties and the eighties. In the remaining period of 30 years, except for a small rise, all the pressure of cumulated primary deficit was absorbed by the (g-i) differential.

The critical contemporary question relates to whether one can continue to rely on the (g-i) differential to provide a reliable cushion, or whether with interest rates being increasingly market determined, the situation warrants fresh examination of the factors behind debt accumulation in India.

Profiles of Growth and Interest Rates

Effective interest rate is derived by dividing actual interest payments during a financial year by the outstanding liabilities at the beginning of that year. This means that the effective interest rate is the weighted average of past interest rates pertaining to debt that are currently being serviced. It implies that even if current interest rates fall, the effective rate will fall more slowly than the current interest rates. Conversely, it will also rise more slowly, in a period where nominal interest rates are rising. Figure 4.2 and Table 4.4 show the steady rise of effective interest rate until the end of the nineties after which it has started falling. Until 1959-60, the nominal interest rate was well below 2 per cent per annum. It generally remained in the range of 3.2 to 3.7 per cent up to 1973-74. Rising steadily since then, the peak was attained towards the end of the nineties with the average rate going above 10 per cent. It is clear that over the long run, the nominal growth rate has been far more volatile than the nominal interest rate. As a result the intra-year variability in the debt accumulation process is largely due to the growth rate volatility.

Figure 4.2

Time Profile of Nominal Growth and Interest Rates

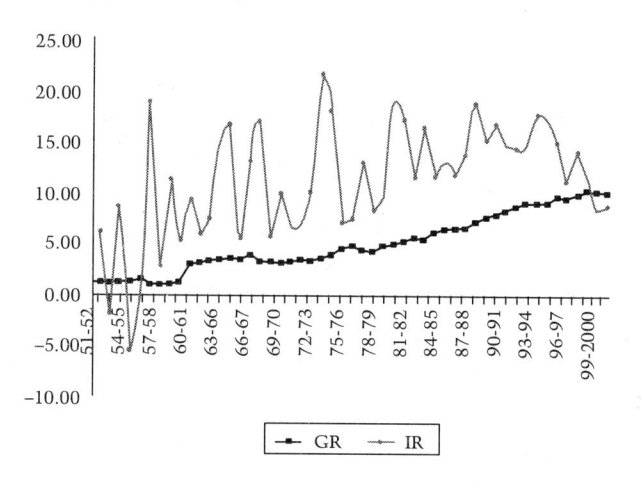

Table 4.4

Debt Relative to GDP and Growth and Interest Rates

(Rs. Crore)

	GDPmp	GDP Growth Rate	Debt-GDP Ratio	Derived Fiscal Deficit to GDP Ratio	Effective Interest Rate
	1	2	3	4	5
1950-51	9934		28.84		
1951-52	10566	6.362	27.56	0.44	1.361
1952-53	10366	-1.893	28.36	0.27	1.253
1953-54	11282	8.837	26.70	0.64	1.388
1954-55	10678	-5.354	30.73	2.52	1.318
1955-56	10873	1.826	32.29	2.11	1.257
1956-57	12951	19.112	29.87	2.76	1.046

contd...

contd...

	1	2	3	4	5
1957-58	13349	3.073	33.78	4.79	1.095
1958-59	14874	11.424	36.26	5.95	1.079
1959-60	15675	5.385	38.66	4.25	1.286
1960-61	17167	9.518	38.12	2.82	3.192
1961-62	18196	5.994	38.28	2.32	3.277
1962-63	19566	7.529	39.27	3.66	3.523
1963-64	22482	14.903	38.72	4.55	3.623
1964-65	26220	16.627	38.61	5.41	3.634
1965-66	27668	5.523	40.95	4.36	3.661
1966-67	31305	13.145	45.86	9.67	4.091
1967-68	36649	17.071	43.27	4.10	3.493
1968-69	38823	5.932	43.40	2.55	3.329
1969-70	42750	10.115	41.74	2.33	3.353
1970-71	45677	6.847	41.24	2.17	3.393
1971-72	48932	7.126	43.82	5.32	3.558
1972-73	53947	10.249	44.35	4.60	3.603
1973-74	65613	21.625	36.99	0.52	3.685
1974-75	77479	18.085	33.96	2.64	4.124
1975-76	83269	7.473	32.90	1.30	4.667
1976-77	89739	7.770	37.45	6.93	5.017
1977-78	101597	13.214	39.54	6.46	4.527
1978-79	110133	8.402	39.48	3.00	4.553
1979-80	120841	9.723	41.55	5.57	5.082
1980-81	143762	18.968	41.56	6.63	5.186
1981-82	168600	17.277	40.44	5.00	5.347
1982-83	188262	11.662	45.08	8.86	5.775
1983-84	219496	16.591	43.40	4.73	5.650
1984-85	245515	11.854	46.21	7.40	6.272
1985-86	277991	13.228	49.46	8.65	6.622
1986-87	311177	11.938	53.52	9.34	6.725
1987-88	354343	13.872	55.19	8.19	6.756
1988-89	421567	18.971	54.50	8.11	7.301
1989-90	486179	15.327	55.16	7.90	7.728
1990-91	568674	16.968	55.31	8.15	8.016
1991-92	653117	14.849	54.30	6.14	8.455
1992-93	748367	14.584	53.71	6.32	8.762
1993-94	859220	14.813	55.63	8.85	9.141
1994-95	1012770	17.871	53.18	5.99	9.218
1995-96	1188012	17.303	51.03	5.69	9.292
1996-97	1368208	15.168	49.38	5.08	9.811
1997-98	1522547	11.280	51.12	6.74	9.714
1998-99	1740985	14.347	51.22	6.52	10.007
1999-2000	1936925	11.255	51.24	5.19	10.607
2000-01	2104298	8.641	52.98	5.81	10.401
2001-02	2296049	9.112	55.36	6.81	10.242

Source: (Basic data): As in Table 4.1 and National Income Accounts.

The real interest rate is derived by deducting from the effective nominal rate, the implicit price deflator of GDP at market prices. Table 4.5 gives the profile of real interest rates since 1951-52. There is considerable volatility in the real interest rate because of fluctuations in inflation. However, one trend is clear. As Figure 4.3 shows, except for few years, the real interest rate has been negative throughout the years during 1951-52 to 1994-95. The turning point seems to have occurred in 1995-96 when the real interest rate became positive. Concurrently, the excess of growth over interest rates, whether real or nominal, started falling in magnitude, becoming negative in 2000-01.

Historically, the real interest rates on government securities were kept low as the government was able to borrow from the domestic market at rates much below the market rates due to a variety of banking regulations including requirements for banks to maintain specified statutory liquidity ratio (SLR) and cash reserve ratio (CRR) and by controlling a number of financial institutions.[5] With the liberalisation of the financial sector, the government is borrowing at rates which are by and large market determined.

The six recent years from 1997-98 to 2002-03 require special attention. The 2002-03 figures are available as revised estimates. The recently announced revised estimates put growth of GDP at factor cost in 2002-03 at 4.3 per cent in real terms and 7.1 per cent at current prices. The effective interest rate on central government liabilities in 2002-03 is estimated to be in the vicinity of 9 per cent. Growth in GDP at market prices is likely to be marginally lower as the buoyancy of indirect taxes continues to be less than one. The central debt-GDP ratio[6] at the end of

---

5. The monetised part of debt is reflected in the centre's outstanding liabilities to the RBI. The central government pays interest to the RBI on its outstanding liabilities. Prior to the Agreement in 1997, government paid to the RBI an interest which was significantly lower than that on the market bonds. However, after the agreement, the government pays to the RBI the same rate as for the market. This led to a significant increase in the RBI's profits which comes back to the central government in the form of dividends from the RBI as part of non tax revenue. As a result, there has been an improvement in the primary deficit. For the earlier years, although some dividends still came to the central government from the RBI, these were of a much lower order. Further, there has been both direct and indirect seignorage in the Indian system in the sense that liquidity is sometimes placed with the banks and financial institutions so as to enable them to lift government bonds.

6. Taking the figure of outstanding liability given as revised estimate for 2002-03 in the Receipts Budget and excluding the figure for small savings shown under 'other liabilities'.

2002-03 is estimated to be 57.6 per cent. Thus, in 2002-03, the interest rate will again be higher than the growth rate. During 1997-98 to 2002-03 the central-debt-GDP ratio has risen by 8.22 percentage points, at an average rate of 1.37 percentage points per year. This is a rate of growth in the accumulation of debt relative to GDP that is more than three times that of the average increment of 0.44 percentage points per year in the previous 46 years.

Table 4.5

Cumulated Changes in Debt, Primary Deficit and Factor Reflecting Excess of Growth over Interest Rate

	Change in Debt-GDP Ratio Cum b (Per Cent Points)	Cumulated Primary Def to GDP Ratio Cum p (Per Cent Points)	Factor Reflecting Excess of Gr over ir Cum w(g-i) (Per Cent Points)
	1	2	3
1951-52	-1.283	0.073	1.356
1952-53	-0.480	-0.008	0.472
1953-54	-2.141	0.272	2.413
1954-55	1.888	2.419	0.531
1955-56	3.447	4.150	0.703
1956-57	1.030	6.630	5.600
1957-58	4.932	11.105	6.174
1958-59	7.418	16.727	9.310
1959-60	9.818	20.538	10.720
1960-61	9.277	22.230	12.953
1961-62	9.439	23.369	13.931
1962-63	10.423	25.780	15.357
1963-64	9.880	29.092	19.212
1964-65	9.766	33.292	23.526
1965-66	12.102	36.309	24.207
1966-67	17.012	44.495	27.484
1967-68	14.428	47.230	32.802
1968-69	14.555	48.420	33.865
1969-70	12.898	49.429	36.530
1970-71	12.393	50.273	37.880
1971-72	14.972	54.225	39.253
1972-73	15.503	57.397	41.895
1973-74	8.141	56.576	48.436
1974-75	5.118	57.927	52.808
1975-76	4.053	57.748	53.695
1976-77	8.606	63.142	54.535
1977-78	10.697	68.106	57.409
1978-79	10.637	69.450	58.813

contd...

contd...

	1	2	3	4	5
1979-80	12.709		73.192	60.483	
1980-81	12.716		78.012	65.296	
1981-82	11.598		81.122	69.524	
1982-83	16.237		87.894	71.656	
1983-84	14.556		90.442	75.887	
1984-85	17.361		95.414	78.053	
1985-86	20.612		101.360	80.748	
1986-87	24.677		107.728	83.051	
1987-88	26.346		112.742	86.396	
1988-89	25.660		117.470	91.810	
1989-90	26.319		121.720	95.401	
1990-91	26.470		126.093	99.623	
1991-92	25.459		128.161	102.702	
1992-93	24.862		130.324	105.462	
1993-94	26.784		134.898	108.115	
1994-95	24.337		136.536	112.198	
1995-96	22.185		138.015	115.830	
1996-97	20.540		138.743	118.204	
1997-98	22.274		141.172	118.899	
1998-99	22.380		143.219	120.839	
1999-2000	22.392		143.529	121.137	
2000-01	24.131		144.439	120.307	
2001-02	26.520		146.279	119.759	

Source: (Basic data): As in Table 4.2.

Figure 4.3

Real Growth and Interest Rates

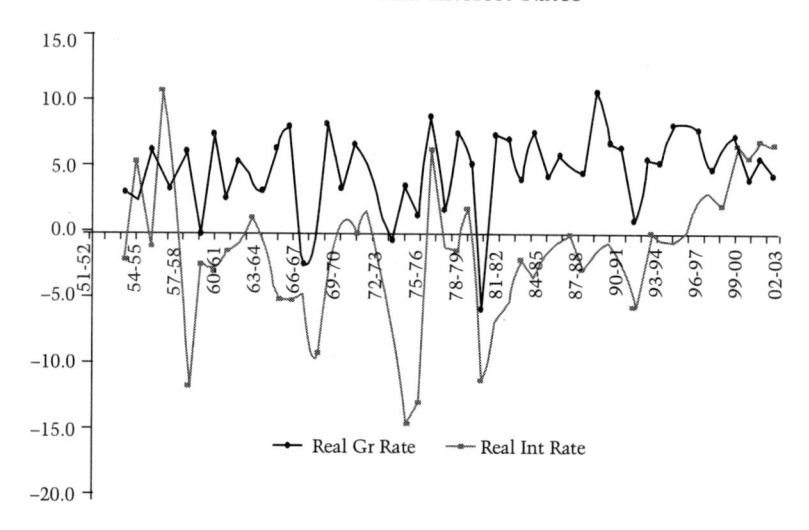

If the reversal in the sign of (g-i) is sustained, it is clear that rather than partially absorbing the impact of cumulated primary deficit, it will add to the accumulation of debt. With the prevailing debt-GDP ratio of around 57 per cent of GDP, every 1 percentage point differential in (i-g) will cause just a little less than 0.57 percentage points of increase in the debt-GDP ratio. Even if the (g-i) differential turns out to be positive, it is likely that the days of a large excess of growth rate over interest rate are over. Therefore, the likelihood of primary deficits getting converted into a rise in the debt-GDP ratio is stronger now. It may also be noted that the effective interest rate for the central government is lower than the corresponding effective rate for the states. The adverse impact of the changes in the (g-i) differential for the states would therefore be even stronger.

An economy where the condition $g = i$ is met is considered 'dynamically efficient' (see e.g., Abel *et al.*, 1989). Lahiri (2001) provides a discussion of the issue in the Indian context. If interest rates are persistently lower in relation to the growth rate, it is due either to excessive capital accumulation relative to other factors or because the real interest (or profit) rate deviates from the marginal product of capital due to financial repression or other market distortions. Writing early in the nineties, Buiter and Patel (1992) observe: "We assume in what follows that while the interest rate can be below the growth rate for extended finite periods of time, the Indian economy is not dynamically inefficient, and there are no social free lunches to be earned by increasing the Public debt". In the context of growing liberalisation, it is not expected that the interest rates could be much below the marginal product of capital for sustained periods of time. Under these circumstances, if the debt-GDP ratio is to be stabilised at its current level, a balance would have to be achieved on the primary account. However, if the debt-GDP has to be brought down, as it has already been considered excessively high in some analyses, a reasonable primary surplus will have to be generated.

It is worth exploring whether in India the real interest rate would overtake the real growth rate on a sustained basis in the near future.[7] In

---

7. Fiscal and primary deficits along with growth and interest rates may be considered as interdependent. Particularly, fiscal deficits may affect interest rates and the level of primary expenditure may affect growth rates. This analysis looks primarily at their historical paths in explaining their relative roles in the process of accumulation of debt. For future projections of the behaviour of debt, the interrelationship among the relevant variable would have to be kept in view. However, this would require detailed modelling to adequately take into account the important interrelationships.

some studies, it has been noted that the possibility of growth rate exceeding the interest rate by a significant margin in the near future is limited. In a recent study, Reynolds (2001) specifies a model where in the 'no-change' scenario the relevant long-term parameters imply that the real interest rate would exceed the real growth rate around 2007-08 on a sustained basis. The recent World Bank Report (2003: 27) provides for a negligible margin between growth and interest rates in both base and reform scenarios in the period 2003-04 to 2006-07. It is notable that the interest rates at which the central government has been able to borrow is the lowest because of the minimum risk perception as well as indirect returns offered through a plethora of exemptions in central taxes. For state governments, the situation is likely to be more adverse. It is critical therefore to get a better understanding of the process of generation of primary deficits.

Accumulation of Primary Deficit

Table 4.6 gives the year-wise profile of the ratio of derived primary deficit to debt during 1951-52 to 2001-02. Except for a few years, central budget never had a primary surplus. The primary deficit to GDP ratio was continuously above 4 per cent during 1984-85 to 1990-91 and again in 1993-94. The primary deficit is the excess of primary expenditure, i.e., total expenditure minus interest payments over revenue receipts. Its capacity to adjust to changes in the relativity of growth and interest rates is limited. Figure 4.4 indicates that the primary deficit to GDP ratio is less volatile and more autonomous than the (g-i) differential. It shows that the maximum build up of primary deficit was in the period from 1979-80 to 1993-94. During this period the primary deficit to GDP ratio remained above 3 per cent except in three years. The peak was reached in 1982-83 when it exceeded 6.5 per cent. However, throughout this period, a build up of the debt-GDP ratio could be contained because of the excess of growth rate over interest rate. The primary deficit to GDP ratio since 1993-94 remained below 2.5 per cent of the GDP and the change in the debt-GDP ratio was modest till 1999-2000 because the growth rate also exceeded the interest rate. The debt-GDP ratio has started rising from 2000-01 because of the combined effect of primary deficit and the negative difference between the growth rate and the interest rate.

Table 4.6

Decomposition of Primary Deficit and Debt Relative to GDP

	Primary Deficit to GDP Ratio (Per Cent)	Change in Debt-GDP Ratio (Per Cent Points)	$w(g\text{-}i)$ $[w=b_{t\text{-}1}/(1+g_t)]$ (Per Cent Points)
	1	2	3
1951-52	0.073	-1.283	1.356
1952-53	-0.081	0.803	-0.884
1953-54	0.280	-1.661	1.941
1954-55	2.147	4.029	-1.882
1955-56	1.731	1.559	0.172
1956-57	2.480	-2.418	4.898
1957-58	4.475	3.902	0.573
1958-59	5.622	2.486	3.136
1959-60	3.811	2.401	1.410
1960-61	1.692	-0.542	2.233
1961-62	1.139	0.162	0.977
1962-63	2.410	0.984	1.426
1963-64	3.312	-0.543	3.855
1964-65	4.200	-0.114	4.314
1965-66	3.018	2.336	0.681
1966-67	8.186	4.910	3.277
1967-68	2.735	-2.583	5.318
1968-69	1.190	0.127	1.063
1969-70	1.008	-1.657	2.665
1970-71	0.844	-0.505	1.349
1971-72	3.952	2.579	1.374
1972-73	3.173	0.531	2.641
1973-74	-0.821	-7.362	6.541
1974-75	1.350	-3.022	4.373
1975-76	-0.179	-1.066	0.887
1976-77	5.394	4.554	0.840
1977-78	4.964	2.091	2.874
1978-79	1.344	-0.060	1.404
1979-80	3.742	2.072	1.670
1980-81	4.820	0.007	4.814
1981-82	3.109	-1.118	4.228
1982-83	6.772	4.640	2.132
1983-84	2.548	-1.682	4.230
1984-85	4.971	2.805	2.166
1985-86	5.947	3.251	2.696
1986-87	6.368	4.065	2.303

contd...

...contd...

	1	2	3
1987-88	5.013	1.669	3.345
1988-89	4.728	-0.686	5.414
1989-90	4.251	0.659	3.591
1990-91	4.373	0.151	4.222
1991-92	2.068	-1.011	3.080
1992-93	2.163	-0.596	2.759
1993-94	4.574	1.921	2.653
1994-95	1.637	-2.446	4.084
1995-96	1.480	-2.153	3.632
1996-97	0.728	-1.645	2.373
1997-98	2.429	1.734	0.695
1998-99	2.047	0.106	1.940
1999-2000	0.310	0.012	0.298
2000-01	0.909	1.739	-0.830
2001-02	1.840	2.388	-0.548

Source: (Basic data): As in Table 4.2.

Figure 4.4

Primary Deficit to GDP Ratio and Excess of Growth over Interest Rates

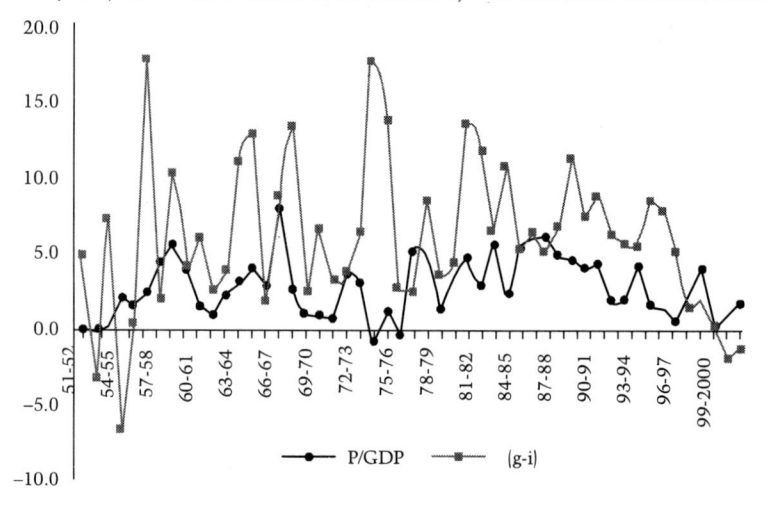

Table 4.7
Inflation, Real Growth and Real Interest Rates

	IPD (GDPmp) 1993-94=100	Inflation Rate (wrt to IPD)* (Per Cent)	Real Gr Rate (Per Cent)	Real Int Rate (Per Cent)	Real Gr Rate Real Int Rate (Per Cent)
	1	2	3	4	5
1950-51	6.69				
1951-52	6.91	3.25	3.11	-1.89	5.00
1952-53	6.60	-4.38	2.49	5.63	-3.15
1953-54	6.77	2.52	6.31	-1.14	7.45
1954-55	6.11	-9.75	4.40	11.07	-6.67
1955-56	6.02	-1.44	3.26	2.69	0.57
1956-57	6.80	12.83	6.28	-11.79	18.07
1957-58	7.03	3.41	-0.34	-2.31	1.98
1958-59	7.29	3.78	7.65	-2.70	10.35
1959-60	7.49	2.64	2.74	-1.36	4.10
1960-61	7.78	3.98	5.54	-0.79	6.33
1961-62	7.95	2.12	3.87	1.15	2.72
1962-63	8.30	4.38	3.15	-0.85	4.01
1963-64	8.99	8.30	6.60	-4.68	11.28
1964-65	9.75	8.55	8.08	-4.92	12.99
1965-66	10.56	8.26	-2.74	-4.60	1.86
1966-67	11.97	13.34	-0.19	-9.25	9.05
1967-68	13.00	8.61	8.46	-5.11	13.58
1968-69	13.31	2.38	3.55	0.95	2.60
1969-70	13.75	3.35	6.76	0.00	6.76
1970-71	13.97	1.59	5.25	1.80	3.45
1971-72	14.72	5.32	1.80	-1.77	3.57
1972-73	16.32	10.89	-0.64	-7.29	6.65
1973-74	19.24	17.90	3.73	-14.21	17.94
1974-75	22.45	16.70	1.39	-12.57	13.96
1975-76	22.10	-1.55	9.02	6.22	2.81
1976-77	23.42	5.96	1.81	-0.94	2.75
1977-78	24.73	5.58	7.64	-1.05	8.69
1978-79	25.35	2.52	5.88	2.03	3.85
1979-80	29.35	15.79	-6.07	-10.71	4.64
1980-81	32.73	11.51	7.46	-6.32	13.78
1981-82	36.09	10.26	7.01	-4.92	11.93
1982-83	38.88	7.72	3.94	-1.95	5.89

contd...

...contd...

	1	2	3	4	5
1983-84	42.33	8.88	7.71	-3.23	10.94
1984-85	45.48	7.42	4.43	-1.15	5.58
1985-86	48.75	7.19	6.03	-0.57	6.61
1986-87	52.05	6.77	5.16	-0.05	5.21
1987-88	56.84	9.21	4.66	-2.45	7.12
1988-89	61.56	8.29	10.68	-0.99	11.67
1989-90	66.70	8.35	6.98	-0.62	7.60
1990-91	73.73	10.55	6.42	-2.53	8.95
1991-92	83.92	13.82	1.03	-5.36	6.39
1992-93	91.34	8.85	5.74	-0.08	5.82
1993-94	100.00	9.48	5.33	-0.34	5.67
1994-95	109.68	9.68	8.19	-0.47	8.65
1995-96	119.52	8.97	8.33	0.32	8.01
1996-97	128.18	7.24	7.93	2.57	5.36
1997-98	136.52	6.51	4.77	3.20	1.57
1998-99	147.29	7.89	6.46	2.12	4.34
1999-2000	152.95	3.85	7.41	6.76	0.65
2000-01	159.86	4.52	4.13	5.89	-1.76
2001-02	165.40	3.47	5.64	6.77	-1.13

Note: * IPD refers to the implicit price deflator of GDP at market prices.
Source: (Basic data): As in Table 4.2.

Summary and Medium-Term Prospects

Although the interest rates have been higher than the growth rates for three consecutive years during 2000-01 to 2002-03, it is possible that in 2003-04, the sign of the (g-i) differential will be reversed again. With the inflation rate expected in the region of 5 to 5.5 per cent, the real interest rate could be in the region of 3.5 to 4 per cent for the central government, given the nominal effective interest rate in the vicinity of 9 per cent. If the growth rate is above 4 per cent, which it is likely to be as the forecasts are in the region of 6 per cent, we should have a positive differential.

In 1996-97, the debt-GDP ratio was about 49 per cent, which was very close to the restructuring target set out by the Eleventh Finance Commission at 48 per cent of GDP (EFC Report, p.21). The cumulative departure away from this target has been due to both continued primary deficits and the sign reversal in the growth/interest rate differential.

A summary of the main findings is given below:

(1) Starting with a debt-GDP ratio of about 29 per cent of GDP at market prices in 1950-51 for the central government, by 2001-02, the debt-GDP ratio had reached a level of 55.36 per cent of GDP, an increase of about 26.5 percentage points. Nearly half of this increased occurred in the first three plans.

(2) Accumulation of central debt relative to GDP, for an unbroken period of 45 years since 1955-56, has been due entirely to cumulated primary deficits relative to GDP with the factor of excess of growth rate over interest rate mitigating its impact in a significant way. This trend has reversed itself during the last three years when the excess of interest rate over growth rate has also contributed to the growth of debt.

(3) A significant part of the potential build up of debt due to cumulated primary deficits was absorbed by the excess of real growth rate over real interest rate as adjusted for the influence of the inflation rate. Most of the intra-year variability in the process of debt-accumulation was due to the volatility of the nominal growth rates.

(4) With liberalisation and the end of the regime of financial repression, large excesses of growth rate over interest rate may not be expected on a sustained basis. Prospects are that the difference will remain in a narrow range, even if the growth rate remains higher than the interest rate.

(5) For stabilising the debt-GDP ratio at current levels, fiscal reforms aimed at attaining a balance on a primary account are imperative. For reducing the debt-GDP ratio, primary surplus will have to be generated on a sustained basis. Hence the need to focus on primary balances in any effort to control the growth in the debt-GDP ratio becomes unavoidable.

(6) The position of state governments would be even more difficult as the effective interest rate is higher in their case.

The authors would like to thank Amaresh Bagchi for helpful comments on an earlier draft of the paper.

Economic and Political Weekly, November 15, 2003.

References

Abel, Andrew B.N., Gregory Mankiw, Lawrence H. Summers and Richard J. Zeckhauser (1989). "Assessing Dynamic Efficiency the Other Way Round: Theory and Evidence", *Review of Economic Studies* 56: 1-20.

Buiter, W.H. and Urjit R. Patel (1992). "Debt, Deficits and Inflation, an Application to the Public Finances of India", *Journal of Public Economics* 47: 172-305, March.

Chrystal, Alec K. and D. Kevin (1987). "Would a Higher Fiscal Deficit Stimulate the Economy?", *Fiscal Studies* 8(1), February.

Comptroller and Auditor General of India (2003). *Report on the Accounts of the Union Government* (No. 1 of 2003).

Government of India (2002). *Indian Public Finance Statistics 2001-02 and earlier issues*. Ministry of Finance.

———. (2003). *Receipts Budget* 2003-04 and earlier years.

Lahiri, A. and R. Kannan (2001). "India's Fiscal Deficits and their Sustainability in Perspective", Proceedings of NIPFP-World Bank Conference on *India: Fiscal Policies to Accelerate Economic Growth*. May 21-22. New Delhi.

Phelps, Edmund S. (1961). "Accumulation and the Golden Rule", *American Economic Review* 51: 638-43. Reprinted in Amartya Sen (Ed.), *Growth Economics, and England*.

Rakshit, Mihir (2000). "On Correcting Fiscal Imbalances in the Indian Economy: Some Perspectives", *Money and Finance*. ICRA.

Rajaraman, Indira and Abhiroop Mukhopadhyay (2000). "Sustainability of Public Domestic Debt in India" in D.K. Srivastava (Ed.), *Fiscal Federalism in India-Contemporary Challenges, Issues before the Eleventh Finance Commission*. New Delhi: Har Anand Publications.

Rangarajan, C., Anupam Basu and Narendra Jadhav (1989). "Dynamics of Interaction between Government Deficit and Domestic Debt in India", *RBI Occasional Papers*, September, also included in Amaresh Bagchi and Nicholas Stern (eds.), *Tax Policy and Planning in Developing Countries*. Delhi: Oxford University Press.

Reynolds, P. (2001). "Fiscal Adjustment and Growth Prospects" in T. Callen, P. Reynolds, C. Towe (Eds.), *India at Crossroads: Sustaining Growth and Reducing Poverty*. IMF.

Shigehara, K. (1995). "Commentary: Long-Term Tendencies in Budget Deficits and Debt" in *Budget Deficits and Debt: Issues and Options*. Proceedings of a Symposium. August 31-September 2. US: Federal Reserve Bank of Kansas City.

World Bank (2003). *India: Sustaining Reform, Reducing Poverty*. Report No. 25797-IN.

5 Fiscal Federalism
Some Current Concerns

Two sets of factors have pushed to the fore discussions on federalism. First is the impact of globalisation and the growing integration of countries on the way federal structures function. If we are moving towards a borderless world, how much boundaries within a country matter or should matter? Federal structures will have to undergo a change in order to be able to respond to the forces of globalisation and international competition that emerges as a consequence. Globalisation is also occurring at a time when the respective roles of government and markets are being rewritten. Private sector and markets are being given a larger space in which to operate, even in countries which have been traditionally state-centered. The role of state as a producer of marketable goods and services is being de-emphasised. However, this has not diminished the role of the government. As is being somewhat paradoxically remarked: "More market does not mean less government but only different government." The critical question is in what way this government is different. Obviously the increasing role of market does alter the rules of the game for the government as a whole and for different levels of government. The second set of factors relates to another trend where the advantages of decentralisation are being emphasised. There has always been a school of thought which has emphasised the importance of sub-national governments and local bodies as an essential part of the democratic process. The 73rd and 74th Amendments to the Indian Constitution in 1988 giving explicit recognition to the roles of local bodies in the governance process are reflective of this trend. Similarly, in the United Kingdom, both Scotland and Wales have their own regional parliaments.

Federalism—As a Form of Government

Federalism is an old concept. Its origin is mainly political. I am neither a political scientist nor a constitutional expert to be able to trace fully the evolution of federalism in various countries. It is, however, well known that the efficiency of government depends, among other factors, on the structure of government. Federalism as a form of government has, therefore, been concerned with functions and instruments that are best centralised and those that are best placed in the sphere of decentralised levels of government. Particularly, in large countries, it has been felt that sub-national governments are required and that only a federal structure can efficiently meet the requirements of people from different regions. Underlying this proposition is the premise that preferences vary from region to region. Thus, the rationale of federalism lies in promoting welfare through decentralisation and sub-national autonomy in combination with the benefits of a large market and size.

In our own country during the Independence struggle, provincial autonomy was regarded as an integral part of the Freedom Movement. However, after Independence, several compulsions including defence and internal security led to a scheme of federalism in which the Centre assumed greater importance. Also in the immediate post-Independence period when the Centre and all states were ruled by the same party and when many of the powerful provincial leaders migrated to the Centre, the process of centralisation gathered further momentum. Economic planning at a nation-wide level and the allocation of resources by a central authority also helped this centralising process. The size of the states in India is largely determined by language. After the formation of linguistic states, the size and population of a state is determined by the number of people speaking the same language. However, more recently in large states where people are speaking the same language, demands have been made for dividing them on grounds of regional neglect. Some of these demands have also been met. A similar evolutionary process has been noted elsewhere. Even in the American case, there has been a transition from the earlier era of 'dualism' where the two tiers had comparable responsibilities to growing centralisation, which according to some writers has passed through successive phases of 'centralising federalism' to 'cooperative federalism', and more recently, to 'creative federalism' where the Central Government continues to take an active part in the state and local problems.

Fiscal Federalism

Fiscal federalism is the economic counterpart to political federalism. Fiscal federalism is concerned with the assignment, on the one hand of functions to different levels of government and on the other with appropriate fiscal instruments for carrying out these functions. It is generally believed that the Central government must provide national public goods that render services to the entire population of the country. A typical example cited is defence. Local governments are expected to provide goods and services whose consumption is limited to their own jurisdictions. The argument here is that output of such goods and services can be tailored to meet the preferences and circumstances of the people in that jurisdiction. Such a process of decentralisation enhances the economic welfare above that which could result from the more uniform levels of such services that are likely under a centralised regime. Apart from the provision of national public goods, the Central government is to be vested with the responsibilities for economic stabilisation and for income redistribution. While income redistribution to some extent is possible even within sub-national government jurisdictions, a truly redistribution effort is possible only at the national level. An equally important question in fiscal federalism is the determination of the specific fiscal instruments that would enable the different levels of government to carry out their functions. This is the 'tax-assignment problem' which is discussed very much in the literature. In determining the taxes that are best suited for use at different levels of government, one basic assumption that is made is in relation to the mobility of economic agents, goods and resources. Very often it is assumed that while there is no mobility across national barriers, there is a much greater mobility at decentralised levels. This proposition holds good only partly in an era of globalisation. Once again, it is generally argued that the decentralised levels of government should avoid non-benefit taxes on mobile units. This has the implication that Central government should have the responsibility to levy non-benefit taxes and taxes on mobile units or resources. Building these principles into an actual scheme of assignment of taxes to different levels of government in a Constitution is indeed very difficult. Different Constitutions interpret differently what is mobile and what is purely a benefit tax. For example, in the United States and Canada, both federal and state governments have concurrent powers to levy income tax. On the contrary, in India, income tax is levied only by the Central government though shared with the states. It is interesting to note that the revenues collected by the federal or Central government vary very sharply among different countries. For example, the federal government collects 69 per cent of the total revenue in Australia, 65 per cent in India and 48 per cent in Canada. Thus, the traditional issues in fiscal federalism have been how to determine the assignment of taxes and responsibilities to different levels of government. Recognising, the possibility of imbalance between resources and responsibilities, many countries have a system of inter-governmental transfers. In fact, inter-governmental transfers constitute a distinctive economic policy instrument in fiscal federalism. For example, inter-governmental transfers as a percentage of provincial or state revenues have been 41 per cent in Australia, 40 per cent in India and 20 per cent in Canada in recent years. Correcting vertical and horizontal imbalances has been a major concern with which fiscal federalism has wrestled with. While actual designs of fiscal transfer systems differ across federations, these constitute experiments in search of satisfying the twin objectives of equity and efficiency in a multi-tiered system of government. Conceptually, the emphasis has been on providing enough resources at the sub-national level to ensure provision of a set of services at comparable or minimum acceptable levels in all jurisdictions. This attempt at 'equalisation' impedes the search for efficiency through relocation of households and firms, but is justified on the grounds of congestibility of service provision and on ethical grounds such as those related to equity. There has also been a consideration of rigidities in the mobility of households, which may itself be a function of education, which is one of the services considered for equalisation.

Fiscal Transfers

Let me further elaborate the implications of these 'old' issues on fiscal federalism in the Indian context before I move on to some of the newer issues.

The roots of fiscal federalism in India go back to the Government of India Acts of 1919 and 1935. While the Act of 1919 provided for a separation of revenue heads between the Centre and the Provinces, the 1935 Act allowed for the sharing of Centre's revenues and for the provision of grants-in-aid to Provinces. The Indian Constitution carried these provisions a step forward by providing for a Finance Commission to determine the distribution between the Union and the states of the net proceeds of taxes and the grants-in-aid to be provided to the states which are in need of assistance. While the Constitutional provisions relating to the functions of the Finance Commissions have remained unchanged, one notable change in the framework of federal fiscal arrangements was brought out by the 80th Amendment which broadened the ambit of the sharable Central taxes. The enlargement of the sharable pool to cover all Central taxes except those listed in Articles 268 and 269 and earmarked cesses and surcharges, has enabled states to share in the overall buoyancy of taxes. It has also provided greater stability to resource transfers as fluctuations in individual taxes are evened out. With the 73rd and 74th Amendments to the Constitution which have provided constitutional support to the process of decentralisation, the Finance Commissions are also required to suggest measures to augment the resources for the *panchayats* and municipalities.

The Indian Constitution lays down the functions as well as taxing powers of the Centre and states. It is against this background that the issues relating to the correction of vertical and horizontal imbalances have been addressed by every Finance Commission, taking into account the prevailing set of circumstances. Central transfers to states are not, however, confined to the recommendations of the Finance Commissions. There are other channels such as those through the Planning Commission as well the discretionary grants of the Central government. The Eleventh Finance Commission recommended that 29.5 per cent of the net proceed of the sharable taxes should go to the states. It suggested that in the over all scheme of transfer, 37.5 per cent of the gross revenue receipts of the Centre should be transferred to the states. One important issue that has been raised in this regard in the light of the recent changes of the economic policy aimed at liberalisation is whether the vertical imbalance has increased or decreased. At least one State government has argued before the Twelfth Finance Commission that assigning a greater role to the market, in economic activity has diminished the function of the Central government as compared with state governments. The shift in economic policy has altered the functions of the both Central and state governments. While the constitutionally mandated functions have remained the same, the emphasis has changed. It is not clear whether the shift in economic policy has necessarily increased vertical imbalance. However, this is an aspect which needs a fuller consideration.

Fiscal transfers require to be guided by certain definitive principles. Most analysts agree that a good transfer system should serve the objectives of equity and efficiency and should be characterised by predictability and stability. Equity can be conceptualised and understood in a number of ways both with respect to its vertical and horizontal dimensions. The considerations that should go in determining the distribution of transferred resources among states have been examined in great length by the various Finance Commissions. Equity issues have dominated such discussions as they should be. The effort has been to identify variables which reflect the equity concerns. Equity factors have had a maximum weight in resource transfer formulae. In designing a suitable scheme of fiscal transfers, three considerations seem relevant— needs, cost disability and fiscal efficiency. Needs refer to expenditures required to be made but not met by own resources. Cost disabilities refer to such characteristics of a state that necessitate more than average per capita cost in service provision due to factors that are largely beyond its control like large areas with low density of population, hilly terrains, poor infrastructure, proneness to floods and droughts. Fiscal efficiency encompasses parameters like maintaining revenue account balance, robust revenue effort, economies of expenditure linked to efficient provision of services and the quality of governance. Equity considerations must in effect aim for ensuring the provision of selected services at minimum acceptable standards across the country. It is seen that on average, the low income states spend only half of the average per person expenditure of high income states in social services. In a competitive environment, states that are able to access the market better are likely to grow faster than others. The growth experience of the 1990s shows that developed states with broad industrial base and developed market institutions and infrastructure have performed much better than those without them. The transfer system has also to take this factor into account. At the same time, 'efficiency' in the use of resource should be ensured and promoted. States that perform more efficiently in the delivery of services or raise more revenues relative to their tax bases should not be penalised. The task of formulating a sound transfer system has to establish a fine balance between equity and efficiency, a system where fiscal disadvantage is taken care of but fiscal imprudence is effectively discouraged.

Competitive and Cooperative Federalism

Much of the mainstream literature on federalism assumes that (i) governments are run by altruistic agents and are essentially benevolent and (ii) different units of the government have essentially a cooperative relationship. Thus, federalism and its corollary—decentralisation is supposed to bring in welfare gains. One school of thought has argued that ideas of cooperative federalism founded on these premises do not always function efficiently and Coasian bargains do not always work.

Existence of competitive relationship between governmental units is a key feature of the literature on competitive federalism. Existence of competition brings in the importance of transaction costs of coordinating policies and their implementation vertically between different levels of government and horizontally between different units within each of the levels. It looks at the system of checks and balances and in such a system, explores the pre-conditions for achieving efficient inter-governmental competition. The efficiency is not merely in terms of providing public services but also in creating a favourable environment in which the markets can function. It is also argued that governments tend to emulate policies of other governments, and the voters and opposition parties benchmark performances of other governments and pressurise their own governments to emulate them. The American tradition is focused more on inducing efficiency by the process of 'voting by feet' where households or firms locate themselves in those jurisdictions where the mix of the publicly provided goods is closer to their preferences. In the original Tiebout formulation, jurisdictional competition leads to increase in efficiency through 'sorting and matching'. Others have suggested that such inter-jurisdictional competition may also serve as a disciplinary device to punish inappropriate market intervention by lower governmental officials.

There is a parallel development in the federalism literature from the political science perspective and that is called the "market preserving federalism". This approach, however, assumes that the various levels of government have a common philosophical approach to the importance of the market. Obviously, if there is a convergence of opinion on the role of the markets, it follows, that the structure must reflect this philosophy and try to act in a way in which the markets are allowed to function effectively. You may recall the famous book in management literature entitled "Strategy and Structure". An essential message of this book is that the structure of any corporate unit must flow from the strategy it has adopted to fulfill its objectives. Government interventions can be market-distorting or market-complementary. For example, administered prices are market-distorting, while a good legal system with enforceable contracts is market-complementary.

The extent and areas in which various levels of government in a country function in a competitive manner are to be determined partly empirically and partly by the nature of the government structures. Sub-national governments such as state governments in India, do compete for capital, both domestic and foreign. That is why the policy framework and infrastructural availability are key elements in this competitive process. However, this competition should not result in a 'race to the bottom' when the States taken as a whole suffer. In fact competition in tax concession leads to serious erosion of revenues. With this realisation, state governments in India have come together to fix floor levels with respect to taxation and to reduce tax concessions. It is no doubt true, not only capital but also people will move to jurisdictions where the provision of services is better. However, one must recognise that there are areas in which such competition may have a limited role. With mobility of people constrained by various considerations, primary health and primary education are some areas in which competition is not possible. However, benchmarking and rating sub-national governments, whether it be in terms of human development or fiscal performance or infrastructural facilities has had a beneficial effect. In some ways, competition and coordination have to co-exist.

In meeting the challenges of globalisation, the Indian federal structure must respond in such a way as to create in the first place a large common market within the country. Restrictions on movement of goods and various other impediments have to go. Reform of the tax system has become essential. Introduction of a nation-wide value added tax (VAT) will require a cooperative agreement among the states. While some states have expressed difficulties in introducing VAT, there is at least an agreement in principle to introduce VAT. We have to move faster in this direction.

The economic policy environment in India has undergone a fundamental change. Transition to an increasingly market based development and opening up of the economy to face global competition will require policy changes, creation of market institutions and a responsive decentralised system of governance. The reform agenda of both the Centre and states should be calibrated in a coordinated manner in the spirit of cooperative federalism. At the same time, it is necessary to recognise that governmental units in the federation have also a competitive relationship. It is important to nurture this competition to secure efficiency gains. Thus, we need both coordination and competition and this makes the challenge formidable.

The traditional concerns of fiscal federalism such as the assignment of taxes and responsibilities as well as the correction of vertical and horizontal imbalances continue to remain important. However, it is necessary to take note of the changes in the environment in which governments operate. Fiscal federalism must enable national and sub-national governments to operate in such a way that it leads to efficiency in the use of resources. This improvement in efficiency must be reflected not only in the services provided by the various levels of government but also in creating an environment in which all economic agents use resources efficiently.

I have spoken only on one aspect of federalism. In fact fiscal dimensions of federalism are only a reflection of the political federal structure. Issues in federalism can be discussed at two levels. At one level, the existing arrangement can be taken as given and then one can proceed to discuss measures that would make the system more efficient and more responsive to the changing times. At another level, one can go deeper and try to re-examine the existing division of responsibilities and powers itself. However, the latter will require amendments to the existing Constitution, if changes are sought for. I find that your discussions will be at both levels. I am sure that these discussions which will be based upon the experiences from various countries will provide additional insights for making federal structures more effective and efficient. I wish your deliberations all success.

Inaugural Address at the International Conference on *Distribution of Responsibilities in Federal Democracies*. New Delhi, November 15, 2003.

6 | Issues Before the Twelfth Finance Commission

In federal fiscal systems, on grounds both of equity and efficiency, resources are generally assigned more to the central government whereas states together with the local governments have the larger responsibilities. The resultant vertical imbalance requires transfer of resources from the Centre to the states. States also have different capacities and needs, and this lends a horizontal dimension to the issue of resource sharing. Neither vertical nor horizontal imbalance is expected to be static. Some of the core provisions regarding sharing of resources are built into our Constitution itself. But changes in the economic and fiscal situation warrant a review of the existing arrangements. The Indian constitution has provided for both continuity and change. The Finance Commission is entrusted with the task of periodically examining these issues according to the constitutional provisions and the terms of reference.

With the setting up of the Twelfth Finance Commission we are once again drawn into the core issues of determining tax devolution and grants. The terms of reference contained in the Presidential Order constituting the Commission also reflect concern about the rapidly deteriorating fiscal scenario. Like the Eleventh Finance Commission, this Commission has also been asked to review the state of the finances of the Union and the states and suggest a plan for restructuring public finances with a view to restoring budgetary balance, maintaining macroeconomic stability, and bringing about debt reduction along with equitable growth. In comparison to the terms of reference for the EFC, the reference to debt reduction and equitable growth is new and emphasises concern with the growing disparities among states even as debt has crossed sustainable thresholds.

It is not as if the issues are entirely new, but the problems are more serious. The balancing of resources against responsibilities is qualitatively different now when governments at all levels are nursing large and rising revenue deficits than when the Centre and some of the better off states had a surplus. There were days when some of the states even had a pre-devolution surplus. The task has become progressively more demanding with successive Finance Commissions. In 1988-89, the base year for the Ninth Finance Commission, the combined revenue deficit of the Centre and states was 2.9 per cent of GDP at current market prices. The combined revenue deficits of the Centre and states for the corresponding base years for the Tenth and Eleventh Finance Commissions were respectively 3.6 per cent of GDP in 1994-95 and 6.3 per cent in 1999-2000. In 2001-02, the combined revenue deficit exceeded 7 per cent of GDP. With current trends indicating continued deterioration, the situation is likely to further worsen by 2004-05, the year immediately preceding the reference period of the Twelfth Finance Commission.

Fiscal Trends

It is useful to look at the overall fiscal trends over a longer period. Considering the 15-year period from 1986-87 to 2000-01, and comparing 3-year averages at both ends, that is for 1986-1989 and 1998-2001, the following major changes in the combined finances of the Central and state governments may be noted:

(i) The tax-GDP ratio fell from a level of about 16 per cent relative to GDP by 1.9 percentage points during this period. The average tax-GDP ratio continues to be just a little above 14 per cent in 2002-03 RE. The decline in the tax-GDP ratio was due to a fall in revenues from the indirect taxes relative to GDP of 2.8 percentage points, which could only partially be compensated by the rise of 0.9 percentage points in the ratio of direct taxes to GDP.

(ii) Since non-tax revenue relative to GDP also fell by a margin of 0.3 percentage points to reach an average level of 2.4 per cent of GDP during 1998-2001, the overall ratio of revenue receipts to GDP fell by 2.2 percentage points.

(iii) In contrast, the combined revenue expenditure of the Central and state governments relative to GDP increased by 1.43 percentage points to reach an average level of 22.9 per cent of GDP during 1998-2001. Interest payments and pensions relative to GDP increased since the late eighties to this period respectively by 2.9 and 0.95 percentage points.

(iv) The resulting imbalance led to an increase in the ratio of revenue deficit to GDP by a margin of 3.6 percentage points. The average level of the combined revenue deficit to GDP in 1998-2001 was 6.4 per cent. It has since increased to cross 7 per cent of GDP in 2001-2002.

(v) Fiscal deficit, which was already at a high level of 8.8 per cent of GDP in the late eighties, increased by a margin of 0.4 percentage points. The quality of fiscal deficit as measured by the ratio of revenue to fiscal deficit deteriorated from 33.0 per cent to 69.0 per cent during the period under reference. In 2001-02, the combined fiscal deficit was in excess of 10 per cent of GDP.

(vi) Capital expenditure relative to GDP fell to the extent of 3.5 percentage points during this period, reaching an average level of 3.2 per cent of GDP.

The deterioration in the revenue account balance of the Centre, states and their combined accounts had started towards the end of the seventies. It was in 1979-80 that the central finances fell into revenue deficit after recording a surplus since 1950-51 in all but two years. The combined account of the Centre and states went into revenue deficit in 1982-83, and that of all states in 1986-87. As noted by the Tenth Finance Commission, almost all the states went through a three-phase deterioration in the revenue account balance. In the first phase up to 1986-87, non-plan account surplus was larger than the plan deficit and to that extent it yielded an overall revenue balance. During 1986-87 to 1991-92, the magnitude of plan revenue deficit increased sharply and it became larger than the non-plan surplus. Since then, both the plan revenue account and the non-plan revenue account have remained in deficit and the deficit has generally been growing in magnitude. Only some of the special category states continued to have a surplus on the plan revenue account. However, this was due solely to the special dispensation for plan assistance where they got 90 per cent as grant credited to their revenue accounts.

Among the reasons generally given for this all round fiscal deterioration, some of the important ones are: revision of salaries and pensions in the wake of the recommendations of the Fifth Central Pay Commission, erosion in the buoyancy of central indirect taxes, and the high nominal interest rates towards the end of the nineties. After the peak growth rate achieved in the mid-nineties, there was also a general slow down in growth towards the end of the nineties, which has continued till 2002-03. In the first three years of the new decade, the growth rates have been estimated at 4.0, 5.6 and 4.4 per cent respectively, which are much less than the range of 7 to 7.5 per cent envisaged by the Eleventh Finance Commission. In fact, in spite of the falling nominal interest rates, it has been noted that for these three years the growth rate has fallen short of the average interest rate on the outstanding liabilities unlike in the previous four decades, when the interest rate was lower than the growth rate. This has meant that the growth in the central debt relative to GDP has been due not only to the primary deficit but also to the sign reversal in the growth-interest rate differential. The situation is worse for the states as in their case the effective interest rate is even higher. In the context of macroeconomic stability at a desired level of growth, determination of sustainable levels of fiscal deficit and debt becomes important.

Sustainability Issues

There has been an interesting debate as to the right level of fiscal deficit and the debt that is sustainable in the Indian context. The Tenth Plan has envisaged the average size of fiscal deficit as 6.8 per cent of GDP during the plan period. The Eleventh Finance Commission had suggested fiscal deficit of 6.5 per cent of GDP as the desirable target to be achieved by 2004-05. The fiscal deficit in 2002-03 is estimated to be more than 10 per cent of GDP. The adverse impact of a large fiscal deficit on the economy should not be underestimated. Despite some initial beneficial effects of deficit, many studies have highlighted the adverse effects that result from rising debt, increasing interest payments, fall in the growth rate of developmental expenditure and the consequent impact on growth rate.

Available analytical models suggest different answers as to the appropriate size of debt and deficit, and an assessment has to be made on the basis of the prevailing empirical situation. In the Keynesian paradigm, government expenditures even if financed by borrowing can have beneficial real effects if there are unemployed resources. The traditional Keynesian framework does not distinguish between alternative uses of fiscal deficit as between consumption and investment expenditure nor does it distinguish between alternative modes of financing, through monetisation or internal or external borrowing. The Keynesian framework recognises the emergence of pure inflation only after the state of full employment is reached. In many developing countries, due to supply side rigidities, the limit is often reached well before full employment, beyond which increments to fiscal deficits do not necessarily add to growth. The Keynesian prescription admittedly works well in the short run and particularly in a situation where unutilised capacities exist. However, persistent fiscal deficits become an impediment to growth, when they begin to impact adversely on saving and investment. Under Ricardian Equivalence, fiscal deficits do not really matter except for smoothening the path of adjustment to expenditure or revenue shocks. However, empirically there has not been much support for this theory.

In the neo-classical perspective, fiscal deficits adversely affect the growth rate, if the implicit reduction in government saving is not fully offset by an increase in the private savings. A net fall in the savings rate puts pressure on interest rate and crowds out private investment. In this context, two factors may be relevant in determining the appropriate level of fiscal deficit, *viz.* private savings ratio, and the ratio of government revenues to GDP. When either of the two is higher, a higher fiscal deficit may be permitted without producing adverse effects of crowding out or putting pressure on the interest payments as a proportion of revenue. Further, it is private savings in the form of financial assets that are relevant. While gross savings by the household sector in India is reasonably high with the average of 19 per cent of GDP in recent years, the transferable savings are a little over half of that. The household sector savings in financial assets in the 1990s has been around 10 per cent of GDP on average. The combined fiscal deficit of Centre and states has been approaching this figure. In the Indian situation, presently, the nominal interest rates may not appear to be under pressure in the wake of the flow of external funds and the substantial fall in private corporate investment. However, the ease with which the Central Government has been able to raise funds from the market should not cloud the fact that several state governments are facing serious problems with respect to borrowing and repaying past loans. In fact we need to study separately for each state the appropriate level of fiscal deficit and sustainable debt. Fiscal deficits of the Central and state governments need to be brought down in a calibrated way by augmenting revenues and pruning expenditures.

For fiscal sustainability, it is required that a rise in fiscal deficit is matched by a rise in the capacity to service the increased debt. It has been argued that from this angle, borrowing for generation of assets may be justified. Apart from the fact that a little less than 70 per cent of borrowing is presently not being spent on capital assets at least of the physical kind, even where there is capital expenditure, the return on assets is negligible. Even the more indirect return through higher growth to match the growing interest liabilities has not been forthcoming. In fact, the high level of fiscal deficit combined with the rising debt-GDP ratio has led to a fall in the aggregate government demand net of transfer payments.

Design of Fiscal Transfers

Fiscal transfers require to be guided by certain definitive principles. A good transfer system should serve the objectives of equity and efficiency and should be characterised by predictability and stability. Equity can be conceptualised with respect to its vertical as well as horizontal dimensions. Efficiency should be conceptualised in the context of a welfare function that may be augmented by government expenditures at different levels. The concept of equalisation is considered to be consistent both with equity and efficiency. It aims at ensuring that citizens of every state are entitled to a common standard of services provided the revenue effort is the same. In India there is wide disparity in the level of services across states. It is seen, for example, that on average, the low income states spend only half of per capita expenditure of high income states in social services. Given the average per capita expenditure adjusted for cost disabilities, equalisation would make up the gap arising due to deficiency in capacity, but not in revenue effort. In a good fiscal transfer system, fiscal disadvantage needs to be taken care of while effectively discouraging fiscal imprudence. The task is to devise a formula that redresses disadvantage but penalises imprudence. The issue before the Commission is to transfer these general principles into concrete terms given the empirical realities.

Vertical Dimension

Fiscal transfers from the Centre to the states take place through the Finance Commission as well as the Planning Commission apart from discretionary transfers through the Central Ministries. The EFC considered that it would be useful to take an overall view as to the extent of total transfers relative to center's gross revenue receipts. The EFC recommended an overall share of 37.5 per cent of the Centre's gross revenue receipts as the extent of total transfer. One issue that requires to be considered is whether there are circumstances that would warrant a change in this recommended overall ratio prescribing the extent of total vertical transfers.

Some long-term trends in the context of the issue of determining the extent of vertical transfers are notable.

(i) The share of the revenue expenditure of the states in the combined revenue expenditure of the Centre and the states, after netting out all inter-governmental flows including transfers, ever since the First Finance Commission period, shows a remarkable stability at around 57 per cent. Averages calculated with reference to the recommendation periods of the earlier Finance Commissions show variations in the range of 56 per cent to 60 per cent (Table 6.1). A similar trend is seen with respect to total expenditure (Table 6.2).

(ii) In comparison, the share of states in the accrual of revenues, i.e. their share in combined revenue receipts after transfers, has been above 60 per cent since the Seventh Finance commission (Table 6.3).

(iii) The share of Centre's debt net of lending to the states in the combined debt of the Centre and the states, which was, on

Table 6.1
Relative Share of Centre and States in Revenue Expenditure

Finance Commissions/Years		Combined	Centre	States	Transfers	Centre Net of Transfers (Rs. Crore)	Centre (Per cent) Relative Shares	States
Average (First)		939.0	441.6	549.4	52.0	389.6	41.7	58.3
Average (Second)		1548.8	833.0	907.2	191.4	641.6	41.6	58.4
Average (Third)		2844.5	1717.8	1535.8	409.0	1308.8	46.1	53.9
Average (Fourth)		4277.0	2481.7	2493.3	698.0	1783.7	41.8	58.2
Average (Fifth)		6899.8	3899.5	4137.5	1137.2	2762.3	40.0	60.0
Average (Sixth)		13585.2	8195.5	7586.6	2196.9	5998.7	44.2	55.8
Average (Seventh)		28904.3	16265.0	16777.1	4137.8	12127.2	42.0	58.0
Eighth	1984-85	47329.1	27047.0	27118.0	6835.9	20211.1	42.70	57.30
	1985-86	56031.0	33608.4	31361.9	8939.4	24669.0	44.03	55.97
	1986-87	66189.0	40725.9	35960.0	10496.9	30229.0	45.67	54.33
	1987-88	77013.9	46167.0	43205.3	12358.4	33808.6	43.90	56.10
	1988-89	89851.5	54106.5	49591.9	13846.9	40259.6	44.81	55.19
Average (Eighth)		67282.9	40331.0	37447.4	10495.5	29835.5	44.2	55.8
Ninth	1989-90	107704.3	64010.8	56831.3	13137.7	50873.1	47.23	52.77
	1990-91	122950.0	73557.0	67860.0	18467.0	55090.0	44.81	55.19
	1991-92	143532.0	82291.0	83611.0	22370.0	59921.0	41.75	58.25
	1992-93	159056.0	92692.0	92150.0	25786.0	66906.0	42.06	57.94
	1993-94	183426.0	108500.0	105440.0	30514.0	77986.0	42.52	57.48
	1994-95	214615.0	122347.0	123749.0	31481.0	90866.0	42.34	57.66

Contd...

Issues Before the Twelfth Finance Commission

...contd...

Finance Commissions/Years	Combined	Centre	States	Transfers	(Rs. Crore) Centre Net of Transfers	(Per cent) Relative Shares Centre	States
Average (Ninth)	**155213.9**	**90566.3**	**88273.5**	**23626.0**	**66940.3**	**43.5**	**56.5**
Tenth							
1995-96	245635.0	139715.0	140499.0	34579.0	105136.0	42.80	57.20
1996-97	282779.0	158811.0	162677.0	38709.0	120102.0	42.47	57.53
1997-98	321144.0	179997.0	181479.0	40332.0	139665.0	43.49	56.51
1998-99	385325.0	216417.0	215994.0	47086.0	169331.0	43.94	56.06
1999-2000	448444.9	248869.3	254858.0	55282.4	193586.9	43.17	56.83
Average (Tenth)	**336665.6**	**188761.9**	**191101.4**	**43197.7**	**145564.2**	**43.2**	**56.8**

Note: Net Transfers on revenue account are derived as the difference between the sum of revenue expenditure of Central and state governments and the combined revenue expenditure.

Net revenue transfers take into account tax devolution and grants. Interest paid by the states to the Centre are included in the revenue expenditure of the states and stand netted out from the revenue expenditure of the Centre.

States include UTs with legislatures. Centre includes UTs without legislatures.

Source: Indian Public Finance Statistics. MoF, Government of India.

Table 6.2
Relative Share of Centre and States in Total Expenditure (Revenue and Capital)

Finance Commissions/Years		Combined	Centre	States	Transfers	(Rs. Crore) Centre Net of Transfers	(Per cent) Relative Shares Centre	States
Average (First)		1276.2	650.4	743.2	117.4	533.0	41.7	58.3
Average (Second)		2433.2	1491.0	1285.8	343.6	1147.4	47.4	52.6
Average (Third)		4499.8	3166.0	2234.3	900.5	2265.5	50.5	49.5
Average (Fourth)		5592.7	4204.7	3295.0	1907.0	2297.7	39.6	60.4
Average (Fifth)		9197.0	5615.3	5230.1	1648.5	3966.8	43.1	56.9
Average (Sixth)		19404.5	12319.6	10250.4	3165.5	9154.1	47.5	52.5
Average (Seventh)		40610.9	24831.1	22381.0	6601.1	18229.9	44.8	55.2
Eighth	1984-85	65303.9	41335.6	34527.5	10559.2	30776.4	47.13	52.87
	1985-86	75458.7	50419.9	39712.0	14673.2	35746.7	47.37	52.63
	1986-87	90292.0	60425.5	45350.1	15483.5	44941.9	49.77	50.23
	1987-88	100248.9	65303.2	53155.0	18209.3	47093.9	46.98	53.02
	1988-89	114533.5	75600.0	59510.9	20577.5	55022.6	48.04	51.96
Average (Eighth)		89167.4	58616.8	46451.1	15900.5	42716.3	47.9	52.1
Ninth	1989-90	136113.0	89321.0	68672.9	21880.9	67440.2	49.55	50.45
	1990-91	153152.0	100884.0	81311.0	29043.0	71841.0	46.91	53.09
	1991-92	172311.0	107903.0	96901.0	32493.0	75410.0	43.76	56.24
	1992-93	196043.0	122518.0	108008.0	34483.0	88035.0	44.91	55.09
	1993-94	223196.0	141690.0	122091.0	40585.0	101105.0	45.30	54.70
	1994-95	254371.0	154641.0	145524.0	45794.0	108847.0	42.79	57.21

Contd...

...contd...

Finance Commissions/Years		Combined	Centre	States	Transfers	(Rs. Crore) Centre Net of Transfers	(Per cent) Relative Shares Centre	States
Average (Ninth)		**189197.7**	**119492.8**	**103751.3**	**34046.5**	**85446.4**	**45.5**	**54.5**
Tenth	1995-96	288562.0	174219.0	163759.0	49416.0	124803.0	43.25	56.75
	1996-97	321165.0	193345.0	184101.0	56281.0	137064.0	42.68	57.32
	1997-98	369193.0	207664.0	209465.0	47936.0	159728.0	43.26	56.74
	1998-99	444511.0	250833.0	247224.0	53546.0	197287.0	44.38	55.62
	1999-2000	515095.8	289400.3	292649.2	66953.8	222446.5	43.19	56.81
Average (Tenth)		**387705.4**	**223092.3**	**219439.6**	**54826.6**	**168265.7**	**43.4**	**56.6**

Note: Net Transfers are derived as the difference between the sum of Centre and state expenditures and the combined expenditure. Net transfers take into account tax devolution and grants, and net borrowing by the states from the Centre. Interest paid by the states to the Centre are included in the expenditure of the states, and netted out from the revenue expenditure of the Centre.

States include UTs with legislatures. Centre includes UTs without legislatures.

Source: *Indian Public Finance Statistics*, MoF, Government of India.

Table 6.3
Share of Central and States in Combined Revenue Receipts After Transfers

	Central Rev. Rec	State Rev. Rec	Total Rev Rec.	Share of Centre	Share of States	As % of GDPmp Centre	As % of GDPmp States
			Rs. Crore	Per cent			
Average (First FC)	413	530	943	43.8	56.2	3.7	4.7
Average (Second FC)	656	920	1576	41.6	58.4	4.1	5.8
Average (Third FC)	1467	1530	2998	48.9	51.1	6.1	6.4
Average (Fourth FC)	1939	2416	4355	44.7	55.3	5.5	6.8
Average (Fifth FC)	2632	4055	6687	39.5	60.5	5.1	7.9
Average (Sixth FC)	6548	8366	14915	44.2	55.8	7.1	9.0
Average (Seventh FC)	11176	17443	28620	39.0	61.0	6.6	10.4
Eighth 1984-85	16996	25658	42654	39.8	60.2	6.9	10.5
1985-86	19465	31831	51296	37.9	62.1	7.0	11.5
1986-87	22825	36043	58869	38.8	61.2	7.3	11.6
1987-88	24741	41920	66661	37.1	62.9	7.0	11.8
1988-89	29798	47343	77141	38.6	61.4	7.1	11.2
Average (Eighth FC)	22765	36559	59324	38.5	61.5	7.1	11.3
Ninth 1989-90	39024	52952	91977	42.4	57.6	8.0	10.9
1990-91	36616	63393	100009	36.6	63.4	6.4	11.1
1991-92	43765	77885	121650	36.0	64.0	6.7	11.9
1992-93	48440	86932	135372	35.8	64.2	6.5	11.6
1993-94	45396	100477	145872	31.1	68.9	5.3	11.7
1994-95	60086	116813	176900	34.0	66.0	5.9	11.5

Contd...

...contd...

	Central Rev. Rec	State Rev. Rec	Total Rev. Rec.	Share of Centre	Share of States	As % of GDPmp Centre	As % of GDPmp States
			Rs. Crore			Per cent	
Average (Ninth FC)	**45555**	**83075**	**128630**	**36.0**	**64.0**	**6.5**	**11.5**
Tenth 1995-96	75695	132432	208127	36.4	63.6	6.4	11.1
1996-97	88837	145288	234124	37.9	62.1	6.5	10.6
1997-98	86152	163912	250064	34.5	65.5	5.7	10.8
1998-99	103118	171289	274406	37.6	62.4	5.9	9.8
1999-00	136816	196729	333545	41.0	59.0	7.1	10.2
Average (Tenth FC)	**98123**	**161930**	**260053**	**37.5**	**62.5**	**6.3**	**10.5**

Source: (Basic Data) *Indian Public Finance Statistics.*

average, a little less than 60 per cent for the reference periods of the Sixth and Seventh Finance Commissions increased to the range of 68-69 per cent for the periods covered by the Ninth and Tenth Finance Commissions.

(iv) Fiscal transfers to the states, through all channels, as percentage of the gross revenue receipts of the Centre increased from an average of 31.4 per cent in the period of the Sixth Finance Commission to 38.0 per cent for the Seventh. It increased further to 39.3 per cent for the period covered by the Ninth Commission before coming down to 35.2 per cent during the period of the Tenth Finance Commission. As percentage of GDP at market prices, fiscal transfers show a decline, falling from the level of about 5 per cent for period covered by the Eighth Commission to 4.8 and 4.1 per cent respectively, for the reference periods of the Ninth and Tenth Finance Commissions (Table 6.4).

Often, there has been a demand that the centrally sponsored schemes should be transferred to the states along with funds. It may be mentioned that this does not imply an increase in the overall ratio, as CSS transfers are part of the total transfers. However, there can be other compelling reasons for transferring at least some of the centrally sponsored schemes to the states along with the funds.

Some forthcoming changes in tax assignments also have a bearing on the issue of vertical sharing. Under Article 268A, specified services will be assigned to the states that will collect and retain the tax-revenue even though the basic law may be made by the Central government. In addition, the set of services that are taxed by the Centre will be shared with the states as specified under Article 268A rather than under Article 270 thus excluding the purview of the Finance Commission. Other important changes relate to the introduction of the state level VAT and the phased withdrawal of the central sales tax. It is important to make an assessment of the revenue implications of these changes.

As already noted, predictability is a significant attribute of a robust scheme of transfers. Since devolution of taxes is recommended in terms of shares of central taxes, and the absolute amounts often fall short of those estimated by the Finance Commission, a suggestion has been made that a minimum amount under tax devolution should be

Table 6.4
Fiscal Transfers as % of Gross Revenue Receipts and GDP at Market Prices

Commission/Years	(As % of Gross Rev Receipts) Share in Cent. Taxes	Total grants	Total transfers	(As % of GDPmp) Share in Cent. Taxes	Total grants	Total transfers
Average (First FC)	**13.4**	**11.9**	**25.3**	**0.662**	**0.603**	**1.265**
Average (Second FC)	**15.0**	**17.7**	**32.7**	**0.966**	**1.149**	**2.115**
Average (Third FC)	**11.8**	**12.4**	**24.1**	**1.070**	**1.128**	**2.198**
Average (Fourth FC)	**14.0**	**15.2**	**29.2**	**1.199**	**1.303**	**2.502**
Average (Fifth FC)	**18.5**	**15.5**	**34.0**	**1.761**	**1.478**	**3.239**
Average (Sixth FC)	**16.0**	**15.4**	**31.4**	**1.787**	**1.731**	**3.518**
Average (Seventh FC)	**22.2**	**15.8**	**38.0**	**2.571**	**1.828**	**4.399**
1984-85	19.7	16.8	36.5	2.353	2.010	4.363
1985-86	21.1	18.9	39.9	2.694	2.412	5.106
1986-87	20.5	17.7	38.2	2.726	2.363	5.089
1987-88	20.6	19.6	40.2	2.709	2.578	5.287
1988-89	19.7	18.5	38.1	2.531	2.376	4.906
Average (Eighth FC)	**20.3**	**18.3**	**38.6**	**2.603**	**2.348**	**4.950**
1989-90	20.3	13.2	33.5	2.721	1.778	4.499
1990-91	20.9	19.0	39.9	2.556	2.322	4.877
1991-92	20.7	18.9	39.5	2.633	2.404	5.037
1992-93	21.7	18.8	40.5	2.743	2.383	5.125
1993-94	22.7	21.2	43.9	2.588	2.424	5.013
1994-95	21.4	17.3	38.6	2.453	1.979	4.432
Average (Ninth FC)	**21.3**	**18.1**	**39.3**	**2.616**	**2.215**	**4.831**
1995-96	21.0	15.3	36.3	2.465	1.792	4.257
1996-97	21.7	14.4	36.1	2.563	1.693	4.255
1997-98	24.6	12.6	37.2	2.860	1.466	4.327
1998-99	20.8	13.3	34.1	2.249	1.441	3.689
1999-00	19.3	12.9	32.3	2.253	1.503	3.757
Average (Tenth FC)	**21.5**	**13.7**	**35.2**	**2.478**	**1.579**	**4.057**

Source: (Basic Data) Indian Public Finance Statistics.

prescribed. Under the provisions of Article 270 only a share for the states in the central taxes is determined. This provides for automatic sharing of the central tax buoyancies. However, states have a genuine problem if growth in central taxes falls short of expectations.

Horizontal Dimension

The considerations that should go in determining the distribution among states have been examined in great length by the various Finance Commissions. Equity issues have dominated such discussions as they are resulting in higher share to relating poorer states (Table 6.5). The effort has been to identify variables which reflect the equity concerns. In designing a suitable scheme of fiscal transfers, three considerations seem relevant—needs, cost disability and fiscal efficiency. Needs refer to expenditures required to be made based on the principle of equalisation but not met by own resources. Cost disabilities refer to such characteristics of a state that necessitate more than average per capita cost in service provision due to factors that are largely beyond its control. Fiscal efficiency encompasses parameters like maintaining revenue account balance, robust revenue effort, economies of expenditure linked to efficient provision of services and the quality of governance.

In combining these considerations into a suitable scheme of transfers, there are both conceptual issues and practical problems. A major concern relates to the weights to be attached to the various factors. Besides, there are problems of choosing appropriate indicators and their measurement. For example, revenue capacity is measured by GSDP even though it is recognised that GSDP is not a perfect correlate of income. Comparability of GSDP estimates prepared by the states is also a contentious issue. Although the Central Statistical Organisation (CSO) provides comparable estimates of GSDP at factor cost at current prices, it remains a compilation of the state estimates after certain adjustments. There has also been the question as to whether GSDP at market prices would serve as a better proxy for income or revenue capacity than GSDP at factor cost. Discussions reveal that the allocation of central indirect taxes net of subsidies according to states still remains an intractable problem. Even the measurement of revenue deficit is not unambiguous any more. Some have argued that a

Table 6.5

Share of States in Central Taxes and Duties and Grants as Recommended by the Finance Commissions

(Percentage Share)

State	First	Second	Third	Fourth	Fifth	Sixth	Seventh	Eighth	Ninth(1)	Ninth(2)	Tenth	Eleventh
1	2	3	4	5	6	7	8	9	10	11	12
Andhra Pradesh	4.22	8.58	9.31	8.05	7.77	8.08	7.30	7.34	6.60	6.83	7.98	7.13
Bihar	11.95	9.09	7.83	6.91	9.57	8.79	10.62	10.70	10.65	10.54	10.88	13.04
Gujarat		3.41	6.50	4.23	4.34	3.84	4.62	3.77	3.19	3.50	3.92	2.76
Haryana				1.19	1.42	1.26	1.48	1.11	1.21	1.13	1.23	0.97
Karnataka	1.44	7.01	6.19	7.48	4.65	3.99	4.82	4.38	4.22	3.83	4.64	4.53
Kerala	0.92	3.62	5.23	6.51	4.38	4.99	3.70	3.27	3.01	3.25	3.41	2.83
Madhya Pradesh	5.92	6.81	6.62	5.60	6.45	5.66	7.66	7.50	6.99	7.40	7.10	8.05
Maharashtra	16.58	10.47	9.12	9.01	9.16	7.40	8.22	6.68	6.71	5.85	6.05	4.46
Orissa	5.16	4.51	7.72	8.03	5.41	6.01	4.72	4.84	4.53	5.21	4.28	4.77
Punjab	5.42	4.95	4.50	2.22	2.13	1.76	2.01	1.64	2.04	1.58	1.58	1.25
Rajasthan	3.64	4.57	5.36	4.52	4.99	5.87	4.33	4.25	4.77	6.15	5.03	5.42
Tamil Nadu	10.01	6.95	7.00	7.17	6.98	5.60	7.21	6.25	6.38	5.85	5.89	4.97
Uttar Pradesh	16.53	13.51	11.29	12.96	14.53	14.04	15.90	15.47	15.83	16.46	15.95	18.05
West Bengal	13.54	9.85	7.15	6.78	8.44	8.57	7.66	8.74	6.99	6.99	6.61	8.10
Total	**103.17**	**93.33**	**93.81**	**90.67**	**90.21**	**85.85**	**90.28**	**85.94**	**83.11**	**84.55**	**84.56**	**86.33**

contd....

...contd...

(Percentage Share)

State	First	Second	Third	Fourth	Fifth	Sixth	Seventh	Eighth	Ninth(1)	Ninth(2)	Tenth	Eleventh
	1	2	3	4	5	6	7	8	9	10	11	12
Arunachal Pradesh									1.11	0.79	0.78	0.53
Assam	4.66	4.33	4.47	5.04	3.65	4.58	2.49	4.07	4.12	3.73	3.67	3.05
Goa									0.34	0.48	0.27	0.19
Himachal Pradesh					0.94	2.12	1.56	1.96	1.86	1.75	2.10	1.72
Jammu & Kashmir		2.34	1.66	2.27	2.17	2.42	1.81	2.84	3.48	3.17	3.23	3.78
Manipur					0.50	1.33	0.93	1.19	1.09	1.02	0.94	0.74
Meghalaya					0.35	0.91	0.64	0.97	0.82	0.78	0.83	0.68
Mizoram					0.00	0.00	0.00	0.00	1.25	0.96	0.80	0.58
Nagaland			0.05	2.01	1.53	1.41	1.15	1.34	1.25	1.17	1.23	1.02
Sikkim					0.00	0.00	0.18	0.26	0.23	0.24	0.31	0.38
Tripura					0.63	1.38	0.96	1.42	1.34	1.35	1.27	1.00
Total	4.66	6.67	6.19	9.33	9.79	14.15	9.72	14.06	16.89	15.45	15.44	13.67
Grand Total	100.00	100.00	100.00	100.00	100.00	100.00	100.00	100.00	100.00	100.00	100.00	100.00

Source: Report of the Eleventh Finance Commission (2000) and Vithal and Sastry (2001).

proportion of grants given to the local bodies should be counted as capital expenditure. Others have argued that expenditure on health and education should be treated as investment in human capital.

The measurement of cost disabilities is also not a straightforward exercise. Some of the cost disabilities are clearly related to exogenous circumstances like the nature of the terrain, the extent of rainfall, and proneness to drought and floods. Other factors like the distance from centers of economic activities, the incidence of diseases, the extent of illiteracy, and the composition of population may also be important. Conceptually, cost norms are required to be developed in respect of these different dimensions for application in determining the norm-based expenditure requirements.

As already mentioned, the notion of efficiency is implicit in an equalisation approach since transfers are related to some standard revenue effort. But some times efficiency indicators are used more directly in the devolution formulae. The two previous commissions who have explicitly introduced some efficiency factors have focused on tax effort and improvement in revenue account balance. There is also the issue of backward looking *vis-à-vis* forward looking indicators of efficiency. Only in the case of Medium Term Reform Facility, incentives are linked to performance. However, there are several inherent difficulties in including forward looking indicators in the distribution formula.

An important issue in the context of transfers under the Finance Commission pertains to the relative role of tax devolution and grants. Tax devolution has a built-in flexibility as it can increase automatically if the central taxes are more buoyant. Conversely, there is risk if their buoyancy falls short of expectations. Grants are ensured as these are fixed in nominal terms. It is easier to target grants towards states or sectors. The flexibility in the case of devolution is limited by the criteria used. Yet states have often expressed a preference for devolution because by definition it is unconditional and comes to the states as a matter of right. Within the subset of grants, grants could be made conditional or purpose specific, although Article 275 grants have generally been unconditional. However, if a move is made towards equalisation of services through grants, conditional grants are inescapable.

In order to address problems of adverse incentives, a normative approach for determining revenues as well as expenditures of the state governments is relevant. Following a historical approach in determining revenues and expenditures leads to what is described as gap filling. Such an approach has built-in adverse incentives inducing the states to under-perform in terms of revenues relative to capacity. They also do not have sufficient incentive to economise in the use of resources. The normative approach can effectively neutralise such adverse incentives. In such an approach, states will be assessed in terms of revenues that they ought to raise given their capacity. Similarly, the expenditures will be in line with their requirements on the basis of cost norms and not driven by the past history of expenditures. Designing a fully normative approach is conceptually straight forward, but applying it in practice has to overcome numerous constraints. Some of the previous Commissions have partially applied a normative approach for determining revenues and expenditures. A fully normative approach requires an assessment of revenues and expenditure for the base year as well as determining the relevant growth norms during the reference period.

Restructuring Issues

The Eleventh Finance Commission (EFC) in its outline for restructuring the public finances of Centre and states has suggested a revenue deficit target of 1 per cent in 2004-05 for the Centre, with the states achieving balance in their budget, and the overall fiscal deficit target was set at 6.5 per cent. The current trends indicate that the economy is far from achieving this target. The overall debt-GDP ratio was supposed to be brought down to 55 per cent from a level of 65 per cent in 1999-2000, i.e. a fall of 10 percentage points. As per the latest data, the combined debt-GDP ratio at the end of 2002-03 is estimated at 76 per cent. Thus, instead of falling, the debt-GDP ratio has risen substantially.

Restructuring public finances aimed at macroeconomic stabilisation and achieving revenue account balance requires a broad analytical framework. The impact of the size and composition of government expenditure on growth, inflation, interest rate and the external account has to be considered in an inter-dependent framework that takes into account feedbacks of first and subsequent round effects. This will require that in terms of methodology, one should go beyond consistency frameworks. Restructuring has to spell out adjustments both on the revenue and expenditure sides. Some hard decisions are required to arrest the persistent rise in the debt-GDP ratio.

Fiscal policies will have to be restructured to facilitate acceleration in growth with macroeconomic stability. Public spending in areas such as roads, water supply, power, primary education and primary health will need to be stepped up to provide the appropriate physical and social infrastructure necessary for accelerating growth. The problem would have been a simple one, had there been some fiscal space for augmenting such expenditure. This unfortunately is not the case. The challenge lies in finding ways of augmenting such expenditures while reducing the overall fiscal imbalances at the same time. Failure to step up expenditure on the necessary items will dampen the growth momentum of the economy. Failure on the fiscal consolidation front, on the other hand, can come in the way of faster growth.

The Fiscal Responsibility Act of the Central government envisages that central revenue deficit will be eliminated by 2007-08. A target for fiscal deficit relating to GDP has not been specified in the Act itself but it may be indicated in the rules to be framed in relation to the Act. Some of the state governments have also shown initiatives in this direction through Fiscal Responsibility and Management legislations. Some notable initiatives are from Karnataka, Maharashtra and Punjab. One may hope that this trend will catch on and other states would also impose explicit self-discipline on themselves through such legislations.

Several state governments have asked for debt relief. Some of the previous Commissions have observed that recommendations regarding debt relief by successive Commissions create anticipations about such measures, which has a built-in adverse incentive. At the same time, the extreme difficulty in which the state finances are placed today calls for fresh consideration of this issue. It is clear that any debt relief will have to be linked to a desired path of deficits in the future. The Planning Commission must also ensure that the size of a State Plan is consistent with a sustainable level of debt, as the State Plans are almost fully financed by borrowing in one form or another.

I have referred in some detail to some of the key issues before the present Finance Commission. There are several issues like the role of the Commission in relation to local bodies and re-examination of the Medium Term Reform Facility which I have not touched upon. It will be the endeavour of the Twelfth Finance Commission to evolve a scheme of fiscal transfers which will give due weightage to the available resources of the Centre and the states and the demands on these resources by both the Centre and the states. The correction of vertical and horizontal imbalances has to be done within a framework of fiscal prudence. A good transfer system must establish an appropriate balance between equity and efficiency, a system in which, as I mentioned earlier, fiscal disadvantage is taken care of but fiscal imprudence is effectively discouraged. Needless to say, that the fiscal responsibility must be shared by both the Centre and the states.

Inaugural Address at the Conference on *Issues Before the Twelfth Finance Commission*, 29th September 2003. New Delhi.
Economic and Political Weekly. Vol.XXXIX No.26, June 26-July 2, 2004.

7. Twelfth Finance Commission Report

Approach and Recommendations

In federal fiscal systems, on grounds both of equity and efficiency, resources are generally assigned more to the Central government whereas states together with the local governments have the larger responsibilities. The resultant vertical imbalance requires transfer of resources from the Centre to the states. States also have different capacities and needs, and this lends a horizontal dimension to the issue of resource sharing. Neither vertical nor horizontal imbalance is expected to be static. Some of the core provisions regarding sharing of resources are built into our Constitution itself. But changes in the economic and fiscal situation warrant a review of the arrangements from time to time. The Indian constitution has provided for both continuity and change. The Finance Commission is entrusted with the task of periodically examining these issues according to the constitutional provisions and the terms of reference.

The Twelfth Finance Commission has recommended a scheme of fiscal transfers that can serve the objectives of equity and efficiency within a framework of fiscal consolidation. The effort needed to achieve fiscal consolidation must be seen as the joint responsibility of the Central and state governments. For achieving vertical and horizontal balance, consistent with the responsibilities of the two levels of governments in respect of providing public and merit goods and services, both the Centre and the states need to raise the levels of revenues relative to their respective revenue bases, exercise restraint in undertaking unwarranted expenditure commitments and prioritising expenditures.

The finances of the Central and state governments, individually and in the aggregate, have evinced large and persistent imbalances in the period preceding the Commission's award period. Not only have fiscal and revenue deficits increased, the proportion of revenue deficit to fiscal deficit has increased. Outstanding debt as a proportion of GDP touched 81 per cent in 2004-05. Four factors have accounted for the continuing deterioration: fall in Centre's tax-GDP ratio compared to the peak levels achieved in the late eighties, substantial increase in the level of salary and pension payments, particularly for the states, in the wake of the recommendations of the Fifth Central Pay Commission, high levels of nominal interest rates in the late nineties combined with the subsequent fall in inflation rates, and the low growth rates in the first three years of the new decade. Besides, the tax devolution to states was less than projected because of the deterioration in the tax-GDP ratio of the centre. While these reasons account for the acuteness of the ailment, there are also underlying structural reasons for the persistence of fiscal deterioration because of the tax structure and expenditure pattern.

Vertical Transfers

In the scheme of fiscal transfers, the correction of vertical imbalance is, to some extent, based on judgment. An assessment has to be made of the gap between resources and responsibilities at the two levels of government. Sometimes it is not recognised that the share of states in the combined revenue receipts undergoes a radical change after tax devolution. For example, during the Tenth Finance Commission's period, the share of states which was 38.6 per cent before transfers became 63.0 per cent after transfers. Taking into account a variety of factors including the historical trends, the Commission had recommended an increase in the share of states in the divisible pool of taxes to 30.5 per cent from the previous level of 29.5 per cent. This increase was also necessary to provide some cushion to states whose share in the total tax devolution might go down as a result of any modifications in the formula of horiøntal distribution. The Commission felt that this increase could be accommodated by the Central government by pruning their activities that fall in the domain of the states. The Commission had raised the indicative limit of overall transfers out of the gross revenue receipts of the Centre from 37.5 per cent to 38 per cent.

Horizontal Transfers

In the context of horiøntal imbalance, the Twelfth Finance Commission felt that the equalisation approach to transfers was appropriate as it was consistent with both equity and efficiency. It has not, however, been possible to implement this approach fully, as the extent of disparities in the per capita fiscal capacities of the states is too large and some of the better-off states are also in serious fiscal imbalance. In the devolution scheme recommended, the Commission has endeavored to strike a balance among different criteria reflecting deficiency in fiscal capacities, cost disabilities, and fiscal efficiency. While the Commission has retained, by and large, the indicators used by the Eleventh Finance Commission for determining the horiøntal transfers, it has altered the weights to some extent. The distance criterion combined with the criterion of population, representing together the needs and deficiency in fiscal capacity have a combined weight of 75 per cent. The cost disabilities get a weight of 10 per cent through area and fiscal performance 15 per cent.

Role of Grants

The Twelfth Finance Commission has increased the proportion of grants to tax devolution in the scheme of transfers. Grants constitute around 19 per cent of total transfers compared to around 13 per cent in the Eleventh Finance Commission. Grants achieve certain purposes which cannot be fulfilled by tax devolution. First, they provide greater stability to revenues of states which became an important issue in the recent period. Second, they enable the application of equalisation principle. The Twelfth Finance Commission has made an effort in this direction by focusing on education and health which are two critical merit services. Third, special purpose and conditional grants can be given which promote specific objectives. It is therefore necessary that in judging the transfer to states, tax devolution and grants should be taken together into account. The coefficient of correlation between comparable GSDP per capita (average of 1999-2000 to 2001-02) and the recommended per capita transfers, comprising tax devolution and all the grants, among the general category states excluding Goa, is estimated at -0.89, which emphasises the redistributive character of the transfers.

A word must also be said about the estimation of non-plan revenue deficit grants. Very often such an approach is called 'fiscal dentistry' or gap filling approach. This approach has been misunderstood. No Commission goes by just the gaps projected by the states. The Twelfth Finance Commission also examined each item of expenditure and adjusted it according to some common normative criteria. These are detailed in the Report. Similarly, adjustments were made for revenue projections as well. Even base year figures were adjusted. An important adjustment made by the Twelfth Finance Commission in the base year figures relates to fiscal capacity. In the final analysis, the pre-devolution non-plan revenue deficit was 25 per cent of the states projections. It has also to be noted that nearly 85 per cent of the deficit grant goes to special category states.

The Commission has laid emphasis on strengthening the local bodies in keeping with the constitutional mandate for effective and autonomous local self-governance, recognising that local bodies must be supported by a scheme of transfers that encourages decentralisation and own effort for raising revenues. The recommended transfers for the local bodies constitute about 1.24 per cent of the shareable taxes and 0.9 per cent of centre's gross revenue receipts.

Debt Restructuring

The Commission has recognised that the debt burden of the states is currently heavy. It has, therefore, recommended a scheme of debt relief, which is in two parts. First, there is the relief that comes from consolidating the past debt and rescheduling it, along with interest rate reduction. The second part consists of a debt write-off, which is linked to the reduction in the absolute levels of revenue deficits. Both reliefs will be available, only if states enact appropriate legislations to bring down the revenue deficit to zero by 2008-09 and commit to reducing the fiscal deficit in a phased manner. With the relief that has been recommended, it should be possible for states to pursue their developmental goals with fiscal prudence. The condition imposed also mitigates the moral hazard problem.

Institutional Changes

The Commission has argued that important institutional changes are required to tackle some of the structural problems in managing government finances. One central change relates to the regime of government borrowing. It has recommended that states, like the Centre, must decide their annual borrowing programme, within the framework of their respective fiscal responsibility legislations. In fact, as the background papers for this Conference indicate that if the state governments move on a path of fiscal correction, the market borrowing programme of the states will be sustainable and should not face difficulties in terms of eliciting the necessary subscription. There is also a need to let the states access the market directly for their borrowing requirements. Such a practice will bring in the needed fiscal discipline. The overall limit to their annual borrowing from all sources should be supervised by an independent body like a Loan Council with representatives from the Ministry of Finance, Planning Commission, Reserve Bank of India, and the state governments. This Council may, at the beginning of each year, announce borrowing limits for each state, taking into account the sustainability considerations into account. Our suggestion for de-linking grants and loans in plan assistance, as these need to be determined on different principles, is part of the reform of the borrowing regime.

Restructuring Public Finance

The scheme of restructuring envisages the fiscal deficit to be reduced to 6 per cent on the combined amount of the Centre and states and revenue deficit to ero by 2008-09. This will result in an increase in the aggregate saving rate as well as an increase in government capital expenditure as a percentage of GDP. In consequence, as aggregate investment rate increases, growth is stabilised at above 7 per cent. The reduction in the revenue deficit by 4.5 percentage points is to be achieved by an increase in the total revenue receipts by 2.9 per cent and a reduction in total revenue expenditure by about 1.6 per cent.

In our plan for restructuring government finances, we expect a positive growth dividend, as revenue deficits relative to GDP progressively fall, implying a fall in government dis-savings, and an increase in the overall savings relative to GDP. A higher tax-GDP ratio combined with higher growth on a sustained basis, and fall in interest payments, create the necessary space for increasing government capital expenditure, and productivity enhancing non-interest, non-salary revenue expenditure. The virtuous cycle of reforms, robust government finances, and an equalising system of fiscal transfers, should help establish a sound federal fiscal system in India.

Inaugural address at the 16th Bi-Annual Conference of the State Finance Secretaries, Reserve Bank of India. Mumbai, April 8, 2005.

Economic and Political Weekly, Vol. XL. No. 31, July 30, 2005.

Part II

Growth and Development

8 | Indian Economy
Challenges and Opportunities

A review of the economy in the recent period throws up several interesting insights. Economic growth has averaged 8.6 per cent per annum over the last four years. Our external payments situation is comfortable, foreign exchange reserves are robust, inflation is benign, the investment climate is promising and our comparative advantage in the knowledge economy is fueling the boom in the service sector. Social indicators have improved too. Life expectancy has gone up as have indicators in health and education. A child born today can expect to live 25 years longer, hope to be more educated, and lead a healthier and more productive life than a child born at the time of Independence. Indeed, if we can sustain an average annual growth rate of 8 per cent, the child of today will see the per capita income of the country multiply more than four fold by the time he/she grows up to be 21.

Challenges Ahead

Yet there are many challenges on the way forward. We need to sustain the present rate of growth, if not accelerate it to higher levels. We need to translate growth into poverty reduction. In other words, we need to generate poverty reducing growth i.e. growth *to* which the poor contribute and *from* which the poor benefit. We need to expand employment opportunities and improve productivity across all sectors of the economy. We need to narrow economic disparities across and within states without compromising on efficiency. We need to improve on social indicators too; India still ranks a low 128th in the UNDP's Human Development Index in the bottom third of the league of nations. The agenda for achieving growth and poverty reduction is formidable requiring as it does focus not only on identifying priority areas for action but also on effective and efficient implementation of the policy agenda. In other words, we need to focus simultaneously on economic growth and on governance.

1991 Reforms—Genesis

In the post-Independence economic history of our country, 1991 is a watershed year. This was the year in which the economy was faced with a severe balance of payments meltdown. In response, we launched a broad ranging economic programme not just to restore the balance of payments but to reform, restructure and modernise the economy. This was entirely appropriate for the external payment crisis and was just the proximate manifestation of a policy regime that has, over the years, tended to give precedence to command and control over productivity, efficiency and entrepreneurship. In the event, the 1991 reforms signalled a shift away from the earlier paradigm.

Economic Reforms—Break with the Past

This break with the past came in three important directions. The first was to dismantle the complex regime of licences, permits and controls that dictated almost every facet of production and distribution—what to produce, where to produce, how to produce and how much to produce. The entrepreneur has now greater freedom to decide on all these choices. The second change in direction was to reverse the strong bias towards state ownership of means of production and proliferation of public sector enterprises in almost every sphere of economic activity. Areas once reserved exclusively for the state have been thrown open to private enterprise. The third change in direction was to abandon our inward looking trade policy. This elusive, and in hindsight ill-advised, quest for self-sufficiency was driven by a belief that there was a value to minimising the economy's external dependence and producing what we need ourselves even if it meant high costs and low efficiency. By embracing international trade, India signalled that it was abandoning its export pessimism and was accepting the challenge and opportunity of integrating into the world economy.

Rationale Underlying Reforms

Although the various elements of the reform agenda may look disparate, there is an underlying rationale running across the broad spectrum of economic reforms. This was to give a greater market orientation to the economy and to let the competitive forces and growth impulses that are the bedrock of a modern, dynamic economy to come into fuller play. Liberalisation removed the barriers to entry and relaxed the plethora of restrictions on production and distribution. Deregulation brought about a more competitive domestic environment while the liberalised trade and foreign investment policy sought to improve international competitiveness. By reducing its entrepreneurial role, the government was yielding economic space to the private sector while also redefining the role of the state.

Stabilisation and Structural Adjustment

Conceptually, the economic reform agenda can be divided into two strands—stabilisation, aimed at redressing the internal and external imbalances in the economy, and structural adjustment aimed at removing the rigidities and inefficiencies in the system and improving its competitiveness. Thus, stabilisation can be attempted and completed quickly while structural adjustment is a medium to long-term process. Stabilisation is macroeconomic in content while structural adjustment encompasses both macro and microeconomic aspects. While stabilisation could be managed by the government acting on its own, structural adjustment is much broader and deeper in scope requiring the proactive involvement of the government at various levels and the people at large.

Uniqueness of India's Reforms

India's economic reforms are unique in two important respects—not because of the content of the reforms but because of the context in which we are pursuing them. First, we are implementing reforms in a democratic context, no matter that it has many flaws. Second, we are pursuing reforms in a decentralising context. This democracy-federalism context oftentimes has meant restraint, even compromise, deliberate decision-making and slow progress. While there are many respects in which we can make our approach to reforms more efficient and purposeful, in an overall perspective, it must be acknowledged that making haste slowly—'crossing the river by feeling the stones', as the Chinese say—has a lot of merit. The participatory and consultative processes inherent in our institutions of meditation and restraint have added to the credibility and robustness of our reforms.

Post-Reform Growth Performance

That the content and process of our economic reforms are on the right track is vindicated by the performance of the economy since the launch of the reforms. Between 1981-82 and 1990-91, i.e. the decade before the reforms, the economy grew at 5.6 per cent on a compound average basis. The year 1991-92 was an outlier because of the balance of payments crisis, and should therefore be omitted for the purpose of discerning trends. In fact, there is every justification for including it in the pre-reform period because it was also a culmination of the policies pursued previously. The effect of the reforms should be judged starting with the economy's performance in 1992-93. Between 1992-93 and 2005-2006, the economy grew at 6.6 per cent on a compound average annual basis, a significant improvement over the pre-reform record. The growth rate was 8.5 per cent in 2003-04, 7.5 per cent in 2004-05, 9 per cent in 2005-06 and 9.4 per cent in 2006-07. The expectation is that in the current year, the growth rate will be close to 9 per cent. It is clear that India has shifted to a higher growth trajectory.

Six Challenges on the Way Forward

At the same time if we are to sustain this rate of growth, and in fact accelerate the growth rate to higher levels and translate that growth to broad-based poverty reduction, we must address some important challenges. I want to reflect on what I think are six of the most important challenges warranting priority attention.

First Challenge—Stepping up Agricultural Growth

First, we need to step up the growth rate of the agriculture sector. We have come a long way from the chronic food shortages and occasional famines that marked our pre-independence and immediate post-independence history. That we have achieved near self-sufficiency in food is a remarkable achievement. But it must also be admitted that our agriculture is characterised by low productivity both of land and labour. The most critical problems are low yields and the inability of the farmers to exploit the advantages of the market because of lack of infrastructure to transport the produce from the farm to the market. Clearly we need to modernise and diversify our agriculture sector by improving both the forward and backward linkages. These will include better credit delivery, investment in irrigation and rural infrastructure, improved cropping pattern and farming techniques and development of food processing industry and cold chains across the entire distribution system. Agricultural growth is critical for expanding employment, generating broad-based growth and sustained poverty reduction.

Second Challenge—Infrastructure Development

The second critical constraint to growth is the infrastructure deficit, more particularly, in power. The infrastructure needs of the economy are large because of the demand generated by economic growth, rise in population, rapid urbanisation as well as the need for making up the accumulated backlog. Provision of infrastructure was once considered to be an exclusive responsibility of the government. Advances in technology which have made unbundling possible, as well as innovative financial products have changed the characteristics of infrastructure provision making both private sector participation as well as competition possible. In order to mobilise the necessary resources and build quality infrastructure, we need to put in place appropriate legal, regulatory and administrative frameworks to attract domestic and foreign investment. We also need to address issues of pricing and cost recovery, with subsidies where required, being made transparent and explicit. This in turn will require the establishment of credible regulation for ensuring fair competition across public and private operators, and for protecting consumer interest, public safety and environmental integrity. Efficient and speedy implementation of projects is critical in all spheres but more in the infrastructure area.

Third Challenge—Fiscal Consolidation

The third critical challenge on the way forward is fiscal consolidation which is a necessary pre-requisite for sustained growth. The negative consequences of excessive fiscal deficits are standard fare of textbook economics as also staple of a current debate in our country.

In India, we have been long conscious of the need for fiscal adjustment both at the Centre and in the states. After much debate, the Centre has enacted the Fiscal Responsibility and Budget Management (FRBM) Act, taking upon itself the obligation, by 2008-09, of reducing fiscal deficit to three per cent of GDP and completely eliminating the revenue deficit. Similarly, in response to the incentives provided by the Twelfth Finance Commission, several states too have enacted their respective fiscal responsibility legislations.

More recently, an argument that has been heard is that the resources required for development may be in excess of the resources that can be made available within the fiscal responsibility restrictions.

There is substance in this argument. Nevertheless, the solution does not lie in throwing away hard won gains by abandoning the FRBMs. The solution lies instead in harmonising the fiscal discipline imposed by the FRBMs with the resources needed for development expenditure. What this harmonisation requires is that both the central and state governments ruthlessly prune their unproductive expenditures, rationalise the plethora of schemes and programmes, and after that identify whether any segment or element of the FRBM targets needs to be rephased to be consistent with the resource requirements for productive expenditures. Frequent tamperings with FRBM targets will erode credibility.

Fourth Challenge—Building Social Infrastructure

The fourth important challenge to growth is investment in social infrastructure—particularly in the twin merit goods of primary education and basic health. There are any number of studies that establish a positive correlation between low levels of poverty and improved indicators of health and education. We need to spend more on education and health. But we also need to spend more efficiently because better education and health are a function not just of the quantum of expenditure but also of the quality of that expenditure.

Fifth Challenge—Managing Globalisation

Next on my list is the challenge of globalisation. Globalisation has been a contentious issue, and often a topic of acrimonious debate as also high profile protests. The scope of this lecture does not permit me to address in detail all the issues surrounding the debate on globalisation. What I do want to emphasise though is that our economies are no longer defined by political boundaries. Globalisation, defined as the free movement of goods, services, ideas and people across borders, is here to stay. No revolution in human history has been totally benign. So it is the case with the globalisation which comes with costs and benefits. We cannot wish away globalisation, nor can we shut our doors and remain indifferent. The only option is to manage globalisation in such a way as to maximise the benefits and minimise the costs. Consider for example our head start in the knowledge economy. We got off the block here ahead of other countries because of our superior technical manpower. But other countries are fast catching up and our comparative advantage will be threatened unless we are continuously ahead of the curve in terms of technical sophistication and competence levels. More than many other developing countries, India is in a position to wrest significant gains from globalisation. Even as we make efforts to modify the international trading arrangements to take care of the special needs of developing countries, we must identify and strengthen our dynamic comparative advantages.

Sixth Challenge—Good Governance

Just to recap, the five challenges on the way forward to accelerating growth and poverty reduction that I have addressed so far are: stepping up agriculture growth, infrastructure development, fiscal consolidation, enhancing the quality and reach of primary education and basic health, and managing globalisation. Identifying these challenges and drawing up plans to address them is the relatively easy part. What is infinitely more difficult is the translation of those policies into action. That brings me to the sixth and final challenge that we need to confront—the issue of governance.

That good governance is at the very heart of economic growth and poverty reduction, and even political legitimacy, is now part of conventional wisdom. However, we did not zero in on this intuitively. The realisation that good governance is critical came as a result of some profound changes in development thinking over the past 50 years. In the 50s and 60s, when many countries of Asia and Africa were emerging out of colonialism, the path to development was widely believed, lay in capital formation. In the 1970s, awareness grew that physical capital was not enough, and at least as important was fulfilling basic human needs. When this too did not produce results, the missing link, it was thought, was improving social capital through education and health. But again there was no breakthrough. The disappointing experience with the debt crisis in Latin America and chronic poverty in Sub-Saharan Africa and South Asia during the 'lost decade' of the 80s threw up the idea that the path to development lay in improving economic management and giving greater play to market forces. Again the results were mixed. Some countries such as those in Latin America posted disappointing results in spite of making the transition to the market fully; on the other hand countries in East Asia performed well despite deviating in important ways from the market model. What made the difference was institutions of governance. The received wisdom is that, for growth and poverty reduction, we need physical and social capital, we need to focus on basic needs, and we need to yield to the market forces in a calibrated manner. These are all necessary, but not sufficient. They will not yield results unless they are accompanied by good governance.

What is good governance? As per textbook definition, good governance is the manner in which the authority of the state is exercised in the management of a country's economic and social resources for maximising welfare. In the ultimate analysis, it is the quality of governance that separates success and failure in economic development. Across countries, application of the same policies in roughly similar contexts has produced dramatically different results. In our own country, we have seen vast differences across states in development outcomes from out of the same mix of development policies. These differences across countries as well as across regions within countries, even as they adopt similar policy packages, arise because of differences in governance. Indeed research shows that per capita incomes and the quality of governance are strongly correlated indicating a virtuous circle in which good governance results in economic development.

Technology

Even as we take action to meet the challenges I have listed, it is important to note that there are some long run factors, the most important of which is technology. History has shown that modern economic growth has been inspired by a rapid and persistent upgradation of technology and scientific knowledge. It is estimated that from one-third to one-half of the growth experienced by the industrially advanced countries has come from technological progress. Thus, technology has emerged as the principal driving force for long-term economic growth. Economic growth results both from slow and steady improvements in technology and from knowledge embodied in physical and human capital as well as from the 'breakthrough' inventions. Breakthrough inventions are, however, unpredictable and such inventions change the direction of almost the entire industrial structure. Schumpeter made a fundamental distinction between invention, which was the discovery of new techniques, and innovation, which consists of the practical application of an invention in production for the market. Invention is the outcome of the efforts of the scientists and technologists, while innovation is the task of the entrepreneur. Production for the market occurs only when the scientist and the entrepreneur join hands.

In India, we need to identify very clearly the areas in which we must concentrate as far as technological advance is concerned. India has been successful in adapting imported technologies to Indian needs and circumstances. We need to do more of this. However, given our resource endowments and capabilities we need to identify areas where the pay-off from R&D efforts will be high.

Sustaining the High Growth

In the context of the high growth achieved in the recent period, a question that is often raised is: Is this high rate of growth sustainable? Two related questions are: is the economy 'over-heating'? Is the growth consumption driven or investment driven? All these are inter-related questions.

In terms of sustaining the high growth over the medium term, some of the macroeconomic parameters are in the right direction. The domestic saving rate of the economy had touched 34.4 per cent of GDP in 2006-07. The gross-investment rate was 35.5 per cent. In fact, the Eleventh Plan projection for the gross-domestic saving rate is 34.8 per cent. This has very nearly been achieved already. Therefore, in terms of saving and investment rates, the conditions for achieving a growth rate of 9 per cent are already there. I have already referred to the various challenges that need to be faced if the high growth rate is to be sustained. Certainly the prospect for achieving a 9 per cent rate of growth in a sustained way is within our grasp.

Is there a short-run problem? The term 'overheating' is used to describe the situation in which the economy is operating at almost the full levels of its capacity. With the actual output pushing against the potential output, the economy begins to show higher inflation and widening current account deficit or both. In the Indian situation, towards the end of last calendar year and in the first quarter of the current year, there were signs of 'overheating' as inflation rate was running nearly one per cent above the usually accepted level of around 5.5 per cent. The trade deficit in the balance of payment also widened. However, these signs have abated. The issue of whether the present growth is propelled by consumption or investment is relevant in this context. One argument has been that the growth over the last few years has been driven largely by consumption demand including demand for homes financed by loans from banking system. It is argued that the consumption demand was fuelled largely by monetary factors such as easy liquidity and low interest rates. One way of testing this hypothesis is to look at the share of incremental consumption and investment in incremental GDP. In the 4 years beginning 2003-04 the share of incremental investment in incremental GDP was 48 per cent, 49 per cent, 52 per cent and 56 per cent. These figures indicate that while upto 2004-05 consumption might have played a major role in the subsequent years investment is playing a leading role. However, looking at the share it is also clear that both consumption and investment have played more or less equal role in driving growth. A consumption boom that lasts for a period has the potential to create an investment boom. The efforts to take care of the impact of 'over-heating' in the short-run must be accompanied by removing structural constraints on growth over the medium term. Contrary to the concerns of 'overheating', in the last two months some concerns have been expressed about the possible slowdown. It is true that some sectors in the economy are showing weaknesses in terms of growth. The rupee appreciation has also its impact both on exports and domestic production. Nevertheless the over all situation still remains buoyant and we should be able to achieve a growth rate between 8.5 per cent and 9 per cent during the year.

Conclusion

To conclude, the Indian economy in the four years beginning 2003-2004 has achieved an overall growth rate of 8.6 per cent. Maintaining a growth rate of 8 to 9 per cent over an extended period is both possible and probable. All the objective conditions are favourable for sustaining such a growth. We need, however, to address the several issues raised earlier, if we have to achieve this growth rate comfortably. Among the six challenges which I had indicated earlier, the three most important are: (a) agriculture, (b) infrastructure, particularly power, and (c) good governance. The importance of accelerating agricultural growth in an economy in which 60 per cent of the people are dependent on agriculture cannot be over emphasised. A higher growth in agriculture will have to come from improved productivity. This will enhance the quality of employment, if not, the quantity. Infrastructure has always been recognised as a key factor in economic growth. In the present context, where we are poised for high growth, improvement in infrastructure and more particularly of the power sector is very critical. Good governance is essential for ensuring that we get the full benefits of the various policy interventions. We need ideas. We need capacity to turn those ideas into policies and programmes. And we need boldness and a sense of purpose to implement those policies and programmes. Ideas, policies and execution form the triad of good governance.

Lecture delivered at Physical Research Laboratory, Ahmedabad, January 2008.

9 Economic Growth and Social Development

Evolution of Thinking on Growth

One can see four or five stages in the evolution of thought on economic growth. The chronological sequence is not without some overlap. In the first stage, the major concern was simply to accelerate economic growth. Growth was identified with the increase in the availability of material goods and services and was to be achieved through capital formation. Better life was identified with enhanced production of goods and services. The need for accelerating growth in this sense was felt even more strongly in developing economies, which started out with very low living standards. Eradication of poverty was to be achieved through faster economic growth. In the second stage, a distinction was made between growth and development. A greater concern with the distribution of income emerged. Development was seen as going beyond mere economic growth and bringing about changes in the structure of the economy. Equitable distribution of the benefits of economic growth became an independent goal. Balanced regional development also became a concern in large economies. In the third stage, the concept of equity was interpreted to mean the provision to everyone of what came to be described as 'basic needs' which included the basic requirements of life such as food, education, safe drinking water and health services. In essence, this approach stressed the need to provide to all human beings the opportunities for a 'richer and more varied life' as one of our plan documents put it. The next stage in the evolution of economic thinking on growth was the emergence of the concept of 'sustainable development' which acquired importance in the context of the environmental degradation caused in the process of economic growth. Sustainable development focuses attention on balancing today's concerns with tomorrow's requirements. In the current stage of thinking on growth, the concept of basic needs has been widened and the objective of growth is set as "human development" which means an improvement in the quality of life of the people. Enhancement of human development should lead on the one hand to the creation of human capabilities through improved health, knowledge and skills and on the other the opportunities for the people to make use of these capabilities. In a broader sense, human development implies human rights and participation and freedom of choice. In addition, the accent has shifted from the mere processes and dynamics of growth to include also the institutions which should deliver the benefits of growth to the poor and disadvantaged. Under this approach, economic growth becomes only one aspect of human development.

Performance of the Indian Economy

The performance of the Indian economy since Independence as measured by the normal indicators of economic growth has been impressive. The Indian economy was literally stagnant during the first half of this century. The growth momentum started with the attaining of independence. The annual growth rate in GDP, however, remained below 4 per cent until the end of 70s. It was only in the 80s that the annual growth rate crossed the 5 per cent figure. Between 1981-82 and 1990-91, the growth rate of the economy was 5.68 per cent per annum. 1991-92 was an exceptionally bad year for reasons well known. If we leave out that year, between 1992-93 and 2004-05 the average growth rate was 6.25 per cent. Even if 1991-92 is included, the growth rate since then would be 5.8 per cent. Because of the fairly substantial growth in population, the growth rate of per capita income was much lower. During the period 1950-51 to 2003-2004 the per capita income, in 1993-94 prices, increased from Rs. 3687 in 1950-51 to Rs. 11798 in 2003-04, registering a growth rate of about 2.18 per cent per annum.

Obviously the growth in national income and per capita income is reflected in a number of social performance parameters such as rise in the literacy rate, the availability of medical and health facilities, expansion in education, etc. The crude death rate per thousand has declined from 22.8 during 1951-1961 to 8.1 in 2002. Life expectancy at birth during this period increased from 41 years to 65.4 years. Infant mortality rate per thousand live births declined from 146 during 1951-1961 to 63 in 2002. The general literacy rate increased from 18.3 per cent of the total population in 1951 to 65.4 per cent in 2001. More hearteningly, during this period the female literacy rate went up from 8.86 per cent to 54.2 per cent. The head count poverty ratio has declined from 54.9 per cent in 1973-74 to 26.1 per cent in 1999-2000.

While the achievements of the post-independence Indian economy are indeed striking in comparison with the record of our performance during the first 50 years of the twentieth century, it has nevertheless fallen short of our expectations. Our performance has also been well short of what has been achieved by other developing countries, particularly, in East Asia triggering the concern that we performed well below our potential. It is only in this decade that India is beginning to be recognised as one among the fastest growing economies.

As measured by the social indicators, the performance of the country is even less impressive. India ranks low in the Human Development Index (HDI). As per the UNDP, *Human Development Report* of 2005, India's rank in 2003 was 127 among a total of 177 countries. It is, however, to be noted that India, with the HDI value at 0.6, is included among the medium human development countries. The three components of the HDI are life expectancy, education and GDP. Of these three, India's life expectancy index at 0.64 is near the world average of 0.70. But with respect to education and GDP, our indices at 0.61 and 0.56 are much lower than the world average of 0.77 and 0.75 respectively. Admittedly, the computation of these indices is debatable. The HDI also does not take into account many other aspects of social development as well as institutional dimensions like the freedoms enjoyed by people in making political and economic choices. The index may thus understate to some extent India's achievements. However, the deprivation in India in terms of health and education facilities has been documented by several other studies as well. According to a recent study, children in the age group of 6-13 not attending school were estimated at 17.80 per cent. Sixty-seven per cent of deliveries were not done in institutions. Twenty-two per cent of the population did not have access to safe drinking water and 14.4 per cent of children were not fully immunised. Nearly 40 per cent of the population was not living in electrified houses. The number of people living below the poverty line is close to 260 million. While in one sense there has been significant progress in the provision of medical and educational facilities as reflected in the improvement in life expectancy and in literacy rates, we still have a long way to go before we can claim a satisfactory level of performance in these areas. This narration leads us to several questions.

Interaction between Growth and Human Development

How far is social progress possible without adequate economic growth? What are the synergies between social development and economic growth? Can expenditures on social sectors by themselves ensure better social progress? What are the organisational and motivational factors necessary to secure better returns from expenditure? What should be the role of the state and the private sector in relation to social development activities?

At a fundamental level there is no conflict between economic growth and social or human development. Economic growth implies improvement in the material well being of people which necessarily includes better health, education and sanitation. However, there are two possible routes to achieve the end of social development. One is to let the economy grow and expect the consequential benefits to accrue to all segments automatically. This approach is often described as 'trickle down'. However, for this to happen, the economy needs to grow strongly. Any moderate rate of growth, as we have had in this country particularly in the first three decades after independence, is unlikely to have a significant impact on the bottom deciles of population. The alternative strategy of development is to focus directly on social infrastructure facilities such as health, education, sanitation and drinking water. No country including India has adopted an exclusive approach. Poverty alleviation programmes of various types were introduced from time to time, besides focusing on providing basic facilities like primary education and health. However, as we have noted, the changes in these areas have not been to the desired extent. In this context, one must also refer to an issue that is being raised whether the new economic policy has in any way contributed to the decline in the provision of these facilities. There is nothing in the new economic policy which dilutes or diminishes the role of the state in the social infrastructure sectors. In fact, the argument has been the other way round. By asking the government to vacate the areas in which markets can function effectively and can be monitored, the government acquires increased financial and administrative resources to pay attention to social infrastructure sectors. As has been somewhat paradoxically remarked, "more market does not mean less Government but only different Government."

While it is true that nutrition, health and education can and should be treated as ends in themselves, there is no assurance that improved health and education will automatically result in higher economic growth. They only create conditions under which growth in the sense of rise in national income can be accelerated. However, enhanced human development expenditures cannot be sustained over a long period unless supported by accelerated economic growth. There are examples of regions and countries where substantial improvements in human development indicators have not necessarily resulted in higher economic growth. When there is a dichotomy between human development indicators and economic development, it can be a source of social tensions. For example, as education spreads, the economy must have the ability to productively absorb the growing number of educated. Economic growth and social development must move in tandem so as to reap the synergic effects of the two moving together.

Needless to say, equity and growth can be mutually supporting. There is enough cross-country evidence to show that economic growth leads to reduction in poverty. By the same token, equity through creating equality of opportunities can accelerate growth by enabling the deprived to reach their full potential. However, in the short-run, there could be possibilities of trade-off which then should be managed in a manner that the long-run potential is not undermined. The design of policies has, therefore, to perform a delicate balancing act. The pro-poor policies necessary as they are to widen the opportunities and capabilities of the poor, must not harm growth in the long-run. Pro-poor polices should include not only income transfers which by their very nature have to be limited but also flow of investment to sectors and areas where poor work and live. Rural development thus assumes major importance. Equally significant are increased access to education, health and other social services.

The *Human Development Report* of 1991 introduced the concept of Human Expenditure Ratio which measures the percentage of national income devoted to human priority concerns such as elementary education, preventive health care, nutrition, water supply and sanitation to analyse how public spending on human development can be designed and monitored. According to the Report, the Human Expenditure Ratio needs to be around 5 per cent, if a country wishes to do well in human development.

Efficiency in Expenditures

Cross-country comparisons on human development expenditure do throw interesting light on the effectiveness of expenditures incurred. According to the *Human Development Report* 1991, both Sri Lanka and India had a similar human expenditure ratio of 2.5 per cent of GDP. In absolute terms, human expenditure per capita in 1988 was $10 for Sri Lanka while it was $9 for India. However, in the ranking of HDI, Sri Lanka ranked 75, whereas India was much lower down at 123rd. Part of the reason for the difference in the ranking could be enhanced expenditure at a certain level over a longer period. As the *Human Development Report* itself admits, "Even Government expenditure cannot be considered in isolation. Its impact depends not just how much money is spent but on how and in what environment it was spent." While human expenditure ratio provides a clue to the seriousness of efforts made, much depends on the efficiency with which the resources allocated are utilised.

Studies on social development expenditures made by several researchers in India show that even where quantitative targets have been achieved, the quality of achievement has not been up to the mark. For example, it is pointed out that though 82 per cent of the population has been provided with safe drinking water, the quantity of water is inadequate in many rural areas and that there are problems of drinking water quality in many areas.

There is one common conclusion that seems to emerge from various studies. Wherever there has been community participation and involvement, programmes have been more successful. Administrative and bureaucratic machinery delivers goods when it is constantly under the purview of local communities. We need to create grassroot level organisations of various types which will generate demand for accountability from various programmes evolved by the government. There is an urgent need to get more out of the resources that are being spent and to achieve the targets both in quantitative and qualitative terms.

By presenting the "Outcome Budget" to the parliament last month, the government responded to a growing concern about the effectiveness in the utilisation of public resources. Making a distinction between outputs and outcomes, the Twelfth Finance Commission (TFC) addressed this issue earlier by saying in its report: "The conventional budget exercises have focused on allocation of resources to different heads, without taking into account how these government expenditures get translated into outputs and outcomes. Outputs are the direct result of government expenditure and outcomes are the final results. Thus, in the context of education, opening a new school or appointing a new teacher is an output and reduction in the rate of illiteracy is an outcome." The TFC added: "A critical part of budgetary reforms must include information on the relationship between expenditures and the corresponding performance in producing real results. Although in the past there have been attempts at introducing performance budgeting, such endeavors have receded in importance. There is need to bring back performance budgeting as an integral part of the preparation and evaluation of budgets, both for the centre and the states. Thus, the management of public expenditures should be guided by economy, efficiency, and effectiveness." Improvements in the health and education delivery systems even at current levels of expenditure can bring about substantial changes in the availability of these services.

Conclusion

Social development and economic growth are not necessarily the same. That is why countries do not rank identically on the income scale and human development scale. Sometimes the differences in the rankings are quite striking. The rank correlation co-efficient between the real GDP per capita Index and the Human Development Index for all 177 countries for 2003 is high at 0.94. This is to be expected since GDP Index is one of the three factors included in the Human Development Index. Also the other two components—life expectancy and education—are closely correlated with GDP. However, taking only Medium Human Development countries, it is seen that the rank correlation co-efficient with GDP Index is lower at 0.60. There are several countries in this group which rank high on the real GDP Index but lower on the Human Development Index and vice versa. However, in the case of India, the difference is small. India ranks 118 on per capita GDP index and 127 on HDI.

Nowadays, the HDI on the model of the global HDI is being computed for different states in India to understand inter-state differences in income and social development. We have now the figures available for 2001. The rank corelation coefficient between the Income Index and the HDI across states in India is positive at 0.76. This coefficient is somewhat similar to the correlation among medium human development countries. This goes to show that there are many states in which there are wide disparities between the two indices. Andhra Pradesh and Haryana rank much higher in the income index than in HDI. Andhra Pradesh ranks 11 in the income index but is as low as 20 in HDI. Similarly, Haryana ranks as high as 3 in the income index but is very low at 17 in HDI. On the contrary, Kerala which ranks 7th in income index ranks 2nd in HDI. There are several states in the north-east which rank very low in the income index but rank reasonably high in HDI. Nagaland is a good example. It ranks as low as 15 in the income index but is high at 5 in HDI. This can be accounted for by the differences in the proportion of public expenditures on health and education and the efficiency with which they are spent. States like UP and Bihar rank low both in income index and human development indices. UP ranks 27 and Bihar 28 in both the indices.

What is the model of economic growth that is appropriate for India? Development has many dimensions. We now know that economic growth is only one aspect. Nevertheless, accelerated economic growth is a necessary condition for achieving many other dimensions of development. Development must ensure equality of opportunities for all. However, equality of opportunities does not necessarily guarantee equalities in incomes. With some people good at converting opportunities into income and others not being so, different individuals will end up with different levels of income. That is why it is necessary to assure every one a minimum level of living along with equality of opportunities. Every person must have his or her basic needs met. These basic needs include access to services such as food, education, health care and shelter. Without sacrificing these goals, the economy must remain efficient. It is only an efficient economy that can generate the surplus necessary to meet the socio-economic goals. We need, therefore, to stress simultaneously the economic development in the conventional sense of accelerating growth rate and social development in the sense of securing for everyone the basic needs. The two have a mutually interacting beneficial impact and the two must be pursued together. These are the two legs on which the country must walk. Any strategy of development, which ignores any one of the two legs, will only make the country limp along. To achieve higher levels of human development in our country, we need a three pronged approach comprising of higher economic growth, a higher proportion of expenditure, particularly public expenditure on social sectors, and efficient utilisation of the funds allocated. Growth and equity should not be posed as opposing considerations. They must be weaved together to produce a coherent pattern of growth. Therein lies the challenge of development.

Valedictory Address delivered at the CESS Silver Jubilee Seminar, Centre for Economic and Social Studies, Hyderabad, January 9, 2006.

10 Economic Growth and Issues of Governance

That good governance is at the very heart of economic growth and poverty reduction, and even political legitimacy, is now part of conventional wisdom. However, we did not zero in on this intuitively. The realisation that good governance is critical came as a result of some profound changes in development thinking over the past 50 years. In the 50s and 60s, when many countries of Asia and Africa were emerging out of colonialism, the path to development, it was widely believed, lay in capital formation. In the 1970s, awareness grew that physical capital was not enough, and at least as important was fulfilling basic human needs. When this too did not produce results, the missing link, it was thought, was improving social capital through education and health. Yet again there was no breakthrough. The disappointing experience with the debt crisis in Latin America and chronic poverty in Sub-Saharan Africa and South Asia during the 'lost decade' of the 80s threw up the idea that the path to development lay in improving economic management and giving greater play to market forces. Again the results were mixed. Some countries such as those in Latin America posted disappointing results in spite of making the transition to the market fully; on the other hand countries in East Asia performed well despite deviating in important ways from the market model. What made the difference was institutions of governance. The received wisdom is that, for growth and poverty reduction, we need physical and social capital, we need to focus on basic needs, and we need to yield to the market forces in a calibrated manner. These are all necessary, but not sufficient. They will not yield results unless they are accompanied by good governance.

What is Good Governance?

What is good governance? As per textbook definition, good governance is the manner in which the authority of the state is exercised in the management of a country's economic and social resources for maximising welfare. In the ultimate analysis, it is the quality of governance that separates success and failure in economic development. Across countries, application of the same policies in roughly similar contexts has produced dramatically different results. In our own country, we have seen vast differences across states in development outcomes from out of the same mix of development policies. These differences across countries as well as across regions within countries, even as they adopt similar policy packages, arise because of differences in governance. Indeed research shows that per capita incomes and the quality of governance are strongly correlated indicating a virtuous circle in which good governance results in economic development.

Nexus between Good Governance and Economic Development

How does good governance impinge on economic development? Anti-poverty programmes may be totally undermined by weak accountability, corruption and 'capture' of the programmes by vested interests. An unsympathetic and oftentimes hostile government-citizen interface may alienate people from the ruling class and erode the government's credibility. Legislation promoting social development (e.g., bonded labour, minimum wages) may come to naught if the laws are not implemented without fear or favour. Efforts to promote private investment may not succeed unless the rules of the game are clear and potential investors see governmental action to be credible, rational, transparent and predictable. Public investment priorities may be distorted by narrow parochial concerns or corrupt motives. Expenditure management systems may flounder because of weak accounting or monitoring systems. Failure to involve people in the development process may erode its benefits and compromise its sustainability.

State and Market

While talking of good governance, it is contextual to refer to the debate thrown up by economic reforms on the role of the government. Liberalisation implies the state yielding economic space to the market. This has given rise to the stereotype view that in the post-reform scenario, the government has a smaller role because the market now takes over part of what the government has been doing. This is a misperception. In the reform context, the government has, not a smaller role, but a different role, and arguably a more critical one. As has been remarked somewhat paradoxically, more market does not mean less government but different government.

Role of the Government

Conceptually, the role of the government in the reform context can be divided into two broad strands. The first strand of the role of the government arises from performing those functions that the government alone can perform. In the transition to a market system, government needs to move out of areas where markets can perform; conversely, government needs to concentrate its efforts and resources in areas where markets do not exist or cannot perform. For example, tasks such as maintaining macro economic stability, promoting equity, securing the right to property are all quintessentially government functions which, to use today's terminology, cannot be outsourced to the market. Then there are government functions which arise as a result of market failure. Market failure represents a set of conditions under which markets fail to allocate resources efficiently because of the myopic nature of the market participants. This happens typically in the provision of public goods, in the case of natural monopolies or in situations where there are externalities or information asymmetries. For example, markets cannot be relied upon to provide external defence or internal security which are public goods. Markets cannot also be relied upon to provide a positive bias in favour of girls' education which has a positive externality, or to prevent pollution which has a negative externality.

The second strand of the role of the government in the reform context is to 'govern' the market to maximise collective welfare. Market economies are not self-regulating. They cannot simply be left on an autopilot with a government watching from the sidelines. The government has a central role in regulating the market. For example, the government has to set in place and enforce a competition law, regulate those utilities which are natural monopolies, has to set standards for quality and safety and has to take initiatives towards consumer awareness and consumer protection. As David Osborne said in his landmark book, *Reinventing Government*, the role of the government is to "steer, but not row."

As succinctly observed in the Discussion Note for the conference of chief secretaries on Effective and Responsive Administration in 1996:

> The unfinished course of economic reforms and the new model of participative governance will require the government to become more caring and responsive both to the needs of a growing economy and to the concerns of the relatively unserved sections. The popular references to a non-interventionist and smaller government cannot be taken to imply the abandonment by the central and state governments of the fundamental obligation of a democratic government to provide an administration which is efficient, effective, clean, corruption-free, freely accessible to the people, and based on simple and transparent procedures.

Good Governance—Characteristics

What does the above statement on governance mean in practical terms? Obviously it covers a wide canvas. Here I will only attempt to reflect on some essential characteristics of good governance, and for the sake of clarity, will group them under three heads: (i) rule of law; (ii) accountability for actions and results; and (iii) combating corruption.

Rule of Law

I need hardly emphasise the importance of rule of law to maintaining an orderly civil society. What is not appreciated though is the link between the rule of law and economic development. Private enterprise cannot thrive if there is no rule of law. Indeed there are surveys to show that at the top of the wish list of private entrepreneurs is not tax sops or purchase and price preferences but a clean law and order situation free of bribery, extortion, and violence so that they can pursue their economic activity.

Rule of law has five distinct characteristics, *viz.*: first, there is a set of laws/rules known in advance; second, the laws/rules are effectively enforced, in other words nobody should be able to get away by breaking the laws/rules; third, the laws/rules are enforced in a transparent and non-discriminatory manner; fourth, there are established institutional mechanisms for making new laws and for amending modifying existing laws to reflect the changing situation; and finally, the processes for making laws are participatory and consultative.

Where do we stand on the rule of law when judged by the above five criteria? While our laws and the law making processes stand the test, it is in the enforcement of the laws that there are serious shortcomings. In particular, there are two widely held perceptions. First, the rich and the powerful can get away by breaking the law because they can 'manipulate' the system. Second, the poor and vulnerable get caught in the spokes of law enforcement even when they are innocent. As a premiere police organisation of the country, you are in a better position to appreciate these perceptions, evaluate to what extent they are valid, and throw up ideas for restoring the faith of the common man in the law enforcement system. The usual and by far the dominant refrain is that the system is compromised because of political interference. Admittedly, that is an issue and a problem. But is that the only issue? Or are there other vested interests? Can it be claimed that if the officers are guaranteed freedom to act free of political interference, they will be able to show better results without being hostage to any other interest? I am aware these are sensitive issues, but it is important for each and every one of us to introspect on whether we are compromising our professionalism, integrity and sense of duty at the altar of personal gain.

A related issue in the context of the rule of law is our procedures for investigation and prosecution. I must confess that my knowledge of the issue is limited, as I have not had the opportunity or the occasion to study this issue in detail. I know that some police officers feel that our procedures are hostage to the culture of a 'soft state' and that the police cannot get the better of crime unless they are allowed to resort to more coercive methods. This is an important issue if also a sensitive one. But in a democracy means are as important as ends and procedures adopted cannot violate the basic principles of rule of law. Order without law can be dangerous.

Accountability for Results and Actions

The government is the trustee of public resources and is responsible for using them for maximising collective welfare. This requires that there are institutional mechanisms not only for determining how the resources are allocated but also for demanding accountability for results. Modern democracies are beginning to embrace a wider and more direct concept of accountability that goes beyond the traditionally established channel of the accountability of the executive to the legislature in a parliamentary democracy. Increasingly, the trend is towards accountability in terms of standards of performance and service delivery of public agencies to citizen groups that the agencies are required to serve.

We have seen several positive movements in the direction of increasing the accountability of the government. First, there has been the deepening of decentralisation through the 73rd and 74th Amendments to the Constitution. Although not commonly perceived as such, decentralisation is an essential component of economic reforms. The rising demand for decentralisation around the world has come as part of the broader process of liberalisation of the economic system. The underlying rationale for liberalisation is similar to that for decentralisation: that power over the production and delivery of goods and services should be rendered to the lowest unit capable of capturing the associated costs and benefits. Decentralisation, if effectively enforced can aid good governance by giving 'voice' to people not only to determine how their common pool resources should be spent but also to demand accountability for those expenditures. It is equally important that delegation must go hand in hand with capacity building.

The second recent initiative towards enforcing accountability for results is the output/outcome budgeting. This is an important reform as it links outlays of expenditure to actual results on the ground. For example, we spend enormous amounts of money on primary schools and teachers, but what use is all this expenditure if there is no improvement in enrolment (which is an output) and in literacy levels (which is an outcome). By explicitly indicating results to be achieved through public outlays, the government is not only imposing a discipline on itself but is also providing a reference frame for rendering accountability.

The third initiative towards enhancing accountability is the right to information. We may have any number of institutions and mechanisms for "supply" of accountability, but that will not be effective unless there is "demand" for accountability. The right to information fills this important gap by providing public access to information relating to the functioning of the public agencies. Although it is not yet clear how the right to information will unfold, early experience is promising. We have several examples from around the country where the right to information has checked malpractices, prevented waste and leakage of resources and enforced accountability for results.

Even as initiatives such as output/outcome budgeting, decentralisation and right to information are all positive steps, they do not, in and of themselves, cover the whole gamut of issues in enforcing accountability for results. In fact, to comprehensively address the issue, three things are important. First, there should be systems to define results to be achieved both at the macro level and at the individual level; second, there should be objective, transparent and value free methods for measuring performance; and third, there should be widely endorsed methods of rewarding performance and penalising failure. Take for example primary education. We have three objectives here: enrolment, retention and minimum levels of achievements. The relevant questions will be the following: Are there systems to define results to be achieved in respect of the three performance indicators? Are the present hierarchical systems appropriate for evaluating the performance of teachers individually, and, collectively, at the school level? How effective are the parents committees, the user watchdog groups, tried out in some states? Have these been empowered appropriately? Do they inspire trust and credibility? Are there incentives for teachers to deliver on the results? Are there penalties for performance deficits and are they deterrent enough? These are the types of issues we need to work on to promote accountability for results. In the final analysis, the system should encourage initiative and innovation. The system as it prevails now promotes, as some one remarked, to do things rightly than to do the right things. This has led to the quip that the file work of the most corrupt bureaucrats is always perfect.

Combating Corruption

Concern about corruption is as old as the history of government. In 350 BC, Aristotle said in *The Politics* that ".to protect the treasury from being defrauded, let all money be issued openly in front of the whole city, and let copies of the accounts be deposited in various wards." There are similar references in Kautilya's *Arthashastra*. Corruption, broadly defined, is the abuse of public office for private gain. Accordingly, this definition covers all the pernicious maladies that most of us confront in every day life—bribery, nepotism, extortion, black-market. The negative consequences of corruption are well known but, as someone put it, not well realised. Corruption is anti-national, anti-development and anti-poor. There are documented studies to show that corruption impedes growth, inhibits potential investment, increases inefficiency and breeds vested interests. Most importantly, corruption, like inflation is a regressive tax and hurts the poor the most. There is a widespread view that corruption is a global phenomenon, that it is part of human nature and not much can be done about it. This is both cynical and defeatist. Admittedly corruption is pervasive across all countries, all cultures and all settings. But it varies in degree, in kind and most importantly on its damaging impact. The costs of corruption in a country such as ours with over 250 million people living in poverty are decidedly much heavier and more tragic than the costs in rich societies where everyone enjoys basic security and livelihood. It is also an important fact that in poorer countries with all round scarcities, corruption is more pervasive.

Although economists are increasingly engaged in the task of estimating the impact of corruption on growth and development, there are no definitive answers. Several studies do show a negative correlation between corruption index and the investment rate or the rate of growth. However, there are three problems associated with such studies: first, there is no standard definition of corruption; second there are as yet no standard ways of quantifying the extent of corruption; most studies base their measure of corruption on surveys of corruption perception; and third, it is difficult to estimate the counterfactual—what would growth have been in the absence of corruption?

Notwithstanding these conceptual and empirical problems, there is wide acknowledgement that, corruption imposes heavy costs on society. In particular, there are five types of costs: (i) loss of public resources through leakages in taxes, duties, fees and other levies; (ii) misallocation of public resources as investment choices are often driven by opportunities for corruption; (iii) low investment because of lower trust and confidence in public institutions; (iv) high costs and low quality of public services; and (v) increased insecurity and vulnerability of the poor, erosion of confidence in public institutions, breakdown of the rule of law, and ultimately threat to the legitimacy of the state itself.

We now know that corruption is not culture specific but is a function of the environment. As Malcolm Gladwell explains on the basis of evidence in his bestseller, *The Tipping Point*, the impetus to engage in a certain kind of behaviour does not come from a certain kind of person but from the context and the environment. If there are opportunities for corruption, some people will succumb to it. And if the chances of getting caught and punished are slim, more people will succumb to it. The incidence of corruption is large and pervasive in our system. Some of you might remember that in the pre-reform regime we used to draw up the production plan on the basis of complex input-output models. The late Prof. Raj Krishna, who was involved at one time with the models, suggested that the input-output matrix cannot be realistic unless it includes "leakage and corruption" as one of the sectors of the economy.

Demand for corruption, i.e., opportunity for corruption, as is well known, is higher in regulated and controlled environments which allow politicians and bureaucrats to dispense patronage. For example, the pre-reform licence-control regime provided opportunities for corruption because of the rents available in dispensing licences, permits and quotas. Similarly, citizen-government interface provides opportunities for corruption. In tax administration, for example, corruption depends on five factors: complexity of tax laws, monopoly power of revenue officials, the degree of discretion available to tax officials, the degree of transparency in the system, and finally the role of the political leadership. Quite evidently, demand for corruption goes down if the opportunities for rent seeking and dispensing patronage are minimised.

The implementation of economic reforms has reduced opportunities for rent seeking. The introduction of e-governance systems has increased transparency. Even as these have been positive developments, the incidence of corruption, especially at the cutting edge level continues to be high. Transparency International, an international watchdog body, ranks India low down in the 88th position in the corruption perception index at par with African economies like Mali, Benin, Gabon and Tanzania. People ask, how come India is growing so fast in spite of so much corruption. That is a wrong question. The right question will be to turn this one on its head and ask, how much faster would India be growing if corruption were controlled.

In fact, corruption has become so entrenched in our system that we have totally acquiesced in it. We accept it as an unavoidable part of our democracy and governance structures. While we denounce corruption in principle, we do not attach any social stigma or enforce any social sanctions against people perceived to be corrupt. The issue of 'tainted ministers' continues to haunt us without a satisfactory solution. We no longer blow the whistle against corruption because we are not confident that the corrupt will be booked and punished. We no longer get agitated against bribes we have to pay because we have already provided for them in our calculations. We are no longer surprised at the high cost of public works or the poor quality of public services because we have internalised corruption in our collective psyche.

As the premier police agency in the country charged with the responsibility of preventing and controlling corruption, you should be asking yourself a number of questions. How come there are so few people caught for corruption when there are many more who are perceived to be corrupt? How come it takes so long to complete prosecution in spite of so many specialised agencies for enforcement and delivery of justice? How come the conviction rate is so poor?

The usual explanations again are the familiar ones: political interference, loose laws, inadequate and poorly trained staff etc. These may all be true, but collectively they still do not offer a satisfactory explanation.

Combating corruption is critical to improve the quality of life of the people. A two-fold strategy is needed to contain corruption. First opportunities for corruption must be reduced. This can happen as we carry forward our economic reforms and reduce all forms of controls which result in rent-seeking opportunities. As scarcity of supply of goods and services is replaced by greater abundance, the pervasive nature of corruption that we see in our country can be restricted. Reforms and growth can go hand-in hand in reducing opportunities for corruption. Second, the government agencies charged with combating corruption must show an increased determination in identifying corrupt officials and politicians and getting them convicted. Unless the conviction rate goes up, indulging in corruption will be treated as a low risk violation. Above all, the public have a major responsibility. They must show in a decisive way their disapproval of people who are corrupt. This is particularly relevant at the time of casting the vote.

Conclusion

To summarise, good governance is a combination of transparent and accountable institutions, strong skills and competence, pecuniary and professional integrity, and a fundamental willingness to do the right thing. The test of good governance is ultimately the quality of service at the cutting edge level. I can hardly overemphasise that good policies are necessary, but not sufficient. They need to be accompanied by good governance. Each and every public functionary, be they part of the executive, judiciary or the legislature has the responsibility of making his or her contribution to good governance. Only then will we be able to achieve our goals of growth and poverty reduction. The art of progress, as the philosopher Whitehead put it, is to preserve order amid change and to promote change amid order.

Seventh D.P. Kohli Memorial Lecture, New Delhi, June 1, 2006.

11 Employment and Growth

Employment and Unemployment Scenario

The National Sample Surveys are the major source of data on the employment-unemployment situation in the country. The results of the latest survey—NSSO 61st Round which covers a period of five years from 1999-2000 to 2004-05 reveals that there have been notable changes in the labour force, workforce and employment pattern in India during this period.

Labour Force and Workforce

The compound annual growth rate of labour force[1] was at an all time high of 2.93 per cent (Table 11.1) in the past two and a half decades. This increase is unprecedented in the sense that not only has labour force growth rate outstripped the population growth rate but also exceeded it by almost two times. An increase in Labour Force Participation Rate (LFPR)[2] was seen across all segments (Table 11.2) with the most significant increase being in the case of female participation rates.

There was a distinct upswing in employment growth[3] from an annual 0.98 per cent (1993-94 to 1999-2000) to 2.89 per cent (1999-2000 to 2004-05), with 60 million jobs having been added in the five-year period

---

1. People who are either 'working' (employed) or 'seeking or available for work' (or unemployed) constitute the labour force.
2. LFPR is the number of persons in the labour force per 1000 persons.
3. All figures of workforce pertain to the usual principal and subsidiary status (UPSS).

Co-authors Padma Iyer Kaul and Seema.

(Table 11.1). These figures have also been confirmed by others (Jeemol and Ravindran, 2007). The signals of this rising trend were also seen in the results of the Fifth Economic Census and NSS 60th Round (thin round).

Table 11.1

Employment and Unemployment (UPSS)

	1993-94	1999-00	2004-05	1993-94 to 1999-00	1999-00 to 2004-05
	in Million			Point to Point Annualised Growth Rate (CAGR)	
Labour Force	381.94	406.05	469.06	1.03	2.93
Workforce	374.45	397.00	457.82	0.98	2.89
Number of Unemployed	7.49	9.05	11.24	—	—
	As a Proportion of Labour Force in Per cent				
Unemployment Rate	1.96	2.23	2.39	—	—

Notes: 1. Figures for 2004-05 are derived from 61st round survey on the basis of data provided by NSSO.

2. Employment in 1993-94 and 1999-2000 is as per *Report of the Task Force on Employment Opportunities* (Planning Commission).

Table 11.2

Labour Force Participation Rate by Gender and Rural-Urban Location (UPSS)

(Per cent)

NSS Round	Rural		Urban	
	Male	Female	Male	Female
1983 to 1993-94 50th Round	56.1	33.0	54.3	16.5
1993-94 to 1999-2000 55th Round	54.0	30.2	54.2	14.7
1999-2000 to 2004-05 61st Round	55.5	33.3	57.0	17.8

Source: Statement 4.1 of NSS Report No. 515.

In contrast to these results, the NSSO 55th Round had shown a deceleration in the growth of employment from 2 per cent per annum in the period 1983 to 1993-94 to less than 1 per cent per annum in the period 1993-94 to 1999-2000 and also an economy-wide decrease in employment elasticity from 0.41 to 0.15. The results led to major concerns about the phenomenon of 'jobless growth' and skepticism on the ability of economic growth to tackle the problem of unemployment.

This period was however marked by an improvement in real earnings across majority of rural and urban occupational groups. The rapid economic growth had a greater impact on the quality dimension of employment than on the quantum of employment (Rangarajan, 2006).

Sectoral Distribution of Employment

A sectoral disaggregation of the workforce shows (Table 11.3) that as expected, there has been a decline in the share of agriculture in employment from 59.8 per cent to 58.4 per cent between the 55th and 61st NSS Round. In terms of absolute figures, the number of workers in this sector has increased with agriculture and allied sectors absorbing almost 30 million of the incremental workforce. These figures are based on data provided by NSS but in an alternative estimate (Sundaram, 2007) the incremental workforce in agriculture is only 18 million in the period 1999-2000 to 2004-05. As per this estimate the share of agriculture in total employment is 56.48 per cent as against 58.4 per cent as per NSS data.

Table 11.3

Employment (UPSS)—Sectoral Shares

(in Million)

Sectors	2004-05	1999-2000	1993-94
Agriculture, Forestry & Fishing	267.57 (58.4)	237.56 (59.8)	242.46 (64.8)
Mining & Quarrying	2.74 (0.6)	2.27 (0.6)	2.70 (0.7)
Manufacturing	53.51 (11.7)	48.01 (12.1)	42.50 (11.3)
Elect., Gas & Water Supply	1.37 (0.3)	1.28 (0.3)	1.35 (0.4)
Construction	25.61 (5.6)	17.62 (4.4)	11.68 (3.1)
Trade, Hotels & Restaurants	47.11 (10.3)	37.32 (9.4)	27.78 (7.4)
Transport, Storage & Communication	17.38 (3.8)	14.69 (3.7)	10.33 (2.8)
Financing, Insurance, Real Estate & Business Services	6.86 (1.5)	5.05 (1.3)	3.52 (0.9)
Community, Social & Personal Services	35.67 (7.8)	33.20 (8.4)	32.13 (8.6)
Total Employment	457.82 (100)	397.00 (100)	374.45 (100)

Notes: 1. Figures for 2004-05 are provided by NSSO based on their 61st round survey.
2. Employment in 1993-94 and 1999-2000 is as per *Report of the Task Force on Employment Opportunities* (Planning Commission).
3. Figures in brackets denote sectoral share in total employment.

As per NSS data the share of the manufacturing sector in employment has marginally declined from 12.1 per cent to 11.7 per cent though in absolute terms the workforce in the sector increased by 5.5 million. The services sector improved its share from 22.7 per cent to 23.4 per cent adding 16.8 million workers in the five year period. Within this sector Trade, Hotels & Restaurants was the largest gainer and accounted for 10 million of the incremental workforce. The most striking feature of the growth in workforce is that across all sectors of the economy, in 2004-05, the absolute number of workers have increased from the 1999-2000 levels.

Occupational Status of Workforce

The survey also throws up some interesting features when we look at the activity status distribution of the workforce (Table 11.4). In the self-employed category the previous trend of decline has now been reversed. Cutting across the rural-urban divide the share of self-employed workers has increased sharply with an offsetting decline in the share of casual labourers. As per our estimate there are about 260 million people who are self-employed. This rise in self-employment has been viewed by some as an indicator of the deterioration in the quality of employment based on the argument that the rise in jobs in this category has been mainly in the unorganised sector where the wage rates are low.

Table 11.4

Distribution of Workforce by Gender, Activity-Status and Rural-Urban Location

(Per cent)

Population Segment	1999-2000			2004-05		
	SE	RWS	CL	SE	RWS	CL
Rural Male	55.0	8.8	36.2	58.1	9.0	32.9
Rural Female	57.3	3.1	39.6	63.7	3.7	32.6
Urban Male	41.5	41.7	16.8	44.8	40.6	14.6
Urban Female	45.3	33.3	21.4	47.7	35.6	16.7

SE – Self-Employed
RWS – Regular Wage/Salaried
CL – Casual Labour
Source: Statement 5.7 of NSS Report No. 515.

Another dimension of the quality of employment is the number of jobs created in the organised sector. Organised employment as measured by DGE&T (Director General of Employment and Training) declined in the first four years of this decade reaching a figure of 26.44 million in 2004 and then increased slightly by 0.1 per cent to 26.46 million in 2005. A closer scrutiny reveals that in the period 2004-05 the public sector employment decreased by 1 per cent while the private sector recorded an increase of 2.5 per cent (Table 11.5). As per some studies, the DGE&T data understates the organised sector workers and a better measure would be the NSS data on the regular wage salary workers. The shares of the RWS workers have risen marginally in rural India while they show a slight decline in urban India. However in terms of absolute numbers the total regular/wage salary workers have increased by a little over 10.7 million in this five-year period (2000-2005) i.e. an annual increment of 2.14 million per annum (Table 11.6). In contrast the average annual increment in the period from 1993-94 to 1999-2000 was lower at 1.46 million (Sundaram, 2007).

Table 11.5

Estimates of Employment in Organised Public and Private Sectors

(Lakh Persons as on March 31st of the Year)

Year	Public	Private	Total
1999	194.15	86.98	281.13
2000	193.14	86.46	279.60
2001	191.38	86.52	277.89
2002	187.73	84.32	272.06
2003	185.80	84.21	270.00
2004	181.97	82.46	264.43
2005	180.07	84.52	264.58

Source: Ministry of Labour & Employment (DGE&T).

Table 11.6

Number of Usual Status Workers by Activity-Status, Gender and Rural-Urban Location

('000)

Population Segment	1993-94 to 1999-2000 SE	RWS	CL	1999-2000 to 2004-05 SE	RWS	CL
Rural Person	1,69,194	20,010	1,15,191	2,06,183	24,260	1,12,395
Urban Person	40,105	38,056	17,237	52,244	45,059	17,308
Males	1,41,468	49,518	86,279	1,67,750	56,405	85,155
Females	67,831	9,468	46,149	90,677	13,364	44,548
Person	2,09,299	59,066	1,32,428	2,58,427	69,769	1,29,703

Source: Sundaram, K. (2007). "Employment and Poverty in India: 2000-05".

Elasticity of Employment

The elasticity of employment measures the sensitivity of employment growth to the GDP growth. The relationship however is not simple and straightforward as factors other than GDP like wage rate, technology and improvements in infrastructure also impact employment growth rates. Notwithstanding this qualification, employment elasticities are commonly used to track sectoral potential for generating employment and in forecasting future growth in employment.

The period from 1993-94 to 1999-2000 was marked by a sharp decline in employment elasticity across all sectors reflecting a deceleration in employment growth rate. This trend has been reversed in the period 1999-2000 to 2004-05. Using the data on sectoral employment growth rate and the sectoral growth rates of GDP it is possible to calculate the sector wise elasticity for the period 1999-2000 to 2004-05 (Table 11.7). A quick comparison with the previous period (1993-94 to 1999-2000) reveals that the aggregate elasticity of employment has practically tripled from a low of 0.15 to a figure of 0.48. This increase in elasticity is seen in all sectors except for Construction and Transport Storage & Communication where the elasticity has declined. At an aggregate level, this increase though very sharp does not seem improbable especially when we compare it to the elasticities in the periods before the 55th NSS Round (Table 11.7).

At a disaggregated level, agriculture seems to have done a complete about turn with the elasticity moving from 0 to 1.52, a figure which is higher than the earlier trends even if we ignore the 55th round as an exception. The other surprise is the mining sector where elasticity grew from 0 to 0.82, between the 55th and the 61st Round, completely contrary to the projections made by the Task Force on Employment Opportunities. This rise however appears to be sustainable. The rising international prices of metals and the resurgence in the steel and aluminum sector have led to addition in production capacities in iron ore, manganese and bauxite. In addition the housing boom may have added to increase in quarrying activities. In the other sectors (if we accept the 55th NSS round as an outlier) the elasticities moved roughly in line with the past trends.

Table 11.7
Elasticity of Employment

Sector	1999-2000* to 2004-05	1993-94 to 1999-2000	1983 to 1993-94	1977-78 to 1983
Agriculture, Forestry & Fishing	1.52	0.00	0.50	0.45
Mining & Quarrying	0.82	0.00	0.69	0.80
Manufacturing	0.34	0.26	0.33	0.67
Elect., Gas & Water Supply	0.33	0.00	0.52	0.73
Construction	0.88	1.00	1.00	1.00
Trade, Hotels & Restaurants	0.59	0.55	0.63	0.78
Transport, Storage & Communication	0.27	0.69	0.49	1.00
Financing, Insurance, Real Estate & Business Services	0.94	0.73	0.92	1.00
Community, Social & Personal Services	0.28	0.07	0.50	0.83
Total Employment	**0.48**	**0.15**	**0.41**	**0.53**

Notes: * 1. Figures for 2004-05 are derived from Table 11.3 based on 61st round survey.
2. All other elasticities are as per *Report of the Task Force on Employment Opportunities*.

In calculating the elasticities the critical factor is the employment levels at the beginning and end of the period for the various sectors. We have relied on the sectoral employment data provided to us by the NSSO. Prof. Sundaram has however independently estimated the employment levels for the various sectors for 2004-05, which differs from the estimates based on NSSO. While there is not much difference in the aggregate level of employment the critical difference is with regard to agriculture. He estimates the employment in agriculture at 258.66 million in 2004-05 (Sundaram, 2007) whereas the estimate based on NSSO is 267.57 million. Consequently the employment elasticity calculated using Prof. Sundaram's data is 0.78 and is different from the figure of 1.52 calculated using NSSO data.

In order to project employment growth it is necessary to make some assumptions about how employment elasticity will move in the future. This is inherently difficult as much depends on technological change which is difficult to predict. In general one would expect that the employment elasticity would continue to fall in sectors where productivity is currently low and is expected to improve and also where technological change is likely to be labour saving. However predicting such changes will be judgemental.

Employment Projections

The Report of the Task Force on Employment Opportunities (2001) had projected, based on certain assumptions, that the economy would be able to achieve the level where the employment will be equal to the labour force in the year 2012.[4] The assumptions were; a 9 per cent GDP growth rate since 1999-2000, 1.5 per cent growth rate of labour force and an aggregate elasticity of employment at 0.22. However the actual growth rate between 1999-2000 and 2004-05 was lower at 6 per cent. Hence in an earlier study the projections were reassessed (Rangarajan, 2006). Assuming an overall elasticity of 0.22 and corresponding sectoral elasticities, the projections showed that with an annual growth rate of 8 per cent in GDP and a labour force growth of 1.5 per cent per annum, it

---

4. The Task Force had made multiple projections based on different assumptions for growth rate of GDP and labour force, but only one, relevant to the current context has been used.

will take up to 2017 to reach the point when workforce equals labour force. However, with a 9 per cent rate of growth of GDP and under the same assumptions of growth in labour force and sectoral elasticities, this point will be reached by 2012. If the GDP growth rate was lower at 8.5 per cent it will take up to 2015 to reach this point.

In addition to GDP growth rate the other important variable for unemployment projections is the labour force. As mentioned earlier the period 1999-2000 to 2004-05 witnessed an unprecedented high growth rate of labour force at 2.93 per cent (CAGR). A substantial contribution to this came from the increase in female participation in the labour force (Table 11.2). The growth rate of labour force for the future will not only be impacted by the increased participation by women but also by the increase in school enrolments. While the former will pull up the labour force growth rate the latter will have a dampening effect. However, with the major emphasis of the government on primary education, the younger age groups are likely to move out of the labour force. Thus the labour force growth is likely to remain at the current level or even marginally reduce in the future.

Actual data on labour force, workforce and unemployment are available in the NSS 61st Round. We now make fresh projections based on the new data available. In order to do this we are making three sets of assumptions regarding the movement of elasticities[5] in the future. This gives us three alternative employment scenarios.

Alternative Employment Projections

Scenario 1

Under this scenario we presume that the elasticities calculated as per the industry wise data on employment provided by the NSSO for the period for 1999-2000 to 2004-05, will prevail for the next few years at the same level. These set of elasticities are shown in Table 11.7. Using an employment elasticity of 0.48 and a labour force growth rate of 2.93 per cent, if GDP growth rate is 9 per cent the projections (Table 11.8) show

---

5. The employment figures for Trade, Hotels and Restaurants and Transport, Storage and Communication have been clubbed together for making projections since the GDP figures from 2005-06 onwards are not available separately for these two sectors.

Table 11.8
Employment Projection—Scenario 1

Sector	Employment in 2004-05 (in Million)	Projected Elasticity (Ratio)	Projected GDP Growth Rate (Per cent)	Employment Growth Rate (Per cent)	Projected Employment in 2006 (in Million)
Agriculture, Forestry & Fishing	267.57	1.52	3.73	5.67	282.74
Mining & Quarrying	2.74	0.82	4.73	3.88	2.85
Manufacturing	53.51	0.34	10.90	3.71	55.5
Elect., Gas & Water Supply	1.37	0.33	6.90	2.28	1.4
Construction	25.61	0.88	12.07	10.62	28.33
Trade, Hotels & Restaurant, Transport, Storage & Communication	64.49	0.45	11.97	5.39	67.97
Financing, Insurance, Real Estate & Business Services	6.86	0.94	10.33	9.71	7.53
Community, Social & Personal Services	35.67	0.28	7.60	2.13	36.43
Total	457.82	0.48	9.13	3.29	482.75
Labour Force	469.06				482.8
Unemployment Rate (Per cent)	2.39				
Labour Force Growth Rate (Per cent)	2.93				
Employment Growth Rate (Per cent)	2.89				

Note: The GDP figures are as per Q/E for 2005-06.

that the economy has already achieved the level where labour force will equal the work force! This conclusion is unrealistic and hence there is a need for a modification in our assumptions which brings us to Scenario 2.

Scenario 2

A closer look at the employment elasticities reveals that the elasticity for agriculture and allied sectors is very high as compared to the earlier trend. Such a high elasticity of 1.52 does not appear to be sustainable and is likely to come down, in line with the past trends. Accordingly the elasticity of agriculture has been moderated to a lower figure of 0.7 for projections. This is also consistent with the elasticity calculated using Prof. Sundaram's estimates of workforce in agriculture for 2004-05. We assume that for the other sectors the actual elasticities calculated as per NSSO data will continue to hold good. Keeping the labour force growth rate at 2.93 per cent and GDP growth rate at 9.1 per cent, our projections show that it will take up to 2009 to reach the point where labour force will equal the workforce (Table 11.9). In the terminal year the total labour force would have grown to 526.50 million while the employment figure would be higher at 529.87 million.

Given the elasticity of employment, the crucial factor in determining the convergence of labour force with workforce, will be the growth rate and its composition. Our estimates show that with an overall growth rate of 8.5 per cent and an agricultural growth rate of 3 per cent, labour force will equal workforce only in 2012. If we keep the overall growth rate at the same level and reduce the agricultural growth rate to 2 per cent, it will take up to 2017 for the convergence to occur.

Scenario 3

The elasticities calculated above are based on a comparison between the 55th and the 61st round. It has been suggested by some (Unni and Ravindran, 2007) that the sharp growth of employment in the recent period may be reflecting a statistical phenomenon of a low base in 1999-2000 and to get a more accurate picture of employment growth, a longer-term period should be considered. Accordingly we have computed the growth rates of labour force and sectoral employment elasticities using a longer period—1993-94 to 2004-05 and the results are laid out in Table

Table 11.9
Employment Projection—Scenario 2

Sector	Employment in 2004-05 (in Million)	Projected Elasticity (Ratio)	Projected GDP Growth Rate (Per cent)	Employment Growth Rate (Per cent)	Projected Employment in 2009 (in Million)
Agriculture, Forestry & Fishing	267.57	0.70	3.73	2.61	296.62
Mining & Quarrying	2.74	0.82	4.73	3.88	3.19
Manufacturing	53.51	0.34	10.90	3.71	61.9
Elect. Gas & Water Supply	1.37	0.33	6.90	2.28	1.5
Construction	25.61	0.88	12.07	10.62	38.35
Trade, Hotels & Restaurant, Transport, Storage & Communication	64.49	0.45	11.97	5.39	79.56
Financing, Insurance, Real Estate & Business Services	6.86	0.94	10.33	9.71	9.94
Community, Social & Personal Services	35.67	0.28	7.60	2.13	38.81
Total	457.82	0.36	9.13	3.29	529.87
Labour Force	469.06				526.50
Unemployment Rate (Per cent)	2.39				
Labour Force Growth Rate (Per cent)	2.93				
Employment Growth Rate (Per cent)	2.89				

11.10. Over the longer period the aggregate elasticity drops to 0.29 as compared to 0.48, a figure we calculated for the 5-year period between 1999-2000 to 2004-05. Notably, this drop is the sharpest in agriculture and mining with the other sectors showing a moderate decrease. Exceptions to this decrease are the Construction and Transport, Storage & Communication sectors where over the longer period the elasticity goes up, instead of falling as in the case of other sectors.

Table 11.10

Elasticity of Employment 1993-94 to 2004-05

Sectors	1993 94*	2004 05**	Rate of Growth of Employment	Elasticity of Employment 1993-94 2004-05	Elasticity of Employment 1999-2000 2004-05
Agriculture, Forestry & Fishing	242.46	267.57	0.90	0.39	1.52
Mining & Quarrying	2.70	2.74	0.13	0.03	0.82
Manufacturing	42.50	53.51	2.12	0.31	0.34
Elect., Gas & Water Supply	1.35	1.37	0.13	0.02	0.33
Construction	11.68	25.61	7.40	0.99	0.88
Trade, Hotels & Restaurant	27.78	47.11	4.92	0.57	0.59
Transport, Storage & Communication	10.33	17.38	4.84	0.45	0.27
Financing, Insurance, Real Estate & Business Services	3.52	6.86	6.25	0.82	0.94
Community, Social & Personal Services	32.13	35.67	0.95	0.13	0.28
Total	374.45	457.82	1.84	0.29	0.48

Source: *1. Report of the Task Force on Employment Opportunities.
**2. Table 11.3.

In making a forecast an alternative will be to use these elasticities derived from the longer period. A theoretical objection to this could be that, it does not give proper weight to recent experience but the advantage is that it enables us to check the consistency of our earlier projections over the longer period also. Notably for this long period both labour force growth rate and employment growth rate came down to 1.88 per cent and 1.84 per cent respectively. These are much lower than the growth rates of 2.93 per cent and 2.89 per cent experienced in the recent period. Using the elasticities and the labour force growth derived from the longer

Table 11.11
Employment Projection—Scenario 3

Sector	Employment in 2004-05 (in Million)	Projected Elasticity (Ratio)	Projected GDP Growth Rate (Per cent)	Employment Growth Rate (Per cent)	Projected Employment in 2008 (in Million)
Agriculture, Forestry & Fishing	267.57	0.39	3.73	1.46	279.46
Mining & Quarrying	2.74	0.03	4.73	0.14	2.75
Manufacturing	53.51	0.31	10.90	3.38	59.12
Elect. Gas & Water Supply	1.37	0.02	6.90	0.14	1.38
Construction	25.61	0.99	12.07	11.95	35.93
Trade, Hotels & Restaurants, Transport, Storage & Communication	64.49	0.51	11.97	6.10	77.03
Financing, Insurance, Real Estate & Business Services	6.86	0.82	10.33	8.47	8.75
Community, Social & Personal Services	35.67	0.13	7.60	0.99	36.74
Total	457.82	0.29	9.13	2.65	501.16
Labour Force	469.06				496.16
Unemployment Rate (Per cent)	2.39				
Labour Force Growth Rate (Per cent)	1.89				
Employment Growth Rate (Per cent)	1.84				

period, a 9.1 per cent growth rate of GDP would enable the economy to reach the point where labour force will equal the workforce by 2008 (Table 11.11). Surprisingly, this result is only marginally different from the one arrived at as per Scenario 2.

The critical factor that will determine the point where the labour force will be equal to the workforce will be the assumptions made about the labour force growth rate. In fact if we use a labour force growth rate of 2.93 per cent for projection this point will be reached in 2013. On the other hand if we assume an alternate figure of labour force growth rate of 2.4 per cent then this point will be reached in 2009.

The above analysis indicates that at 9.1 per cent GDP growth rate, even under very conservative assumptions, the economy will reach a level where workforce will match labour force within a one year time frame.

These projections have two obvious limitations. Firstly, that they do not take into account the impact of technological changes. These changes can however alter the capital–labour ratio and impact the sectoral elasticity and employment growth. Secondly, the demand for labour is projected independent of the supply leaving no scope for accounting for adjustments by way of changes in real wages and productivity. Despite this, the projections provide some useful insights that are summarised below:

i. Agriculture will still account for more than half of the total workforce in the country in the terminal year irrespective of the scenario we choose. Its share declines from 60 per cent in 1999-2000 to 58 per cent in 2004-05 and to 56 per cent in 2008 (Scenario 3).[6] While this decline *per se* is desirable but its slow pace raises important questions on the productivity and remunerations in this sector.

ii. The secondary sector has a share of 18-20 per cent in the terminal year, and as expected manufacturing leads with an employment share between 11-12 per cent with construction coming second with 6-8 per cent employment share.

---

6. Even as per Scenario 2 the share of agriculture in the terminal year remains at 56 per cent.

iii. The employment share of the services sector is 23-24 per cent and within the sector, Trade, Hotels, Transport and Communication is the largest employment provider, accounting for 14-16 per cent of the total workforce. The second largest employer is the Community, Social and Personal services that have a 7 per cent share.

These employment shares are in sharp contrast to the employment shares in the developed countries where share of agriculture in employment is only 5 per cent. Closer home even in China agriculture has yielded share to the other sectors at a faster pace.

Conclusion

The employment scenario has undergone a fundamental change. As per the 61st Round of NSS, employment in the period 1999-2000 to 2004-2005 has increased at an annual rate of 2.89 per cent. This is in sharp contrast to the annual growth rate of 0.98 per cent in the period 1993-94 to 1999-2000. This sharp increase in employment growth is also corroborated by other studies. Along with the sharp increase in employment the labour force has also increased dramatically. The unadjusted employment elasticity for the latest period is 0.48. Even after adjusting the sectoral elasticities to lower figures, it is seen that with a GDP growth rate of 9.1 per cent, by 2009 the workforce will become equal to labour force. Growth has been a major driving force in achieving a higher level of employment.

The analysis of the data thrown up by the Survey and Projections indicates that bulk of the increase in employment has happened in the informal sector and agriculture still accounts for a large percentage of the workforce. This trend is a cause for concern as the relatively low wages and lack of social security here translate into the phenomenon of 'working poor' i.e. workers in the BPL households. In other words, the congruence of labour force and workforce by itself does not guarantee elimination of poverty. The new challenge is one of improving the total factor productivity in the informal sector and in agriculture so that there is a significant improvement in the emoluments of those who are employed, that is, in the quality of employment.

References

Ministry of Statistics and Programme Implementation (2004-05) (2006). *Employment and Unemployment Situation in India, July 2004-June 2005, NSS 61st Round.* New Delhi. September.

———. (2007). *Informal Sector and Conditions of Employment in India, July 2004-June 2005, NSS 61st Round.* New Delhi. April.

National Commission for Enterprises in the Unorganised Sector (2007). *Report on the Conditions of Work and Promotion of Livelihoods in the Unorganised Sector.* August. New Delhi: Academic Foundation.

Planning Commission (2001). *Report of Task Force on Employment Opportunities.* New Delhi. June.

Rangarajan, C. (2006). *Employment and Growth.* Madras School of Economics. Monograph 2/2006.

Sundaram, K. (2007). "Employment and Poverty in India: 2000-2005", *Economic and Political Weekly*, July 28.

Unni, Jeemol, G. Raveendran (2007). "Growth of Employment (1993-94 to 2004-05): Illusion of Inclusiveness?" *Economic and Political Weekly*, January 20.

12 Rural Employment Guarantee Scheme

Physical and Financial Planning

The Employment Guarantee Scheme (EGS) underlying the National Rural Employment Guarantee Act is by far one of the largest social safety-net programmes launched anywhere in the developing world. The EGS is also historic for we now have for the first time a demand driven scheme across the country unlike the several supply driven schemes of the past. It is ambitious in its scope and size, and is an affirmation of our collective desire that the benefits of growth must be broad based and inclusive, and that growth can be sustainable only when the poor contribute 'to' growth and benefit 'from' growth. Let me also add that having some people left behind while others move on is not only unacceptable but also destabilising.

The EGS guarantees a minimum of 100 days of wage employment in every financial year to every rural household as an employment of last resort. In the lead up to the adoption of the bill by the parliament, there was a lot of debate and discussion in the media and in public fora on almost every aspect of the bill. I personally found following that debate to be very rewarding, as it was rich, informed, educated and, of course, contentious. This debate was a testimony not only to the intellectual capital that goes into the shaping of our public policy but also reflective of our commitment to openness, freedom of expression and pluralism of ideas.

Just to recapitulate, the following are some of the main issues that drove and shaped the debate.

(i) Should the wage rate under the EGS be the minimum wage rate, or some other rate that will be above or below the minimum wage? What is the wage rate that will be optimal in terms of making the scheme self-selecting?

(ii) Should the guarantee be restricted to 100 days per year or should it be open ended?

(iii) Should the scheme be restricted to only one adult per household regardless of the size of the household?

(iv) Should the scheme be restricted to families below the poverty line or should it be open to all?

(v) Should the scheme be implemented in 150 or 200 districts to start with or should it cover entire country in one go?

(vi) What exactly will be the cost of the scheme and where will the funds come from? Given that the estimated cost of the scheme varies from Rs. 10,000 to Rs. 36,000 crore—roughly one per cent of GDP—is this the most efficient use of the money? Are there better and more effective ways of spending such a large amount of money to achieve the objective of poverty reduction? Will welfare be maximised if we spend this money on education and health instead?

(vii) What will be the implications of such a large and open-ended expenditure commitment to managing the fiscal and revenue deficits especially in the context of the obligations under the Fiscal Responsibility and Management Act (FRMA)?

(viii) Do we have the administrative capacity, and the monitoring and accountability systems to implement a scheme of this size?

(ix) Given our experience with similar schemes such as food for work and drought relief, should we not be concerned about waste, leakage and corruption, especially given the weak monitoring systems and lax accountability mechanisms?

(x) To what extent should the EGS focus on asset creation? Furthermore, does the focus on asset creation erode the guarantee dimension of the EGS?

(xi) What should be the role and responsibilities of the panchayati raj institutions in the EGS? In particular, should the *Gram Panchayats* uniformly be the only instrumentality for delivering the EGS regardless of the varied track record and capacity levels in the PR institutions across the country or should we settle for asymmetric decentralisation?

This listing of issues will not be complete unless I also mention that some economists and commentators have even called into question the justification for an open-ended universal employment guarantee scheme of this type on the ground that there is no evidence to show that the rural employment situation has worsened in the recent period.

Several analysts have drawn attention to the fact that National Sample Survey Estimates of unemployment rates show that in 1999-2000 those who reported themselves as being 'usually unemployed' during the year were barely two per cent of the male labour and less than one per cent of the female labour force. The 'usual' unemployment rates have not shown any sustained trend either for males or females over the 20 year period. The NSS surveys, however, show that under employment figures—as measured by the proportion of days in a year in which those actively seeking working do not find it—are much higher around seven per cent for both males and females. These figures nevertheless do not show any definite trend. The levels in 1999-2000 were the same as in 1977-78 for males. There was, however, an improvement in the case of females. While there has been no deteriorating trend and in fact there may have been some improvement, the levels are still a cause for concern and redressing this remains a major challenge. While the lasting solution to employment generation will lie in accelerating over all growth, this may happen only slowly. Targetted employment schemes such as the EGS become necessary till such time the over all growth is able to fully meet the demand for work from rural labour force.

Now that the parliament has enacted the legislation, many of the policy issues have been settled. The Act, as finally passed, guarantees at least 100 days of wage employment per year on demand to every rural household. The wages to be paid are the minimum wages applicable for agricultural labour in the respective states till such time that the central government specifies a wage rate which will not be less than Rs. 60 per day. In the event of failure to redeem the guarantee, the state government is mandated to pay an unemployment allowance to the employment seeker. The scheme is to be implemented in 200 poor and backward districts in the first phase. The Central government bears the cost of guaranteed wages, up to three-fourths of the cost of material, and the wages of skilled and semi-skilled workers. The state governments are to meet the balance one-fourth of the costs of material and semi-skilled and skilled labour as well as the payment of employment allowance.

The Act as finally passed by the parliament balances the various trade offs and reflects some of the advice that emerged from the public debate. For example, at the draft stage there was debate, as I said earlier, on whether the scheme should be restricted to households below the poverty line which would have entailed elaborate mechanisms for means testing. Under the Act as finally passed, the scheme is open to all with no restrictions on whether the household is below or above the poverty line. This is wise as this is an acknowledgement that only the poor with no alternative will come forward to undertake unskilled labour and the scheme will run on a self-selecting basis. Also this will eliminate the huge transaction costs underlying means testing.

With the policy issues behind us, the task ahead is to move on to implementation so as to deliver the intended benefits to the poor and unemployed in the country. The important components involved in the implementation of EGA are, (a) selection of beneficiaries and the wage rate; (b) design of system and institutions for implementation of the scheme; (c) provision of resources and the pattern of funding; (d) capacity building for effective implementation of the scheme; and (e) safeguard against corruption with regard to the use of fund and the selection of beneficiaries. By any reckoning this is a complex and formidable challenge and requires 'out of the box' thinking and action.

I want to raise some issues that we should be addressing on the way forward to implementation of the EGS. For conceptual clarity I will group them under four headings: (i) physical and financial planning; (ii) delivery systems and capacity building; (iii) asset creation; and (iv) monitoring and experience sharing.

Physical and Financial Planning

In order to deliver on the guarantee, it is imperative that at the field level there is an understanding of the supply and demand patterns of labour. Needless to say, the supply of labour is region specific and is a function of the seasonal pattern, seasonal conditions, the ruling market wage and the general outlook of the economy. Some of these are obviously more variable than others. We learn from the Maharashtra experience, for example, that in times of distress it is the women who seek the protection of the employment guarantee while the men-folk move on to neighbouring villages or districts in pursuit of wage rates which are higher than the wage rates under the employment guarantee scheme. It is lessons of experience such as this that we need to factor into in planning for the implementation of the EGS. From the supply side it is necessary to have a shelf of schemes with all the necessary physical and financial estimates done so that they are ready for grounding at short notice. Failure to be ready will entail not only waste and inefficiency but also payment of unemployment allowance. Minimising the amount of unemployment allowance paid should, in fact, be one of the yardsticks for measuring the efficiency of implementation.

Streamlining financial systems and procedures will be another complex task. There should be enough funds at the field level for payment of wages in the context of an uncertain estimate of how many people will in fact be seeking the guaranteed employment. This means that the flow of funds from the state to district to the village level should be smooth. An important question in this context is should funds be channeled through the existing systems or is there need to design alternate systems? How can this be done without eroding fiduciary accountability? Non-availability of funds at the required time can seriously impair the effectiveness of the Scheme. We should avoid such a contingency.

Delivery Systems and Capacity Building

Let me now turn to some thoughts on delivery systems and capacity building. *Gram Sabhas* and panchayat raj institutions have been given a pivotal responsibility under the Act. The village, intermediate and district *panchayats* are designated principal authorities for planning and implementation of the EGS. The *Gram Panchayats*, GPs for short, are responsible for the identification of schemes acting upon the recommendations of the *Gram Sabha*, for vetting and costing them and for having them approved by the programme officer. *Gram Panchayats* also have to register eligible adults of every household in their jurisdiction and issue registration cards to each of them. *Gram Panchayats* are also responsible for monitoring and social audit.

Criticism for the role assigned to the *Gram Panchayats* in the implementation of the EGS has come from two sides. From one side it has been argued that the *Gram Panchayats* have been given a very limited role in the EGS and have been subordinated to the programme officer. It is contended that the programme officer, being an official of the state government not owing any allegiance to the *panchayat*, can undermine the autonomy and accountability of the *panchayats* and thereby the implementation of the EGS. The arguments in favour of giving a larger role to the *panchayats* are the standard ones: greater accountability, better appreciation of local needs and lower transaction costs. From the other side, there has been criticism that *panchayats* have been made the main delivery system for the EGS uniformly across the country ignoring the reality that the Panchayat Raj system has not evolved to the same degree of experience, capacity and awareness across the country. In some states and in parts of some states, GPs have come into their own exercising autonomy and managing finances responsibly and rendering accountability with a sense of integrity. On the other hand, there are states and pockets of states where GPs have been captured by powerful elites to the detriment of democratic decentralisation. Given this reality, should we have a uniform pattern of delivery of EGS by the GPs across the country or should we settle for asymmetric decentralisation whereby the role to be performed by the GPs depends on their proven capacity and demonstrated track record? I am aware this is a sensitive and contentious issue but one that needs to be debated transparently. My own personal view is that panchayati raj institutions constitute the most effective vehicle for the implementation of the Employment Guarantee Scheme and we need to make all efforts to strengthen them. We should explore alternatives only if GPs fail in their performance.

No matter whether the EGS is delivered through the GP or through some other mechanism, its implementation demands a significant amount of record keeping and documentation. For example, documentation is necessary for identification and registration of eligible beneficiaries, the number of days of employment delivered to each household, the list of persons to whom unemployment allowance, if any, has been paid and the quantum thereof, the man-days of work invested in each project, etc. Similarly capacity is required at the GP level for identifying projects, preparing the cost and labour demand estimates and in measuring physical out-turns.

The need for training in a variety of skills, techniques and management practices is quite obvious. What are the areas in which training will be required? How can it be best delivered? How can the lessons of experience in one district or state be documented and disseminated widely? These are some questions which need to be addressed.

There is the question of accountability both for efficiency in the utilisation of funds as well as fiduciary integrity. There are some inbuilt safeguards in the EGS such as the requirement that all wages in cash or unemployment allowance shall be made directly to the person concerned in the presence of independent persons of the community on pre-announced dates. There is also a requirement for monitoring by state and district level agencies as well as by NGOs. Even as these are improvements over many of our existing practices, they are by no means foolproof. There is no substitute for continued vigilance and threat of serious penalty in case of corruption, waste or leakage. Technology in general and e-governance practices in particular may help us in this regard. This is another area where we need to do innovative thinking.

Asset Creation

Let me now move on to issues under the broad area of asset creation. Schedule 1 (clause 1) of the Act says: "Creation of durable assets and strengthening the livelihood resource base of the rural poor shall be an important objective of the scheme." Clause 2 of the schedule also indicates nine focus areas of the scheme in order of priority. The list of focus areas includes water conservation and water harvesting, drought proofing, flood control and road connectivity.

Drawing from the Maharashtra experience, some commentators have suggested that emphasis on asset creation might compromise the guarantee dimension of the scheme. This is so because of the unpredictability of the demand for EGS work with respect to location, timing, number of workers and duration of their seeking the employment guarantee. The tension between employment guarantee and asset creation is a valid concern and needs to be acknowledged. The statutory obligation to guarantee employment should get priority over asset creation. Nevertheless the huge outlay on the scheme, which could potentially go up to as much as one per cent of GDP, cannot be justified unless there are assets to show for it. De-emphasis of asset creation can also encourage corruption. In fact, we should use the opportunity provided by the new Scheme to improve rural infrastructure which is imperative for accelerating growth.

While on the subject of asset creation, it is also necessary to pay attention to maintaining the assets created under the EGS because every rupee spent on maintenance has a higher benefit-cost ratio than a rupee spent on investment. Should EGS funds not be used for maintenance of assets created under the EGS or indeed under any other scheme?

Monitoring and Experience Sharing

Finally, let me turn to monitoring the implementation of the EGS. The importance of monitoring hardly bears any reiteration. India is a vast and complex country which in many ways is an advantage. It offers scope for a diversity of experiences and practices. We should capitalise on this, by initiating right at the beginning of implementing the EGS, a monitoring system which will be a repository of the experiences and best practices across the country so that these can then be disseminated to all others. I also want to add that we have to do a lot of "learning by doing". It is not as if every detail of EGS has been thought through and every question resolved. Implementation will throw up hundreds of issues for which we need to find answers efficiently and flexibly. The EGS is not meant to be and should not be converted into a top driven programme where every minute detail is predetermined in a straitjacketed fashion. Indeed I believe there will be a lot of lessons thrown up from the bottom. We will have to keep our eyes and ears and importantly our minds open, reflect on these experiences, respond flexibly to the operational challenges and refine the implementation of the EGS as we move on.

Conclusion

Despite several weaknesses, our administration has proved that it can deliver on the most exacting tasks under challenging circumstances. Our administration conducts elections and carries out census in the remotest parts of the country in inhospitable terrain and unfriendly climate. Our administration delivers relief and rehabilitation in times of natural disasters such as floods, droughts or earth quakes with commendable efficiency. Indeed, the way we responded to the task of tsunami relief where other affected countries have fallen short is a tribute to the talent and capacity in our administration. Woefully the same administration fails us in the routine tasks of day-to-day implementation of development programmes. This certainly is not for want of capacity but because of system shortcomings. The task for the Administrative Reforms Commission is to see how the enormous talent and capacity available in our administration can be constructively deployed for the collective good of the nation. Managing the EGS is a challenge set in that context.

The tasks that lies ahead in implementing the Employment Guarantee Act are enormous. Effective implementation requires (1) demand based budgeting, (2) advanced planning to offer work on demand, and (3) inter-sectoral planning of projects. There is also need for a clear definition of the roles and responsibilities of the various agencies involved in the process of implementation.

Inaugural Address delivered at National Institute of Public Finance and Policy. New Delhi, December 19, 2005.

13 State, Market and the Economy

The Shifting Frontiers

Among the issues of public policy, the one that has attracted the widest attention has been the issue of state *versus* market in economic development. The issue has once again assumed importance in the context of economic reforms and structural adjustment that are currently under way in many countries. The goal of development is improvement in the quality of life of people. But on the means to achieve this goal, perceptions and approaches have been changing over time. This has led to a continuous reappraisal of the roles of state and market in the development process. This question obviously does not admit of a categorical 'either-or' answer. It is neither feasible nor desirable to argue for a total withdrawal of government from all spheres of economic activity or to advocate total state intervention in all areas of economic life. What needs to be determined is the optimal state-market mix. Apart from the general principles governing the merits and demerits of state and market intervention, the mix can vary from country to country depending on the historical experience of the functioning of the state and markets. While recognising that state and market have separate but interconnected roles to play, the emerging view is that the market must be allowed to work wherever it can function efficiently and the state must step in wherever the market does not succeed. In the course of this paper an attempt has been made to provide the broad contours of this debate, derive lessons from international experience and provide a framework for determining the appropriate mix.

Developments in the Literature

The literature on the respective roles of state and market is long and interesting. From the days of Adam Smith to the present, notable contributions have been made by distinguished economists from various schools of thought. The earliest proponent of free trade was Adam Smith who was writing against the background of a strong mercantilist tradition. Adam Smith told us: "It is not from the benevolence of the butcher, the brewer or the baker, that we expect our dinner but from their regard to their own interest" (Smith, 1776). It was not as if Smith did not recognise human motives other than 'self love'. The author of the *Wealth of Nations* was also the author of *Theory of Moral Sentiments*. Nevertheless, he felt that the outcome of the pursuit of self-interest need not be chaotic. Indeed, it can be orderly; individual optimum can lead to social optimum. It was this thought which led Adam Smith to make the celebrated statement that in pursuing his own advantage, each individual was "led by an invisible hand to promote an end which was no part of his intention." Adam Smith also said that the state should undertake three main tasks: "defending its citizens from the violence and invasion of other independent societies, protecting every member of society from the injustice or oppression of every other member of it, and erecting and maintaining certain public works and public institutions which can never be in the interest of any individual or small number of individuals to erect and maintain, because the profit would never repay the expense though it may frequently do much more than repay it to a great society" (Smith, 1776). While the first two activities relating to defence and justice are clearly definable, the third role assigned to the state is indeed open to many interpretations. It can in a sense cover all economic activities in which there are 'externalities', situations in which there is a divergence between private and social returns or private and social costs.

The idea of state minimalism acquired a further interpretation in welfare economics, where it was argued that as long as the competitive market forces were allowed a free play, an economy would obtain a state where it was impossible to improve a person's well-being without affecting another person. This is the well known "Pareto optimality". So long as the state does not rank the welfare of one group of people over another group, market forces themselves are capable of attaining an optimal state. In other words, without gross inequalities, there is no need for any state intervention. There are, however, certain caveats to the above assertion, the most important being that there should be no production and consumption externalities, in the sense that production and consumption of any particular product must have little effect on people other than the producers and consumers concerned. However, presence of externalities does not necessarily warrant state intervention; in general some institutional arrangements could do as well.[1] The idea of free markets and state minimalism also received support from the Austrian School of Fredrich Hayek and Ludwig Von Mises. The Austrian school argued that markets enjoyed 'information' and 'incentive' superiority.

The major criticism of state minimalism came from Keynes in the wake of the Great Depression of 1930s. While Keynes himself was a strong believer in individual initiative and enterprise, he recognised the role of the state in maintaining a level of effective demand which was necessary to ensure full employment. He argued that market forces by themselves could not result in full employment. He pleaded for active state investment to fill the gap between the actual level of investment and the level of investment that was required to maintain full employment.

The intervention of state in the economy has also been advocated by other writers for different reasons. For example, there are economists who have argued that state, as an institution, has a role to monitor the actions of individuals since in the absence of some superior authority, a section of the participants may contravene the rules and try to obtain profit. The importance of state intervention has also found support in the works of economists who regard the state as 'trustee of the poor'. It has been argued that the ultimate aim of development is to enhance the quality of life of the people which can result either from the trickle down effect of growth or from direct state intervention in providing basic needs. They find the latter strategy more effective and therefore advocate the need for state intervention to promote literacy, health care

---

1. The well known contribution in this regard has been that of Ronald Coase who had argued (Coase, 1960) that so long as the parties involved could readily make and enforce contracts in their mutual interest, no state intervention was necessary to get the efficient outcome. In his view, the problem of externalities was only a problem of 'transaction costs' and that if there were externalities but no transaction costs, there could be no problem since the parties would always bargain to the efficient solution. He recognised that some of the solutions might be imperfect and that the answer lay in choosing among a variety of inefficient alternatives, private and governmental.

and nutrition. After discussing the distinction between 'negative' and 'positive' liberties, Dreze and Sen (1995) write:

> A similar—though not identical—distinction can be made about the readings of the government's 'duties' *vis-a-vis* the citizens. The negative roles consist in preventing what are taken to be bad developments (for example, outlawing monopolistic arrangements), whereas positive roles concern supporting constructively the efforts of the citizens to help themselves (for example, by arranging public education, by redistributing land, by protecting the legal rights of disadvantaged groups). Leaving out extremist advocacies, most political theories tend to provide room for both positive and negative roles of the government, but the relative importance that is given to the respective spheres can vary greatly.

Sukhamoy Chakravarty at one time drew attention to different types of market failures that are possible. The concept of market failure according to him can be broadly classified into four principal groups:

> first, competitive equilibrium may not necessarily exist, given the relevant structural conditions that characterise many underdeveloped economies; secondly, even when conditions for the existence of competitive equilibrium at a point of time are satisfied, in the absence of a system of competitive futures markets, the amount of information conveyed by an existing price system is inadequate for carrying out investment planning on an efficient basis; thirdly, even when one assumes away all problems connected with the existence of competitive equilibrium, the market mechanism may exhibit gross deviations in terms of 'optimality' in view of the greater importance of factors such as externalities, imperfections in the factor market, etc, in the case of underdeveloped economies; and finally, the market mechanism may give rise to a distribution of incomes which give rise to a profile of savings and growth which is likely to differ from the socially desirable time path of savings (Chakravarty, 1993).

The instrumentalities for correcting market failure will have to depend on the nature of market failure.

The effectiveness of the state or market in economic intervention cannot be argued in vacuum. Much depends on the nature of the state and the structure of markets. History is replete with instances of state terrorism. Even in the economic arena, the state has acted in many countries in the interest of the men in power rather than in the interest of the people in general. This happens more often under non-democratic forms of government, though it is possible even in democracies for the power structure to tilt in favour of some. Equally, the efficiency of markets depends on market structure. In theory, much of the benefits of markets flow from competitive equilibrium or full or near-full market clearing. In practice, this may not happen. In fact, some economists claim that since market processes generate only restricted competition or asymmetric information, they cannot result in efficiency. The conditions of perfect competition under which all participants are price-takers may not be achieved. But so long as markets can encourage competition by allowing the entry of new participants, market expansion becomes possible with improved efficiency. At least firms are kept under constant pressure. Besides these issues, there is the wider question of the compatibility between the political structure and market structure.

Government Intervention and Planning

The developments in literature were paralleled by certain historical experiences. The Fifties were probably the heyday of government intervention. One can discern three distinct, but not necessarily mutually incompatible, streams of thought and developments culminating in this situation. The first was clearly the process of putting Keynesian macroeconomics into action. The second was the success story of the command economies under the socialist regimes of the USSR and eastern Europe. The third was the birth of planning in the newly independent third world economies.

The adoption of macroeconomic principles with a predominant interventionist character in the post second world war period was the outcome of acceptance of the Keynesian doctrine that in capitalism full employment was not automatic and that if investment fell short of savings, government intervention was necessary to correct the situation. What Keynes was seeking was modified capitalism. Keynes wrote:

> ...whilst it indicates the vital importance of establishing certain central controls in matters which are now left in the main to individual initiatives, there are wide fields of activity which are unaffected. The state will have to exercise a guiding influence on the propensity to consume, partly through its scheme of taxation, partly by fixing the rate of interest and partly, perhaps, in other ways. Furthermore, it seems unlikely that the influence of banking policy on the rate of interest will be sufficient by itself to determine an optimum rate of investment. I conceive therefore that a somewhat comprehensive socialisation of investment will prove the only means of securing an approximation to full employment; though this need not exclude all manner of compromises and of devices by which public authority will co-operate with private initiative. But beyond this, no obvious case is made out for a system of state socialism which would embrace most of the economic life of the community. It is not the ownership of the instruments of production which is important for the state to assume. If the state is able to determine the aggregate amount of resources devoted to augmenting the instruments and the basic rate of reward to those who own them, it will have accomplished all that is necessary (Keynes, 1936).

The post-second world war period saw a strong recovery and robust growth of market-based economies of the west, spurred by strong public expenditure and technical progress. But slowly inflation started creeping. Public sectors of most of these economies became large and the national debt as a percentage of GDP began to rise sharply. The coexistence of inflation and stagnation began to erode the faith in the benign role of state intervention and in the Keynesian framework of analysis.

The success story of the command economies was another critical determinant in shaping public opinion about state intervention. The Soviet Union was transformed from a backward economy to a modern industrialised economy. The system was also able to ensure for the entire population the basic necessities of life. At a theoretical level, it was demonstrated by economists like Oscar Lange and Abba P Lerner that the outcomes of the socialist economies and private capital economies can be made equivalent in certain areas, if so desired. But these systems ran into severe problems, once the basic essentials were met and there was a diversification of demand. The centralisation of economic decision-making which was important in the command economy, proved inadequate and too slow in the context of the rapidly expanding economy. Inefficiencies crept into the system and shortages of various types began to develop. This eventually led to a complete transformation of the system.

However, in the 1950s and 1960s the command economies were certainly hailed as examples of what the state intervention can do in improving the living standards. Though the success of the command economies influenced the birth of planning in the third world economies, the basis for economic planning was seen in terms of production or consumption externalities. In this context, a distinction was made of the functioning of markets in three different areas. These were: (i) allocation of a given stock of consumer goods; (ii) allocation of production with given stock of equipment, land and labour; and (iii) allocation of investment on the assumption of a given stock of labour and land. It was argued that the price mechanism worked perfectly in terms of allocation of a given stock of consumer goods, while it worked less perfectly, but tolerably well, even in the second market where the assumption of a given stock of consumer goods was replaced by a flow of supply of these goods with a given stock of equipment, materials and labour. It is, however, in relation to allocation of investment that the market was considered to be inefficient in the developing economies. Long gestation periods, lumpy investment and absence of immediate profitability were reasons adduced to support state entrance in the production sector. In fact, government intervention in production was even seen as a pre-requisite for private sector to expand, emphasising thereby the 'crowding in' rather than 'crowding out' effect of public expenditure.

Thus, in the 1950s and 1960s, the dominant view in the literature on development economics was that the government had an important role to play and that it must undertake activities that would compensate for market failure. Market failure was perceived particularly in the area of allocating resources over time that is for investment because of the 'myopic' nature of the market participants. The literature also emphasised the importance of coordination that aggregate planning could achieve. It is this line of reasoning that led most developing countries, including India, to formulate economy-wide plans.

Historical Experiences: East Asia, Russia and India
East Asia

To anyone interested in the issue of economic growth and the role of state, the experience of the east Asian countries provides a striking example. These countries have been able to grow fast over the last three decades and achieve a level of per capita income approximating to that of middle income industrialised developed nations. To what does one attribute the extraordinary progress made by these countries? It is accepted by all that governments in these countries intervened strongly for faster development. Policy interventions took many forms. Even as they intervened actively to regulate the entry and exit of firms, determine production priorities and make extensive use of subsidies, they also adopted a policy of export promotion. In fact, the intervention was not market-excluding but market complementary. At the same time these countries made the biggest investment in human resource development. South Korea achieved universal elementary education in 1965. However, even in these countries, many attempts at direct intervention in fixing production priorities misfired and they had to be abandoned. The domestic market remained less competitive. But the compulsions of export promotion tried to limit the fallout of the monopolistic character of production system.

The recent meltdown in the east Asian economies has raised a question whether the crisis amounts to a failure of the market. It is true that the markets failed to detect some of the weaknesses in the functioning of the system in these countries and punish them; in fact, the markets overlooked these deficiencies. In that sense, the crisis is an example of market failure. However, it is also a case of government failure, as the governments in these countries failed to fulfil some of their responsibilities. Regulation of markets and more particularly financial markets has always been regarded as one of the major responsibilities of the state. The Achilles heel of the crisis was the financial sector. A major factor now identified in causing the crisis relates to the weaknesses in the financial sector. Banks and non-banks were not subject to effective prudential regulation and supervision or asset-liability management. Neither the government nor the market emerges well out of the crisis which is a failure of government and market.

Russia

The collapse of communism in Russia and some of the east European countries also holds certain important lessons for the roles of state and market. There is no doubt that the communist system was able to eradicate poverty and ensure to the bulk of the population the basic requirements of life. However, the system was not able to cope up with the situation of rising and diversified demand. It is instructive to turn to Gorbachev, who, in explaining the shortcoming of the old communist economic machinery, comments:

> It is above all the lack of inner stimuli for self-development. Indeed through the system of plan indices, the enterprise receives assignments and resources. Practically all expenses are covered, sales of products are essentially guaranteed and, most importantly, the employees' incomes do not depend on the end results of the collective's work: the fulfillment of contract commitments, production quality and profits. Such a mechanism is likely to produce medium or even poor quality of work, whether we like it or not. How can the economy advance, if it creates preferential conditions for backward enterprises and penalises the foremost ones?(Gorbachev, 1987).

Early efforts on restructuring the Soviet economy were met with severe resistance. The experiment of *Perestroika* failed and the system itself underwent a total collapse. Russia and some of the east European countries are still to recover from this shock and the transition to a new order has been painful. Understandably, there have been backlash effects with some nostalgic references to the earlier period. However, even where communists have come back to power, they have called themselves 'reformed' communists. It is interesting to note what the Russian communist leader Gennady Zuganov has said:

> A return to state monopoly is impossible. Total control by the state of the entire economy led us to the crisis...We see our main task as creating conditions in which people see the benefit of working whether they are in the state or private sector rather than drinking and stealing (Zuganov, 1995).

He added that the government led by his resurgent group would encourage mixed state and private enterprises, a concept totally rejected by the traditional Communist Party. Clearly, not only has the rigidity of the earlier ideology disappeared but market has been recognised to have an influence on shaping the society's well being.

India

In keeping with the spirit of the times, India too went for economy-wide planning in 1951. The basic urge of course was to accelerate the process of economic growth. The planners had to define right at the beginning the respective roles of state and the market. The First Plan went into this question at great length and it is interesting to note what the planners had to say nearly 50 years ago:

> This brings us to the problem of the techniques of planning. A possible approach to the problem is, as mentioned earlier, through a more or less complete nationalisation of the means of production and an extensive system of governmental controls on the allocation of resources and on the distribution of the national product. Judged purely as a technique of planning, this may appear a promising line of action. But, viewed against the background of the objectives outlined above, and in the light of practical considerations, such an expansion of the public sector is, at the present stage, neither necessary nor desirable. Planning in a democratic set up implies the minimum use of compulsion or coercion for bringing about a realignment of productive forces. The resources available to the public sector have, at this stage, to be utilised for investment along new lines rather than in acquisition of existing productive capacity. Public ownership of the means of production may be necessary in certain cases; public regulation and control in certain others. The private sector has, however, to continue to play an important part in production as well as in distribution. Planning under present conditions, thus means, in practice, an economy guided and directed by the state and operated partly through direct state action and partly through private initiative and effort (Government of India, 1951).

While the various Plans recognised the role that the private sector could play, the major thrust was on state guidance. It resulted in the creation of an elaborate licensing machinery and a set of planned targets for industry and other activities based on what was considered to be an optimal allocation of scarce resources. Price controls became ubiquitous and markets were shunned. The planned process of economic development did achieve tangible results in terms of accelerating economic growth. Compared to a near stagnation of national income in the previous 40 years, Indian economy grew between 3 to 4 per cent in the period following the initiation of planning in 1951. The savings rate increased from a meagre 10 to 24 per cent. The country was able to build a diversified industrial structure capable of producing a variety of basic, capital and consumer goods. However, the growth rate itself fell short of Plan targets as well as the rates achieved by many other countries. Public enterprises instead of generating surpluses for the state for investment had to seek budgetary support. While there is no compelling reason why public sector enterprises cannot function efficiently, the structure and the accountability system were not conducive to promote efficiency. Public accountability is a double-edged sword. While, on the one hand, it helps to keep the managers of public enterprises responsible, too much of it can inhibit autonomy and innovation. The right balance has been difficult to find. Ministers and ministries are loath to distance themselves from these enterprises. The extensive control mechanism including multitudes of controls on investment and production not only fragmented capacity but also reduced competition. An import substitution approach compounded the problem and the rising level of capital-output ratio till the early 1980s, confirmed the need for a more efficient use of capital. In the wake of the balance of payments crisis of 1991, these factors compelled the policy makers to reassess the nature of the mix of state and market and the kind of instruments to be used to bring about change. In fact, the approach document of the Eighth Plan submitted in May 1990 which preceded the current economic reforms observed:

> The return to the regime of direct, indiscriminate and detailed control in industry is clearly out of the question. Past experience has shown that such a control system is not effective in achieving the desired objective. Also the system is widely abused and leads to corruption, delays and inefficiency (Government of India, 1990).

Even in the area of human resource development, the record of India has not been impressive, though showing substantial improvement over the level at the time of independence. The fault for this cannot be laid at the door of the present phase of liberalisation. The distortions in priorities occurred earlier. A much stronger effort towards human resource development in the 1960s and 1970s would have made substantial difference.

Conclusion

In any economic system, state can play many roles. One can at least identify three such roles: (i) as a producer of goods and services, (ii) as a regulator of the system, and (iii) as a supplier of 'public goods' or 'social goods' like primary education and health. The first role as a producer of goods and services finds expression in the system of planning with public enterprises engaged in productive activities, if not in all the sectors of the economy, but at least in the critical areas called the 'commanding heights' of the economy. The second role of 'regulator' gives to the state the super authority that sets the rules of the game. In fact, the quality of the economic performance of markets depends critically on the quality of public intervention through regulation. This is in fact a market complementary role. The third possible role of state is that of a 'welfare provider'. This role prompts the state to support private initiatives, through the provision of required infrastructure and through vigorous efforts at human development to enhance the capability of the masses. This can be regarded as a 'facilitator' role with state intervening in areas where markets cannot perform effectively. The basket of activities that state takes up will be a composite of these various roles and the composition of the basket can vary over time even for a country.

Countries in general are moving away from the role of state as a producer of goods and services. A major reason for the emergence of skepticism regarding the benefits of state intervention in this area has been the growing perception that government failures on account of political factors and bureaucratisation may, in many cases, exceed market failures. Given the importance of incentive-reward system in achieving consistent improvement in efficiency, it is felt that markets may provide better incentive frame-work in many activities. Closely related to these institutional factors is the belief that a competitive environment tends to create a better climate conducive to enhancing efficiency.[2]

The decreasing role of state as a producer of goods and services and the increasing role of market in such areas simultaneously enhance the role of state as a 'regulator' and facilitator. Tony Blair and Gerhard Schroder (1999) summed up the position by remarking, "the state should not row but steer". The analogy may not be perfect. But the message is clear. State can play a better role in setting the direction rather than driving. That is why the paradoxical statement, 'more market does not mean less government but different government'. The regulatory role of the government in the financial and other sectors has assumed added importance in the context of the east Asian and other crises. The regulatory role comes into play in order to maintain competitive conditions in the market. Increasing attention is being paid to introducing appropriate legislation in all countries to maintain competition. Anti-trust laws are getting strengthened. In the context of globalisation and borderless trade, greater coordination among supervisory agencies is also being put in place. The 'facilitator' role corresponds closely to the third area mentioned by Adam Smith where state intervention may become necessary. However, even here there is a changing perception. It is no longer necessary for the state to participate directly in the investment in physical infrastructure. Private investment under a suitable regulatory and tariff authority may yet fill the need, even though direct investment by the state in the emerging economies in these areas will be dominant for quite some time. But in the area of social infrastructure such as health and education, the role of the state is clearly seen, even though intervention may take many forms.

---

2. The issue of creating an appropriate rewards system is not a new one. Marx wrestled with the problem of work motivation and the conflict between the principle of 'need' and that of 'desert'. But he simply concluded that the socialist society would graduate from 'each according to his ability' to 'each according to his needs'. Lerner, however, saw the contradiction more clearly and said that "the principle of equality would have to compromise with the principle of providing such incentives as would increase the total of income available to be divided" (Lerner, 1944).

Operationally, the two important issues that arise are whether and when the state should shift the responsibility to the markets and secondly if that is to be done how the transition should be managed. It is very clear that these are issues that can be addressed only contextually and it is difficult to prescribe a single model applicable to all countries and at all times. As Paul Streeten (1995) has indicated, the transitions to be managed are three-fold: (i) from excessive to reduced state intervention; (ii) from intervention in the wrong areas to those areas neglected previously; and (iii) from one form (of reliance on quantity controls) to another (reliance on prices) as an instrument of policy. These transitional arrangements are not that easy; this can be seen from the problems faced by Russia and east European countries. A whole new scheme of institutional arrangements including legal framework becomes necessary.

The major question of determining how much of state intervention still remains. One test for determining the respective roles of state and market is the application of the concept of comparative advantage. Given a particular objective, it may be possible to examine the comparative advantage of state instruments *versus* market instruments in achieving the objective. Within state intervention, it may be necessary to examine whether ownership by government or regulation is the most effective method for achieving the desired objective. In some activities unbundling of funding and providing the service can be attempted and the advantage of combining government and market in different proportions can be explored. Thus, for example, an elementary school may be fully funded by the government and run by the government; an elementary school may be fully funded by the government but run by the private management; both funding and provision may be done in private sector but government may support targeted children who cannot afford to pay for the private facility. In this context, it may be noted that discussions on the functioning of the economic and social system are usually centred around the roles of state and market. These two do not exhaust all organisational mechanisms. Even in relation to economic activities, the role of voluntary organisations which are not influenced exclusively by profit motive may become increasingly relevant.

The serious question which we have to address is not one of either state or market, but one of how much state intervention, what kind and by what means. As a general rule markets must be allowed to function where price signals clearly work in achieving efficiency. State intervention becomes necessary only in areas where markets do not exist or where they cannot perform efficiently. Mixed economy is a reality the world over. The crucial factor for determining the mix is that of comparative efficiency. It is necessary to create a matrix of activities and the kind of intervention and determine for each activity what form of intervention is best. As an illustration, the activities can be broadly classified as manufactures, physical infrastructure, social infrastructure and financial and other services. Forms of intervention can be divided into two—market and state. State intervention can be further classified into direct investment, regulatory, indicative and unbundling. The intensity of intervention may have also to be specified.[3] This type of exercise should be done at all levels of government and for all activities. With limited resource availability, government should reallocate resources more in areas where it has a comparative advantage over the market and vacate those where it has less of an advantage. A mix that was relevant at one stage of development need not be appropriate at a later stage. The ultimate test is not ideology but what works best under a given set of circumstances.

---

3. The matrix can take the following form:

Activities Intervention	Manufactures	Physical Infrastructure	Social Infrastructure	Financial and Other Services
Market				
State				
(a) Direct investment				
(b) Regulatory				
(c) Indicative				
(d) Unbundling				

References

Blair, Tony and Gerhard Schroder (1999). *The Third Way—Die neue Mitte*.

Chakravarty, Sukhamoy (1993). "Theory of Development Planning: An Appraisal" in *Selected Economic Writings*. Oxford.

Coase, Ronald (1960). "The Problem of Social Cost", *Journal of Law and Economics* (3)1: 1-44, October.

Dreze, J. and A. Sen (1995). *India Economic Development and Social Opportunity*. Oxford.

Gorbachev, Mikhail (1987). *Perestroika*. London: Collins.

Government of India (1951). *The First Five-Year Plan: A Draft Outline*. New Delhi: Planning Commission.

———.(1990). *Approach to the Eighth Five-Year Plan: 1990-95*. New Delhi: Planning Commission.

Keynes, John Maynard (1936). *The General Theory of Employment, Interest and Money*. London: Macmillan.

Lerner, A.P. (1944). *The Economics of Control*. London: Macmillan.

Smith, Adam (1776). *An Inquiry into the Nature and Causes of Wealth of Nation*. Modern Library Edition. London. 1937.

Streeten, Paul (1995). *Thinking about Development*. Cambridge University Press.

Zuganov, Gennady (1995). Zuganov made this statement in the course of an interview at the Davos World Economic Forum, Reported in *Asian Age*. April 2.

This is an expanded version of the author's Principal S.V. Desai Memorial Lecture 2000 and H.C. Mathur Memorial Lecture 1996. The author is very grateful to Y.V. Reddy for many stimulating discussions on the subject. His thanks are also due to K.U. Bhaskar Rao and Sunando Roy for their significant help.

Economic and Political Weekly, April 15, 2000.

14 National Statistical Commission

An Overview of the Recommendations

Collection of numerical data for the purpose of understanding the behaviour of various socio-economic variables has a long history. The origin of the term 'statistics' is associated with this concept, which is to describe the state. Of course, statistics, as a scientific discipline, goes beyond enumeration. Statistical inference is an important part of the discipline. However, inference will be fruitless, if the basic data are faulty or inaccurate or unreliable. That is why we have to pay attention to data collection in all its dimensions. A good statistical system is a prerequisite for sound decision-making and for the formulation and monitoring of public policies.

India, in accordance with its federal structure, has created a statistical system, which is both decentralised and centralised. Large-scale statistical operations such as Population Census, Economic Census and nationwide sample surveys are centralised. In addition, the compilation of macroeconomic aggregates like national accounts, price indices and industrial production are largely central activities. However, the state governments and statistical organisations of the state are also engaged in collecting and generating data on a number of variables. Even where the responsibility for policy formulation lies with the central ministries, the actual collection of data may be done by the state governments through their agencies. For example, in the case of agricultural statistics, the crop area and yield data are collected by state governments through various schemes initiated by the central Ministry of Agriculture. There is, therefore a need for a high degree of coordination between the central statistical authorities and the state-level organisations. The Statistics Wing of the Ministry of Statistics and Programme Implementation in the Government of India is the nodal agency for coordination of statistical activities and maintenance of statistical standards. For coordination with states and union territories, it operates through state directorates of economics and statistics.

The Indian statistical system has over the years built an elaborate statistical infrastructure to capture the wide variety of data generated by a very large and decentralised economy. However, due to its over dependence on the administrative set up and traditional records, the system has not been able to keep pace with the demands of statistical requirements. The process of development has also brought in significant structural changes in the economy, which need to be captured by the statistical system. While the scientific basis for the generation of data and the methodologies adopted may not be in question, in many cases, what has brought about a decline in the quality and reliability of the statistics generated by the system is the inability of the present system or procedure of collecting data to meet the quality standards.

Apart from the quality of data, there are other problems such as data gaps, duplication leading to conflicting statistics and inordinate delays in transmission and publication of data. In the field of agricultural statistics large data gaps exist with reference to the output of fruits and vegetables and other minor crops, and estimates of meat, meat products and fish. The results of 16th Livestock Census, scheduled to be completed in 1997, are still not available for a number of states. The representativeness of the Index of Industrial Production (IIP) has been considered as questionable due to *inter alia* inadequate information on the small-scale sector. One of the perennial issues relating to national income in our country has been the difference between the National Accounts and National Sample Survey (NSS) estimates on consumption expenditure. In the area of external sector statistics also, the reconciliation of the data on exports and imports between the Directorate General of Commercial Intelligence and Statistics (DGCI and S) and the Reserve Bank of India (RBI) is essential. Further, the present system has not been able to provide adequate information on basic socio-economic indicators required for micro level planning. For example, although the Civil Registration System was envisaged as a mechanism to provide annual estimates of the infant mortality rate, birth rate, death rate, etc, at the district level, it has failed and, as a result, such estimates are not available at the decentralised level. No reliable information is available on many aspects in the health sector like problems of the aged, contribution of private sector to health care, disease-specific expenditure on health, etc. The whole area of services sector is undergoing far-reaching changes with the application of information technology. More of intangible goods are getting exchanged. However, huge data gaps exist with reference to such transactions.

Approach of the Report

The commission after examining the present system of collection and dissemination of statistics relating to different sectors of the economy adopted a five-fold approach to bring about improvements:

- First, reform in the administrative structure of the Indian statistical system and upgrading its infrastructure so as to ensure its autonomy.
- Second, improvement of the present system of collection of data, in relation to data that are currently being generated.
- Third, exploration of alternative techniques, in relation to the existing statistics, if the present system for collecting data is under strain for whatever reasons.
- Fourth, identification of new data series that may be generated in keeping pace with the expanding economy.
- Fifth, evolution of appropriate methodologies for collection of data, in relation to the new data requirements.

Administration of Indian Statistical System

At the moment, as the system operates, there is no effective coordination either horizontally among the different departments at the centre or vertically between the Centre and the states. The responsibilities for the horizontal and vertical coordination and maintenance of statistical standards rest with the ministry of statistics and programme implementation. However, it is found that this ministry is not in a position to ensure that the ministries and all state governments adhere to certain commonly accepted procedures. The task has become more difficult as the post of the director-general of the Central Statistical Organisation remains vacant since September 1997. The lack of an effective and adequately empowered coordination mechanism is a major weakness in the system. Besides, there is no policy-making body or authority on statistics for evolving a national statistical strategy.

For reform of administration of the Indian statistical system, the commission is of the view that an independent statistical authority free from political interference having power to set priorities with respect to core statistics is needed to ensure quality standards of statistical processes. Such an authority will also improve the coordination among different agencies collecting data. Though the National Advisory Board on Statistics was constituted with this objective, its impact has been minimal. In view of this, the commission has recommended the creation of a permanent and statutory apex body—National Commission on Statistics (NCS)—through an act of parliament, independent of the government in respect of policy-making, coordination and maintaining quality standards of core statistics. The NCS will have a chairman and four expert members all of whom would be eminent statisticians or social scientists and they will act on the advice of a number of technical committees on various subject areas.

The presence of an administrative machinery within the government is necessary to implement and sustain the policies evolved by the proposed NCS. The commission has, therefore, proposed the restructuring of the existing Statistics Wing of the Ministry of Statistics and Programme Implementation into a full-fledged department of the ministry to be known hereafter as the National Statistical Organisation (NSO). The head of the NSO will be the National Statistician and will be the secretary to the Government of India. He or she will also be the secretary to the National Commission on Statistics. The NSO will comprise three offices and a wing, namely, the Central Statistical Office, National Sample Survey Office, Data Storage and Dissemination Office and Consultancy Wing. The NSO will be responsible for implementation and maintenance of statistical standards as laid down by the NCS besides carrying out various other functions such as the compilation of National Accounts, apart from facilitating national and international coordination, publication of core statistics, the conduct of methodological research and studies, as well as arranging the training of statistical personnel and maintenance of a 'warehouse' for core statistics.

There is an increasing demand for professional statistical activities within the government. The commission has, therefore, recommended the creation of a body—the Consultancy Wing—under the National Statistical Organisation to utilise the expertise available within the government in the setting up of a commercial wing for professional statistical activities.

A lack of coordination among the different ministries and departments of the Central government leads ultimately to poor and unproductive statistical advice to the concerned administrative ministries and departments. To remedy this situation, the commission recommends the appointment of statistical advisers in important ministries and departments in order to make available sound statistical inputs and advice for the purposes of policy formulation and decision-making under the technical guidance of the National Statistician.

Some of the state directorates of economics and statistics do not play a nodal role in the coordination of statistical activities within the state and lack survey sampling and data processing capabilities. To improve the coordination within the state statistical systems, the state directorates of economics and statistics must be made responsible for technical coordination with all state departments in respect of the content, methodology and dissemination of statistics. The Conference of Central and State Statistical Organisations is another instrument which would provide a forum for regular interaction among the Central and state statisticians. In some of the states, as the statistical cadres are generally fragmented, the constitution of an organised state statistical cadre is urgently required. For strengthening the statistical system in the states, the commission has recommended a centrally-sponsored scheme with the specific objectives of developing survey and data-processing capabilities in the states.

As quality issues hinge on the professional capabilities of the officers and staff engaged in producing national statistics, an important objective of the Indian statistical system is to promote professionalism in the Indian Statistical Service (ISS). At the moment, there is no mechanism either for providing appropriate training to the official statisticians or for promoting specialisation among the officers of the ISS. The commission, therefore, has recommended the provision of appropriate training facilities for improving the skills of the ISS officers. Further, the career of an officer should be so planned that he or she can specialise in some specific areas, gradually narrowing down the areas of specialisation over the years. There is also a need for harmonisation between the choice of individual specialisation and the goals of the organisation and for orienting the transfer and training policies consistent with the goals of specialisation. Moreover, the commission has noted that there is stagnation in the career prospects of ISS officers due to bleak promotional avenues, which has adversely affected the system. The commission has, therefore, recommended a one-time measure of promoting the stagnant ISS officers so as to inspire them to enhance their output. This apart, periodic cadre review has been recommended with a view to re-structure the cadre from its existing broad-base to the model cadre structure recommended by the Fifth Central Pay Commission.

The system lacks legal backing for the statistical activities. The present Collection of Statistics Act, 1953 is weak. In addition to ensuring the reliability of statistics and the efficiency of operations, a strong Act, in accordance with the federal structure of the country, should also take into account the informants' rights to privacy. Recognising the role of information technology for processing, transmission and dissemination of data, the commission has recommended the establishment of strong communication links between the NSO and all other related statistical offices including the states' statistical offices through one or more Internet service providers or virtual private network.

Agricultural Statistics

Though India has a long tradition of comprehensive crop statistics, at present a steady deterioration in the quality of data on crops, which are traditionally covered under the system of agricultural statistics has occurred. In addition to this, there are several data gaps on new crops and ancillary agricultural activities. Despite impressive and commendable achievements in agriculture over the years, there is a growing concern over the quality of agricultural statistics that are now available. Statistics of crop production—both area and yield—are based on scientifically designed methodologies. These designs have been arrived at after considerable experimentation and discussion among scholars of international repute. However, the present status of crop statistics is far from satisfactory. There have been frequent revisions of crop estimates and they have been quite steep on a number of occasions. The publication of final estimates on crop production is considerably delayed. The quality of land use and crop data has suffered seriously for a variety of reasons. Village officials who play a key role in collecting land use statistics do not attach much importance to this work. Higher-level revenue officials too do not pay adequate attention to this activity at the time of supervision. All these factors have contributed to the deterioration in the quality of crop statistics even though efforts have been made to bring about improvements through the Timely Reporting Scheme (TRS) and the Improvement of Crop Statistics (ICS) Scheme. Thus the pillars on which the entire edifice of agricultural statistics rest have been weakened. The commission has, therefore, made a reassessment and examined the methodology as well as the organisational improvements required for improving agricultural statistics.

The major reason for the poor quality of area statistics is the failure of the *patwari* agency to devote adequate time and attention to the *girdawari* operations while yield estimates suffer on account of the poor performance of field operations. The heavy workload of the primary agency contributes substantially to the poor quality and delay in the availability of agricultural statistics. In order to reduce the workload, it may not be an appropriate proposition to increase the number of primary workers, at this juncture, due to financial constraints.

At present, the area statistics are generated through complete enumeration in the temporarily settled states while in the permanently settled states these are arrived at through a sample of 20 per cent villages covered by the Establishment of an Agency for Reporting Agricultural Statistics (EARAS) scheme. The commission's assessment is that adequate improvements in the quality and timeliness of area statistics can be achieved if the *girdawari* is declared as a programme of high priority and the *patwari* is mandated to carry out the crop inspection, according to the prescribed time schedule, more importantly in the case of the 20 per cent villages under TRS and EARAS, if necessary by sparing him from other duties during that period. In addition to this, intensive supervision of the *patwari's* work by higher-level revenue officials as well as by the technical staff of the scheme for ICS with accountability for any lapses should be ensured. Once the TRS and EARAS are put on such sound footing, it is possible to use the results for framing not only the advance estimates but also the final estimates of crop area. Further, the commission is of the view that data from a 20 per cent sample is large enough to estimate crop area with a sufficient degree of precision at the all-India, state and district levels. The commission has, therefore, recommended that crop area forecasts and final area estimates issued by the ministry of agriculture should be based on the results of the TRS in the temporarily settled states and on those of EARAS in the permanently settled states. The revised system for the estimation of crop areas will also reduce the workload of the primary data collecting agencies and improve the quality of their work.

The role of the scheme for ICS in locating the deficiencies in the system of crop statistics is quite significant. The ICS reports which act as a cross-check on the work done by others have brought to light several discrepancies and deficiencies in quantitative terms. Despite the fact that the ICS has commented on the quality of crop statistics with reference to individual states, there have not been much improvements in the quality. Therefore, there is a need for exploring the feasibility of using the ICS data for working out a correction factor to be applied to official statistics of crop area to generate alternative estimates of the same.

At present, primary statistics of crop production are collected and compiled by the state governments and consolidated for the nation as a whole by the union ministry of agriculture. The ministry compiles the crop production figures and releases a number of forecasts of crop production. The present system of release of the forecasts has been found to be subjective. The commission is of the view that it is necessary to make an objective forecasting based on timely and detailed information on crop condition, meteorological parameters, water availability, crop damage, etc. Though the ministry of agriculture has been working in this direction, organisational strengthening with professional statisticians and experts in other related fields is required. While the use of remote sensing technology does offer an alternative route for the regular flow of crop statistics, there are a number of issues that require to be sorted out before this can become extensively operational. Meanwhile, the existing programmes of remote sensing technology must be pursued with active cooperation from the concerned agencies.

The data collected through Agricultural and Livestock Censuses are required for identifying and formulating policies and programmes for the rural population. However, as the results of these censuses are not available in time, this defeats the very purpose for which these censuses are conducted. The major reasons for the delay in the availability of the results from these censuses are the gigantic nature of the task, the heavy workload on the part of the primary agencies and a lack of adequate administrative and technical supervision over the work of primary agencies. To circumvent these problems, there is a need for conducting the censuses not as complete enumeration but as sample censuses. Further, no relationship has been worked out based on the data collected through these two censuses because they are conducted independently with different field agencies, reference periods and basic units of enumeration. In view of several operational and substantive gains, the commission has recommended the integration of the Livestock and Agricultural Censuses.

Industrial Statistics

The Annual Survey of Industries (ASI) has been the principal source for most of the basic statistics of the industrial sector. The frame of factories, which the ASI uses for conducting the survey, is based on the list of factories maintained by the Chief Inspectors of Factories (CIF). The commission has observed that a large number of units, which are qualified for inclusion in the CIF's list, have not been included and at the same time many defunct units have not been removed. The data generated by the ASI system based upon this deficient ASI frame do not therefore depict the true situation of organised industrial sector. Urgent steps should be taken for making the ASI frame more comprehensive by including in it all units that are eligible for registration with the CIF, followed by an appropriate updating mechanism. With the objective of generating reliable benchmark estimates at the disaggregated level, of providing an efficient weighting diagram for revision of the base year of Index of Industrial Production and also of updating the ASI frame, the commission has recommended a one-time census of units eligible for registration.

The estimates of different variables of industrial statistics derived by the ASI are often associated with large sampling and non-sampling errors. To enhance the credibility and utility of these estimates, sampling errors need to be published along with the estimates of important survey characteristics. Further, a periodic review of the sampling design and of the sample size in the ASI must be undertaken with the objective to improve the precision of the estimates at the industry-group levels.

Estimates of the growth rates of industrial production based upon the Index of Industrial Production are extensively used for policy-making at various levels in the government and also for decision-making in the banking and corporate sectors. The importance of IIP is further increased due to the fact that it is the only indicator generated every month and disseminated on a wide scale. Concern has been expressed over the large divergence between the quick and the final estimates of the IIP. The commission has made a critical appraisal of the quality of the monthly IIP as an economic indicator of the general level of industrial activity in the economy. The functioning of the source agencies providing the primary data of industrial production to the CSO is afflicted with a number of serious deficiencies. The product coverage of IIP and the administrative and institutional framework for primary data collection are much below the desirable standards. In the new policy regime of liberalisation of the industrial sector, the governmental machinery's ability to induce a good response from the industrial units for providing statistics on a monthly basis has been considerably eroded. The available legal backing by the Industrial Development and Regulation Act has also not yielded the desired response. The commission therefore recommends that the quality of the IIP must be improved by toning-up the statistical wings of the source agencies, in particular, within the Department of Industrial Policy and Promotion (DIPP) of the ministry of industry, which has a considerable share in the weighting diagram. Further, the commission has recommended exploring the possibilities of constructing an additional IIP based on bigger units, for which collection of data could be streamlined in a more effective manner than in the case of the entire industrial sector.

The need for harmonisation of the activity, product and trade data has been evident for quite some time, as this would enable a cross-classification of activity and product data. At present, there is no uniformity in the codes being used by the organisations dealing with the collection and processing of product-level data, compelling the user to refer to different documents. In this context, the commission has felt the need of an urgent finalisation of the unique coding system developed by the central Board of Excise and Customs (CBEC) based on the Harmonised System and emphasised its simultaneous adoption by all the producer and user organisations concerned with product-level data. To give wide publicity, the information on coding structure should also be made available on an extensive basis through websites and publications. The use of national classification would eliminate the multiplicity of product-level coding systems and would also enable a study of the flow of output through various economic systems apart from a cross-classification of activity and product data.

Services Sector Statistics

With the services sector's growing share in the nation's GDP, the need for establishing a well-organised mechanism that can maintain a sound statistical database for this can hardly be overemphasised. The task becomes difficult given the vastness of the sector, its heterogeneous nature as well as fast-changing composition with the frequent emergence of new services and the exit of obsolete ones. Thus the evolving of an appropriate survey methodology for collection of data from the vast services sector is a real challenge.

As regards Follow-up Enterprise Surveys on the services sector conducted by the ministry of statistics and programme implementation are concerned, data users perceive that the survey estimates of gross value added per worker for different sub-sectors are sometimes unrealistic. These problems should be addressed by way of carrying out methodological research to find out innovative methods of data collection. The commission has recommended the setting up of a unit in the proposed National Sample Survey Office of the National Statistical Organisation to regularly undertake studies for bringing about improvements in the survey methodologies, including the method of data collection. Further, for the emerging areas like software exports, e-commerce, entertainment sector, and related fields, the commission has recommended the development of a suitable methodology for estimating their contribution in employment, gross value added, etc.

The existing Follow-up Enterprise Surveys on the services and other sub-sectors (excluding manufacturing and repairing sub-sectors), carried out by the ministry of statistics and programme implementation, take into account all types of enterprises (other than those in the public sector), irrespective of their size, under the same survey year. This approach to data collection might not lead to proper representation of bigger units in the sample causing distortion in the estimated results. Thus the survey estimates are likely to be subject to a large margin of sampling error. To overcome this problem, the commission has recommended the carrying out of a survey of 'bigger' units in sub-sectors other than manufacturing and repairing. For complete coverage of the sub-sectors, the residual category of relatively smaller units should be surveyed through the existing Follow-up Enterprise Surveys. As trade and services figure in the state list, the commission has also recommended the evolving of an appropriately decentralised survey mechanism in collaboration with state directorates of economics and statistics.

The latest classification of economic activities, i e, National Industrial Classification 1998 (NIC-98), that includes activities relating to services, accepts the major features of the International Standard Industrial Classification (ISIC) 1990 (Revision 3). A comparison of the NIC-98 with the World Trade Organisation's List of Services reveals that some of the emerging activities are not specifically listed in the NIC-98. The commission has, therefore, recommended developing a mechanism to identify such activities on a regular basis and for assigning them proper codes within the framework of NIC.

Infrastructure Statistics

In developing a proper statistical database for the infrastructure sector, a major hurdle is the absence of a clear definition of "infrastructure". The commission has defined the term by identifying certain characteristics. The commission has also observed large data gaps in the infrastructure sector and recommended measures to bridge such gaps. In order to improve the accessibility of such data for policy-makers and other data users, the commission has recommended that the ministry of statistics and programme implementation should publish data on all infrastructure activities in a single document.

Road transport is one of the important activities of the Infrastructure sector. But the database for this sub-sector is quite weak. Thus a proper data collection mechanism should be evolved to strengthen the database.

Power is another vital sub-sector where the statistics need improvement. The commission has recommended that the state governments should be asked to collect data pertaining to the finances of the state electricity boards. Further, the electricity authorities at the state and union territory level should publish the data for the electricity-generating units, including those in the private sector, under their respective jurisdictions.

Quantification of the infrastructural activities in the form of an index would help policy-makers and researchers. The commission has therefore recommended the construction of two types of indices in this regard. While the first one, called "Infrastructure Index", will provide a summary measure of the growth of infrastructure, the second one, namely, "Infrastructure Utilisation Index", will indicate the extent of utilisation of identified infrastructure facilities.

Socio-Economic Statistics

The commission took note of the problems on various aspects included in the socio-economic sector statistics and assessed the current status of these for the country in the areas of education, health and family welfare, manpower and employment, environment, population characteristics and gender with regard to reliability, timeliness and adequacy of data available in these areas and have made specific recommendations for improving the system.

The commission is of the view that in each of these areas, there are major deficiencies of data, which can be largely attributed to the near collapse of the Administrative Statistical System. The deficiencies common to all the sectors include: poor quality of data, inordinate delays, lack of effective checks, incomplete coverage, poor implementation of provisions of Acts, low priority and general apathy to statistical activities, inadequate infrastructure and staff for statistical work, lack of computerisation and its use in data compilation, processing and dissemination of data produced by different agencies. As a result, routine data on schools, students enrolled, hospitals, medical and para-medical personnel, births and deaths occurring in the population are just not collected due to a lack of proper emphasis on these items of information and the administrative back up for a compilation and analysis of the required data.

In the area of population statistics, the Population Census is one of the most comprehensive sources of information on the size, distribution, living conditions and demographic characteristics of the population. Even though the provisional population totals on limited data are released within a month of the completion of fieldwork, a considerable delay in the processing and release of detailed final results still persists, which undermines the immense utility of this gigantic exercise. The results released early are considered as provisional figures. Therefore, it is essential to have an advance calendar for the entire census operations so that all reports are released and disseminated within a time frame of three years.

The commission also highlighted the need to integrate databases relating to the administrative units of the country. Attempts should also be made to develop uniform unique area codes for districts, blocks and villages at the national level. This exercise has been attempted in the recent census. These codes should also include geo-codes, which should be sufficient to locate them in a map.

The recent democratic decentralisation process initiated by the 73rd and 74th Amendments giving greater responsibilities and powers to the *panchayats* and *nagar palikas* as the third tier of governance offers a new window of opportunity for local planning, effective implementation and monitoring of various social and economic development programmes in the country at the local levels. The national statistical system should assist the various developmental agencies in this challenging requirement and it is therefore important to establish a system of data collection from the block level onwards and also their dissemination to the local bodies on one hand and further flow upwards to the district and above levels. To facilitate this, a statistical functionary is necessary, who would be the outermost peripheral link at *taluka* headquarters with a networked computer for data entry, maintenance of block-level databases, simple tabulations and speedy data transmission to higher authorities in an appropriately summarised pre-designed format.

A minimum list of variables or indicators that should be collected at village level should be identified and a system of their compilation and aggregation should be established. Similarly, the variables and indicators required for aggregation at the district, state and national levels should also be identified. The community block should be the first level of aggregation for village level information. The commission has recommended that the data compiled by all government departments at the village and block level in respect of the identified variables or indicators should be supplied to the Block Statistical Assistant periodically, who will maintain the block level data and also disseminate the same to the *panchayats* and local bodies on the one hand and to the district authorities on the other hand. A system for ensuring a regular flow of information from all the government departments to the block level statistical personnel should be established.

In the area of health and family welfare statistics, the three departments of health, family welfare and Indian System of Medicines and Homeopathy of the ministry of health and family welfare have a separate system of data collection in their respective areas, while the Registrar General of India is responsible for collection and dissemination of vital statistics through its system of registration of vital events. The commission has recognised that an efficient Health Management Information System (HMIS) is a prerequisite for studying the problems of health and diseases, effective administration of health services and evaluation of effectiveness and efficiency of various health programmes. It is, therefore, essential that a comprehensive assessment of the HMIS as it operates, be undertaken by setting up of a committee and examining in detail the data requirements of the states and the Centre. Similarly, detailed data on morbidity and mortality that form the core of data requirements for any health planning strategy are lacking and periodical morbidity surveys must be conducted to meet the data requirements of public health planners and epidemiologists. The computerisation of hospital records both in the public and private sector is needed for generation of the requisite data on health conditions. Further, recognising the increasing participation of private sector in providing health care services both in the rural and urban areas, the integration of the information from this sector with that of the government sector is urgently needed. It is also necessary to regulate the private health sector to ensure quality of services to the public and therefore the centre should formulate a regulatory model Act including provisions for submission of periodical statistical returns. Further, National Family Health Surveys similar to those conducted in 1992-93 and 1998-99 should be conducted periodically using national resources, if funds are not available from any other agency.

The country has a well-established system of civil registration through an elaborate machinery right up to the district level and below for registration of vital events under the Registration of Births and Deaths Act. The civil registration system has the potential to generate vital rates for district level and below and form the basis for planning health and family welfare programmes at the local level as required in the 73rd and 74th Amendments. The system is however deficient and suffers from poor coverage and quality in registration. In the country as a whole the registration coverage is only 53 per cent for births and only 48 per cent for deaths and the problem is more acute in the rural areas and in a few states. There are many administrative and management factors responsible for this poor registration. The commission is of the view that the responsibility for registration of births and deaths should be vested with *panchayats* and *nagar palikas* in a phased manner starting with the states where panchayati raj institutions are well in place. The system should be a proactive one by increased involvement of local-level government functionaries and the local bodies. The computerisation of the system of civil registration would also solve the problem of compilation of information that has to flow regularly into the statistical system.

The need for information on the fast-changing composition of the labour market has been growing for appropriate assessment of demand and supply of labour in different sectors of the economy. Labour and employment statistics are generated largely through the implementation of various labour laws and regulations by the states and Centre. For the unorganised sector, the National Sample Survey Organisation and Central Statistical Organisation are collecting and disseminating labour and employment-related data by conducting periodic sample surveys. The Registrar General and Census Commissioner of India is also publishing data decennially on workers and those seeking work through its census operations. The data collected by the Ministry of Labour through states suffer from very poor response in submission of returns, delays in filing the returns, poor quality, undercoverage and time lag in publication of results. The large number of returns to be submitted by the primary units adds to the reluctance of the unit owners for a prompt response. The poor implementation of the penal provisions of the Acts for non-submission of returns by the implementing agencies has been another area of concern.

The problems are largely administrative in nature and the agencies concerned should give adequate priority to the statistical aspects in the implementation of the Acts. Further, simplification and rationalisation of various returns is also required apart from use of information technology in the compilation and processing of data by the states. The role of employment exchanges in the changing jobs scenario needs to be assessed and redefined as a placement agency and source of labour-market information. Further, the provisions of various labour Acts should be vigorously implemented and if required, legal provisions should be strengthened and penalties on defaulters made more stringent to act as a deterrent. The renewal of licence of the units should be subject to satisfactory submission of returns in the past.

Education being key to the process of human development in the country, statistics on education becomes crucial in the formulation of development policies. Ministry of Human Resource Development is the main agency for producing statistics on school education, which are collected through the states. The All-India Educational Survey conducted by the NCERT is another important source of statistics on school education in the country. In its review of the educational statistics system, the commission took note of the deficiencies of quality, reliability, time lag and weak infrastructure in the collection and dissemination of education data. The system can be improved by strengthening the practice of record keeping, vigilant data scrutiny and verification and computerisation of district-level information. Quite a few data gaps exist in relation to educational planning, and these should be collected and published by the agencies concerned. In the area of technical and higher education the problems are still more acute as the agencies involved are collecting data for specific purposes without any coordination with the ministry of human resource development. In this area, the regulating bodies such as University Grants Commission, All-India Council of Technical Education, the Department of Agricultural Research and Education, National Council of Teacher Education and Department of Health through the Medical and Dental Councils should be made responsible for collecting and disseminating the requisite data. Further, the infrastructure for collection and dissemination of education statistics needs to be strengthened at the Centre and the states by providing adequate statistical manpower and other facilities of computer hardware and software. For collecting and compiling all educational statistics, the International Standard Classification of Education (ISCED, 1997) developed by United Nations Educational and Scientific Organisation (UNESCO) should be used to ensure standardisation and comparability of data across the states and internationally.

The improvement in gender statistics can be achieved by ensuring that statistics related to individuals are collected, compiled, analysed and presented by sex and age so as to reflect issues related to women and men in society. A gender perspective is needed in all traditional statistical fields. This implies that gender statistics cannot be produced and improved in isolation. Such work must be integrated with the development of the overall data collection system. Improvement of content, methods, classifications and measurements should be made part of the ongoing efforts to improve the sources of statistics namely, censuses, surveys and administrative systems. The department of women and child development should play a proactive role and strengthen its statistical set-up.

The need for conservation of environment and the related concept of sustainable development has attracted the attention of the entire world and is becoming a guiding principle of developmental planning. Environment statistics is in its nascent stage in the country and as such there is a need to build up an efficient system for the collection of environment statistics and developing environmental indicators based on the international framework provided by the United Nations Statistics Division. The CSO has already taken initiatives in this direction; however, Ministry of Environment and Forests should take the primary responsibility for collection and dissemination of environment statistics and the CSO should continue to play the coordinating role.

Financial and External Sector Statistics

The deregulation of financial markets has accelerated the pace of financial innovations and brought forth the need for regular and timely flow of qualitative financial statistics for pursuing sound macroeconomic policies as well as promoting financial stability. In the context of the recent financial crises, the traditional issues in financial statistics such as timeliness in dissemination, accuracy, transparency, harmonisation, international comparability, etc, have come into sharper focus. In addition, many unconventional issues relating to classification, valuation and measurement of financial transactions have also attracted attention. An efficient use of financial statistics requires greater harmonisation of financial statistics with other related system of accounts such as national accounts, balance of payment statistics, etc. The need for data standardisation, wider coverage and higher frequency has become important from the viewpoint of analysis and the establishment of linkages among various market segments. Since financial markets are much more information driven, timeliness in dissemination of reliable information assumes special importance.

The international initiative in this direction has resulted in the IMF establishing the Special Data Dissemination Standards (SDDS) in April 1996, in order to enhance the timely availability of comprehensive statistics relating to the real, fiscal, financial and external sectors of the economy. As a subscriber to SDDS, the concerned agencies in India have made concerted efforts to adhere to the data standards of SDDS. With the use of technology, it is possible to quickly disseminate data to a wider range of users. With a larger role for markets and increasing cross-border financial flows, transparency has assumed significance not only for market participants, but also for regulators. Apart from transparency, timeliness and quality of the information made available, as public good have also assumed importance. Alignment with international standards in economic, banking and financial areas is critical for the enormous efficiency enhancing value that this offers. A further emergence of new institutions in the regulatory sphere poses new opportunities and challenges.

The commission while making its recommendations on financial and external sector statistics took into account this changing environment. It noted that an institutional infrastructure already exists in India for collection and dissemination of statistics on these sectors. The Reserve Bank of India (RBI) is the principal though not the sole agency for collection and dissemination of statistics in respect of financial and external sector statistics. It collects and disseminates these data through its various publications, website and press releases. The other major public sector agencies and institutions that collect, compile and disseminate financial statistics are the Ministry of Finance, Securities and Exchange Board of India (SEBI), National Bank for Agriculture and Rural Development (NABARD) and Industrial Development Bank of India (IDBI). The Insurance Regulatory and Development Authority (IRDA) would have an important role in collection and dissemination of data with regard to the insurance sector. The commission has noted that many of these institutions have been taking into account the changing environment and modifying their data collection formats from time to time. For instance, the modalities for the collection of data on the external sector have been modified as per the recommendations of the High Level Committee on balance of payments, 1993 (chairman, C Rangarajan). The commission also noted that by and large, the data available on financial and external sectors in India are in conformity with relevant international manuals on external, monetary and financial statistics. However, the commission identified some areas that need further refinement to suit the unique needs of Indian economy, the recent institutional development in the financial sector especially the developments in financial markets. In particular, the commission has identified the needs in respect of data relating to fiscal, informal sector, insurance and e-commerce.

The monetary and financial statistics as well as data relating to commercial banks published by RBI are reliable, adequate and reasonably timely. Since there are differing perceptions on the concepts of monetary aggregates, RBI should publish the time series on components of money at a disaggregated level so as to enable analysts to construct their own series. The RBI, in consultation with IDBI, should introduce necessary returns from financial institutions (FIs) for compilation of liquidity and other financial aggregates. RBI should consider publication of data on average holding of cash reserves by commercial banks for the reserve maintenance period, residual maturity of term deposits with the commercial banks, inter-bank cheque clearances and maintain uniformity in the classification of occupation in borrowal accounts in Basic Statistical Returns (BSR) in conformity with National Industrial Classification (NIC) 1998 of CSO. In addition, Locational Banking Statistics (LBS) and Consolidated Banking Statistics (CBS) on international claims of banks should be compiled and published by RBI. There are deficiencies in respect of data relating to non-banking finance companies (NBFCs) and the informal financial sector, which need to be addressed by RBI urgently. For deposit taking NBFCs, periodical returns should be collected, consolidated and data disseminated on a systematic basis. A one-time census of NBFCs covering all companies incorporated with the Department of Company Affairs (DCA) should be conducted. The coverage of the AIDIS needs to be improved by pooling the estimates of central and state samples on the one hand and by increasing the sample size on the other. The CSO should conduct enterprise surveys separately for financial service enterprises and provide data needed to derive value-added details as also the details of credit. There is a need for NABARD to improve the quality and timeliness of data relating to Regional Rural Banks (RRBs) as well as cooperative banks and also to initiate surveys on financial data relating to non-governmental organisations (NGOs) and self-help groups (SHGs).

While SEBI should continue to have the primary responsibility for collection and dissemination of data in respect of capital markets, there is a need for improvement in data with regard to private placement and daily dissemination of data by all stock exchanges in a standardised format. SEBI should provide an estimate of all-India market capitalisation at regular intervals and consolidated data of share-brokers and share-broking firms. There is also need to widen the coverage of data on mutual funds operations. The primary responsibility for collection and dissemination of data in respect of the insurance sector should naturally rest with IRDA. The data should be consolidated by different categories of insurance, e g, life, non-life, reinsurance, pension and super-annuation, health, crop and others.

While the data disseminated by RBI on the government securities market compares well with international standards, there is a need to improve the coverage and timeliness of data with regard to certain money market instruments such as commercial papers (CP) and certificate of deposits (CD). As the data on money and the government securities market are critical not only for the market participants, but also for RBI in its own day-to-day monetary management, with further improvement in technology such as implementation of the negotiated dealing system (NDS), full-scale operationalisation of very small aperture terminal (VSAT), such data should be made available on a real time basis. Keeping in view the impact of fiscal policy on the real, financial and external sectors of the economy, there is scope for further improvement in terms of coverage, classification and dissemination. The details of actuals of Internal and Extra Budgetary Resources (IEBR) should be published in the budget. The state government should make available to the public the data on major fiscal variables on a monthly basis. A research unit should also be set up in the Central Board of Direct Taxes (CBDT) to undertake research studies on various aspects of tax planning. There is also a need for establishment of a data warehouse for fiscal statistics.

While the balance of payments statistics compiled and released by RBI are broadly consistent with the international standards, and are disseminated widely and in a timely manner, certain discrepancies in data have, however, persisted and certain new areas have emerged which need further attention. For instance, there are continuing discrepancies in merchandise trade data, both exports and imports, between the Directorate General of Commercial Intelligence and Statistics (DGCI and S) and RBI. There is also a need for more detailed data on trade in services, which has emerged as an important component of balance of payments. A technical group with the participation of concerned agencies should examine the data reporting mechanism for software exports. RBI should improve the coverage of short-term credit in external debt by inclusion of data on suppliers' credit up to 180 days. RBI should re-orient its methodology for compilation of data on International Investment Position (INIP) by making increasing use of flow data wherever the stock data are not readily available with a view to generating quarterly data with a time lag of six months. In view of electronic commerce being a new and fast growing way of conducting business, there is a need for developing an appropriate methodology by closely monitoring the international trends and multilateral initiatives for data compilation. It is also necessary to conduct surveys covering e-commerce providers for data on income, expenditure, value added, etc.

Notwithstanding the progress made so far by the concerned agencies, namely, RBI, SEBI, NABARD, IDBI, IRDA and Ministry of Finance, there is a need to focus on the areas recommended by the commission so as to further strengthen the process of collection, compilation and dissemination of the financial and external sector statistics.

Price Statistics

Changes in the prices of goods and services affect different segments of the population differently. Thus measuring prices and their rate of change over time has become crucial to almost every economic issue, from the conduct of monetary policy to measuring inter-temporal and inter-regional economic progress. Central and state government agencies collect the primary data on prices for varied purposes. The data on prices, both for the wholesale price index and consumer price indices, are not satisfactory. On account of existing deficiencies, such as involvement of multiple data collection agencies, use of varying concepts and definitions, non-existence of an exclusive field agency, non-standard specifications, repetition of prices due to non-response, and the meagre honorarium to data collectors, the commission has recommended the unification of the system of price data collection so that the mechanism should take into account the requirements of all central agencies compiling price indices. This would enhance the reliability and credibility of price data.

On the issue of compilation of the Wholesale Price Index (WPI), the commission has recommended that the revision of base year must be undertaken more frequently so as to capture the changes in industrial structure on account of liberalisation. The services sector has presently developed to such an extent now that it contributes significantly to country's GDP. On account of the non-inclusion of services sector in the existing WPI, the development of a separate price index for services sector is recommended. Ultimately, this should be merged with the WPI, once the services sector index is stabilised and its robustness is established. The Consumer Price Index (CPI) is widely used for a variety of purposes and is also viewed as an indicator of the effectiveness of government economic policies. However, in the absence of an all-India CPI, the WPI is currently used as a measure of inflation in India, though it is an inadequate indicator. The commission has recommended the development of all-India consumer price indices for rural and urban areas.

Corporate Sector Statistics

The growing importance of the corporate sector calls for a greater transparency and availability of data. Furthermore with the withdrawal of various direct regulatory functions of the government such as industrial licensing, import licensing, capital issues and exchange controls, a number of avenues of collection of data have ceased to exist while the need for data for the success of indicative planning, forecasting and for research purposes has grown. Finally, the onset of the knowledge-based sectors or the new economy requires better reporting standards of certain attributes to help monitor the national economic performance and its future outlook.

In the DCA, the Registrars of Companies (ROCs) are primarily responsible for provision of the basic information on the corporate sector and the statistical machinery in the ROCs is inadequate to deal with this task. The frame of the corporate sector maintained by the ROCs is highly inadequate and the available information is not properly processed for wider dissemination. Therefore, the commission recommends a one-time census of all registered companies by the DCA, which will help to create a frame by eliminating closed or defunct companies and also to facilitate the estimation of population parameters. The ROCs, vested with the responsibilities for allotting the Corporate Index Number (CIN), should monitor the submission of annual reports rigorously for a proper implementation of the Act and for purposes of annual updation of the frame as well as improvement of the database. The DCA and ROCs should process information available in the company balance sheets and produce more comprehensive information on the different aspects of the corporate sector for monitoring and policy formulation. The scope of the standards of disclosure and reporting of data should be improved by including additional variables in the annual reports and the balance sheets of the companies. The commission has made specific recommendations in this regard.

National Accounts Statistics

The National Accounts Statistics (NAS) provides the framework for an internally consistent description of the macro economy based on the data generated by practically the entire statistical system in the country. The estimates of national or state domestic product and related aggregates and accounts are derived statistics that draw on the basic data available from various primary sources. The primary data sources fall in two broad categories: those data generated as a by-product of public administration system (land records, enforcement of various laws regulating economic activities, collection of customs duties, etc) and those collected directly from the economic agents through sample surveys or censuses carried out by the official agencies of the Central and state governments. For certain newly-emerging activities such as software, where the official system of primary data collection is not currently in place, the NAS also draw on selective non-official sources. While alternative standard methods of estimating national accounts aggregates, namely, income, expenditure and commodity-flow, are suggested to provide independent checks, data limitations often do not permit these independent consistency checks. Hence, certain internal consistency checks provided by national accounts identities are used to derive certain components as residuals. Wherever independent methods are employed, discrepancies usually appear. In such cases, a judgment is exercised about the relative reliability between the estimates obtained by independent methods and the most reliable one is taken to provide the control total and discrepancies with reference to control total are recorded as 'errors and omissions'.

The credibility of National Accounts Statistics in the 1990s came to be questioned on two counts. First, there were frequent and often large revisions in the sectoral or aggregate estimates for the same year released at different points of time. The reason has been traced to the large revisions carried out by the various primary source agencies supplying data for national accounts. The commission has made recommendations to improve the quality of primary data collected by the reporting source agencies as also to put in place certain institutional correctives to minimise large revisions. Secondly, there have been frequent charges, sometimes made by the officials themselves, that a very large degree of underestimation of the level of gross or net domestic product exists. This is partially true because of the absence of official data-collecting machinery for some of the new activities like software and floriculture, which have expanded since the economy was liberalised in 1991. However, as in other countries, indirect estimation methods and use of non-updated rates, ratios and norms that go into the estimation of GDP have unknown (downward or upward) biases. The commission has, therefore, approached this criticism in the context of improving the database and procedures of estimation of GDP (including the updation of rates, ratios and norms) while suggesting mechanisms of data collection for as yet uncovered or inadequately covered newly emerging activities.

After analysing the methods of estimation, data sources and deficiencies in NAS at the sectoral, sub-sectoral and regional levels, the commission, while making recommendations, has emphasised the following five points:

- improving the quality, reliability and timeliness of the existing direct estimates of NAS aggregates;
- updating the rates, ratios and norms used in various aggregates by conducting geographically dispersed type studies at as frequent intervals as possible;
- conducting benchmark surveys with experimentation in survey methods for improving indirect estimates of NAS aggregates;
- guidelines for improving the regional accounts for state directorates of economics and statistics (DESs); and
- institutionalising frequent interaction between National Accounts Division of the Central Statistical Organisation and DESs and working out a joint programme of improvement.

The major weakness in the estimation of GDP by industry lies in estimating the contribution of the large number of unorganised and small self-employed enterprises in manufacturing and services, where the basic problems are those of irregular income streams, multiple activities undertaken during a year, absence of business accounts, and frequent entries and exits of units. While benchmark enterprise surveys currently provide the available database, the characteristic features mentioned above pose formidable challenges of survey design, survey methodology and survey practices. It is therefore recommended that, periodical benchmark surveys of unorganised enterprises be continued while simultaneously conducting pilot studies for improving the technical survey design methods and practices.

The estimates of private final consumption expenditure (PFCE) presented in the National Accounts Statistics relate to the expenditure made by the households and non-profit institutions serving households (NPISHs). These are, therefore, not strictly comparable with the consumption expenditure of households revealed by the NSS surveys. In the absence of availability of direct data on the consumption expenditures made by both the households and the NPISHs, the estimates of PFCE are made through indirect methods through the commodity-flow approach. This approach has been adopted due to the absence of income-expenditure surveys on NPISHs. It is recommended that periodical surveys and type studies be conducted to collect income and expenditure data on NPISHs. The second major weakness in the PFCE estimates is the usage of large number of rates and ratios, like the marketable surplus ratios of agricultural commodities, transport margins, etc, which are outdated. It is for this reason that the commission has recommended periodical and geographically dispersed type study.

The major data gap in the estimation of government final consumption expenditure (GFCE) is lack of analysis of the budgets of local bodies, due to their size and non-availability of finalised accounts of these bodies in time. This leads to undercoverage of GFCE. In view of this, it is recommended that the state directorates of economic and statistics should analyse the budgets of the local bodies every year for estimating all the national accounts aggregates including GFCE.

The major problems in the estimation of saving and capital formation relate to the private corporate sector, residual method of estimation of household saving, non-availability of data on NPISHs and local bodies, and use of large number of rates and ratios. The problems in the estimation of saving and investment of the private corporate sector have been traced to the doubts about the representative character of the sample companies and inadequacies in the blow-up factor. The commission has recommended taking corrective steps on the corporate sector in the form of analysis of balance sheets with wider coverage of companies. The other important weakness in the estimation of saving and investment relates to the indirect residual estimation of savings in the form of physical assets undertaken by household enterprises and own account un-incorporated enterprises for which decennial all-India debt and investment surveys provide benchmark estimates. It is therefore recommended to conduct income expenditure surveys of households and to conduct regular benchmark surveys of enterprises to provide direct estimates of household saving and estimates of investment by the enterprises.

The weaknesses in the compilation of regional accounts are the absence of state-level IIP, absence of annual surveys on enterprises, absence of indicators to move forward the benchmark estimates, particularly in the case of services sectors, and non-availability of data at state level on private corporate sector. It is therefore, recommended that states should compile IIP for their states, and pool the centre (of NSSO) and state sample to improve the quality of benchmark survey results on unorganised manufacturing and services sectors, as also on the workforce estimates. The recommendations made on the corporate sector statistics, local bodies and NPISHs, when implemented would provide estimates for this sector at state level as well, for the purpose of estimates of state domestic product, capital formation and district domestic product.

Conclusion

The commission after analysing the deficiencies of the Indian statistical system in terms of its administration and technical requirements has made several recommendations to revamp the statistical system. It may be legitimate to question how the recommendations would bring about improvements in the timeliness, reliability and adequacy of the Indian official statistics and contribute to its credibility in public perceptions and debates. In this context it may be stated that the loss of credibility in official statistics especially in the 1990s prompted the appointment of the National Statistical Commission with a wide-ranging terms of reference. The reasons were traced to: (a) deterioration in administrative statistics at the primary level; (b) weakening of the institutional mechanisms of vertical coordination between the Centre and the states; and (c) a similar weakening of the lateral coordination between the Ministries at the Centre and the Central Statistical Organisation. The recommendations on individual subjects aim at stemming the deterioration in the administrative statistical system and to improve it over time. Similarly, a revival or strengthening of the established institutional mechanisms of vertical coordination has also been recommended along with several suggestive guidelines for improving the state statistical systems. This would go a long way towards restoring the vertical coordination. The commission has recommended wide-ranging changes in the top structure of the Indian Statistical System to provide correctives for identified systemic deficiencies. In doing so, the commission has taken into consideration the proposed 'mission statement' as given below:

> The mission of the Indian Statistical System shall be to provide, within the decentralised structure of the system, reliable, timely and credible social and economic statistics, to assist decision-making within and outside the government, stimulate research and promote informed debate relating to conditions affecting people's life.

The proposed establishment of the National Commission on Statistics as a nodal policy-making and supervisory non-official body with statutory backing and assisted by subject specific expert groups as also its executive organ namely, the National Statistical Office with well-defined implementing powers and headed by a national statistician are meant to strengthen coordination in the decentralised statistical system at various levels. The proposed new institutional arrangement of statistical advisers in the various central ministries with the responsibility of supplying the core statistics would help not only in ensuring coordination, but also in ensuring the standards and carrying out statistical audit. The systemic view of the essentially decentralised Indian statistical system reflected in the recommendations of the commission would help to improve the credibility along with timeliness, reliability and adequacy. The improvements suggested would lay the foundation of a strong, robust and responsive statistical system that would cater to the needs of its various stakeholders and for enabling scientific decision-making using statistics, which is the basic requirement for good governance.

The National Statistical Commission was set up in January 2000 to examine critically the deficiencies of the present statistical system and to recommend measures to correct the deficiencies. The commission submitted its final report in August 2001. The commission comprised C. Rangarajan as chairman and the following as members: V.R. Rao, S.M. Vidwans, J. Roy, Prem Narain, Rakesh Mohan, V.R. Panchamukhi, Y. Venugopal Reddy, K. Srinivasan, S.D. Tendulkar, A.B.L Srivastava and Fredie Ardeshir Mehta. Vaskar Saha functioned as the secretary to the commission. The report of the commission comprises two volumes dealing with various subject areas including the administrative structure of the Indian statistical system. Volume two of the report which contains detailed recommendations run to approximately 700 pages. This is a slightly expanded version of chapter two of the report. The full report of the commission is now available at the website: *www.nic.in/stat*

Economic and Political Weekly, October 20, 2001.

Part III

Sectoral Issues:
Industry, Power, Banking and Agriculture

15 Paradigm Shifts in Industrial Policy

Introduction

All developed countries have gone through a process of transformation, which meant a shift from agriculture to industry. Between 1870 and 1930, the proportion of active population employed in agriculture had declined from 54 per cent to 23 per cent in the US, from 85 per cent to 51 per cent in Japan, and from 42 per cent to 25 per cent in France. Given this historical development world over, it is not surprising that growth was identified with industrialisation in the developing economies. The Indian planners, however, went a step further and talked of industrialisation with an emphasis on heavy industries. The Second Five Year Plan (1956-1961) gave expression to it, when it said that the Plan "accords high priority to industrialisation and especially to the development of basic and heavy industries." It was no doubt recognised that for the process of industrialisation to start, there has to be a transfer of resources from agriculture. The Second Five Year Plan recognised this clearly when it said "development involves a transfer of part of the working force from agriculture to secondary and tertiary activities, but this, in turn, presupposes an increase in productivity in agriculture itself, if the food and raw material requirements of a developing economy are to be met" (Government of India, 1956). However, in actual fact the realisation that inadequate agricultural growth and insufficient availability of wage goods including foodgrains could act as a restraint on industrial growth came only later. The industry-agriculture relationship was mainly seen in terms of agriculture making available the required raw materials. Once again, the recognition of the importance of agricultural growth and rural incomes as a source of demand for industrial goods, thereby fuelling industrial growth, came later.

Pre-Reform Industrialisation Paradigm

The process of industrialisation in India in the first four decades was governed by two considerations—import substitution and industrial licensing. Import substitution constituted a major plank of India's foreign trade policy and, therefore, of industrialisation. Planners more or less chose to ignore the option of foreign trade as an engine of India's economic growth. This was primarily due to the then widely prevalent view that exports could not be a significant factor in economic growth of developing economies—a perspective that came to be termed "export pessimism" in the literature. A further impetus to the inward orientation was provided by the existence of a vast domestic market. In retrospect, it is clear that the policy makers not only underestimated the export possibilities but also the import intensity of the import substitution process itself. As a consequence, India's share of total world exports declined from 1.91 per cent in 1950 to a mere 0.53 per cent in 1992.

The inward looking industrialisation process did result in high rates of industrial growth between 1956 and 1966, as may be observed from Table 15.1. However, several weaknesses of such a process of industrialisation soon became evident, as inefficiencies crept into the system and the economy turned into an increasingly 'high-cost' one. Over a period of time, this led to a 'technological lag' and also resulted in poor export performance.

Foreign trade policy issues became the focus of intensive discussion in the early 1980s. It came to be realised that a scheme of import licensing under which imports were permitted only to the extent that domestic production fell short of domestic demand irrespective of difference in cost and prices would lead to inefficiency. The view gained ground that a more liberal policy of imports of capital goods and technology would enable India to reap the benefits of international division of labour.[1] The attempt, therefore, was to move away from import substitution *per se* towards

---

1. For instance, the *Report of the Committee on Trade Policies* (Government of India, 1984) stated that it was difficult to determine the optimum of openness of the economy added that "import liberalisation would be useful insofar as it would reduce monopoly profits, eliminate obsolete technologies and place an outside limit on import-competing activities where the domestic resource costs are too high."

efficient import substitution, so that considerations relating to cost and efficiency were incorporated in the overall policy framework. It also became increasingly clear that production for export could not be isolated from production for the home market.

Table 15.1

Annual Growth Rate in the Index of Industrial Production

(Unit: All figures in per cent)

Period	General Index	Basic Industries	Capital Goods	Intermediate Goods	Consumer Goods
1951 to 1955	6.7	30.9*	-	5.8	3.4
1956 to 1960	5.7	4.7*	-	9.8	2.9
1961 to 1965	9.0	10.5	19.7	7.2	5.0
1966 to 1970	3.7	6.2	-1.4	4.0	4.0
1971 to 1975	3.6	5.3	5.4	1.8	1.6
1976 to 1980	4.8	5.1	5.2	-	4.9
1981-82 to 1985-86	7.3	8.4	7.1	6.3	6.7
1986-87 to 1990-91	8.4	7.4	15.8	5.5	6.6
1991-92 to 1995-96	6.1	6.5	6.0	6.1	6.0
1996-97 to 2000-01$	5.7	4.2	7.7	7.1	5.5
1992-93 to 1996-97	7.4	6.8	8.9	8.5	6.6
1997-98 to 2001-02$	5.1	4.1	4.7	5.8	5.5

Notes: * Figures represent investment goods industries, which are the basic and capital goods industries.

$ Refers to Base Year 1993-94=100 and all other periods since 1981-82 refers to Base Year 1980-81=00.

Sources: Rangarajan (1982; 1994); RBI (2001-02). *Handbook of Statistics on Indian Economy, 2001*, and the *Annual Report, 2001-02*.

Another important element in the process of industrialisation was a system of industrial licensing under which a licence was required before setting up any large unit. This practice had roots in the belief that resources could be best allocated only by a planning authority and that licensing was the best way to manage limited resources. While the industrial licensing system underwent some changes in terms of threshold levels and types of products, it formed an essential part of government policy until the end of the 1980s.

New Economic Policy

The year 1991 is an important landmark in the economic history of post-Independent India. The country went through a severe economic crisis triggered by a serious balance of payments situation. The crisis was converted into an opportunity to introduce some fundamental changes in the content and approach to economic policy. The response to the crisis was to put in place a set of policies aimed at stabilisation and structural reform. While the stabilisation policies were aimed at correcting the weaknesses that had developed on the fiscal and the balance of payments fronts, the structural reforms sought to remove the rigidities that had entered into the various segments of the Indian economy. The structural reforms introduced in the early 1990s broadly covered the areas of industrial licensing, foreign trade, foreign investment, exchange rate management and the financial sector. From the point of view of industrialisation, changes in the areas of licensing and foreign trade and investment had important implications. Even before the onset of reforms, the problems associated with industrial licensing were well recognised. The approach document of the Eighth Plan (1991-1996) submitted in May 1990 had remarked: "A return to the regime of direct, indiscriminate and detailed controls in industry is clearly out of question. Past experience has shown that such control system is not effective in achieving the desired objective. Also the system is widely abused and leads to corruption, delays and inefficiency" (Government of India, 1990). One early step that was undertaken as part of the structural reform process was to dispense with licensing. Changes in foreign trade policy focussed on reducing the tariff rates and dismantling quantitative controls over imports. The tariff rates have been brought down in stages. Some caution in this regard had become necessary to enable the Indian industries set up behind high protective tariff walls to adjust to the changed situation. The policy towards foreign investment underwent a significant change with foreign investors given the freedom to own majority shareholding over a wide spectrum of industries.

Without going into details, the common thread running through the various policy measures introduced since 1991 has been the improvement of the efficiency of the system. The thrust of the New Economic Policy has been towards creating a more competitive environment in the economy as a means to improving the productivity and efficiency of the system. This was to be achieved by removing the barriers to entry and the restrictions on the growth of firms. While the Industrial Policy of 1992 sought to bring about a greater competitive environment domestically, the counterpart Trade Policy set out in the same year, sought to improve international competitiveness subject to the degree of protection offered by the tariffs. The private sector was to be given a larger space to operate in as much as some of the areas, reserved exclusively earlier for the public sector were now to be opened to the private sector. In these areas, the public sector would have to compete with the private sector, even though the public sector might continue to play the dominant role in the foreseeable future. What was sought to be achieved was the improvement in the functioning of the various entities, whether they were in the private or in the public sector.

Trends in Industrial Production

Before focussing on the challenges before industrialisation in the liberalised regime, let us take a brief look at the pattern and rate of growth of industrialisation in our country in the last five decades. Table 15.1 provides the basic data on the growth rate. In the 1950s, the average annual rate of growth of industrial production was 6.2 per cent. In the 1960s, while the first half had a very high growth rate, the second half showed a sharp decline. This deceleration in growth rate continued through the 1970s. Thus, over the 15-year period 1966-1980, the rate of industrial growth was at a modest annual rate of 4 per cent. The growth rate picked up substantially in the decade of the 1980s, when the average annual growth rate was 7.8 per cent. There was a collapse of the industrial growth rate in 1991-92 and a small growth in 1992-93 (Tables 15.2, 15.3 and 15.4). Since 1992-93, the average annual growth rate till the end of that decade was 6.0 per cent. While the period 1992-93 to 1996-97, had an annual growth rate of 7.4 per cent, in the subsequent period the growth rate came down and the average for the next five years is only 5.1 per cent[2] (Table 15.1).

---

2. It may be noted that the sharp decline in industrial production occurred in 1997-98 according to the earlier index of industrial production (Table 15.4). This is also corroborated by the National Accounts Statistics (Table 15.4). However, according to the new index of industrial production (Base 1993-94=100) the break happened only in 1998-99 (Table 15.4).

Table 15.2

Annual Growth Rates of Index of Industrial Production: Use-based Classification

Year	General	Basic Goods	Capital Goods	Intermediate Goods	Consumer Goods	Consumer Durables	Consumer Non-durables
Base: 1980-81=100							
Weight	100.00	39.42	16.43	20.51	23.65	2.55	21.10
1981-82	9.3	10.9	6.7	3.7	13.8	10.9	14.1
1982-83	3.2	7.0	3.7	1.0	-1.6	9.1	-2.8
1983-84	6.7	6.0	11.7	9.8	1.6	16.1	-0.4
1984-85	8.6	11.1	3.0	9.7	7.2	27.3	5.1
1985-86	8.7	6.8	10.6	7.5	12.5	18.7	11.5
1986-87	9.2	9.3	18.2	4.1	6.1	13.7	3.6
1987-88	7.3	5.5	15.9	2.7	9.8	7.6	10.3
1988-89	8.7	9.9	7.1	11.7	3.9	22.3	0.1
1989-90	8.6	5.4	21.9	4.3	6.5	2.4	7.5
1990-91	8.2	6.9	16.0	4.7	6.8	10.7	5.8
1991-92	0.6	6.5	-8.5	-2.1	1.0	-10.9	4.0
1992-93	2.3	2.6	-0.1	5.4	1.8	-0.7	2.4
1993-94	6.0	9.4	-4.1	11.7	4.0	16.1	1.4
1994-95	9.4	5.6	24.8	3.7	8.7	10.2	8.3
1995-96	12.1	8.3	17.9	11.8	14.3	36.1	8.8
1996-97	7.1	8.2	5.9	9.8	4.1	5.4	3.1
1997-98	4.2	7.0	-4.0	6.9	4.6	9.9	2.9
Base: 1993-94=100							
Weight	100.00	35.57	9.26	26.51	28.66	5.36	23.30
1994-95	9.1	9.6	9.2	5.3	12.1	16.2	11.2
1995-96	13.1	10.8	5.4	19.3	12.8	25.8	9.8
1996-97	6.1	3.0	11.4	8.1	6.2	4.6	6.6
1997-98	6.6	6.8	5.8	8.0	5.5	7.8	4.9
1998-99	4.1	1.7	12.6	6.1	2.2	5.6	1.1
1999-2000	6.7	5.5	6.9	8.8	5.7	14.1	3.2
2000-01	5.1	3.9	1.7	4.5	8.0	14.6	5.8
2001-02	2.8	2.7	-3.4	1.6	6.0	11.5	4.1

Sources: RBI (2001-02). *Handbook of Statistics on Indian Economy, 2001* and *Annual Report 2001-2002*.

Table 15.3

Annual Growth Rates of Index of Industrial Production and its Components

Year	Mining & Quarrying	Manufacturing	Electricity	General
\multicolumn{5}{c}{*Base: 1980-81=100*}
Weight	11.46	77.11	11.43	100.00
1981-82	17.7	8.0	10.2	9.3
1982-83	12.4	1.3	5.7	3.2
1983-84	11.8	5.7	7.6	6.7
1984-85	8.8	8.0	12.0	8.6
1985-86	4.1	9.7	8.5	8.7
1986-87	6.2	9.4	10.3	9.2
1987-88	3.7	7.9	7.6	7.3
1988-89	7.9	8.7	9.5	8.7
1989-90	6.3	8.6	10.9	8.6
1990-91	4.5	8.9	7.8	8.2
1991-92	0.6	-0.8	8.5	0.6
1992-93	0.6	2.2	5.0	2.3
1993-94	3.5	6.1	7.5	6.0
1994-95	7.5	9.8	8.5	9.4
1995-96	7.4	13.6	8.1	12.1
1996-97	0.4	8.6	3.9	7.1
1997-98	4.9	3.6	6.9	4.2
\multicolumn{5}{c}{*Base: 1993-94=100*}
Weight	10.47	79.36	10.17	100.00
1994-95	9.8	9.1	8.5	9.1
1995-96	9.8	14.1	8.1	13.1
1996-97	-2.0	7.3	4.0	6.1
1997-98	7.0	6.6	6.6	6.6
1998-99	-0.8	4.4	6.4	4.1
1999-2000	1.0	7.1	7.3	6.7
2000-01	3.7	5.4	4.0	5.1
2001-02	1.3	2.9	3.1	2.8

Sources: As in Table 15.2.

Table 15.4

Industrial Growth Rates—Index of Industrial Production and National Accounts

Year	Index of Industrial Production 1980-81=100	Index of Industrial Production 1993-94=100	National Accounts* 1993-94=100
1981-82	9.3		8.8
1982-83	3.2		7.3
1983-84	6.7		8.8
1984-85	8.6		6.4
1985-86	8.7		4.6
1986-87	9.2		8.1
1987-88	7.3		6.9
1988-89	8.7		9.8
1989-90	8.6		11.2
1990-91	8.2		6.8
1991-92	0.6		-1.2
1992-93	2.3		4.1
1993-94	6.0		6.4
1994-95	9.4	9.1	11.3
1995-96	12.1	13.1	12.9
1996-97	7.1	6.1	8.2
1997-98	4.2	6.6	3.0
1998-99		4.1	2.8
1999-2000		6.7	4.2
2000-01		4.9	6.2
2001-02		2.8	2.9

Note: * Refers to value added in industry, that is, mining & quarrying, manufacturing and electricity, gas & water supply.

Sources: As in Table 15.2.

The composition of India's industrial output has also undergone considerable change (Table 15.5). The share of basic and capital goods combined had reached a peak of 55.8 per cent of total output in 1980-81. It has since then come down. In the Index of Industrial Production (IIP) with the base 1993-94, their share has come down to 44.8 per cent. The composition of output has greater significance in a closed economy than in an open economy. In a closed economy, the output of basic and capital goods has a link with investment. However, this need not necessarily be so in an open economy in which output composition reflects more the comparative advantage.

Table 15.5
Weights of Major Industrial Groups in IIP

Groups	1956= 100	1960= 100	1970= 100	1980-81= 100	1993-94= 100
Basic Goods	22.13	25.11	32.28	39.42	35.57
Capital Goods	4.71	11.76	15.74	16.43	9.26
Intermediate Goods	24.59	25.88	20.95	20.51	26.51
Consumer Goods	48.37	37.25	31.03	23.65	28.66
Consumer Durables		5.68	2.92	2.55	5.36
Consumer Non-durables		31.57	28.11	21.10	23.30

Sources: RBI *Report on Currency and Finance,* various issues, and the *Handbook of Statistics on Indian Economy, 2001.*

While analysing the growth in industrial production one must also look at the performance of the service sector. The growth rate of the service sector has shown a steady increase over the last five decades. The annual growth rate of the service sector was 6.7 per cent in the 1980s and 7.5 per cent in 1990s (Tables 15.6 and 15.7). In fact, it was only in 1990s that the growth rate of the service sector has exceeded that of the industrial sector.

Another aspect of the industrialisation process in the post-liberalisation period has been the steady flow of foreign direct investment (FDI). In 1991, the level of FDI flows into the country was $ 97 million. Through the 1990s it increased from year to year and reached a peak of $ 3,557 million in 1997-98. After some set back during the next three years, it has again started increasing. In 2001-02, the FDI inflows increased to $ 3,904 million, an increase of 67 per cent over the previous year. In 2002-03, up to the end of October, FDI inflows were at $ 1,984 million, marginally lower than that for the same period last year.

Thus in the post-liberalisation period, the total inflow of FDI has amounted to $ 23,710 million as at the end of October 2002. The total of portfolio inflows aggregate $ 23,022 million, over the same period, of which $ 9,019 million came in as proceeds of issuance of Global Depository Receipts (GDR) and American Depository Receipts (ADR) by Indian companies. The total inflow through the Foreign Institutional Investor (FII) during this period aggregates $ 12,792 million. Though the purchase of shares by FIIs may not add to investment directly, there is the possibility that those from whom the shares were bought might have utilised these funds for investment.

Table 15.6

Annual Growth Rates of Components of Gross Domestic Product
At factor cost and constant (1993-94) prices

(Unit: All figures in per cent)

Year	Agriculture & Allied	Industry	Services	Total Gross Domestic Product
1971-72	-1.9	3.6	3.1	1.0
1972-73	-5.0	4.2	2.9	-0.3
1973-74	7.2	3.9	1.8	4.6
1974-75	-1.5	3.3	3.4	1.2
1975-76	12.9	4.2	7.8	9.0
1976-77	-5.8	8.4	5.3	1.2
1977-78	10.0	5.7	5.7	7.5
1978-79	2.3	11.2	5.4	5.5
1979-80	-12.8	-2.4	1.1	-5.2
1980-81	12.9	2.0	5.7	7.2
1981-82	5.3	8.8	5.4	6.0
1982-83	-0.7	7.3	4.8	3.1
1983-84	9.6	8.8	5.5	7.7
1984-85	1.5	6.4	6.0	4.3
1985-86	0.7	4.6	7.7	4.5
1986-87	-0.6	8.1	6.8	4.3
1987-88	-1.3	6.9	6.4	3.8
1988-89	15.5	9.8	7.2	10.5
1989-90	1.5	11.2	8.6	6.7
1990-91	4.1	6.8	6.1	5.6
1991-92	-1.5	-1.2	4.5	1.3
1992-93	5.8	4.1	5.1	5.1
1993-94	4.1	6.4	6.9	5.9
1994-95	5.0	11.3	6.9	7.3
1995-96	-0.9	12.9	10.0	7.3
1996-97	9.6	8.2	6.7	7.8
1997-98	-2.4	3.0	9.8	4.8
1998-99	7.1	2.8	8.0	6.6
1999-2000	1.3	4.2	9.4	6.1
2000-01	-0.2	6.2	5.0	4.0
2001-02	5.7	2.9	6.2	5.4

Sources: As in Table 15.2.

Table 15.7

Growth Rates of Components of Gross Domestic Product:
Annual Averages
At factor cost and constant (1993-94) prices

(Unit: All figures in per cent)

Period	Agriculture & Allied	Industry	Services	Gross Domestic Product
1991-92 to 1995-96	2.5	6.7	6.7	5.4
1996-97 to 2000-01	3.1	4.9	7.8	5.9
1992-93 to 1996-97	4.7	8.6	7.1	6.7
1997-98 to 2001-02	2.3	3.8	7.7	5.4

Notes : Averages of annual rates of growth.
Sources: As in Table 15.2.

New Challenges

Globalisation and Competition

Changes in the foreign trade and foreign investment policies have altered the environment in which Indian industries have to operate. The path of transition is, no doubt, difficult. A greater integration of the Indian economy with the rest of the world is unavoidable. We must recognise that there are many countries, which are knocking at the doors of the World Trade Organisation (WTO) to enter. It is important that Indian industry be forward looking and get organised to compete with the rest of the world at levels of tariff comparable to those of other developing countries. Obviously, the Indian government should be alert to ensure that Indian industries are not the victims of unfair trade practices. The safeguards available in the WTO agreement must be fully utilised to protect the interests of Indian industries. India must take a proactive stand in the next round of trade negotiations and articulate its own demands. These would focus on what it wants from the global trading system, such as prohibition of unilateral trade action, establishing symmetry between the movement of capital and natural persons and zero tariffs in industrialised countries on labour intensive exports of developing countries.

Indian industry has a right to demand that the macroeconomic policy environment should be conducive to rapid economic growth. The configuration of policy decisions in the recent period has been attempting to do that. It is, however, time for Indian industrial units to recognise that the challenges of the new century demand greater action at the enterprise level. They have to learn to swim in the tempestuous waters of competition and away from the sheltered waters of the swimming pools. India is no longer a country producing goods and services for the domestic market alone. Indian firms are becoming and have to become global players. At the minimum, they must be able to meet global competition. The search for identifying new competitive advantages must begin earnestly. India's ascendancy in Information Technology (IT) is only partly by design. However, it must be said to the credit of policy makers that once the potential in this area was discovered, the policy environment became strongly industry friendly.

How do India and Indian firms maintain a competitive edge? Analysing India's comparative advantage in engineering *vis-a-vis* China, a leading Indian industrialist[3] has commented that in products that involved flexible manufacturing with a high level of product and industrial engineering, multi vendor co-ordination and continuous improvement, the Chinese faired badly. They have been reported to excel at manufacturing processes that involve both relatively fewer steps, and doing so on a large scale. The commentator adds that what India lacks in mass manufacturing capacities can be made up by her capabilities in design innovations and by moving up the value chain. It is worth pondering over this comment. Experts from the various industries must judge the validity of this statement. However, this is just one illustration. Over a wide spectrum of activities, India's advantage, actual and that which can be realised in a short span of time must be drawn up. Of course, in a number of cases, it will require building plants on a global scale. But, this need not necessarily be so in all cases. In fact the advent of IT is modifying the industrial structure. The revolution in telecommunications and IT is simultaneously creating a huge single market economy, while making the parts smaller and

---

3. Gopal Srinivasan of TVS in an interview had made the remark that the Chinese threat was overstated (Srinivasan, 2001).

more powerful. In today's environment, the primary focus has to be on the strategy and quality of microeconomic business management and the goal must be to achieve higher levels of efficiency and productivity. A new productivity culture must emerge and with it an organisational structure and incentive system that promote productivity. In this context, it is worth noting the turnaround in productivity, which the USA has achieved during the last decade.

Productivity Growth

Higher productivity in the industrial sector helps to achieve faster economic growth. A recent study on sources of output growth in developing countries found that about 60-70 per cent of per capita growth is explained by capital accumulation, about 10-20 per cent by human capital and the remaining is explained by improvement in Total Factor Productivity (IMF, 2000). Industrial growth in India, like many developing countries has seldom witnessed rapid productivity growth. Technically, productivity growth is usually measured in terms of Total Factor Productivity (TFP) growth. TFP is nothing but the ratio of output to a combination of all inputs used.

Several research studies have gone into the issue of productivity growth in Indian industry in the 1980s and in the post-liberalisation period. Unfortunately there is no unanimity with regard to the conclusions. Results differ based on the methodology and data used. While several studies earlier found a substantial growth in productivity in the 1980s, some recent studies throw doubt on these conclusions. In the post-liberalisation period, one would a priori expect an improvement in productivity growth. However, one difficulty in analysing productivity performance in the post-liberalisation period is the lack of adequate observations. Even the few limited studies do not go beyond 1998. One detailed study of selected manufacturing industries finds a substantial improvement in the productivity growth (Trivedi *et al.*, 2000). The same study finds an improvement of productivity in manufacturing in general. Similarly, a study which makes use of data on 487 firms come to the conclusion that, there is credible evidence of improvement in productivity in the post-reform period (Kathuria, 2002). On the contrary, another study examining the productivity of the selected manufacturing groups facing significant tariff reduction using data on 2300 firms does not find evidence of acceleration of productivity growth in the post-reform period (Balakrishnan et al., 2000). A more recent study found evidence of a positive growth in TFP in Indian manufacturing sector in the post-reform period. The TFP growth is estimated at 3.4 per cent per annum for the period 1991-92 to 1997-98. However, this was a shade lower than the TFP growth of 3.8 per cent per annum during the 1980s (Ahluwalia et al., 2002)

Technology Intensity

Technology is the lifeblood of industry. Future progress will be propelled by technology, as it has been so in the past. The Indian manufacturing sector must be fully in tune with the latest development in technology. It is in this context that one must note with concern the declining trend in the ratio of Research and Development (R&D) expenditures. The proportion of national resources spent on R&D by India has fallen steadily from a peak of 0.98 per cent in 1988 to 0.66 per cent in 1997. The bulk of R&D expenditure in India is accounted for by the public funded R&D institutions with industry spending only 28 per cent of national R&D expenditure. The decline in the proportion in national R&D expenditure may be due to the budgetary squeeze. However, even the rate of growth of R&D expenditure by industry has declined in the 1990s. A recent study analysing the trend in the R&D expenditure as a proportion of turnover of 4,209 companies shows that the proportion of R&D expenditure has gone down from 0.868 per cent in the pre-reform period to 0.835 per cent in the post-reform period (Kumar and Aggarwal, 2000). The bulk of the decline is on account of local firms. The R&D intensity of these firms declined from 0.90 per cent to 0.831 per cent. Normally, it is expected that outward orientation will result in greater in-house R&D. Even adaptation of imported technology will require R&D efforts. It is necessary that industry associations make an in-depth analysis of R&D expenditures.

Road Map for Indian Industry

What we need today is a road map for the Indian industry. It must delineate the path different industries must take to achieve productivity and efficiency levels comparable to the best in the world. Of course, we must have our priorities. We must know where we have a distinct comparative advantage as in the case of IT (or biotechnology - BT). We must also know where the pay off is highest in terms of employment. Agro-processing industries need a more focussed attention in this regard. In effect, what we require is a strategic plan for the growth of industries. The plan should address in relation to each major industry issues relating to technology upgradation, size and structure of firms and export potential. While industry specific policies may be indicated, the focus must be on how to improve the functioning of individual enterprises to reach international standards. Where we cannot achieve such standards, we must be willing and honest enough to say so. However, the goal must be how through a combination of technology modernisation and changes in organisational structure which promote productivity, Indian industry can compete effectively in the world market. The 'old economy' dominates the Indian industry. We should not let the old economy to become 'older'. Cement, steel and textiles will not vanish. We must rejuvenate and revitalise the old economy with the new economy tools. All said and done, IT is an intermediate product. The task of preparing such plans or vision documents can be performed by any number of organisations. Even the Planning Commission, which has a responsibility to chalk out medium-term strategy can undertake this task. Perhaps industry associations with the help of industry leaders and experts should prepare these documents. The purpose of these documents should not be to set targets. They ought to be qualitative in character. Mere identification of growth prospects is not enough. These documents should go deeper and pinpoint requisite actions at the enterprise level. It must kindle the spirit of entrepreneurship combined with excellence. As an eminent critic put it, the world cannot marginalise India; but India can marginalise herself (Bergsten, 1999). We must guard ourselves against this danger.

The recent slowdown in industrial production has caused much concern. After a strong growth between 1993-94 and 1996-97, there has been a steady decline in the growth rate. It is only the strong growth in the service sector that has helped to offset this trend and keep the overall growth rate at a reasonable level. Usually the employment elasticity of the service sector is high. However, the type of employment generated depends on the nature of services that grow. For example, the strong growth in IT[4] can generate demand only for the relatively higher skilled.

One must have some understanding of the causes of the decelerating trend in industrial production in the last four years, if measures to counter the trend are to be taken. The slowdown in 1997-1998 and 1998-99 can to some extent be explained by the substantial building up of capacities in the previous three years. In fact, the investment: GDP rate reached its peak value of 26.53 per cent in 1995-1996. However, the continued weakness needs additional explanation.

The familiar argument of imports being a cause of deceleration of domestic production is not substantiated because the import growth rate was weak. In fact, there is a positive correlation between growth rate in imports and industrial production (Tables 15.8 and 15.9). External demand has an important impact in an increasingly open economy. The deceleration in world trade growth since 2001 must have had some effect on domestic industrial production. Another factor that may have contributed to the deceleration of industrial production, is the deceleration in agricultural growth rate. The growth rate in agriculture between 1992-93 and 1996-97 was 4.7 per cent while between 1997-98 and 2001-02 it was 2.3 per cent. The period since 1996-97 is marked by a decline in investment rate (Table 15.10). While public investment declined from its peak value of 8.7 per cent in 1993-94 to 7.1 per cent in 2000-01, private corporate investment declined from its peak value of 9.6 per cent in 1995-1996 to 5.9 per cent in 2000-01. In raising the growth rate of the economy we need to focus on investment. While investment demand is part of aggregate demand, it is not so much the stimulation of overall demand as that of investment *per se* which is crucial for ensuring and sustaining faster growth.

---

4. Including what is coming to be described in a generic fashion as Business Process Outsourcing (BPO)—encompassing software development, back offices, call centres, true design and process development.

Table 15.8
Year-on-Year Rates of Growth of Imports in Terms of its Value in US Dollars

(Unit: per cent)

Commodity	1990-91	1991-92	1992-93	1993-94	1994-95	1995-96	1996-97	1997-98	1998-99	1999-2000	2000-01	2001-02
Iron and Steel	-12.9	-32.2	-2.5	2.1	46.4	24.3	-5.2	3.7	-25.2	-10.5	-18.2	6.9
Non-Ferrous Metals	-13.9	-44.5	15.9	21.4	49.8	25.9	22.3	-16.8	-35.1	-8.5	-2.4	21.0
Capital Goods	**10.4**	**-27.5**	**7.1**	**37.8**	**22.4**	**35.2**	**-4.0**	**-1.3**	**2.7**	**-10.9**	**-0.3**	**4.2**
Manufactures of Metals	16.4	-22.6	11.8	22.3	15.6	34.9	13.7	2.8	16.9	6.6	-3.7	4.4
Machine Tools	37.2	-34.3	-3.9	-6.9	38.2	74.1	41.2	-19.6	-17.8	-24.6	-16.2	-11.9
Machinery except Electrical and Electronic	8.8	-30.6	13.4	13.9	44.9	43.9	-7.1	-0.6	-15.9	-9.8	-1.3	9.4
Electrical Machinery except Electronic	-12.8	-33.6	31.3	-75.3	23.2	53.7	-15.8	16.3	11.3	4.0	9.9	23.3
Electronic Goods					34.6	42.7	-18.7	46.6	6.5	25.8	25.3	13.6
Computer Goods			24.4	175.1	142.2	177.1	-30.1	-01.5	-4.4	21.2	-13.2	-
Transport Equipment	4.6	-60.1	-13.1	27.0	-12.3	-0.8	34.3	-29.2	-24.1	42.4	-38.4	-12.4
Project Goods	36.5	3.2	12.3	11.2	14.2	29.0	-11.4	-17.9	54.5	-63.3	-24.2	-24.5
Non-Oil Imports	3.1	-22.2	12.3	11.2	29.5	28.3	-0.2	14.5	8.0	3.0	-5.9	6.3
Total Imports	**13.4**	**-19.4**	**12.7**	**6.5**	**22.9**	**28.0**	**6.7**	**6.0**	**2.2**	**17.2**	**1.7**	**1.1**

Source: As in Table 15.2.

Table 15.9

Rate of Growth of Imports of Investment Related Products Averages of Annual Rates

(Unit: per cent)

Commodity	1993-94 to 1996-97	1997-98 to 2001-02
Iron and steel	16.9	-8.7
Non-Ferrous metals	29.9	-8.3
Capital Goods	**22.9**	**-1.1**
Manufactures of metals	21.6	5.4
Machine tools	36.6	-18.0
Machinery except electrical & electronic	23.9	-3.7
Electrical machinery except electronic	-3.6	12.9
Electronic goods	19.5	23.6
Computer goods	96.4	26.3
Transport equipment	49.1	-12.3
Project goods	14.7	-15.1
Non-Oil imports	17.2	5.2
Total Imports	**16.0**	**5.6**

Source: As in Table 15.2.

In enhancing the level of investment, I would like to emphasise four critical factors:

- First, all investment decisions are based on future prospects. Continuation of economic policy thus becomes the key to sustaining expectations in the right direction. There has to be a consensus on the core elements of economic policy among decision-makers, legislators and political leaders.

- Second, if the 'feel good' factor is to be restored as a stimulant of 'animal spirits', good governance has an important role to play. Investors need to be assured of dynamism and efficiency in overall governance.

- Third, for generating a general mood of optimism, it may be useful for the government to bring together in one place in the budget the investment that will be made by the various departments and ministries. A consolidation of this can be called 'investment budget'. The present classification in the budget of 'capital' and 'revenue'

Table 15.10

Annual Growth Rates of Domestic Investment and of its Components
(At Current Prices)

(Unit: per cent)

Year	Total*	Household	Private Corporate	Public
		Gross Capital Formation		
1970-71	15.8	7.1	2.3	6.4
1971-72	16.9	7.5	2.5	7.0
1972-73	16.2	6.5	2.5	7.2
1973-74	16.7	6.7	2.5	7.5
1974-75	18.3	7.4	3.5	7.4
1975-76	19.0	7.0	2.6	9.4
1976-77	19.1	7.8	1.5	9.8
1977-78	18.7	8.4	2.3	8.0
1978-79	20.7	9.4	2.1	9.2
1979-80	21.4	8.8	2.5	10.0
1980-81	18.7	7.8	2.4	8.4
1981-82	22.4	6.9	5.4	10.1
1982-83	21.7	5.6	5.4	10.7
1983-84	19.7	6.8	3.2	9.7
1984-85	21.6	7.0	4.2	10.4
1985-86	23.7	7.6	5.2	10.8
1986-87	23.2	7.0	5.0	11.2
1987-88	22.1	9.1	3.5	9.5
1988-89	23.7	10.3	3.9	9.5
1989-90	23.7	10.1	4.0	9.5
1990-91	24.1	10.6	4.1	9.3
1991-92	21.9	7.4	5.7	8.8
1992-93	23.8	8.8	6.5	8.6
1993-94	21.3	7.4	5.6	8.2
1994-95	23.4	7.8	6.9	8.7
1995-96	26.5	9.3	9.6	7.7
1996-97	21.8	6.7	8.0	7.0
1997-98	22.6	8.0	8.0	6.6
1998-99	21.4	8.4	6.4	6.6
1999-2000	23.3	9.6	6.5	7.1
2000-01	22.9	9.9	5.9	7.1
	Averages Over Periods			
1971-72 to 1975-76	17.6	7.0	2.8	7.8
1976-77 to 1980-81	19.7	8.4	2.2	9.1
1981-82 to 1985-86	21.9	6.9	4.7	10.4
1986-87 to 1990-91	23.5	9.7	4.1	9.7
1991-92 to 1995-96	23.7	8.2	7.1	8.3
1996-97 to 2000-01	22.4	8.7	6.8	6.9
1992-93 to 1996-97	23.2	7.9	7.6	7.6
1993-94 to 1997-98	23.1	7.8	7.8	7.5

Note: *unadjusted for errors & omissions.
Source: As in Table 15.2.
  National Accounts Statistics 2002

expenditures does not correspond to the economist's concept of investment.

- Fourth, one important factor contributing to the confidence of investors is stability in the rates of taxation and tariff rates. Unexpected downward revisions in tariffs make a lot of difference to profit calculations. While reduction in tariff rates to bring them in tune with levels prevailing in other developing economies is an important element of the reform process, there is need to inject stability in the rates. When the next change is made, it must be made clear that rates would remain at that level for at least a period of three to four years. Stability in tariff rate can have a significant favourable impact on investment decisions. A similar logic applies to stability in the rates of taxation.

References

Ahluwalia, I.J., Shubham Chaudhuri and Saumitra Chaudhuri (2002). "Trade Liberalisation, Productivity and Export Performance: A Study of the Indian Manufacturing Sector in the 1990s". (mimeo).

Agarwal, R.N. (2001). "Technical Efficiency and Productivity Growth in the Central Public Sector Enterprises in India during 1990s", *Discussion Paper Series* No. 28/2001. New Delhi: Institute of Economic Growth.

Balakrishnan, Pulapre; K. Pushpangadan and M. Suresh Babu (2000). "Trade Liberalisation and Productivity Growth in Manufacturing: Evidence from Firm-Level Panel Data", *Economic and Political Weekly*: 3679-82, October 7.

Bergesten, C. Fred (1999). "India and the Global Trading System", *Fourteenth EXIM Bank Commencement Day Annual Lecture*. Mumbai. March 10.

Government of India (1956). *The Second Five Year Plan (1956-1961)*. New Delhi: Planning Commission.

———. (1984). *Report of the Committee on Trade Policies* (Chairman: Abid Hussain), Ministry of Commerce.

———. (1990). *Approach Paper: The Eighth Five Year Plan (1991-1996)*. New Delhi: Planning Commission.

———. (2002). *National Accounts Statistics 2002*. New Delhi: Central Statistical Organisation, Ministry of Statistics & Programme Implementation.

International Monetary Fund (2000). *World Economic Outlook—Asset Prices and the Business Cycle*. May. Washington D.C.

Kathuria, Vinish (2002). "Liberalisation, FDI and Productivity Spillovers: An Analysis of Indian Manufacturing Firms", *Working Paper Series* No. E/220/2002. New Delhi: Institute of Economic Growth.

Kumar, Nagesh and A. Aggarwal (2000). "Liberalisation, Outward Orientation and In-house R&D Activity of Multinational and Local Firms: A Quantitative Exploration for Indian Manufacturing", *Discussion Paper Series* No. 18/2000. New Delhi: Institute of Economic Growth.

Kuznets, Simon (1966). *Modern Economic Growth: Rate, Structure and Spread*. New Delhi: Oxford and IBH Publishing Co.

Maizels, Alfred (1970). *Growth and Trade*. NIESR Students' Edition 1. London: Cambridge University Press.

Mitra, Arup (1999). "Total Factor Productivity Growth and Technical Efficiency in Indian Industries", *Economic and Political Weekly* 34(31): M98-105, July 3.

Neogi, C. and B. Ghosh (1998). "Impact of Liberalisation on Performance of Indian Industries: A Firm Level Study", *Economic and Political Weekly* 33(9): M16-24, February 28.

Pradhan, G. and K. Barik (1999). "Total Factor Productivity Growth in Developing Economies: A Study of Selected Industries in India", *Economic and Political Weekly* 34(31): M92-97, July 31.

Rangarajan, C. (1982). "Agricultural Growth and Industrial Performance in India", *Research Report* No. 33. Washington D.C.: International Food Policy Research Institute.

———. (1994). "Industrial Growth: Another Look", in Deepak Nayyar (ed.) *Industrial Growth and Stagnation: The Debate in India*. OUP.

———. (2002). "Globalisation and its Impact", *ICRA Bulletin—Money and Finance* 2(8): 36-54, January-March.

Srinivasan, Gopal (2001). A comment made in *Businessworld* 20(37): 16-22. January.

Trivedi, Pushpa; Anand Prakash and David Sinate (2000). "Productivity in Major Manufacturing Industries in India: 1973-74 to 1997-98", *RBI-DRG Study* No. 20. Mumbai: Reserve Bank of India.

16 Banking Sector Reforms in India

India has presently entered a high-growth phase of 8-9 per cent per annum, from an intermediate phase of 6 per cent since the early 1990s. The growth rate of real GDP averaged 8.6 per cent for the four-year period ending 2006-2007; if one considers the last two years, the growth rates are even higher at over 9 per cent. There are strong signs that the growth rates will remain at elevated levels for several years to come. This strengthening of economic activity has been supported by higher rates of savings and investment. While the financial sector reforms helped strengthening institutions, developing markets and promoting greater integration with the rest of the world, the recent growth phase suggests that if the present growth rates are to be sustained, the financial sector will have to intermediate larger and increasing volume of funds than is presently the case. It must acquire further sophistication to address the new dimensions of risks.

It is widely recognised that financial intermediation is essential to the promotion of both extensive and intensive growth. Efficient intermediation of funds from savers to users enables the productive application of available resources. The greater the efficiency of the financial system in such resource generation and allocation, the higher is its likely contribution to economic growth. Improved allocative efficiency creates a virtuous cycle of higher real rates of return and increasing savings, resulting, in turn, in higher resource generation. Thus, development of the financial system is essential to sustaining higher economic growth.

Banking in the Pre-Reform Period

It is useful to briefly recall the nature of the Indian banking sector at the time of initiation of financial sector reform in India in the early 1990s.

This would facilitate a greater clarity of the rationale and basis of reforms. The Indian financial system in the pre-reform period, i.e., upto the end of 1980s, essentially catered to the needs of planned development in a mixed economy framework where the government sector had a domineering role in economic activity. The strategy of planned economic development required huge development expenditures, which was met through the dominance of government ownership of banks, automatic monetisation of fiscal deficit and subjecting the banking sector to large pre-emptions—both in terms of the statutory holding of government securities (statutory liquidity ratio, or SLR) and administrative direction of credit to preferred sectors. Furthermore, a complex structure of administered interest rates prevailed, guided more by social priorities, necessitating cross-subsidisation to sustain commercial viability of institutions. These not only distorted the interest rate mechanism but also adversely affected financial market development. All the signs of 'financial repression' were found in the system.

There is perhaps an element of commonality in terms of such a 'repressed' regime in the financial sector of many emerging market economies at that time. The decline of the Bretton Woods system in the 1970s provided a trigger for financial liberalisation in both advanced and emerging markets. Several countries adopted a 'big bang' approach to liberalisation, while others pursued a more cautious or 'gradualist' approach. The East Asian crises in the late 1990s provided graphic testimony as to how faulty sequencing and inadequate attention to institutional strengthening could significantly derail the growth process, even for countries with otherwise sound macroeconomic fundamentals.

India, in this context, has pursued a relatively more 'gradualist' approach to liberalisation. The bar was gradually raised. Each year the central bank slowly, in a manner of speaking, tightened the screws. Nevertheless, the transition to a regime of prudential norms and free interest rates had its own traumatic effect. It must be said to the credit of our financial system that these changes were absorbed and the system has emerged stronger for this reason.

Contours of Reforms

Financial sector reforms encompassed broadly the institutions, especially, banking, development of financial markets, monetary fiscal and external sector management and legal and institutional infrastructure.

Reform measures in India were sequenced to create an enabling environment for banks to overcome the external constraints and operate with greater flexibility. Such measures related to dismantling of administered structure of interest rates, removal of several pre-emptions in the form of reserve requirements and credit allocation to certain sectors. Interest rate deregulation was in stages and allowed build up of sufficient resilience in the system. This is an important component of the reform process which has imparted greater efficiency in resource allocation. Parallel strengthening of prudential regulation, improved market behaviour, gradual financial opening and, above all, the underlying improvements in macroeconomic management helped the liberalisation process to run smooth. The interest rates have now been largely deregulated except for certain specific classes, these are—savings deposit accounts, non-resident Indian (NRI) deposits, small loans up to Rs.2 lakh and export credit. Without the dismantling of the administered interest rate structure, the rest of the financial sector reforms could not have meant much.

As regards the policy environment on public ownership, the major share of financial intermediation has been on account of public sector during the pre-reform period. As a part of the reforms programme, initially there was infusion of capital by government in public sector banks, which was subsequently followed by expanding the capital base with equity participation by private investors up to a limit of 49 per cent. The share of the public sector banks in total banking assets has come down from 90 per cent in 1991 to around 75 per cent in 2006—a decline of about one percentage point every year over a 15-year period. Diversification of ownership, while retaining public sector character of these banks has led to greater market accountability and improved efficiency without loss of public confidence and safety. It is significant that the infusion of funds by government since the initiation of reforms into the public sector banks amounted to less than one per cent of India's GDP, a figure much lower than that for many other countries.

Another major objective of banking sector reforms has been to enhance efficiency and productivity through increased competition. Establishment of new banks was allowed in the private sector and foreign banks were also permitted more liberal entry. Nine new private banks are in operation at present, accounting for around 10-12 per cent of commercial banking assets. Yet another step towards enhancing competition was allowing foreign direct investment in private sector banks up to 74 per cent from all sources. Beginning 2009, foreign banks would be allowed banking presence in India either through establishment of subsidiaries incorporated in India or through branches.

Impressive institutional reforms have also helped in reshaping the financial marketplace. A high-powered Board for Financial Supervision (BFS), constituted in 1994, exercise the powers of supervision and inspection in relation to the banking companies, financial institutions and non-banking companies, creating an arms-length relationship between regulation and supervision. On similar lines, a Board for Regulation and Supervision of Payment and Settlement Systems (BPSS) prescribes policies relating to the regulation and supervision of all types of payment and settlement systems, set standards for existing and future systems, authorise the payment and settlement systems and determine criteria for membership to these systems.

The system has also progressed with the transparency and disclosure standards as prescribed under international best practices in a phased manner. Disclosure requirements on capital adequacy, NPLs, profitability ratios and details of provisions and contingencies have been expanded to include several areas such as foreign currency assets and liabilities, movements in NPLs and lending to sensitive sectors. The range of disclosures has gradually been increased. In view of the increased focus on undertaking consolidated supervision of bank groups, preparation of consolidated financial statements (CFS) has been mandated by the Reserve Bank for all groups where the controlling entity is a bank.

The legal environment for conducting banking business has also been strengthened. Debt recovery tribunals were part of the early reforms process for adjudication of delinquent loans. More recently, the Securitisation Act was enacted in 2003 to enhance protection of creditor rights. To combat the abuse of financial system for crime-related activities, the Prevention of Money Laundering Act was enacted in 2003 to provide the enabling legal framework. The Negotiable Instruments (Amendments and Miscellaneous Provisions) Act 2002 expands the erstwhile definition of 'cheque' by introducing the concept of 'electronic money' and 'cheque truncation'. The Credit Information Companies (Regulation) Bill 2004 has been enacted by the Parliament which is expected to enhance the quality of credit decisions and facilitate faster credit delivery.

Improvements in the regulatory and supervisory framework encompassed a greater degree of compliance with Basel Core Principles. Some recent initiatives in this regard include consolidated accounting for banks along with a system of Risk-Based Supervision (RBS) for intensified monitoring of vulnerabilities.

The structural break in the wake of financial sector reforms and opening up of the economy necessitated changes in the monetary policy framework. The relationship between the central bank and the Government witnessed a salutary development in September 1994 in terms of supplemental agreements limiting initially the net issuance of ad hoc treasury Bills. This initiative culminated in the abolition of the *ad hoc* Treasury Bills effective April 1997 replaced by a limited ways and means advances. The phasing out of automatic monetisation of budget deficit has, thus, strengthened monetary authority by imparting flexibility and operational autonomy. With the passage of the Fiscal Responsibility and Budget Management Act in 2003, from April 1, 2006 the Reserve Bank has withdrawn from participating in the primary issues of Central government securities.

Reforms in the government securities market were aimed at imparting liquidity and depth by broadening the investor base and ensuring market-related interest rate mechanism. The important initiatives introduced included a market-related government borrowing and consequently, a phased elimination of automatic monetisation of Central government budget deficits. This, in turn, provided a fillip to switch from direct to indirect tools of monetary regulation, activating open market operations and enabled the development of an active secondary market. The gamut of changes in market development included introduction of newer instruments, establishment of new institutions and technological developments, along with concomitant improvements in transparency and the legal framework.

Processes of Reform

What are the unique features of our reform process? First, financial sector reform was undertaken early in the reform cycle in India. Second, the banking sector reforms were not driven by any immediate crisis as has often been the case in several emerging economies. Third, the design and detail of the reform were evolved by domestic expertise, while taking on board the international experience in this regard. Fourth, enough space was created for the growth and healthy competition among public and private sectors as well as foreign and domestic sectors.

How useful has been the financial liberalisation process in India towards improving the functioning of institutions and markets? Prudential regulation and supervision has improved; the combination of regulation, supervision and safety nets has limited the impact of unforeseen shocks on the financial system. In addition, the role of market forces in enabling price discovery has enhanced. The dismantling of the erstwhile administered interest rate structure has permitted financial intermediaries to pursue lending and deposit taking based on commercial considerations and their asset-liability profiles. The financial liberalisation process has also enabled to reduce the overhang of non-performing loans: this entailed both a 'stock' (restoration of net worth) solution as well as a 'flow' (improving future profitability) solution.

Financial entities have become increasingly conscious about risk management practices and have instituted risk management models based on their product profiles, business philosophy and customer orientation. Additionally, access to credit has improved, through newly established domestic banks, foreign banks and bank-like intermediaries. Government debt markets have developed, enabling greater operational independence in monetary policy making. The growth of government debt markets has also provided a benchmark for private debt markets to develop.

There have also been significant improvements in the information infrastructure. The accounting and auditing of intermediaries has improved. Information on small borrowers has improved and information sharing through operationalisation of credit information bureaus has helped to reduce information asymmetry. The technological infrastructure has developed in tandem with modern-day requirements in information technology and communications networking.

The improvements in the performance of the financial system over the decade-and-a-half of reforms are also reflected in the improvement in a number of indicators. Capital adequacy of the banking sector recorded a marked improvement and stood at 12.3 per cent at end-March 2006. This is a far cry from the situation that prevailed in early 1990s.

On the asset quality front, notwithstanding the gradual tightening of prudential norms, non-performing loans (NPL) to total loans of commercial banks which was at a high of 15.7 per cent at end-March 1997 declined to 3.3 per cent at end-March 2006. Net NPLs also witnessed a significant decline and stood at 1.2 per cent of net advances at end-March 2006, driven by the improvements in loan loss provisioning, which comprises over half of the total provisions and contingencies. The proportion of net NPA to net worth, sometimes called the solvency ratio of public sector banks has dropped from 57.9 per cent in 1998-99 to 11.7 per cent in 2006-07.

Operating expenses of banks in India are also much more aligned to those prevailing internationally, hovering around 2.1 per cent during 2004-2005 and 2005-06. These numbers are comparable to those obtaining for leading developed countries which were range-bound between 1.4-3.3 per cent in 2005.

Bank profitability levels in India have also trended upwards and gross profits stood at 2.0 per cent during 2005-06 (2.2 per cent during 2004-05) and net profits trending at around 1 per cent of assets. Available information suggests that for developed countries, at end-2005, gross profit ratios were of the order of 2.1 per cent for the US and 0.6 per cent for France.

The extent of penetration of our banking system in our country as measured by the proportion of bank assets to GDP has increased from 50 per cent in the second half of nineties to over 80 per cent a decade later.

Way Ahead

While we have made a significant progress, let me highlight a few issues that I believe would need significant attention in the near term.

The first is the issue of consolidation. The emergence of titans has been one of the noticeable trends in the banking industry at the global level. These banking entities are expected to drive the growth and volume of business in the global segment. In the Indian banking sector also, consolidation is likely to gain prominence in the near future. Despite the liberalisation process, state-owned banks dominate the industry, accounting for three-quarter of bank assets. The consolidation process in recent years has primarily been confined to a few mergers in the private sector segment, although some recent consolidation in the state-owned segment is evident as well. These mergers have been based on the need to attain a meaningful balance sheet size and market share in the face of increased competition, driven largely by synergies and locational and business-specific complementarities. Efforts have been initiated to iron out the legal impediments inherent in the consolidation process. As the bottom lines of domestic banks come under increasing pressure and the options for organic growth exhaust themselves, banks in India will need to explore ways for inorganic expansion. This, in turn, is likely to unleash the forces of consolidation in Indian banking. However, there are two caveats. First, any process of consolidation must come out of a felt need for merger rather than as an imposition from outside. The synergic benefits must be felt by the entities themselves. The process of consolidation that is driven by fiat is much less likely to be successful, particularly if the decision by fiat is accompanied by restrictions on the normal avenues for reducing costs in the merged entity. Thus, any meaningful consolidation among the public sector banks must be driven by commercial motivation by individual banks, with the government and the regulator playing at best a facilitating role. Second, the process of consolidation does not mean that small or medium sized banks will have no future. Many of the Indian banks are of appropriate size in relation to the Indian situation. Actual experience shows that small and medium sized banks even in advanced countries have been able to survive and remain profitable. These banks have survived along with very large financial conglomerates. Small banks may be the more natural lenders to small businesses.

The second issue is related to capital adequacy. Basel I standards have been successfully implemented in India and the authorities are presently moving towards adoption of Basel II tailored to country's specific considerations. Adoption of Basel II norms will enhance the required capital. Besides, banks' assets will grow or will have to grow in tandem with the growth of the real sectors of the economy. The public sector banks' ability to meet the growing needs will be inhibited, unless the government is willing to bring in more capital. At present, the share of the government in the public sector banks cannot go below 51 per cent. While there is some scope for expanding capital through various modalities, tier-I capital, that is equity, is still critical. While this constraint may not be binding immediately, sooner or later it will be. If growth is modest, retained earnings may form an adequate source of supply. However, when growth is rapid which is likely to be the case, there is need for injection of equity, enlarging the shareholding. In this situation, the government will have to make up its mind either to bring in additional capital or move towards reducing its share from 51 per cent through appropriate statutory changes. A third alternative could, however, be to include in the definition of government such entities as the Life Insurance Corporation that are quasi-government in nature and are likely to remain to be fully owned or an integral part of the government system in the future. However, even to do this an amendment is needed in the statute.

The third aspect concerns risk management. The most important facet of risk in India or for that matter in most developing countries markets remains the credit risk. Management of credit risks is an area which has received considerable attention in recent years. The new Basel accord rests on the assumption that an internal assessment of risks by a financial institution will be a better measure than an externally imposed formula. The economic structure is undergoing a change. The service sector has emerged as major sector. Assessing credit risk in lending to service sectors needs a methodology different from assessing risks while lending to manufacturing. There are other areas of lending such as housing and consumer credit which will need new approaches. Equally important will be the area of management of exchange risk. Besides enabling customers to adopt appropriate exchange cover, banks themselves will have to ensure that their exposure is within acceptable limits and is properly hedged. The entire area of risk management encompassing all aspects of risk including credit risk, market risk and operational risk will have to receive prime attention.

The fourth and final concern I want to refer to is improvement in customer service. Banks exist to provide service to customers. With the introduction of technology, there has been a significant change in the way banks operate. This is a far cry from the situation that existed even 15 years ago. The induction of technology has enabled several transactions to be processed in a shorter period of time. Transmission of funds to customers takes less time now. ATMs provide easy access to cash. Nevertheless, it is not very clear whether the customers as depositors and users of other banking services are fully satisfied with the services provided when they come to a bank. This is an area, which must receive continuous attention. The interface with the customers needs to improve.

Provision of credit is a basic function of banks. The effective discharge of this function is part of the intermediation process. The sectoral deployment of credit must keep pace with the changes in the structure of the economy. The banking industry in India must equip itself to be able to assess and meet the credit needs of the emerging segments of the economy. In this context, two aspects require special attention.

First, as the Indian economy gets increasingly integrated with the rest of the world, the demands of the corporate sector for banking services will change not only in size but also in composition and quality. The growing foreign trade in goods and services will have to be financed. Apart from production credit, financing capital requirements from the cheapest sources will become necessary. Provision of credit in foreign currency will require in turn a management of foreign exchange risk. Thus, the provision of a whole gamut of services related to integration with the rest of the world will be a challenge. Foreign banks operating in India will be the competitors to Indian banks in this regard. The foreign banks have access to much larger resources and have presence in many parts of the world. Therefore, Indian banks will have to evolve appropriate strategies in enabling Indian firms to accessing funds at competitive rates. Another aspect of global financial strategy relates to the presence of Indian banks in foreign countries. Indian banks will have to be selective in this regard. Here again the focus may be on how to help Indian firms acquire funds at internationally competitive rates and how to promote trade and investment between India and other countries. We must recognise that in foreign lands, Indian banks will be relatively smaller players. The motivation to build up an international presence must be guided by the route Indian entities take in the global business.

Second, despite the faster rate of growth of manufacturing and service sectors, bulk of the population still depends on agriculture and allied activities for its livelihood. In this background, one cannot over-emphasise the need for expanding credit to agricultural and allied activities. While banks have achieved a higher growth in provision of credit to agriculture and allied activities last year, this momentum has to be carried further. In this context, it has to be noted that credit for agriculture is not a single market. Provision of credit for high-tech agriculture is no different from providing credit to industry. Provision of credit to farmers with a surplus is also of similar nature. Commercial banks in particular must have no hesitation in providing credit to these segments where the normal calculation of risk and return applies. It is only with respect to provision of credit to small and marginal farmers, special attention is required. They constitute a bulk of the farmers and accounting for a significant proportion of the total output.

The National Sample Survey Organisation has recently released a Report entitled, "Indebtedness of Farmer Households". This Report contains a wealth of data relating to the extent and nature of indebtedness. As per NSSO data 51.4 per cent of the total farm households did not have access to credit. Another fact that emerges is that there is a substantial difference between marginal and sub-marginal farmers on the one hand and the rest of the farmer households on the other regarding the purpose for which loans are obtained and the sources of credit. For all farmer households taken together, at the all-India level, institutional sources were responsible for providing 57.5 per cent of the total credit. But as far as farmer households owning one hectare and less, this proportion is only 39.6 per cent. For all farmer households, the proportion of loan going for production purposes is 65.1 per cent as against 40.2 per cent for marginal and sub-marginal farmer households. Thus, for sub-marginal and marginal farmers, the proportion of production loan is lower than for all farmers. Similarly, the proportion of institutional credit is lower for sub-marginal and marginal farmers than for all farmers. This, in fact, is true of every state of the country. Thus, a critical issue is how to meet the credit requirements of marginal and sub-marginal farmers. What changes do we need to introduce so that credit can flow to this class of farmer households?Can the banking system through its present mode of distribution of credit meet this challenge?Should we think in terms of banks supporting other institutions who are in a better position to lend to marginal and sub-marginal farmers?Banks need to think hard on how to effectively use the 'facilitator and correspondent' models. These models have great potential to reach out to small borrowers and depositors. In any case, a re-look at the organisational structure of our rural branches is called for. Banks need to think deeply on how to meet this challenge of meeting the credit needs of marginal farmers. Financial inclusion is no longer an option; it is a compulsion.

The task to be fulfilled by the Indian banks is truly formidable. At one end we expect banks to be able to lend billions of rupees to large borrowers. At the same time we want them to be able to deliver extremely small loans to meet the requirements of the small borrowers. We must reflect on the kind of organisational structure and human talent that we need in order to achieve these twin goals which are at the two extreme ends of the spectrum of lending.

The first phase of banking sector reform has come to a close and we are moving on to the second phase. In the years to come, the Indian financial system will grow not only in size but also in complexity as the forces of competition gain further momentum and as financial markets get more and more integrated. As globalisation accelerates, the Indian financial system will also get integrated with the rest of the world. As the task of the banking system expands, there is need to focus on the organisational effectiveness of banks. To achieve improvements in productivity and profitability, corporate planning combined with organisational restructuring become necessary. Issues relating to consolidation, competition and risk management will remain critical. Equally, governance and financial inclusion will emerge as key issues for India at this stage of socio-economic development.

First R.K. Talwar Memorial Lecture—2007, Indian Institute of Banking & Finance, July 31, 2007.

17 Financial Inclusion

Some Key Issues

Nature of Inclusion

Financial inclusion denotes delivery of credit and other financial services at an affordable cost to the vast sections of the disadvantaged and low-income groups. The various financial services include savings, credit, insurance and payments and remittance facilities. It will be wrong to classify all those who are not borrowing from the organised financial system as excluded. What is relevant is that those who want credit should not be denied the same provided they are bankable. The criterion of being bankable should not be interpreted narrowly to exclude the vast majority. The objective of financial inclusion is to extend the scope of activities of the organised financial system to include within its ambit people with low incomes. Through graduated credit, attempts must be to lift the poor from one level to another so that they come out of poverty. Financial inclusion may, therefore, be defined as a process of enabling access to timely and adequate credit and other financial services by vulnerable groups such as weaker sections and low-income groups at an affordable cost.

Extent of Exclusion

NSSO data reveal that 45.9 million farmer households in the country (51.4 per cent), out of a total of 89.3 million households do not access credit, either from institutional or non-institutional sources. Further, despite the vast network of bank branches, only 27 per cent of total farm households are indebted to formal sources (of which one-third also borrow from informal sources). Farm households not accessing credit from formal sources as a proportion to total farm households is especially high at 95.91 per cent, 81.26 per cent and 77.59 per cent in the North-Eastern, Eastern and Central Regions respectively. Thus, apart from the fact that exclusion in general is large, it also varies widely across regions, social groups and asset holdings. The poorer the group, the greater is the exclusion.

Institutional Changes

The question before us is how to extend the scope of activities of the organised financial system to include low income groups. The institutions which currently provide financial services in the rural areas include branches of commercial banks, regional rural banks, cooperative societies and micro-finance institutions. What is required now is not creating new institutions for extending their outreach but finding ways and means to effect improvements within the existing formal credit delivery mechanism and evolve new models for extending outreach. In a broad sense, we need to address issues on the supply side as well as demand side. The formal banking system, the rural cooperatives and non-governmental organisations must be strengthened organisationally to extend their outreach. The financially excluded sections require products which are customised to meet their needs. Financial exclusion is also caused by demand side issues. Unless steps are taken on the demand side, that is in the "real sectors", mere supply side solutions from the financial sector will not work. Credit is necessary for this, but not sufficient. Credit has to be an integral part of an overall programme aimed at improving the productivity and income of small farmers and other poor households. Putting in place an appropriate credit delivery system to meet the needs of marginal and sub-marginal farmers must go hand in hand with efforts to improve the productivity of such farm households.

Let me place before you some thoughts on strengthening the credit delivery system in rural areas of commercial banks, regional rural banks and micro finance institutions.

Commercial Banks

The commercial banks have a large outreach. There are, at present, 33,500 commercial bank branches in rural and semi-urban centers in the country. The critical question is how to make these rural branches more effective in terms of delivering credit to the small and the very small borrowers. I list below some approaches in this regard.

First, a critical factor required for providing credit to marginal and sub-marginal farmers as well as other small borrowers is the empathy of the bank officers. Rural lending requires a specific type of organisational ethos, culture and attitude. Rural branches of banks have to be farmer-friendly. Lending to the low-income groups needs motivated bank staff. Such motivation is a function of attitude and beliefs as well as a system of incentives. The possibility of creating a separate cadre of rural bank employees does not appear to be feasible. Several studies have shown that there is a positive co-relation between the extent of training undergone by the managers and their overall attitude. More needs to be done in this regard.

Second, rural branches must go beyond providing credit and extend a helping hand in terms of advice on a wide variety of matters relating to agriculture and other allied activities. We may have to think in terms of branches on the lines of agricultural development branches of SBI where advice on farm and non-farm issues were provided by technical staff attached to the branches. As the Committee on Financial Inclusion has suggested, at least, one branch of the lead bank at the block or *taluka* level can be designated as a nodal branch to address the issue of exclusion. These branches must be strengthened with technical staff for provision of developmental services in the farm and non-farm sectors. All banks could make use of the advice provided by such branches.

Third, in districts where the population per branch is much higher than the national average, commercial banks may be encouraged to open branches. 139 districts in 15 states have been identified by the Reserve Bank as inadequately served by the banking system.

Fourth, there is need for the simplification of the procedures in relation to granting of loans to small borrowers. In some cases, enabling legislations have to be passed. Stamp duty exemption for loan documents relating to small borrowings is also needed. On the whole, a simplified document for the grant of small loans must be evolved. Some steps have already been taken in this regard by NABARD.

Fifth, the SHG-bank linkage scheme has proved to be an effective way of providing credit to very small borrowers. This needs to be further strengthened. The SHG-bank linkage programme has worked well and has contributed significantly to financial inclusion. The cumulative number of groups financed by the banking system is close to 2.3 million. The financial inclusion attained through SHGs is sustainable and scalable on account of its various positive features. One of the distinctive features of the SHG-bank linkage programme has been the high recovery rate. However, the spread of SHGs is very uneven and is more concentrated in southern states. This regional imbalance needs to be corrected and special efforts in this regard may have to be taken by NABARD. SHGs also need to graduate from mere providers of credit for non-productive purposes to promoting micro enterprises. Several state governments have been very active in the promotion of SHGs. However, there is no need to provide any interest rate subsidy to SHGs. Banks do provide them credit at reasonable rates of interest. The financial support of the state governments could be better directed towards building appropriate capacities in the self-help groups and providing technology support and marketing facilities. There are other quality issues which have arisen in the wake of the sharp quantitative expansion. These need to be addressed. Federations of SHGs at village and *taluka* levels have certain advantages. However, the disadvantage is that banks may lose their direct contact with SHGs, if federations act as intermediaries between the financing banks and SHGs. Perhaps, the best course of action would be to make the federations act as facilitators rather than as financial intermediaries. Federations, if they emerge voluntarily from amongst SHGs, must be encouraged.

Sixth, even though SHG-bank linkage has emerged as an effective credit delivery channel to the poor clients, there are segments within the poor who are left out such as share croppers/oral lessees/tenant farmers, whose loan requirements are much larger but who have no collaterals to fit into the traditional financing approaches of the banking system. To service such clients, Joint Liability Groups (JLGs), an upgradation of SHG model, could be an effective way. The Committee on Financial Inclusion had recommended that the adoption of the JLGs concept could be another effective method for purveying credit to small farmers, marginal farmers, tenant farmers, etc. and thereby reduce their dependence on informal sources of credit.

Finally, the business facilitator and correspondent model needs to be effectively implemented. In order to increase the outreach of the banking sector, the Reserve Bank have permitted banks to use the services of specified institutions as intermediaries for providing banking services. However, this scheme has not taken off. This model has a high potential. Banks must take the initiative to remove the obstacles that come in the way of an extended use of facilitators and correspondents. Rules, at present, permit not only institutions but also certain category of individuals to function as business facilitators. This list can be further expanded to include such people as ex-service men as has been done recently. At present, individuals are not allowed to function as business correspondents. Perhaps, a relaxation can be made here. I believe this has also been done recently by RBI. Individuals who have served as bank facilitators and have shown to have a satisfactory record may also be used as business correspondents. In fact, the appointment of well-chosen individuals holds out the best promise in this regard. However, one critical issue in the effective use of this model revolves around as to who should bear the additional transaction costs resulting from the employment of facilitators and correspondents. There has to be some flexibility with respect to the charging of interest rate. These transaction costs can still be accommodated within the present stipulation that the interest rate charged should not exceed the PLR.

Regional Rural Banks

Regional rural banks were originally conceived as low cost institutions having rural bias, local feel and pro-poor focus. The original assumption regarding the low cost nature of these institutions was belied. In fact, they soon turned into loss making institutions. With the changes introduced in the post-liberalisation period, there is a remarkable turn around in the financial performance of the RRBs. RRBs are yet another instrument to achieve the goal of financial inclusion. At present, RRBs have close to 15,000 branches in rural areas. The share of RRBs in the loan account of all scheduled commercial banks in rural areas is an impressive 37 per cent. However, they account for only 21 per cent of the total credit outstanding in rural areas implying thereby that the clientele comprises of small borrowers. RRBs have done well also in relation to the promotion of SHGs.

Of the total 22.4 lakh SHGs credit linked by the banking industry, 33 per cent linkage is done by RRBs. Strengthening of the RRBs could be one major policy intervention for promoting greater financial inclusion. The operations of RRBs could be expanded to 80 hitherto uncovered districts. I understand action is already being taken in this regard. RRBs may also usefully adopt the business facilitator and business correspondent model to achieve greater inclusion.

Role of Technology

In the task of making banking services available to everyone, technology has an important role to play. The required outreach into interiors with low operational costs is only possible with the use of appropriate technology. Technology has to be leveraged to create channels beyond branch network to reach the unbanked and to extend to them banking services similar to those dispensed from branches. In short, technology has to enable the branch to go to the customer instead of the other way round. The RBI has set up an Advisory Group for IT enabled financial inclusion to facilitate development of information technology solutions for delivery of banking services. It is understood that the Group will prescribe certain minimum parameters and standards that are essential for setting up robust technology solutions. The essential ingredients of all the models under consideration include:

a. the issue of a smart card to the client in the village on which all the transactions are recorded;
b. a hand-held terminal with the business correspondent at the village level; and
c. a Central Processor Unit (CPU) linking the smart cards and BC terminals with the banks.

It is necessary to ensure that every transaction made is accompanied by a print out being provided to the farmers or other clients. The operating costs of these models are expected to be minimal and can be easily absorbed by banks. As the transaction increases in volume it will become easier to absorb the incremental operating costs. More importantly, the costs of the technology solutions will be substantially lowered if the infrastructure is shared. The Report of the Committee on Financial

Inclusion has recommended the setting up of a Technology Development Fund. The Central budget has also made a provision for this. This fund can be utilised to strengthen the technology base for financial inclusion.

Micro Financial Institutions

Micro finance institutions play a significant role in ensuring financial inclusion. There are several legal forms of micro finance institutions (MFIs). There are about 1000 NGO-MFIs, 3000 cooperative MFIs and about 20 company MFIs. However, the company MFIs are the major players accounting for over 80 per cent of the micro finance loan portfolio. Ten such MFIs are reported to have an outreach of 1,00,000 micro finance clients. However, an overwhelming majority of MFIs are operating on a smaller scale with clients ranging between 500 to 1,500 per MFI. The geographical distribution of MFIs is skewed with concentration in southern India where the rural branch network of banks is also strong. It is estimated that MFIs added, during the year 2006-07, three million new borrowers and this takes the total coverage to 10.5 million borrowers.

With respect to the operations of MFIs, a number of issues have arisen in the recent period. One such issue relates to the rate of interest. It is recognised that the transaction costs for delivering credit to very small borrowers are high. Also to the extent to which various advisory services are provided, the cost further goes up. It is necessary for MFIs to separate the pure interest costs from other costs which are charged to the borrowers because of the additional services provided. Overall it is necessary to ensure that the burden on the borrower is not such as to make him default. MFIs need to ensure that the earnings capacity of the borrowers is sufficiently enhanced enabling them to bear the cost of borrowing. Taking a holistic view, it is necessary for micro finance institutions to keep the overall cost to the borrowers maintained at a level that is consistent with the repaying capacity of the borrowers.

As the Committee on Financial Inclusion has recommended, there is a need to recognise a separate category of microfinance—non-banking finance companies (MF–NBFCs). This should be done without any relaxation on the start up capital. They should also be subject to all the regulatory prescriptions applicable to NBFCs. Such MF-NBFCs could be defined as NBFCs that provide credit upto a specified amount to the borrowers. Consistent with the definition of micro finance that is prescribed in the new bill, it may be specified that MF-NBFCs are those with 80 per cent of the assets of in the form of microcredit of upto Rs. 50,000 for agriculture, allied and non farm activities and in the case of housing, loans upto Rs. 1,50,000, per individual borrower, whether given through a group mechanism or directly. The supervision of MF-NBFCs could be delegated to NABARD by RBI. These MF-NBFCs could be recognised as business correspondents of banks for providing savings and remittance services. They will not, however, serve as correspondents on the lending side as there could be a conflict of interest.

For the micro finance movement to gather momentum, it is necessary that all the various legal forms of micro finance institutions should be encouraged. Each legal form has its own special advantages. However, it needs to be noted that even the most successful micro finance institutions in the corporate sector depend to a large extent on funding by the banks. Thus, the banks will continue to play a key role either directly or indirectly in micro finance.

National Rural Financial Inclusion Plan

The Committee on Financial Inclusion has recommended that a National Rural Financial Inclusion Plan may be launched with a clear target to provide access to comprehensive financial services, including credit, to at least 50 per cent of financially excluded households, say 55.77 million by 2012 through rural/semi-urban branches of Commercial Banks and Regional Rural Banks. The remaining households, with such shifts as may occur in the rural/urban population, have to be covered by 2015. Semi-urban and rural branches of commercial banks and RRBs may set for themselves a minimum target of covering 250 new cultivator and non-cultivator households per branch per annum, with an emphasis on financing marginal farmers and poor non-cultivator households. This is an achievable target.

Looking at the picture as a whole, two initiatives that will bring about a significant surge forward of the micro finance sector will be the growth of the bank-SHG linkage programme and the induction of individuals as business correspondents. The two will constitute the main pillars of the future development of bank related micro finance, even as other forms of micro finance institutions will continue to grow. The goal of making a significant progress towards financial inclusion seems attainable. Financial inclusion is no longer an option but a compulsion.

18 Agricultural Credit

Reaching the Marginalised Farmers

The two major policy shifts, which have had far reaching implications and transformed the banks in the country were the Nationalisation of Banks in 1969 and the Financial Sector Reforms initiated since 1991-92. While nationalisation ensured that banking services reached the unbanked areas through rapid expansion of the branch network, the latter reforms ensured that public sector banks developed a market orientation and became financially strong and healthy through adoption of sound banking norms and practices.

Banking Reforms and their Impact

The reform measures included: reduction in the statutory liquidity ratio (SLR) and cash reserve ratios (CRR), recapitalisation of public sector banks (SCBs and RRBs), adoption of prudential norms with a focus on capital adequacy ratio, rationalisation of branch licensing and, deregulation of interest rates. During the post reform period, a number of activities were included under the priority sector to make it more broad based. Thus, the ongoing financial sector reform programme aims at promoting a diversified, efficient and competitive financial sector with the ultimate objective of improving the allocative efficiency of available resources, increasing the return on investments and promoting accelerated growth of the real sector of the economy.

The reform measures did have a positive effect on the performance and financial health of the banks. The ratio of operating profits to total assets went up from 1.25 per cent during 1993-94 to 2.67 per cent during 2003-04 while net profit as a percentage of total asset also improved drastically from (–) 0.83 in 1993-94 to 1.13 in 2003-04 for all the scheduled commercial banks. The non-performing assets (NPA) of the banking sector had also come down with the gross NPAs as a proportion to gross advances declining from 23.2 per cent in 1992-93 to 7.2 per cent in 2003-04.

Credit to Agriculture

Contrary to general impression, in relation to agriculture as well, a number of initiatives were taken in the post liberalisation period. Banks were required to prepare Special Agriculture Credit Plans in which banks set for themselves targets for disbursements taking into account the over all increment in credit indicated by the Reserve Bank. Innovative credit products were also introduced during the period with a view to improving the reach of institutional credit. The SHG-Bank linkage programme, launched in 1993-94 for providing micro-finance to the rural poor, has facilitated linking of banks with more than 16.18 lakh SHGs by March 2005. It is heartening that 90 per cent of these are exclusive women groups. The introduction of the Kisan Credit Card (KCC) scheme was a step towards simplifying the procedures for providing timely and adequate short-term institutional credit to farmers as well as reducing the transaction costs to bankers. The number of cards issued has increased in each successive year since its inception and reached a total of over 510.8 lakh cards by the end of March 2005.

The period since 1991-92 has seen a fairly rapid expansion of credit to agriculture. Available data indicate that the flow of credit to agriculture by commercial banks and RRBs taken together increased from Rs. 5,402 crore in 1991-92 to Rs. 60,022 crore in 2003-04 (Table 18.1). This implies a compound annual growth rate of 22.2 per cent. In fact, as compared with commercial banks including RRBs, the flow of credit from the cooperative sector was much slower through this period. The compound annual growth rate of credit for agriculture from cooperative institutions was only 13.7 per cent. There has been a substantial rise (32.49 per cent) in the flow of credit from all agencies in 2004-05 over the previous year. Despite this increase in agricultural credit, it has to be acknowledged that the targets set for agriculture credit of 18 per cent of net bank credit has not been achieved. It is, however, important in this context to take note of the fact that this as well as the other targets for credit flow were introduced at a time when the

Table 18.1

Agency-wise Ground Level Credit Flow to Agriculture Sector

Rupees Crore

Agency/Year	1991-92	1992-93	1993-94	1994-95	1995-96	1996-97	1997-98	1998-99	1999-2000	2000-2001	2001-2002	2002-2003	2003-2004	2004-2005	CAGR 91-92/03-04 %
(i) Co-operative Banks	5797	9378	10117	9406	10479	11944	14085	15957	18260	20718	23524	23636	26959	30638	13.67
(ii) Regional Rural Banks	596	831	977	1083	1381	1684	2040	2460	3172	4220	4854	6070	7581	11718	23.61
(iii) Commercial Banks	4806	4960	5400	8255	10172	12783	15831	18443	24733	27807	33587	39774	52441	72886	22.04
RRB+Commercial Banks	5402	5791	6377	9338	11553	14467	17871	20903	27905	32027	38441	45844	60022	84604	22.22
(i+ii+iii)	11199	15169	16494	18744	22032	26411	31956	36860	46165	52745	61965	69480	86981	115242	18.63

Source: NABARD. *Annual Reports* 2002-03 and 2004-05.

pre-emption of deposits in the form of reserve requirements was very large. The number of accounts in direct advances to agriculture by commercial banks as at the end of March 2004 at 192.3 lakh, showed a decline of more than six lakh accounts as compared to the number of such accounts by end-March 1995.

Credit to Marginal Farmers

The study on "Indebtedness of Farmer Households", recently brought out by the NSSO contains a wealth of data relating to the extent and nature of indebtedness. One interesting fact that emerges is that there is a substantial difference between marginal/sub-marginal farmers and the rest of the farmer households regarding the purpose for which loans are obtained and the sources of credit. For all farmer households taken together, at the all India level, institutional sources provided 57.7 per cent of the total credit (Table 18.2). But as far as farmer households owning one hectare and less, this proportion (derived through appropriate weighting) was only 48.2 per cent indicating that a large proportion of such households were dependent on non-institutional sources for their credit needs. The proportion of credit for production purposes was lower at 47.2 per cent for marginal and sub-marginal farmers as compared to 65.1 per cent for farm households (Table 18.3). It is also seen that in 12 states accounting for 61 per cent of total marginal and sub-marginal, the proportion of institutional credit to total credit is less than the proportion of production credit to total credit. This means that in the case of marginal and sub-marginal farmers in these states, even their production credit requirement is not fully met by institutions.

This situation of the marginal and sub-marginal farmers being denied access to adequate institutional credit raises a number of critical questions. Is it that these groups of farmers are unviable credit propositions to banks and therefore considered too risky?How do we strengthen the capability and capacity of such farmers to improve the productivity of their farms so that banks consider them as "bankable" and farmers find the loans "repayable"?What changes do we need to introduce so that credit can flow to this class of farmer households?Can the banking system through its present mode of credit delivery meet this challenge?Should we think in terms of banks supporting other intermediaries or institutions, which are

Table 18.2

Per 1000 Distribution of Outstanding Loan (in Rs.) by Source of Loan for Each Size Class of Land Possessed by Farmer Household

All India

Size Class of Land Possessed	Government	Co-operative society	Bank	Agricultural/ Professional Money Lender	Trader	Relatives and Friends	Doctor, Lawyer and Other Professionals	Others	All
(1)	(2)	(3)	(4)	(5)	(6)	(7)	(8)	(9)	(10)
<0.01	19	53	154	473	40	231	10	20	1000
0.01-0.40	40	145	248	318	49	149	14	37	1000
0.40-1.00	38	170	320	308	46	91	7	20	1000
1.01-2.00	17	205	354	259	42	88	8	26	1000
2.01-4.00	15	226	410	234	47	51	4	14	1000
4.01-10.00	13	230	445	167	61	56	15	12	1000
10.00+	17	232	427	172	106	40	0	6	1000
All Sizes	**25**	**196**	**356**	**257**	**52**	**85**	**9**	**21**	**1000**

Source: Data drawn from page A-96 of the NSSO Report No. 498.

Table 18.3

Per 1000 Distribution of Outstanding Loan (in Rs.) by Purpose of Loan for Each Size Class of Land Possessed by Farmer Household

All India

Size Class of Land Possessed	Capital Expenditure in Farm Business	Current Expenditure in Farm Business	Non-farm Business	Consumption Expenditure	Marriages and Ceremonies	Education	Medical	Other Expenditure	All
(1)	(2)	(3)	(4)	(5)	(6)	(7)	(8)	(9)	(10)
<0.01	151	57	77	212	224	3	130	147	1000
0.01-0.40	133	95	123	146	201	10	72	220	1000
0.40-1.00	241	227	103	105	133	13	41	137	1000
1.01-2.00	326	320	46	87	99	5	24	93	1000
2.01-4.00	388	347	47	50	89	7	13	59	1000
4.01-10.00	411	398	23	59	50	5	12	41	1000
10.00+	457	325	32	48	29	15	37	57	1000
All sizes	**306**	**278**	**67**	**88**	**111**	**8**	**33**	**108**	**1000**

Source: Data drawn from page A-81 of the NSSO Report No. 498.

in a better position to lend to marginal and sub-marginal farmers? We need to find answers to these to ensure that these farmers get their rightful share.

Strategy for Enhanced Credit to Marginal Farmers

The formulation of any strategy for providing credit access to small and marginal farmers must recognise the fact that the market for rural credit is not a single market. The rural credit market is a differentiated or segmented one with the small and marginal farmers with different needs and priorities at one end of the spectrum and the large farms with a commercial orientation at the other end. Provision of credit for commercial agriculture is no different from providing credit to industry and the provision of credit to farmers with the surplus is also of a similar nature. Commercial banks in particular should have no hesitation in providing credit to those segments where the normal calculations of risk and returns apply. Only with respect to the provision of credit to small and marginal farmers and persons with low income, is special attention required. Low-income groups generally do not have the necessary capabilities to deal with organised credit institutions, nor do they have enough collateral to offer as security to banks, especially in the context of a security oriented lending system. The strategies for meeting the credit requirements of the small and marginal farmers will have to be thought in terms of policies, credit delivery mechanism and credit products, which meet the requirements of this segment of the rural credit market. While evolving such strategies, the composite needs of these groups of farmers such as credit, technology, input supplies, market information and consumption need to be taken into account.

It is well known that banking is about financial intermediation and managing risks. No business enterprise is immune from risks; banks are no exception to this rule. The banker has to minimise his risks by building up the capabilities and skills of the farmer to operate viably in a risky environment through an appropriate coping mechanism.

A critical factor required for providing credit to marginal and sub-marginal farmers is the empathy of the bank officer who needs to build a relationship banking with this clientele. Rural lending requires a specific type of organisational ethos, culture and attitude. Rural branches of banks have to be farmer friendly. Whether the present cadre of officers in rural branches have the required attitude is an important question. A study in Madhya Pradesh supported by DFID indicated fairly high level of dissatisfaction of the rural branch officials with regard to their work situation. Further, the dissatisfaction level was higher for rural branch managers with an urban background, and managers with less than 15 years experience were more negative than those with longer service. Positive correlation was observed between the extent of training undergone by the managers and their overall attitude.

Apart from the need for empathy, rural branches must go beyond providing credit and extend a helping hand in terms of advice on a wide variety of matters relating to agriculture. As in micro-finance, rural credit is all about credit plus services by the bank. The agricultural officers must provide services that will help in making agriculture an integrated activity with appropriate backward and forward linkages through providing "farm advisory services". We must, perhaps, revisit the model of agricultural development branches/farm clinics promoted during the Green Revolution period. Such branches had agricultural experts attached to them to give advice to farmers. This model was not pursued vigorously later in the hope that such advice and help would come from state governments through their extension agencies. That has not happened. We may have to think in terms of restructuring the rural branches of commercial banks so that credit will be supplemented by expert advice. A beginning has been made by some of the commercial banks in this regard through recruiting agricultural graduates from the campus. The personnel policies of these banks need to be tailored to meet the career aspirations of these recruits so that they do not switch over to the general banking services as had happened in the past. The restructuring of rural branches requires focused attention.

The linkage model of the micro-finance programme promoted by NABARD could be thought of for replication for extending more credit to the marginal and sub-marginal farmers. Groups of marginal and sub-marginal farmers could act as Joint Liability Groups, serving as a collective guarantor for the loans extended by banks through executing joint liability agreements making them severally and jointly liable for the repayment of loans. A pilot project in this regard, I understand, is under implementation in seven states.

Another approach is to use civil society organisations (CSO) outside the formal banking system as vehicles for agricultural credit delivery. Such CSOs would include NGOs, Farmer Clubs, SHGs or corporates engaged in rural development as part of their corporate social responsibility. Also functioning cooperatives can be used under this approach. As a recent Report of the RBI has pointed out, this approach can be operationalised under two models: the 'business facilitator' model and the 'business correspondent' model. The business facilitator model involves banks reducing their transaction costs by outsourcing to an existing institution/ person the whole gamut of functions relating to identification of borrowers and processing of loans. The business correspondent model is a further extension of the facilitator model where the intermediary also takes on the functions of credit disbursal and recovery. Outsourcing some of the banking functions has its own risks. Nevertheless, this is an approach that merits further consideration.

The use of such intermediary organisations must, however, supplement and not substitute banks' own initiative to provide credit to such farmers. Banks can take courage and indeed pride from the fact that out of the total institutional lending at the all India level, commercial banks account for 62 per cent. Indeed in 20 out of 27 states, commercial banks have shares higher than the all India average of 62 per cent. The relative institutional dominance is uniform across all farm sizes. Even in the case of lending to sub-marginal and marginal farmers, commercial banks dominate over cooperatives. In the case of marginal farmers at the all India level, commercial banks account for 61 per cent as against cooperatives, which have a share of 32.2 per cent. Thus, the commercial banks have a legitimate role to play in the provision of rural credit and they should not abdicate this responsibility.

Returning to the issue of improving the credit absorptive capacity of marginal and sub-marginal farmers, their low agricultural productivity may be due to a variety of factors such as poor agro-climatic conditions and uneconomic size of their holdings. In looking at the problem of increasing the flow of credit to marginal and sub-marginal farmers, it is important not to treat this as a pure supply side problem. There is need to address simultaneously the demand side issues, that is, of improving the productivity of such farms. Credit is necessary for this but not sufficient. Credit has to be an integral part of an overall programme aimed at improving the productivity and income of such farmers. Putting in place an appropriate credit delivery system to meet the needs of marginal and sub-marginal farmers must go hand in hand with efforts to improve the productivity of such farm households. It is this integrated approach which will provide a solution to the problems of these farm households. Banks have to go beyond the traditional role of purveyors of credit and become collaborators with others in finding a holistic solution. Banking in India today is in a resurgent mood and let us make the banking systems a dynamic vehicle for spurring economic activity all around.

Valedictory Address at Bankers' Conference (BANCON) 2005, November 12, 2005, Kolkata.

19 | Regulation of Tariffs in the Power Sector

Power is one of the key inputs required for sustained economic growth. In fact, the demand for power grows at a much faster rate than the rate of growth of the national product. The elasticity of demand is now close to 1.2. Over the years, India has done well in creating new generation capacities, extending the transmission and distributing network and making electricity available to a large section of the society. Electricity generation in the country which was only 4.1 billion units in 1947 increased to about 350 billion units by 1995, registering a compounded annual growth rate of 7.5 per cent. It has, since then, increased to 500 billion units in 2000-01. Despite this, the power sector has been afflicted by serious shortage of supply in relation to demand particularly in some states. Electricity cannot be easily imported (though not completely ruled out) or stored and hence creation of generation capacity domestically is critical for meeting the country's demand for power. State Electricity Boards (SEBs) or their successors are saddled with problems arising from poor state of their distribution network, low quality of service, tariffs not covering costs, rampant theft, high subsidy and cross subsidy and poor revenue recovery from consumers. From a recent study of the Planning Commission, it is found that the estimated commercial losses of State Electricity Boards (SEBs) without subsidy during 2001-02 were Rs. 33,177 crore as compared to Rs. 11,305 crore during 1996-97. The commercial losses with subsidy payable by state government for the above years are Rs. 24,837 crore and Rs. 4,674 crore, respectively. Those states that are compensating the Electricity Boards for their commercial losses through subventions are facing a huge dent in the state finances. Their revenue deficits are rising. On the other hand, states that are not financially supporting the power sector are facing restriction in supply from central generators, as the defaults to these suppliers are mounting. It is an unfortunate fact that the current operations of SEBs remain unviable. Revenue realisation per unit of power produced is much less than the average cost of production and supply, with the result the SEBs are running deficits. There is a large transmission and distribution loss ranging from 20 to 50 per cent of the supplied energy. No lasting solution to the problems of the power sector is possible without making the current operations of the SEBs or their successors financially viable. The prevailing conditions in the power sector would not only cause serious damage to the electricity industry but also cripple the finances of the state governments.

Elements in the Power Reform Process

Because of its monopolistic nature, the electricity industry has always been subject to regulation. The first legislation of electricity in India was enacted as early as 1910. In the wake of economic reforms introduced in 1991, reforms in the power sector assumed importance. The objective of the reform process is to make the industry viable and efficient. To achieve this objective, the state governments have enacted legislations to enable setting up of regulatory authorities, restructuring of the electricity industry along functional lines and creating opportunities for private participation in the electricity industry both in the spheres of generation and distribution. It is significant to note that these are common themes in the power reform process in almost all countries. Obviously there are several issues in restructuring and regulation unique to each country. However, there is a commanality of approach.

In 1991, the first policy statement with regard to reform of the electricity sector was announced involving private sector participation in the generation of electricity. The setting up of a regulatory framework was an integral part of the restructuring of the industry. Orissa initiated the process in 1995 and many other states have followed suit by enacting suitable legislations and set up independent regulatory bodies to govern the industry. In 1998, the Central Electricity Regulatory Commission Act was passed and the Central Regulatory body was formed to generally regulate the functioning of the Central sector players and inter-state supply.

Role of Regulatory Commissions

The mandate to the regulatory commissions is usually wide. It goes very much beyond the determination of tariffs. For example, Section 11 of the Andhra Pradesh Electricity Reform Act specifies a wide gamut of functions aimed at the development of the electricity industry. In effect the Act wants the Commission to take measures conducive to the development and management of the electricity industry in an efficient, economic and competitive manner. Nevertheless, tariff fixation remains the chief tool for achieving the results. It is in this context that the enunciation of long term tariff principles assumes importance. Obviously tariff levels cannot be set for many years to come as many elements that form part of the cost such as fuel prices keep changing from year to year. However, by laying down the tariff fixation methodology and the principles on specific aspects such as loss reduction, and incentives and disincentives, efficiency can be promoted.

Tariff Fixation

Fixation of tariffs in the electricity industry is a complicated exercise. The literature on the subject is large. However, for a regulator, one important question to ask is: if pricing is to be based on a cost plus formula, how should costs be determined? Costs, as stated, by the licensees cannot simply be accepted. There must necessarily be a certain normative element. Without such a normative element, it can only end up in a high cost situation. One perplexing question before all the regulators has been the determination of T&D loss i.e., transmission and distribution loss. In some states these losses have been creeping up instead of coming down. Of course, one common reason cited for not being able to determine precisely these losses is that the flow of power to agriculture is not metered. It is high time that the regulators as well as electricity boards initiated appropriate steps to determine technical losses and commercial losses. If metering is essential for this purpose, the regulators must insist on this. Technological answers are available for reducing technical losses. Commercial losses are only an euphemistic expression for theft. Quite clearly, a reduction in T&D losses even by a few percentage points can bring about considerable improvement in the financial position of electricity boards. Inter-state comparisons in this regard can also provide the basis for action. In this context, it may be desirable to fix certain targets of efficiency in respect of T&D losses which could be achieved over a multi-year period. This is not uncommon in the case of price fixation for other commodities such as fertiliser or chemicals.

Price Discrimination

In the supply of power, price discrimination is inevitable. Even in a normal situation when a monopoly supplier faces different markets, prices differ from one market to another. Monopoly power and price discrimination have been described as Siamese Twins. However, in the Indian context, it is not only the different demand curves in the different markets but also socio-economic considerations that lead to different prices. Subsidies are once again inevitable in such a situation. However, the issue to be addressed is how subsidies can be fashioned to meet well defined target groups and how they can coexist with efficiency and prevention of waste. There must be a recognition that there are limits to cross subsidisation.

In determining the cost to various users, there are obviously many problems. Determination of the cost to serve is not easy in a multi-user situation. An appropriate formula must be adopted for determining wheeling charges as well as other costs while fixing the cost for supplying to a particular type of user.

Tariffs and Competition

Needless to say, many of the regulatory measures including tariff fixation that are currently followed are within the traditional mould of regulating monopolies. The cost-based regulation may need a relook as regulatory commissions move towards creating conditions for more competition. Many states are following the single buyer model. In this model generation is first unbundled, followed by transmission, distribution and much later of retail supply. Under the prevailing model, the single buyer which is the Transmission Company purchases all power and sells it to the distribution companies. At present, Power Purchase Agreements are screened by the regulators to ensure that bulk supply cost does not go up disproportionately. It is also a fact that in a single buyer model, investment in generation will be forthcoming only under 'take or pay' contract. Distribution companies even when they are privatised remain smaller private monopolies. Under a competitive regime which may prevail at the generating and distribution levels, the role of the regulator will completely change. His role as a tariff fixer may wither away. However, that future is nowhere in sight. Nevertheless, regulators must explore how competition can be enhanced at each stage. How can the industry transit from 'competing for the market' to 'competing in the market'?Some have argued that competition in generation can be introduced, if generators are allowed to sell directly to large consumers. This can accentuate the problems of SEBs. However, this issue needs to be examined in all its implications.

Other Issues

There are other matters which are partly of administrative nature which are of concern to regulators. In some states, governments have either stayed the orders of the Commission or instructed the utilities not to comply with the orders of the Commission. This defeats the very purpose of creation of Independent Regulatory Commissions. In some cases, tariffs are asked to be reduced by the government without providing required subsidy. The jurisdiction of courts over the orders passed by Regulatory Commissions is also a contentious area. Should the jurisdiction extend to all aspects of the orders or should it be restricted only to some? In the meanwhile it will be in the interest of regulators to provide detailed reasoning for their orders so that the public can have a better appreciation of their task.

Conclusion

The appropriate fixation of tariff is a difficult exercise. Several considerations come into play. The regulators have a three fold task of ensuring: (a) efficiency in operations, (b) affordable price to the consumers and (c) adequate flow of capital to the sector. While in the long run, all these objectives may be congruent, in the short run, they may not. Regulators may have to balance the interest of consumers on the one hand with that of the share holders on the other. They face the daunting task of making the sector financially viable while safeguarding the interest of the consumer.

Extracted from the Address delivered at the Conference of Power Regulators held at Hyderabad, August 30, 2002.

20 The Widening Scope of Insurance

What is Insurance?

An insurance contract provides risk coverage to the insuree. A purchaser of insurance pays a fixed premium in exchange for a promise of compensation in the event of some specified loss. Insurance is bought because it gives peace of mind to the holders. This comfort level is important in personal and business life. Though the primary purpose of insurance is to provide risk coverage, when the contract period extends over a long time, as in the case of life insurance, premium payments comprise of two components—one for buying risk coverage and the other towards savings. This bundling together of risk coverage and savings is peculiar to life insurance and is more common in developing countries like India. In the industrially advanced countries, this is not necessarily so and short duration life insurance contracts without a savings component are equally popular. In the developing economies because of the savings component and the long nature of the contract, life insurance has become an important instrument of mobilising long-term funds. The savings component puts the life insurance in direct competition with other financial institutions and savings instruments.

The total investment portfolio of the insurers in India as at the end of March, 2005 was Rs. 4,65,864 crore. The total premium collected by the insurers both life and non-life in 2004-05 was Rs.1,00,335 crore. The major contribution came from life insurance. The insurance penetration i.e., premia as percentage of GDP was 3.17 per cent in 2004. While this ratio is steadily increasing, it is far below the world average of 8.06 per cent. This shows the vast potential that exists.

Insurance and Growth

Insurance and economic growth mutually influence each other. As the economy grows, the living standards of people increase. As a consequence, the demand for life insurance increases. As the assets of people and of business enterprises increase in the growth process, the demand for general insurance also increases. In fact, as the economy widens the demand for new types of insurance products emerges. Insurance is no longer confined to product markets; they also cover service industries. It is equally true that growth itself is facilitated by insurance. A well-developed insurance sector promotes economic growth by encouraging risk-taking. Risk is inherent in all economic activities. Without some kind of cover against risk, some of these activities will not be carried out at all. Also insurance and more particularly life insurance is a mobiliser of long-term savings and life insurance companies are thus able to support infrastructure projects which require long-term funds. There is thus a mutually beneficial interaction between insurance and economic growth. The low income levels of the vast majority of population has been one of the factors inhibiting a faster growth of insurance in India. To some extent this is also compounded by certain attitudes to life. The economy has moved on to a higher growth path. The average rate of growth of the economy in the last three years was 8.1 per cent. This strong growth will bring about significant changes in the insurance industry.

At this point, it is important to note that not all activities can be insured. If that were possible, it would completely negate entrepreneurship. Professor Frank Knight in his celebrated book *Risk Uncertainty and Profit* emphasised that profit is a consequence of uncertainty. He made a distinction between quantifiable risk and non-quantifiable risk. According to him, it is non-quantifiable risk that leads to profit. He wrote, "It is a world of change in which we live, and a world of uncertainty. We live only by knowing something about the future; while the problems of life, or of conduct at least, arise from the fact that we know so little. This is as true of business as of other spheres of activity." The real management challenges are uninsurable risks. In the case of insurable risks, risk is avoided at a cost.

Assessment of Risks

An important function of an insurer is to assess the average level of risk borne while offering a product. This assessment depends upon a variety of factors and actuarial calculations become necessary. This is a highly technical area involving theories of probability. The premium charged by an insurer is based on the calculated average risk. Obviously this premium will be high for people who perceive themselves to be in a low risk category. However, for insurance as an activity to succeed, the population to which a product is offered must consist of categories with different degrees of risk. That is why the larger the coverage, the lower the average risk and lower the premium. Diversification is the way to reduce the average risk.

Regulatory Framework

As in the case of all financial institutions, insurance is an activity that needs to be regulated. This is so because the smooth functioning of business depends on the trust and confidence reposed by the customers in the solvency of the financial institutions. Insurance products are of little value to customers, if they cannot trust the company to keep its promise. The regulatory framework in relation to the insurance companies seeks to take care of three major concerns: (a) protection of consumers' interest, (b) to ensure the financial soundness of the insurance industry, and (c) to help the healthy growth of the insurance market. So long as insurance remained the monopoly of the government, the need for an independent regulatory authority was not felt. However, with the acceptance of the idea that there can be private insurance entities, the need for a regulatory authority becomes paramount. With the passing of the Insurance Development and Regulatory Act in 2000, the insurance regulatory authority has become a statutory authority. Protecting consumer interest involves proper disclosure, keeping prices affordable, some mandatory products and standardisation. Most importantly, it has to make sure that consumers get paid by insurers. From the consumers' point of view, the most important function of the regulatory authority will be to ensure quick settlement of claims without unnecessary litigation. With respect to solvency and financial health, regulations will have to be introduced to ensure that insurance companies follow appropriate prudential norms such as solvency margins. Large funds are under the custody of the insurers and they get invested to produce additional returns. The management of these funds is important to the insurer, the insured and the economy. Entry into the insurance industry must also be regulated with suitable capital adequacy norms. The third role should be one of development. The insurance industry in India has a large potential and the framework of regulation must enable the industry to tap this vast potential.

IRDA over the last decade has brought into force a number of regulations which are well conceived. They have received wide spread appreciation. The recent decision of IRDA to move to a free tariff regime for several general insurance products is welcome. The prescription of tariff is contrary to market principles and insurance products need to be priced based on market forces.

The reform of the insurance sector is part of the overall economic reform process that is underway. The basic philosophy underlying the new economic policy is to improve the productivity and efficiency of the system. This is sought to be achieved partly by creating a more competitive environment. The growth of the real economy depends upon the efficiency of the financial sector. A greater element of competition is being injected into the financial system as well.

All regulators need to keep in mind that there is a fine distinction between regulations and controls. Regulations lay down norms while controls have a propensity to micromanage institutions. Regulators must take care to ensure that regulations do not slide into controls.

The insurance industry in our country underwent a big change in 2000 when private participants were allowed into the industry along with a streamlined regulatory and supervisory regime. There are at present 14 private life insurance companies along with LIC and 12 entities in non-life sector. There is evidence to show that competition has done good to insurance industry. The rate of growth of the industry in the post liberalisation period has been faster. It has also developed in terms of product innovation and the use of alternative distribution channels.

Conclusion

The insurance sector has a vast potential not only because incomes are increasing and assets are expanding but also because the volatility in the system is increasing. In a sense, we are living in a more risky world. Trade is becoming increasingly global. Technologies are changing and getting replaced at a faster rate. In this more uncertain world, for which enough evidence is available in the recent period, insurance will have an important role to play in reducing the risk burden that individuals and businesses have to bear. In the emerging scenario, the insurance industry must pay attention to (a) product innovation, (b) appropriate pricing, and (c) speedy settlement of claims. The approach to insurance must be in tune with the changing times.

The mission of the insurance sector in India should be to extend the insurance coverage over a larger section of the population and a wider segment of activities. The three guiding principles of the industry must be to charge premium no higher than what is warranted by strict actuarial considerations, to invest the funds for obtaining maximum yield for the policy holders consistent with the safety of capital, and to render efficient and prompt service to policy holders. With imaginative corporate planning and an abiding commitment to improved service, the mission of widening the spread of insurance can be achieved.

Convocation Address at the Institute of Insurance and Risk Management, Hyderabad, July 27, 2006.

21 Reforming the Pension System

Demographic Changes

The issue of pension has assumed great significance because of certain demographic changes. Thanks to recent developments in medical and healthcare, life expectancy at birth in India has increased considerably. More and more people are living beyond the age of 60. It is estimated that the share of the aged in the total population will rise from 6.4 per cent in 1991 to 8.9 per cent in 2016. In absolute numbers, this will mean an increase from 54.7 million to 113.0 million during this period. Today people in India at age 60 are expected to live beyond 75 years of age. This implies that on an average an Indian worker must have adequate resources to support himself and his wife for approximately 15 years after his retirement. This is indeed a challenge. We have to find ways and means through which the growing number of aged can be taken care of during the period of retirement.

Existing Coverage of Pensions

A pension scheme is basically a promise by a sponsor to the plan member for provision of income security in the form of pension in the post retirement period for consideration received during the working life. The sponsor of the pension plan can be the employer which may include Government, a Union or a Trust. As we survey the pension scenario in our country, it is possible to identify four distinct groups. First, there is the group of people whose income during their working life is so low that they cannot provide for their non-working life. These people can be covered only by social security nets. The second group comprises civil servants of the Central and state governments who are assured of a pension based on final salary. The third group comprises workers in certain industrial and other establishments who are compulsorily covered under the Provident Fund—Pension Scheme. The fourth group comprises workers not covered under the Provident Fund Scheme as well as independent professionals who will have to save enough during their working life to take care of their needs in the post retirement period. There are problems associated with pension arrangements in relation to each of these groups.

The government even now operates a number of schemes under which pension is paid to destitute persons aged 65 and above. However, these are not well coordinated and the percentage of people covered is very small. The extent to which government can provide assistance to such people will depend upon the fiscal resources and the overall policy. However, the need for a broad based social assistance scheme cannot be under played.

The pension provided to the civil servants come under the category of non-contributory 'defined benefit' pension schemes. Pension spending on government servants has risen dramatically in recent years. The pensions spending of the Central government as percentage of GDP has doubled between 1995 and 2000. In 1998 the wage bill of the civil servants constituted 4.8 per cent of the GDP while the pension bill was equivalent to 1.3 per cent of the GDP. Government servants do not explicitly contribute to the pension scheme and no fund is accumulated. The system operates on a pay-as-you go basis. There are serious apprehensions on the sustainability of the present arrangement. Unless some system of funding is initiated, the burden at some point can become tough to bear. In fact, in the case of all obligations where re-payment or payment is expected to be made over several years, the creation of a sinking fund becomes essential. The reform as far as the government servants' pension scheme is concerned must be towards creating some funding arrangement. Whether or not the pension formula itself must undergo a change will be a policy decision.

Approximately 49 per cent of the non-government salaried workers in the formal sector are covered by Compulsory Provident Funds. These mandatory 'defined contribution' plans cover, however, only 177 industries. Even within these specified industries only establishments employing 20 or more persons need to provide provident fund benefits to employees. The major problems associated with the Compulsory Provident Fund Schemes are low rates of return and poor accumulation. It is estimated that over the last decade provident funds in India have earned a return of only little over 2.5 per cent above inflation rate for their members. Since the rules governing withdrawals are excessively permissive, the accumulation has been low. Consequently there has been a failure to reap the benefits of compounding over decades and providing for old age. More often workers have viewed their contribution as a tax shield rather than savings that will benefit them later.

The fourth group comprising workers and professionals not covered by any Provident Fund Scheme or Pension Schemes have to save on their own in order to take care of their needs in the post retirement period. That is why some of the savings instruments get tax relief. Approximately 90 per cent of the workers are not covered by any Pension Scheme. The Public Provident Fund Scheme was created to take care of such workers as well as self-employed. It has had no big impact.

Issues in Pension Reform

As mentioned earlier, social safety nets for people below the poverty level will depend upon the fiscal resources of the government. As far as the Pension Scheme for government servants is concerned, governments both at the Centre and the states will have to think afresh on how to deal with their unfunded pension liabilities. A High Level Expert Group has suggested that in relation to newly recruited civil servants a 'defined contribution' scheme should be introduced combined with a minimum commitment.

As regards the existing Compulsory Provident Fund Cum Pension Scheme, the reform must be in the direction of ensuring a better return through improved funds management and increasing accumulation of the individuals by tightening the provisions relating to withdrawals. As the contribution rates are already high, there is hardly any scope to raise this rate. A higher accumulation will have to be achieved by securing a higher rate of return. This can happen, if there are professional fund managers. Introduction of specialised agencies for fund management approved by the regulator must be an important part of pension reform.

Apart from these three groups, there is a large class of workers and professionals who need pension cover. It is here, there will be scope for new private pension schemes. The potential is high. In fact, the new pension schemes can be set up by a wide variety of entities. For example, in the US, college teachers have their own Pension Fund which is managed by the Teachers' Association. Some of the eminent economists have headed this organisation. Teachers are given the option of deciding what percentage of their contribution will be conservatively managed and how much can be put in aggressively managed schemes. The conservatively managed scheme is known as Teachers Insurance and Annuity Association and the aggressively managed scheme is called College Retirement Equities Fund. I understand that similar organisations exist for professionals like Doctors in the US. Pension Funds are long-term funds. A person saves through his working life. People will be willing to contribute to such a scheme only if they have confidence in the entities promoting such a scheme. Credibility to deliver is, therefore, extremely important and credibility can come only if there is a regulatory authority overseeing the functioning of the schemes. The growth of pension funds in our country will, therefore, depend upon how strong the regulatory system is. I am happy to know that IRDA may be entrusted with the responsibility of overseeing the pension schemes. Management of pension funds has a close similarity to the management of life funds. The pension schemes if properly managed can give to the members a high rate of return. But they should not gamble in this process. That is why the regulation of the portfolio becomes important. Any pension plan must be clearly governed by a set of prudential regulations and must operate through a scheme of trustees who hold a fiduciary duty to the participants. Every one who is capable of saving is very much interested to save enough for his post working life. Individuals will opt for private pension schemes if the entities can earn the trust of the people. A well-designed and effective pension system will provide much needed income security to the aged and in this process enhance savings in the economy and promote economic growth. The reform of the pension system must move in the direction of (a) conforming to 'defined contribution' system (b) creating 'safety walls' around the assets created out of funds and (c) establishing a strong regulatory system.

Address at Seminar on Pension with a Special Focus on India, Institute of Insurance and Risk Management. Hyderabad, August 29, 2002.

Part IV

External Sector and Globalisation

22 | Globalisation and its Impact

Introduction

Globalisation has become an expression of common usage. Unfortunately, it connotes different things to different people. To some, it represents a brave new world with no barriers. For some others, it spells doom and destruction. We need to have a clear understanding of what globalisation stands for, if we have to deal with a phenomenon that is willy-nilly gathering momentum.

As we begin analysing the implications of globalisation, several questions arise. What is globalisation? Is it purely an economic concept? Is this a new phenomenon? What are the benefits of globalisation? Who gets hurt in the process of globalisation? Is globalisation intrinsically inequitous? Is it possible for individual countries to isolate themselves from globalisation? What are the complementary institutions and policies that countries can build to protect themselves or to gain maximum benefits? Where does India stand in this race for globalisation? Is she a potential gainer or loser?

Broadly speaking, the term 'globalisation' means integration of economies and societies through cross country flows of information, ideas, technologies, goods, services, capital, finance and people. The essence of globalisation is connectivity. Cross border integration can have several dimensions—cultural, social, political and economic. In fact, some people fear cultural and social integration even more than economic integration. The fear of "cultural hegemony" haunts many. However, we use the term globalisation in this paper in the more limited sense of economic integration which can happen through the three channels of: (a) trade in goods and services, (b) movement of capital and (c) flow of finance. Besides, there is also the channel through movement of people.

Historical Development

Historically, globalisation has been a process with highs and lows. During the Pre-World War I period of 1870 to 1914, there was rapid integration of the economies in terms of trade flows, movement of capital and migration of people (Tables 22.1, 22.2 and 22.3). The 19th century had witnessed some revolutionary breakthroughs in communication and transport with the emergence of railroad, steamship and telegraph (Frankel, 2000). Keynes wrote in 1920 "What an extraordinary episode in the progress of man that age was which came to an end in August 1914!... The inhabitant of London could order by telephone, sipping his morning tea in bed, the various products of the whole earth.....he could at the same time and by the same means adventure his wealth in the natural resources and new enterprise of any quarter of the world...". The Pre-World War I period witnessed the growth of globalisation mainly led by the technological forces in the fields of transport and communication. There were less barriers to flow of trade and people across the geographical boundaries.[1] Indeed there were no passports and visa requirements and very few non-tariff barriers and restrictions on fund flows (Streeten, 1998). The pace of globalisation, however, decelerated between the First and the Second World Wars. The inter-war period witnessed the erection of various barriers to restrict free movement of goods and services (Maizels, 1970 and Frankel, 2000). Most economies thought that they could thrive better under high protective walls. After World War II, all the leading countries resolved not to repeat the mistakes they had committed previously by opting for isolation. Although after 1945, there was a drive to increased integration, it took a long time to reach the pre-World War I level. In terms of percentage of exports and imports to total output, the US could reach the pre-World War level of 11 per cent only around 1970. Most of the developing countries which gained Independence from colonial rule in the immediate post-World

---

1. According to Streeten (2001), there were much less barriers to immigration during 1870-1913, and that sixty million Europeans moved to Americas, Australia or other area for new settlement. According to Kuznets (1972), "...through most of the nineteenth and in the early twentieth century emigration from Europe was essentially voluntary, unrestricted, and in response to greater economic opportunities in the country of destination... During the nineteenth and early twentieth centuries, when intercontinental emigration was high and unimpeded by legal restrictions either at origin or at destination, the identity of the countries in Europe with high migration proportions changed continuously."

War II period followed an import substitution industrialisation regime. The Soviet bloc countries were also shielded from the process of global economic integration. However, times have changed. In the last two decades, the process of globalisation has proceeded with greater vigour. The former Soviet bloc countries are getting integrated with the global economy. More and more developing countries are turning towards outward oriented policy of growth. Yet, studies point out that trade and capital markets are no more globalised today than they were at the end of the 19th century.[2] However, there are more concerns about globalisation now than before because of the nature and speed of transformation. What is striking in the current episode is not only the rapid pace but also the enormous impact of new information technologies on market integration, efficiency and industrial organisation.

Table 22.1

World Trend in Trade 1876-1959

Index No. 1913=100

Period	Trade Volume	
	Manufacturing	Primary Produce
1876-80	31	31
1896-1900	54	62
1911-13	94	97
1926-30	113	123
1931-33	81	116
1934-35	84	114
1936-38	100	125
1948-50	132	116
1951-53	178	133
1954-56	216	156
1957-59	251	182

Source: Maizels (1970).

Original Sources: 1. Industrialisation and Foreign Trade, League of Nations. Geneva, 1945.

2. Lewis, W.A. (1952). "World Production, Prices and Trade, 1870-1960", *Manchester School* 20(2).

---

2. The share of exports in GDP for 16 major industrial countries was 18.2 in 1900 and 21.2 in 1913. In 1992, the share was still lower at 17 per cent for the industrial countries (Streeten, 1998). While international investment flows as measured by absolute value of current account exceeded 3 per cent of GDP before 1914, they slumped to less than half that level in 1930s and only after 1970 began to move decisively upward—reaching 2.3 per cent in 1990-1996 (Obstfeld, 1998).

Table 22.2
Net Capital Flows as Percentage of GDP

Period	US	UK	Japan	France	Germany	Canada	Australia
1870-89	0.7	4.6	0.6	2.4	1.7	7.0	8.2
1890-1913	1.0	4.6	2.4	1.3	1.5	7.0	4.1
1914-18	4.1	3.1	6.8	*	*	3.6	3.4
1919-26	1.7	2.7	2.1	2.8	2.4	2.5	4.2
1927-31	0.7	1.9	0.6	1.4	2.0	2.7	5.9
1932-39	0.4	1.1	1.0	1.0	0.6	2.6	1.7
1940-46	1.1	7.2	1.0	*	*	3.3	3.5
1947-59	0.6	1.2	1.3	1.5	2.0	2.3	3.4
1960-73	0.5	0.8	1.0	0.6	1.0	1.2	2.3
1974-89	1.4	1.5	1.8	0.8	2.1	1.7	3.6
1990-96	1.0	2.0	2.2	0.7	1.9	4.1	4.0

Note: The figures refer to mean absolute value of current account as percentage of GDP.
* Not Available.
Source: Obstfeld (1998).

Table 22.3
Intercontinental Migration, 1801 to 1955

(in millions)

Items	1801-1820	1821-1850	1851-1880	1881-1910	1911-1940	1946-1955
1. Emigration from Europe						
Total Flow per Decade						
(a) Gross	0.12	0.98	2.89	8.49	5.39	na
(b) Net	0.12	0.90	2.37	5.89	3.32	4.36
As Percentage of Population						
(a) Gross	0.1	0.4	1.0	2.2	1.1	na
(b) Net	0.1	0.4	0.8	1.5	0.7	0.8
2. Immigration into US						
(a) Gross	0.12	0.82	2.57	5.91	3.46	1.95
(b) Net	0.12	0.75	2.11	4.10	2.13	1.70
As Percentage of Population						
(a) Gross	1.7	5.5	7.2	8.5	3.0	1.3
(b) Net	1.7	5.9	5.9	5.9	1.9	1.1

Source: Kuznets (1972).

Gains and Losses from Globalisation

The gains and losses from globalisation can be analysed in the context of the three types of channels of economic globalisation identified earlier.

Trade in Goods and Services

According to the standard theory, international trade leads to allocation of resources that is consistent with comparative advantage. This results in specialisation which enhances productivity. While the classical theory of comparative advantage was based on assumptions of perfect competition, constant returns to scale and fixed technology, the "new trade theory" which takes into account imperfect competition, increasing returns to scale and changing technology also comes to the conclusion that openness leads to improved rates of growth (Frankel, 2000). The new trade theory talks of dynamic gains from international trade. It is accepted that international trade, in general, is beneficial and that restrictive trade practices impede growth. That is the reason why many of the emerging economies which originally depended on a growth model of import substitution have moved over to a policy of outward orientation. Obviously, even in relation to trade in goods and services, there is one concern. Emerging economies will reap the benefits of international trade only if they reach the full potential of their resource availability. This will probably require time. That is why international trade agreements make exceptions by allowing longer time to developing economies in terms of reduction in tariff and non-tariff barriers. Special and differential treatment has become an accepted principle.

Movement of Capital

Capital flows across countries have played an important role in enhancing the production base. This was very much true in 19th and 20th centuries. Capital mobility enables the total savings of the world to be distributed among countries which have the highest investment potential. Under these circumstances, one country's growth is not constrained by its own domestic savings. The inflow of foreign capital has played a significant role in the development in the recent period of the East Asian countries. The current account deficit of some of these countries had exceeded 5 per cent of the GDP in most of the period when growth was rapid. In fact, at the peak, the foreign capital inflow into Malaysia in 1993 was 17.4 per cent of its GDP, while in Thailand in 1995 it was 12.7 per cent of the GDP (Rangarajan, 2000a). Capital flows can take either the form of foreign direct investment or portfolio investment. For developing countries the preferred alternative is foreign direct investment. Portfolio investment does not directly lead to expansion of productive capacity. It may do so, however, at one step removed. Recent events have shown that portfolio investment can be volatile particularly in times of loss of confidence. That is why countries want to put restrictions on portfolio investment. However, in an open system such restrictions cannot work easily. Even in relation to foreign direct investment, two aspects have raised concerns. First, there is always the fear that some part of the domestic economy will be controlled by external factors. In India, it is very often referred to as the "East India Company Syndrome". However, there is an increasing realisation on the part of transnational companies also not to act in a manner inconsistent with the policies of countries in which investment is made. Even in recent East Asian crisis it was found that foreign direct investment was a stable element. While to some extent fresh capital inflow was moderated, there was no outflow of foreign direct investment (Rangarajan, 2000b). The second aspect of concern in relation to foreign direct investment has been the fact that a significant part of foreign direct investment has been in the form of cross border mergers and acquisitions.[3] It is felt that FDI entry through the take over of domestic firms is less beneficial because such foreign acquisitions do not add to the productive capacity but simply transfer ownership and control from domestic to foreign hands. While this is correct, it overlooks the fact that the funds released to the domestic entrepreneurs because of the acquisition can be utilised for expanding capacity by the domestic entrepreneurs. Whether or not mergers and acquisitions lead to technological upgradation in the short-term is not clear. However, it is reported that over the longer term, effects could be different. Cross border mergers and acquisitions can be followed by transfer of new or

---

3. The ratio of the value of cross border M&As to FDI inflows in developing countries has risen from one-tenth in 1987-1989 to more than one-third in 1997-1999. Among developing regions, the ratio is the highest in Latin America and the Caribbean: it increased from 18 per cent to 61 per cent between these two periods, while in developing Asia it increased from 8 per cent to 21 per cent between the same periods (United Nations, 2000).

better technology, when acquired firms are restructured to increase the efficiency of their operations. As recent events in India have shown while foreign direct investment is beneficial, public policy will have to be extremely careful in setting the conditions under which private capital is invited. Seeking guarantees and providing guarantees are inconsistent with an open system. Risk taking is the basic element of entrepreneurial spirit.

Financial Flows

The rapid development of the capital market has been one of the important features of the current process of globalisation. While the growth in capital and foreign exchange markets have facilitated the transfer of resources across borders, the gross turnover in foreign exchange markets has been extremely large. It is estimated that the gross turnover is around $ 1.5 trillion per day worldwide (Frankel, 2000). This is of the order of hundred times greater than the volume of trade in goods and services. Currency trade has become an end in itself. The expansion in foreign exchange markets and capital markets is a necessary prerequisite for international transfer of capital. However, the volatility in the foreign exchange market and the ease with which funds can be withdrawn from countries have often created panic situations. The most recent example of this was the East Asian crisis. Contagion of financial crises is a worrying phenomenon. When one country faces a crisis, it affects others. It is not as if financial crises are solely caused by foreign exchange traders. What the financial markets tend to do is to exaggerate weaknesses. Herd instinct is not uncommon in financial markets. When an economy becomes more open to capital and financial flows, there is even greater compulsion to ensure that factors relating to macroeconomic stability are not ignored. This is a lesson all developing countries have to learn from East Asian crisis. As one commentator aptly said "The trigger was sentiment, but vulnerability was due to fundamentals" (Reddy, 2000). In this context, it has been emphasised that opening of the capital account need not preclude moderate controls, either price based or regulatory, on capital flows. Controls should be selective, designed to achieve the specific objective of containing speculative capital. While there is, no doubt, that countries benefit by capital flows, the need to keep a watchful eye on foreign exchange markets becomes essential. What applies to trade may not necessarily apply to finance in full measure. However, while stringent capital controls may be adopted as a temporary shield as part of crisis management, they cannot be a permanent solution (Rangarajan, 2000b).

Concerns and Fears

On the impact of globalisation, there are two major concerns. These may be described as even fears. Under each major concern there are many related anxieties. The first major concern is that globalisation leads to a more inequitous distribution of income among countries and within countries. The second fear is that globalisation leads to loss of national sovereignty and that countries are finding it increasingly difficult to follow independent domestic policies. These two issues have to be addressed both theoretically and empirically.

The argument that globalisation leads to inequality is based on the premise that since globalisation emphasises efficiency, gains will accrue to countries which are favourably endowed with natural and human resources. Advanced countries have had a head start over the other countries by at least three centuries. The technological base of these countries is not only wide but highly sophisticated. While trade benefits all countries, greater gains accrue to the industrially advanced countries. This is the reason why even in the present trade agreements, a case has been built up for special and differential treatment in relation to developing countries. By and large, this treatment provides for longer transition periods in relation to adjustment. However, there are two changes with respect to international trade which may work to the advantage of the developing countries. First, for a variety of reasons, the industrially advanced countries are vacating certain areas of production. These can be filled in by developing countries. A good example of this is what the East Asian countries did in the 1970s and 1980s. Second, international trade is no longer determined by the distribution of natural resources. With the advent of information technology, the role of human resources has emerged as more important. Specialised human skills will become the determining factor in the coming decades. Productive activities are becoming "knowledge intensive" rather than "resource intensive". While there is a divide between developing and the advanced countries even in this area—some people call it the digital divide—it is a gap which can be bridged. A globalised economy with increased specialisation can lead to improved productivity and faster growth. What will be required is a balancing mechanism to ensure that the handicaps of the developing countries are overcome.

Apart from the possible inequitous distribution of income among countries, it has also been argued that globalisation leads to widening income gaps within the countries as well. This can happen both in the developed and developing economies. The argument is the same as was advanced in relation to inequitous distribution among countries. Globalisation may benefit even within a country those who have the skills and the technology. The higher growth rate achieved by an economy can be at the expense of declining incomes of people who may be rendered redundant. In this context, it has to be noted that while globalisation may accelerate the process of technology substitution in developing economies, these countries even without globalisation will face the problem associated with moving from lower to higher technology. If the growth rate of the economy accelerates sufficiently, then part of the resources can be diverted by the state to modernise and re-equip people who may be affected by the process of technology upgradation.

The second concern relates to the loss of autonomy in the pursuit of economic policies. In a highly integrated world economy, it is true that one country cannot pursue policies which are not in consonance with the world-wide trends. Capital and technology are fluid and they will move where the benefits are greater. However, this is not a new phenomenon. For example, in the days of gold standard, maintenance of the external value of the currency in terms of gold content became paramount. Domestic monetary policy actions were subordinated to this overriding consideration. In fact, the fixed exchange rate system under the Bretton Woods arrangement also imposed similar constraints. In a more or less fixed exchange rate regime, no country can allow its inflation rate to be out of alignment with the inflation rate in the rest of the world. Of course, the flexible exchange rate regime which is now prevalent, gives a little more autonomy in the pursuit of domestic monetary policy. It is, however, impossible for any country to have domestic autonomy, fixed exchange rate and free capital flows. This is the famous impossible trinity. Similar to the limitations of monetary policy in an open economy, the process of globalisation imposes some constraints on fiscal policies of countries as well. Multilateral commitments have led many developing countries to reduce import duties which traditionally have been a major source of revenue. Free capital mobility results in tax competition among countries. At any rate, no country wants its tax regime to be less attractive for investment. While fiscal autonomy in this sense is reduced, the overall fiscal impact will depend on the elasticity of revenues to GDP and the impact of globalisation on growth of GDP and the tax base. As the nations come together whether it be in the political, social or economic arena, some sacrifice of sovereignty is inevitable. The constraints of a globalised economic system on the pursuit of domestic policies have to be recognised. However, it need not result in the abdication of domestic objectives.

Another fear associated with globalisation is insecurity and volatility. When countries are inter-related strongly, a small spark can start a large conflagration. Panic and fear spread fast. The only hope here is that despite integration, different parts of the world economy can be at different phases of the business cycle. In fact, until recently there had been a lag between the time the US reached the peak of the cycle and the European Union reached it. Such non-synchronised movements have had a beneficial effect. However, we are now facing for the first time since the 1980s the first synchronised downturn. There is greater insecurity because of the constant drive towards efficiency and competition. The downside to globalisation essentially emphasises the need to create countervailing forces in the form of institutions and policies at the international level. Global governance cannot be pushed to the periphery, as integration gathers speed.

Empirical evidence on the impact of globalisation on inequality is not very clear. The share in aggregate world exports and in world output of the developing countries has been increasing. In aggregate world exports, the share of developing countries increased from 20.6 per cent in 1988-1990 to 29.9 per cent 2000 (IMF, 2001 and Table 22.4A). In fact, in comparing the share of the developing countries over time, care has to be taken to compare the share of the same set of countries over the entire time frame. In fact, four of the countries which are now classified as newly industrialised Asian economies, are excluded from developing countries when data on developing countries are presented in the various documents. We have included these four countries in the category of developing countries while computing the share and comparing the trend. Similarly the share in aggregate world output of developing countries has increased from 17.9 per cent in 1988-1990 to 40.4 per cent in 2000 (IMF, 2001 and Table 22.4B). The growth rates of the developing countries both in terms of GDP and per capita GDP have been higher than those of the industrial countries. These growth rates have been in fact higher in the 1990s than in the 1980s. All these data do not indicate that the developing countries as a group have suffered in the process of globalisation. In fact, there have been substantial gains. But within developing countries, Africa has not done well and some of the South Asian countries have done better only in the 1990s.[4]

Table 22.4A

Share in Aggregate World Exports

(per cent)

Year	Major Industrial Countries*	Developing Countries**	Asia	Africa
1988-90	55.5	20.6	10.8	2.0
1995	50.0	26.9	17.5	1.8
2000	47.7	29.9@	19.1	2.1

Note: * Major Industrial Countries include US, Japan, Germany, France, Italy, UK and Canada.

** Developing Countries also includes Newly Industrialised Asian Economies.

@ Excluding share of Israel which is shifted to Industrial Countries group.

Source: Various Issues of *World Economic Outlook*, IMF.

---

4. It is not easy to answer the question whether globalisation has led to a more unequal distribution of income in the world. Even if one were able to establish that the distribution of income globally had become more unequal in the 1990s, it is difficult to trace this purely to globalisation. Apart from this, there are two other issues. First, there is the issue whether incomes of countries should be measured by actual exchange rates or purchasing power parity rates. Second, there is the issue whether all countries should be treated equal or given weights according to their respective population. Inequality measured by deciles, indicates that, between 1988 and 1993, the share of world income going to the poorest 10 per cent of the world's population fell from 0.88 per cent to 0.64 per cent, whereas the share of richest 10 per cent rose from 63.7 per cent to 66.9 per cent (Wade, 2001). However, the limitation of the measure of deciles is that, it focuses only on the extreme 20 per cent observations of the population. This measure ignores the improvement in economic performance of developing countries of Asia and western hemisphere, which lie in the middle of the distribution. In fact, the worsening of the income distribution may be due to the extremely low growth of certain countries particularly in the Sub-Saharan Africa. However, even according to the study by Wade, the Gini coefficient which takes into account the entire spectrum of distribution of income shows no deterioration, if countries are weighted by respective population and purchasing power parity exchange rates are used. There are also studies which show that the number of people in extreme poverty as measured by people below a certain poverty line has declined.

Table 22.4B

Share in Aggregate World Output

(per cent)

Year	Major Industrial Countries*	Developing Countries**	Asia	Africa
1988-90	62.7	17.9	7.2	1.7
1995	46.2	41.2	24.4	3.3
2000	45.4	40.4@	25.0	3.2

Note: * Major Industrial Countries include US, Japan, Germany, France, Italy, UK and Canada.
  ** Developing Countries also includes Newly Industrialised Asian Economies.
  @ Excluding share of Israel which is shifted to Industrial Countries group.

Source: Various Issues of *World Economic Outlook*. IMF.

While the growth rate in per capita income of the developing countries in the 1990s is nearly two times higher than that of industrialised countries (Table 22.5), in absolute terms the gap in per capita income has widened.[5] As for income distribution within the countries, it is difficult to judge whether globalisation is the primary factor responsible for any deterioration in the distribution of income. We have had considerable controversies in our country on what happened to the poverty ratio in the second half of 1990s. Most analysts even for India would agree that the poverty ratio has declined in the 1990s. Differences may exist as to what rate at which this has fallen. Nevertheless, whether it is in India or any other country, it is very difficult to trace the changes in the distribution of income within the countries directly to globalisation.

India and the External Sector

India's economic policy towards foreign trade and foreign investment in the first four decades after India's Independence was restrictive. Import

---

5. The level of GDP per capita in developing countries has increased from US $ 2,170 in 1990 to US $ 3,260 in 1998 with a compound growth rate of 5.2 per cent. In between the same periods, the level of GDP per capita in OECD countries has increased from US $ 16,040 to US $ 20,360 registering a compound growth rate of 3.0 per cent. These figures show that, although the growth rate of per capita income of developing countries is much higher than that of OECD countries during 1990-1998, the gap between the respective levels of per capita income has widened from US $ 13,870 in the year 1990 to US $ 17,100 in the year 1998 (UNDP, 2000).

Table 22.5

Key Average Growth Rates

Items	Major Industrialised Countries*		Developing Countries**		Asia		Africa	
	1982-1991	1991-2001 $	1982-1991	1991-2001 $	1982-1991	1991-2001 $	1982-1991	1991-2001
GDP Growth Rate	3.1	2.8	4.3	4.5	6.9	7.4	2.2	2.8
Per Capita GDP Growth Rate	2.3	2.0	2.0	3.8	5.0	6.0	-0.7	0.3
Exports Growth Rate (Volume)	5.1	5.9	4.2	8.7	8.4	11.3	2.8	2.9
Imports Growth Rate (Volume)	5.8	6.7	1.9	8.2	6.6	9.3	1.2	3.5

Note: * Major Industrial Countries include US, Japan, Germany, France, Italy, UK and Canada.
**Developing Countries does not include Newly Industrialised Asian Economies and Israel in the group of developing countries since 1997.
$ figures for 1991-2001 are based on the projections for the year 2000 and 2001.
Source: *World Economic Outlook*, May 2000 IMF.

substitution constituted a major element of country's foreign trade and industrial policies. The approach to foreign investment was equally constrained. The deficit on the current account was met mainly by borrowing and particularly from official sources. India's share in world exports which stood at 1.85 per cent in 1950 fell to 0.58 per cent in 1992.[6] In the wake of the economic crisis that overtook the country in 1991, the approach to and content of economic policy underwent a far reaching change. This change was reflected in trade and investment policies. An outward orientation began to emerge. Tariff rates have been steadily brought down while quantitative controls have been dismantled. Foreign investment policy has become proactive. Majority ownership by foreign investors is allowed over a wide spectrum of industries. Authorised foreign institutions

---

6. India's share in world exports experienced a declining trend since 1950 up to 1980. Afterwards, the share started increasing slowly from 0.4 per cent in 1980 to reaching 0.67 per cent in 2000-01 (Table 22.8). It can also be noted that, India's share in the world trade was as high as close to 4 per cent during 1860-1889 (Kuznets, 1972). During the first four decades since Independence, India's exports share in the GDP remained almost constant, where as India's share in world exports witnessed a declining trend (Table 22.8). This phenomenon is due to the fact that, the world exports were increasing at a faster rate than the growth rate of India's GDP.

are allowed to invest in Indian stock markets. The exchange rate of the rupee is by and large determined by the forces of supply and demand, although the central bank does intervene to avoid instability and volatility.

How has the Indian economy fared as a result of the steady opening up? India's growth rate has definitely been higher in the period following 1992-93, even though there are concerns about falling growth rate in the last two years. In relation to the external sector, the situation has been comfortable. The current account deficit which peaked to 3.2 per cent of GDP in 1990 has been declining and is remaining around only one per cent of GDP in the last few years. The foreign exchange reserves of the country has been increasing and stands today at $ 55.6 billion. The import growth rate has not shown any alarming rise. The increasing integration has not resulted in a jolt to the economy. On the contrary, the broad macroeconomic indicators have shown an improvement. However, many concerns have been raised in relation to the impact of globalisation on Indian industries, agriculture in general and food security in particular and on the stability of the financial sector.

While recognising the fact that the Indian economy in the last decade has become more open, it is also necessary to note that the Indian economy is much less open than many other economies. Taking the most commonly used indicator of openness which is the proportion of import and export of goods and services to GDP, it is seen that this ratio has increased from 15 per cent in 1980 to 25 per cent in 1998.[7] However, this ratio of 25 per cent is much smaller than many other countries. For small countries like Malaysia and Singapore with a high outward orientation, this ratio exceeds 200 per cent. Among the industrially advanced countries, the United States is the only country which has a ratio similar to that of India (Table 22.6). Tariff levels are another indicator of openness. Here again, while India's weighted mean tariff rate has come down from 49.8 per cent in 1989-90 to 29.5 per cent in 1999, it is still high compared with many other countries (Table 22.7). While the weighted average tariff rate is nil for Hong Kong and Singapore, it is as low as 2.7 per cent in European Union countries and 2.8 per cent in the US. However, it is of significance to note that the standard

---

7. Compared to this, the ratio of sum of merchandise exports and imports to NDP in India was 18.83 per cent and 19.57 per cent in the year 1894 and 1899, respectively (Brahmananda, 2001).

deviation of the tariff rates in the US is high at 11.4 per cent which means that the rates on certain products are very high (World Bank, 2001).

Table 22.6

Foreign Trade as Percentage of GDP

Country	1970	1999
US	11	24
Canada	43	84
Japan	20	19
UK	44	53
France	30	50
Germany	*	57
Italy	32	49
EU	3.6	2.7
HongKong	181.0	261.0
Singapore	232	*
Korea	37	77
India	8	27

Note: Foreign Trade refers to exports and imports of goods and services.
Source: *World Development Indicators, 2001*. World Bank.

Table 22.7

Tariff Barriers in Different Countries

Country	Weighted Mean Tariff (All) 1988/89/90	Weighted Mean Tariff (All) 1999	Standard Deviation 1988/89/90	Standard Deviation 1999	Weighted Mean Tariff (Primary) 1988/89/90	Weighted Mean Tariff (Primary) 1999	Weighted Mean Tariff (Manfd.) 1988/89/90	Weighted Mean Tariff (Manfd.) 1999
US	4.1	2.8	6.7	11.4	2.1	2.0	4.5	2.9
Canada	6.5	3.2	7.0	22.3	2.4	5.9	7.2	2.9
Japan	3.3	2.3	8.0	7.3	3.7	4.0	2.9	1.4
EU	3.6	2.7	5.6	5.0	2.8	1.8	4.1	3
Hong Kong	0.0	0.0	0.0	0.0	0.0	0.0	0.0	0.0
Singapore	0.5	0.0	2.2	0.0	0.0	0.0	0.6	0.0
Korea	13.8	5.9	8.1	5.9	8.1	5.5	16.9	6.1
India	49.8	29.5	43.8	12.4	26.0	24.9	69.9	32.3

Source: *World Development Indicators, 2001*. World Bank.

Framework of Policy

What should be India's attitude in this environment of growing globalisation? At the outset it must be mentioned that opting out of globalisation is not a viable choice. There are at present 142 members in the World Trade Organisation (WTO). Some 30 countries are waiting to join the WTO. China has recently been admitted as a member. What is needed is to evolve an appropriate framework to wrest maximum benefits out of international trade and investment. This framework should include (a) making explicit the list of demands that India would like to make on the multilateral trade system, (b) measures that rich countries should be required to undertake to enable developing countries to gain more from international trade and (c) steps that India should take to realise the full potential from globalisation.

Demands on the Trading System

There is considerable concern about the next round of negotiations in the WTO. Developing countries including India should project strongly their viewpoint. Without being exhaustive, the demands on the multilateral trading system should include (1) establishing symmetry as between the movement of capital and natural persons, (2) delinking environmental standards and labour related considerations from trade negotiations, (3) zero tariffs in industrialised countries on labour intensive exports of developing countries, (4) adequate protection to genetic or biological material and traditional knowledge of developing countries, (5) prohibition of unilateral trade action and extra territorial application of national laws and regulations, and (6) effective restraint on industrialised countries in initiating anti-dumping and countervailing action against exports from developing countries (Ganesan, 1999).

Concerns have been expressed about the impact of present WTO arrangements on Indian agriculture. However, under the present provisions, the degree of protection enjoyed by Indian agriculture is below what is permissible. In fact, in relation to some agricultural products, very recently the import duty was increased considerably. On the contrary, Indian agricultural products can gain greater market access in the advanced countries, as the tariff barriers come down in those countries. This expectation has not been fulfilled so far. The developed countries have played a clever game by taking recourse to 'Green Box' and 'Blue Box' provisions. But possibilities do exist for expanding the market for Indian agricultural products.

Negotiations are not that easy. We have to give in some areas to gain in others. The manoeuvering abilities of developed countries to steer the international trading system in the direction of meeting their own needs and concerns cannot be underestimated. They have shown themselves to be crafty in this area. However, what is important is the approach. We must stay and fight whether they be intellectual property rights or public policy considerations. Doha showed some success in this direction. But the benefits of being part of the larger system should not be lost sight of.

Rich Country Initiatives

The purpose of the new trading system must be to ensure "free and fair" trade among countries. The emphasis so far has been on "free" rather than "fair" trade. It is in this context that the rich industrially advanced countries have a role to play. They have often indulged in "double speak". While requiring developing countries to dismantle barriers and join the main stream of international trade, they have been raising significant tariff and non-tariff barriers on trade from developing countries. Very often, this has been the consequence of heavy lobbying in the advanced countries to protect 'labour'. Although average tariffs in the United States, Canada, European Union and Japan—the so called Quad countries—range from only 4.3 per cent in Japan to 8.3 per cent in Canada, their tariff and trade barriers remain much higher on many products exported by developing countries. Major agricultural food products such as meat, sugar and dairy products attract tariff rates exceeding 100 per cent. Fruits and vegetables such as bananas are hit with a 180 per cent tariff by the European Union, once they exceed quota. Even in the case of dismantling the Multi-Fibre Agreement (MFA), it is stretched up to 2005 and has been back loaded so that much of the benefits will accrue to countries like India only towards the end (Stern, 2001). In fact, these trade barriers impose a serious burden on the developing countries. It is important that if the rich countries want a trading system that is truly fair, they should on their own lift the trade barriers and subsidies that prevent the products of developing countries from reaching their markets. It is important that these issues are brought to the forefront of the discussions at all international fora.

Actions by India

The third set of measures that should form part of the action plan must relate to strengthening India's position in international trade. India has many strengths, which several developing countries lack. In that sense, India is different and is in a stronger position to gain from international trade and investment. India's rise to the top of the IT industry in the world is a reflection of the abundance of skilled manpower in our country. It is, therefore, in India's interest to ensure that there is a greater freedom of movement of skilled manpower. At the same time, we should attempt to take all efforts to ensure that we continue to remain a frontline country in the area of skilled manpower. India can attract greater foreign investment, if we can accelerate our growth with stability. Stability, in this context, means reasonable balance on the fiscal and external accounts. We must maintain a competitive environment domestically so that we can take full advantage of wider market access. We must make good use of the extended time given to developing countries to dismantle trade barriers. Wherever legislations are required to protect sectors like agriculture, they need to be enacted quickly. Infact, we had taken a long time to pass the Protection of Plant Varieties and Farmers' Rights Bill. We must also be active in ensuring that our firms make effective use of the new patent rights. South Korea has been able to file in recent years as many as 5000 patent applications in the United States whereas in 1986, the country filed only 162 (Bergsten, 1999). China has also been very active in this area. We need a truly active agency in India to encourage Indian firms to file patent applications. In effect, we must build the complementary institutions necessary for maximising the benefits from international trade and investment.

Conclusion

Globalisation, in a fundamental sense, is not a new phenomenon. Its roots extend farther and deeper than the visible part of the plant. It is as old as history, starting with the great migrations of people across the great land masses. Only recent developments in computer and communication technologies have accelerated the process of integration, with geographic distances becoming less of a factor. Is this 'end of geography' a boon or a bane? Borders have become porous and the sky is open. With modern technologies which do not recognise geography, it is not possible to hold back ideas either in the political, economic or cultural spheres. Each country must prepare itself to meet the new challenges so that it is not bypassed by this huge wave of technological and institutional changes.

Nothing is an unmixed blessing. Globalisation in its present form though spurred by far reaching technological changes is not a pure technological phenomenon. It has many dimensions including ideological. To deal with this phenomenon, we must understand the gains and losses, the benefits as well as dangers. To be forewarned, as the saying goes, is to be forearmed. But we should not throw the baby with bath water. We should also resist the temptation to blame globalisation for all our failures. Most often, as the poet said, the fault is in ourselves.

Table 22.8

India's Exports Performance since Independence

(per cent)

Year	Share in World Exports	Year	Share in GDP
1950	1.85	1950s	6.0
1960	1.03	1960s	4.0
1970	0.64	1970s	6.0
1980	0.42	1980s	6.0
1990	0.52	1990-91	5.7
1995	0.63	1995-96	9.0
2000-01	0.67	2000-01	10.1

Source: 1. *Fifty Years of Indian Parliamentary Democracy, 1997*. Lok Sabha Secretariat, New Delhi.
2. *Economic Survey, 2001-02*. Government of India.
3. *Medium Term Export Strategy, 2002-2007*. Government of India.

Risks of an open economy are well known. We must not, nevertheless, miss the opportunities that the global system can offer. As an eminent critic put it, the world cannot marginalise India. But India, if it chooses, can marginalise itself. We must guard ourselves against this danger. More than many other developing countries, India is in a position to wrest significant gains from globalisation. However, we must voice our concerns and in cooperation with other developing countries modify the international trading arrangements to take care of the special needs of such countries. At the same time, we must identify and strengthen our comparative advantages. It is this two-fold approach which will enable us to meet the challenges of globalisation which may be the defining characteristic of the new millennium.

References

Bergsten, C. Fred (1999). "India and the Global Trading System", *Fourteenth EXIM Bank Commencement Day Annual Lecture.* Mumbai, March 10.

Bhalla, A.S. (Ed.)(1998). *Globalisation, Growth and Marginalization.* Ottawa: IRDC.

Brahmananda, P.R. (2001). *Money, Income, Prices in 19th Century India.* Mumbai: Himalaya Publishing House.

Debroy, Bibek (1996). *Beyond the Uruguay Round: The Indian Perspective on GATT.* New Delhi: Response Books.

Dunning, John H. (1994). "Globalisation, Economic Restructuring and Development", *6th Raul Prebisch Lecture.* Geneva: UNCTAD.

Feldstein, Martin (2000). "Aspects of Global Economic Integration", *NBER Working Paper.* September.

Frankel, Jeffrey A. (2000). "Globalisation of the Economy", *NBER Working Paper*, August.

Ganesan, A.V. (1999). "Presidential Address" delivered at the *Fourteenth EXIM Bank Commencement Day Annual Lecture.* Mumbai, March 10.

Government of India (2002). *Economic Survey 2001-02.* New Delhi: Ministry of Finance.

———. (2002): *Medium Term Export Strategy 2002-2007.* New Delhi.: Ministry of Commerce and Industry.

IMF (2000). *World Economic Outlook.* May. Washington DC.

———. (2001). *World Economic Outlook*, October. Washington DC.

Keynes, John Maynard (1920). *The Economic Consequences of Peace.* New York: Harcourt Brace and Howe.

Kuznets, Simon (1972). *Modern Economic Growth: Rate, Structure and Spread.* New Delhi: Oxford and IBH Publishing Co.

Lok Sabha Secretariat (1997). *Fifty Years of Indian Parliamentary Democracy.* New Delhi.

Maizels, Alfred (1970). *Growth and Trade.* NIESR Students' Edition. London: Cambridge University Press.

Nayyar, Deepak (1995). "Globalisation: The Past in Our Present", Presidential Address at the *Seventy-Eighth Annual Conference of Indian Economic Association.* December 28-30.

Obstfeld, Maurice (1998). "The Global Capital Market: Benefactor or Menace", *Journal of Economic Perspective* 12(4): 9-30.

Panitchpakdi, Supachai (2001). "If You Are in WTO Fold, You'll be Heard", Interview with *The Economic Times*, September 25.

Raghavan, Chakravarthi. "What is Globalisation?", *Third World Resurgence* 74.

Rangarajan, C. (2000a). "Understanding the East Asian Crisis" in C. Rangarajan, *Perspective on Indian Economy: A Collection of Essays*. New Delhi: UBSPD.

———. (2000b). "Capital Account Liberalisation and Control: Lessons from the East Asian Crisis", in C. Rangarajan, *Perspective on Indian Economy: A Collection of Essays*. New Delhi: UBSPD.

Reddy, Y.V. (2000). "The Asian Crisis: Asking the Right Questions" in Y.V. Reddy, *Monetary and Financial Sector Reforms in India*. New Delhi: UBSPD.

———. (2001). "Globalisation and Challenges for South Asia", B.P. Koirala India-Nepal Foundation Lecture at Kathmandu. *RBI Bulletin*. June.

Ricupero, Rubens (1997). Is there Life after Globalisation?Prospects for Development in the 21st Century", *Southern Economist*, June.

Sen, Amartya (2001). "A World of Extremes: Ten Theses on Globalisation", *The Times of India*, July 16.

Stern, Nicholas H. (2001). "Globalisation, the Investment Climate, and Poverty Reduction", Lecture at ICRIER. New Delhi. March 27.

Streeten, Paul (1998). "Globalisation: Threat or Salvation?', in A.S. Bhalla (Ed.), *Globalisation, Growth and Marginalization*. Ottawa: IRDC.

———. (2001). "Integration, Interdependence, and Globalisation", *Finance & Development* Washington DC: IMF.

UNDP (2000). *Human Development Report, 2000*. New Delhi: OUP.

United Nations (2000). *World Development Report 2000—Cross-border Mergers and Acquisitions and Development*. New York.

World Bank (2001). *World Development Indicators 2001*. Washington DC.

The author is thankful to Shri Amaresh Samantaraya for his assistance.

23 Global Imbalances and Policy Responses

Introduction

Although the world economy has grown at a satisfactory rate in the last three years, there is concern, and uncertainty about the future, because of the global imbalances—the large current account deficit of the US and surpluses elsewhere—which have reached unprecedented levels. The current account deficit of the US, estimated at 6.4 per cent of GDP for 2006, is the largest in the nation's history. There has been no large industrial country that has ever run persistent current account deficits of the magnitude posted by the US since 2000 (Edwards, 2005a). The growing external imbalances has necessitated the US building up a large net debtor foreign investment position while Japan, the European Union (EU) and emerging Asia have built up creditor positions. Interestingly, the large current account deficit has so far not led to a significant depreciation of the dollar, as it has been financed with little evidence of risk premia by the increased availability of global liquidity.[1] As a result, US interest rates (long-term) have been low, consumer spending resilient and corporate profits high, despite high oil prices.

Is it a Cause for Concern?

Is the large global imbalance a cause for concern? While views differ, the dominant refrain is that such a wide gap in the current account of the most powerful economy in the world has the potential for destabilisation. Both adjustment and non-adjustment have

---

1. The US Federal Reserve's broad real dollar exchange rate index fell by roughly eight per cent between November 2000 to November 2005 (Obstfeld and Rogoff, 2005).

Co-author A. Prasad.

associated problems.[2] The sustainability of the US current account deficit depends obviously on how long investors will be willing to finance it. In fact, some estimate that with unchanged policies and exchange rate, the US current account deficit can expand to between 8 to 12 per cent of GDP by 2010 (Cline, 2005; Roubini and Setser, 2004; and Mann, 2004 cited from Truman, 2005). There is a view that this order of deficit can be sustained, the most notable proponent being Greenspan (2003). Dooley, Garber and Folkerts-Landau (2003) argue that the US current account deficit is optimal and does not require any adjustment in the fiscal or current account balances nor in exchange rates.[3]

It has also been argued that since the return on US foreign assets exceeds the cost of servicing US liabilities, the US current account deficit is sustainable (Cooper, 2004). Although the US had a negative net international investment position of $ 2.5 trillion, the US enjoys a net positive rate of return. US residents earned $ 36 billion more on their investments abroad than they paid out on foreign investments in the US in 2004 and $ 7 billion more in 2005 (US Treasury Report, 2006).[4]

---

2. Historically, the present situation reminds one of 1960s. In the 1950s, the imbalance in world payments consisted principally of the coexistence of a large deficit in the US balance of payments and surpluses in a number of other industrial countries. The US deficit was supposed to have been temporary and hence welcomed as a way to redress the chronic world dollar shortage of the early post-war period. But it became a source of concern after 1965. By August of 1970, the net US reserve position had deteriorated to the point where the liabilities to foreign authorities exceeded the US official reserves by almost US $ 30 billion. On August 15, 1970 the US suspended the conversion and announced that it would no longer exchange dollar for gold. This was followed by a period of chaotic exchange rate movements.

3. The authors wrote a series of articles beginning June 2003 that came to be known as "Bretton Woods II" view. The authors drew parallels between the current global imbalances and the Bretton Woods system. The authors argued that the Asian countries (which they called periphery countries) were pursuing a development strategy of export-led growth supported by undervalued exchange rates, capital controls and official capital outflows in the form of accumulation of reserve asset claims on the center country (US). This was similar to the situation in the 1950s (Japan and Europe were the periphery and the US was the center country). The economic emergence of a fixed exchange rate periphery in Asia, according to the authors reestablished the US as the center country in the Bretton Woods international monetary system.

4. In 2004, according to Hausmann and Sturzenegger, the US got $ 30 billion more on its overseas investments than it paid on its external debts, which implies about $ 600 billion of assets (with a 5 per cent return). Yet formally the US had $ 2.5

contd...

The substantial weakening of the US dollar against other currencies during 2002-2004 did help create large valuation gains in respect of the non-dollar denominated assets of entities resident in the USA and valuation losses in their dollar denominated liabilities. The extent of the differential in returns between assets and liabilities, which Hausmann and Sturzenegger (2005) term as "dark matter" has had the effect of reducing the trade deficit concomitantly and helped stabilise the external payments position of the USA.[5] There is the further argument that the US has achieved a permanent increase in the productivity and profitability of investments and this could facilitate its current account financing.

Notwithstanding these optimistic arguments, there is now a large body of literature supporting the view that the large US current account deficit is not sustainable in the long run (Roubini and Setser, 2004; Obstfeld and Rogoff, 2005; Bernanke, 2005; Truman, 2005).

Historically, in 'large countries' that have gone through major economic reversals, the decline of GDP growth per capita on average has been in the range of 3.6 to 5.0 per cent in the first year of the structural adjustment. Three years after the initial adjustment, GDP growth will still likely to be below its long run trend (Edwards, 2005a). There is an overwhelming concern that an abrupt unwinding of the imbalances could threaten global economic and financial stability. Going forward, the scope for positive net factor payments from abroad and sizeable valuation effects are limited (Geithner, 2006a).[6] Lane and Milesi-Ferretti (2005) show that the US had relied on capital gains to stabilise its external position during the past few years. Looking forward, this cannot be sustained unless sizeable differences in rates of return exist between US external assets and liabilities.

---

contd...
    trillion in (net) external debt, which implies (again with a 5 per cent return) net payments of $ 125 billion. Dark matter, as defined by these authors is the gap between the assets implied by the fact that the US receives more on its international investments than it pays on its external debt (the investment income line in the balance of payments is positive, or at least was) and the United States' formal debt position.

5. The US investments abroad are in foreign currencies while its liabilities are in dollars. Hence, even a slight depreciation of the dollar will earn a higher rate of return on US assets than that earned by foreign firms in the US.

6. The US Treasury is of the view that while the large negative international investment position of the US will probably generate outflows on investment income in the near future, these outflows are not likely to be massive.

As Geithner (2006b) has forcefully articulated, it would not be appropriate to assume that global savings have moved across borders to their most productive uses, raising concerns about the sustainability of the US deficit. An abrupt adjustment scenario presented by the IMF (*World Economic Outlook*, September 2005a) suggests that an abrupt and disorderly adjustment could result in an increase in protectionism and a global slowdown with severe consequences to several countries. Such an abrupt adjustment could come from a sudden shift by central banks in portfolio preference away from US assets which would force a large real depreciation of the dollar, and a sharp correction of the trade balance. Together with the rise in protectionism, this could lead to strong inflationary pressures, triggering significant monetary tightening in the short term, which would have an adverse effect on GDP growth. In this scenario, emerging Asia could experience a sharp real appreciation of national currencies, deterioration in trade and current account balances and a slowdown in growth. Similar impact will be felt in Japan, Euro area countries, and to a lesser extent other developing regions.

It will obviously be unwise to let these imbalances mount until a sudden change in sentiment triggers an abrupt adjustment. An orderly unwinding of the global imbalances is decidedly preferable. The broad contours of the policies required for such a smooth adjustment are also recognised even though there is no consensus on the relative priorities attached to different policy interventions. Besides, there is no certainty about when and with what vigour each country will act.

Status of Global Imbalances

The current account deficit of the US has doubled between 2000 and 2006. The doubling of oil prices since last year has led to some changes in the pattern of imbalances, with the combined surpluses of oil producing countries now equal to roughly half the US current account deficit. Thus, the large current account deficit of the US has a corresponding surplus in the external accounts of other countries, including oil exporters such as Russia and Saudi Arabia, countries of emerging Asia, and most particularly China. The biggest change among the surplus countries between 2000 and 2006 has been in China and oil exporters.[7]

---

7. The increase in oil exporters oil exports revenue as a per cent of own GDP was 40 per cent between 2002-2005 and 1 per cent of world GDP.

Table 23.1

Current Account Imbalances

(US $ Billion)

	2000	2005	2006
USA	−416.0	−805.0	−864.0
Euro-zone	−41.9	+2.5	−23.8
Japan	+119.6	+163.9	+140.2
Asia	+46.1	+155.4	+159.5
Of which: China	+20.5	+158.6	+173.3
Middle East	+70.0	+196.0	+240.9
Of which: Oil Exporters	+148.8	+347.4	+423.7
Russia	+46.8	+86.6	+106.0

Note: + Denotes Surplus/− Denotes deficit.
Source: IMF (2006). *World Economic Outlook*, April.

Factors Behind the Current Account Deficit of the US

There are varying explanations for global imbalances depending on which side of the macro-identity one is looking at. Some look at factors causing the US current account deficit (US consumption, growth, etc.), or factors causing the US capital account surplus (strong US productivity growth) or causes for the saving-investment imbalance (US fiscal deficit) Forbes (2005).

The analysis of the determinants of current account imbalances usually follows four common tracks, *viz.*, trade balance, saving-investment divergence, domestic demand and capital flow. The first approach traces the current account balance (reflected in the trade balance) essentially to income and relative prices. This leads to a focus on the relative demands in the home country and abroad and on exchange rates. The widening of the current account deficit has been frequently attributed to the strength of the dollar and hence it's increased purchasing power in the mid-1990s. The second approach characterises the current account balance as identical to the difference between savings and investment. Under this approach, the recent deterioration of the US current account has largely been attributed to the decline in US domestic savings, and in particular of household and public savings. The third track stresses on the deterioration in current

Table 23.2

Major Imports and the Top 10 Sources of Imports into the US (2005)

Category of Import	Value in US $ Billion
Petroleum Products	252
Capital Goods (Excluding Automotive Products)	380
Automotive Products	240
Consumer Goods (Excluding Autos and Food)	407
Country of Importation	**Per Cent of Total**
Canada	17.2
China	14.6
Mexico	10.2
Japan	8.3
Federal Republic of Germany	5.1
United Kingdom	3.1
South Korea	2.6
Taiwan	2.1
Venezuela	2.0
France	2.0
Malaysia	2.0

Source: US Treasury. *Report to Congress on International Economic and Exchange Rate Policies.*

account as arising from the gap between domestic demand and output. The fourth perspective explains the current account deficit as equal to the net inflow of capital from abroad and views the large and growing current account deficit as driven by supply of capital from overseas. The above four tracks are evidently merely alternate ways of characterising the current account balance. They do not explain the fundamental causes.

To appreciate the fundamental causes of the global imbalances, it would be useful to briefly review the events leading to build up of current account deficit in the US after 1995. The US current account deficit rose between 1996 and 2002 along with an effective appreciation of the dollar exchange rate. Between the third quarter of 1995 and the first quarter of 2002, the real exchange rate of the dollar appreciated by 33 per cent and the current account deficit increased from about 1.5 per cent of GDP to just below 4 per cent of GDP. The dollar exchange rate seemed to have appreciated due to capital inflows attracted by high rates of return caused by productivity growth. This encouraged higher consumption and lower savings. This trend was fuelled further by the fiscal deficit which started emerging after 2000. Up to 2004, the US interest rates were also low.

Several economists have identified the US fiscal imbalances and foreign exchange intervention by Asian central banks to be the fundamental causes of the imbalances (Truman, 2005; Roubini and Setser, 2004). The re-emergence of fiscal deficit in the USA, along with the pre-existing current account deficit has prompted reference to the 'twin-deficits' hypothesis, according to which, the fiscal deficit reduces public savings and therefore national savings which get reflected in the current account balance. The fact that the US general fiscal deficit was about 4.0 per cent of GDP in 2005 and its net private savings was a negative 1 per cent of GDP has added credence to this view.[8] However, from a longer-term perspective, empirical evidence on the linkage between fiscal and current account deficits is mixed.[9] Bernanke (2005) has pointed out that the twin deficit argument does not explain why countries in Europe and Japan are running current account surpluses and fiscal deficit during the same period.

A contrarian explanation downplays the role of fiscal deficit and highlights the importance of a 'global saving glut' (particularly in emerging markets) (Bernanke, 2005). Bernanke has argued that the US current account deficit is driven by a global savings glut rather than lack of US savings.[10] Yet others (Chinn and Ito 2005; Rajan, 2006) have argued that that the real problem is investment restraint and it would be misleading to term the situation as a 'savings glut'. Whether it is the savings glut or low investment demand, the saving-investment gap has led to significant current account surpluses in Asia. But it might seem too far-fetched to blame the Asian countries with a strong preference for

---

8. The saving rate began falling in the early 1990s as households increased their consumption in response to their rising level of wealth arising from an increase in stock prices and rising housing prices.
9. It is important to note that during 1996 to 2000, when the US was running a current account deficit, the Federal Budget was in a surplus.
10. Bernanke (2005) argued that a combination of diverse forces created a significant increase in the supply of global saving ('global saving glut') which helps to explain both the increase in the US current account deficit and low level of real interest rates.

saving and hold them responsible for the excessive consumption or investment in the countries that have a current account deficit (Issing, 2005).

Productivity shocks have been identified as one of the key driving forces behind the current account movements.[11] The robust productivity outlook in the US relative to other countries, it is claimed, is consistent with the increase in the US current account deficit. Productivity gains in the US since the mid-1990s triggered huge capital inflows and high consumption expenditure, resulting in the large trade deficit (Mann, 2002).

The proponents of the financial intermediation theory argue that the uncoordinated response after the Asian crisis led to many emerging market economies to build large reserves that resulted in ample global liquidity in search of investment opportunities. A number of factors were at play simultaneously that together led to the preference for US assets. These were: (a) high productivity growth in the US, (b) sluggish economic performance in Europe and Japan, (c) booming house prices fueled by low interest rates and (d) weak investment in emerging Asia with the exception of China.

It has also been argued that low interest rates in the US have played an important role in stimulating consumption in the US. High consumption and high residential investments in America have allowed the US to act as an engine of growth for the world since 2001 and this growth was financed by capital inflows. Chinn and Ito (2005) suggest that the widening of the US deficit over the last ten years is at least partly attributable to the run-up in stock prices. In the view of Knight (2006), this US role as 'consumer of last resort' has also sustained and augmented the global imbalances.

Redressing Global Imbalances

It is clear that an orderly correction in the imbalances can be achieved only through coordinated action on exchange rate, fiscal and monetary policy actions by different countries. This would be a

---

11. Ferguson Jr (2005) points out that labour productivity growth surged from about one and a half per cent annually in the two decades preceding 1995 to roughly 3 per cent in the period since then.

combination of depreciation of the US dollar, reduced consumption, increasing national savings and reducing fiscal deficit in the US, and increasing domestic demand and greater flexibility in exchange rates in parts of the world outside the US. All these changes will not occur quickly; neither is it desirable. At present, the US is the dominant engine of global growth. A sharp reduction in the US fiscal deficit or a sudden large deprecation of the US dollar could impact growth and lead to a global recession. Japan is just getting out of its recession and an abrupt withdrawal of fiscal stimulus in Japan can adversely affect growth. Even a large appreciation of the *renminbi* may not by itself do much in terms of correcting the global imbalance, but it could have an adverse impact on the Chinese domestic economy.

Fiscal Policy

The nature of adjustment varies depending on whether it is analysed from the savings-investment side or from the side of trade adjustment. Although all these approaches tend to yield a consistent result, the focus on savings-investment balance suggests that the main policy levers should be the fiscal deficit and structural policies that influence private savings. The central issue is how the reduction in the US fiscal deficit would affect the external current account and whether this would lead to a fall in the value of dollar, and if so by how much. From an accounting perspective, a decrease in the fiscal deficit should lead to an adjustment in the current account. Roubini (2005b) holds that an orderly global rebalance requires both expenditure switching through a nominal and real depreciation of currencies and expenditure reduction reflecting a reduction in the fiscal deficit.[12] Issing (2005) argues that there is a relatively weak relationship between fiscal balances and current account balances for the US and across several countries. His paper surveys several studies on the issue and points out that most empirical studies find elasticities between fiscal balances and current account positions of around 0.0 to 0.3 for the US.[13] This implies that a

---

12. The 1980s saw the mergence of twin deficits. The authors draw comfort from the evidence that the adjustment was achieved through a reduction in the fiscal deficit and fall in the dollar.
13. See for instance, Erceg, Guerrieri and Gust (2005), who suggest that a one dollar reduction in the federal budget deficit would cause the current account deficit to decline by less than 20 cents.

decline to 4 per cent fiscal deficit from a balanced budget in the US since 2000 contributed only between 0.0 to 1.2 percentage points of the current account deficit.[14] A recent US Treasury Occasional Paper (Barth and Pollard, 2006) cites point estimates for the response of the current account deficit to a budget balance ranging from 0.1 to 0.44. Chinn and Ito (2005), however, argue that budget balances play an important role in the determination of current account balances.[15] From past experience, it looks as though a correction in the budget deficit will only lead to a small reduction in the current account deficit, but fiscal correction is desirable since it will improve government savings.[16,17] At the same time as Rato (2006) has warned, substantial fiscal correction in the US without concomitant measures in other parts of the world to increase domestic demand could reduce global demand. Merely raising taxes or cutting expenditure in the US without adjustment in the exchange rate could result in a reduction in domestic demand and lower imports without any increase in exports, which would have an adverse impact on growth.

Monetary Policy

The US current account deficit is in part a result of faster growth of domestic demand in the US than in the Euro area, Japan and a host

---

14. Issing explains the weak link between fiscal and current account deficits in the US through the Ricardian Equivalence theory which implies that a change in the fiscal position should have no effect on the current account, as it gives rise to an equal adjustment in private sector net savings. However, applying the elasticities of 0.0 to 0.3 in the current context, Issing concludes that the rise in the US fiscal deficit in recent years may have played a role in explaining the worsening US current account deficit.

15. The authors do not rule out a coefficient as high as 0.40 at conventional significance levels, which means that a 6 percentage point swing in the budget balance would result in a 2.4 percentage point swing in the current account balance.

16. Kumhof, Laxton, and Muir (2005) calibrate it to the US economy, showing that a permanent improvement of one percentage point in the fiscal balance would generate an average current account improvement of about one half of one percentage point of GDP over 10 years.

17 Roubini (2005b) shows that of the 6 per cent fiscal change in 2000-2004, 4.6 per cent of it was due to a fall in revenues and 1.4 per cent was due to increase in spending. He points out that tax revenue in 2004 were the lowest in 50 years. He holds the strong view that the US fiscal path is unsustainable and if not corrected will lead an unsustainable public debt.

of emerging economies. It is also the result of a number of negative factors such as the fiscal deficit and negative US household savings. The latter is ascribed by some to the accommodative monetary policy until June 2004, high liquidity and the ability of households to leverage. The US Federal Reserve seems to be sceptical about the ability of monetary policy to contribute to the adjustment of global imbalances. In fact the Federal Open Market Committee in 2004 had concluded that "Members of the Committee noted that monetary policy was not well equipped to promote the adjustment of external imbalances but could best contribute to maintaining an environment of price stability that would foster maximum sustainable economic growth. Fiscal policy had a potentially larger role to play by promoting an increase in national saving, but the adjustment would involve shifts in demand and output both domestically and abroad, and changes in fiscal policy would not be sufficient to foster the adjustment."

In theory, the level of interest rates influences the rate of savings. There is evidence (Issing, 2005) to suggest that low or negative US real interest rates may have partly contributed to the decline in private savings. It is also possible that the wealth effect from equity holdings could have contributed to higher consumption and lower savings. In fact, the paper shows a correlation coefficient of 0.48 between personal savings and real interest rates during 1980-2004 and 0.56 between net savings rate and real short-term interest rates. This raises the issue of the role of monetary policy in addressing global imbalances. The transmission channel will be through interest rates curtailing aggregate demand and raising the level of private savings. It could be argued that the transmission channel will be weak since the increase in policy interest rates in the US has not transmitted to the long end of the yield curve. Further, even if long-term interest rates rise, that will result in an increase in interest payments while its impact on private savings would be limited. Some argue that a tight monetary policy and higher interest rates would slow down the external adjustment process via dollar appreciation caused by large capital inflows. However, there is a view (Truman, 2005) that monetary policy has a role to play in slowing the growth of total domestic demand relative to growth of total domestic supply or domestic output. In fact this is the core function of monetary policy. Control of inflation is sought to be achieved normally through containing aggregate demand. Only in this case the ultimate objective is reduction in current account deficit.

Expanding Domestic Demand Outside the US

Steps to boost growth and investment in Europe are part of the solution to global imbalances.[18] Over the last 10 years, domestic demand in the Euroarea has expanded annually a full 1.8 percentage points more slowly than that in the USA. This gap is equivalent of the USA adding an economy the size of France or the United Kingdom in about 10 years, if the same gap is maintained (US Treasury Report to Congress, 2006). A key feature of adjusting global imbalances will be expanding demand relative to output in Europe, Japan, and many parts of developing Asia.[19] Structural reforms that involve reforming their healthcare and pension systems, liberalising their labour markets and boosting productivity have been advocated. Undertaking structural reforms to boost the efficiency of the largely non-tradable services sector which plays a significant role in the economy would help raise growth. It is important to recognise that faster growth abroad helps only if it is relatively concentrated in non-tradable goods (Obstfeld and Rogoff, 2005). It is important that demand in the Euroarea should come through stronger growth. Similarly both Japan and China must revive their domestic demand and move from an export-led growth to a domestic demand-led growth. Oil producing countries can play their part by increasing investments in oil related activities as also by increasing domestic productive spending with consequent impact on their current account imbalances.

Exchange Rate Policies

A question that needs to be addressed is whether it is possible to reduce the US current account deficit without exchange rate changes. Past experience shows that a more competitive dollar can substantially

---

18. Europe's single monetary policy also has led to divergences in that since all countries face the same nominal interest rates, slow growing economies with low inflation have higher real interest rates while faster growers have lower real interest rates (*The Economist*, August 18, 2005).

19. IMF 2005 estimates that a half per cent increase in real GDP growth in Japan would reduce the US current account deficit by about 0.2 per cent after three years.

reduce the trade deficit.[20, 21] The rule of thumb presumes that a 10 per cent real effective depreciation of the dollar brings about a correction of 1 per cent of GDP in the current account deficit of the US. However, recent research also documents a sustained decline in the exchange rate pass-through to US import prices by more than half. In the final analysis, changes in the fiscal position of the USA, changes in the saving-investment balances in the world and changes in productivity and growth in different regions will all have to be translated into reducing the current account deficit of the USA. Feldstein (2006) explains that with the reversal of the low interest rate policy of the US, the sustained downtrend in the household savings is likely to be soon reversed. The conversion of higher savings to reduced current account deficit will require an increase in US exports and shift in consumption from imports to domestically produced goods and services. This can only come from a lower dollar.[22]

It is also not certain that a significant increase in domestic demand in Japan, Europe and Asia would necessarily lead to a rebalancing of the US trade account. Currently, the level of US imports is twice that of its exports. Even if US exports and imports were to grow at the same pace, due to this base effect, the trade gap will continue to widen. Statistical studies suggest that for every percentage point that the GDP of the US grows, imports grow somewhat less than twice as fast, while for every percentage point that foreign economies grow, US exports grow only a little more than a percentage point (US Treasury Report to Congress, 2006).[23] Estimates show that a 20 per cent change in the real trade-

---

20. Feldstein (2006) points out that the last big fall of the dollar, a 37 per cent decline in the mid-1980s, was followed by a 40 per cent fall in the trade deficit.
21. Sebastian Edwards (2005b) analyses that the 1987-1991 current account adjustment in the US was characterised by a steep depreciation of the dollar (about 30 per cent in real trade weighted terms), an increase in inflation, a rise in interest rates, a decline in GDP below trend rate and an increase in the rate of unemployment above trend rate. This was the impact when the adjustment was significant but gradual.
22. Without a lower dollar Feldstein warns that the higher savings rate would mean slower growth, and rising unemployment which could lead to protectionist pressures.
23. Tracing the current account balances of the US between 1973 and 2004, Edwards (2005a) shows that a pattern of negative correlation between the trade weighted real value of the dollar and the current account deficit. Periods of strong dollar

contd...

weighted dollar exchange rate will only lead to a 2 percentage point reduction in the current account deficit of the US (Obstfeld and Rogoff, 2005). These authors emphasise that the greater part of the adjustment will have to come from saving and productivity shocks.

An international monetary system can function effectively only if both surplus and deficit countries allow their currencies to respond to the situation. The gold standard mechanism broke down because of the asymmetric behaviour of the gold gaining and gold loosing countries. While various studies may show somewhat weak response to exchange rate changes, they are nevertheless an integral part of the solution.

While US must act, surplus countries more particularly China, must let their currencies appreciate.[24]

Indian Response

In a broad sense, India has not contributed to the global imbalances. India had a modest current account deficit both in 2004-05 and 2005-06. This deficit may continue through the current year. However, in relation to the US, it has a surplus. Once again, this surplus is small compared to the US's overall deficit. India's exchange rate has been fluctuating. The official policy is not to intervene in the market except to reduce undue volatility. In the recent period, the rupee has depreciated against the dollar, after having appreciated earlier. India's good growth performance is largely propelled by domestic demand even though external sector is assuming increasing importance. Thus, India's situation is dissimilar to that of China. While no action is required on the part of India as part of a coordinated action to reduce the global imbalances, action by the US and other countries could create a

---

contd...
 have tended to coincide with periods of larger current account deficits and periods of dollar depreciation are associated with improving current account deficit, the contemporaneous coefficient of correlation between the two being –0.53. Against this, it is notable that although the dollar depreciated between 2002 and 2004 against a number of currencies, the current account deficit worsened.
24. An appreciation of the Chinese currency is likely to have an impact on global imbalances not only through the reduction in the US-China current account imbalance but also by allowing other Asian countries to appreciate (*Asia-Pacific Regional Outlook*, 2005b, IMF).

situation for which India must have an appropriate response. If monetary policy is further tightened in the US, it will have an impact on the capital flows to India. While some reduction in the capital flows to India will not matter, as the level of foreign exchange reserves is already high, we must watch the situation so that the reduction is not of the order which will hinder the financing of the current account deficit. The process of correction, if successful, will lead to some relative reduction in the expansion of global trade and hence, we must take appropriate steps to improve the competitiveness of our exports. It is also in India's interest to ensure that correction to the global imbalance is smooth and not abrupt.

Conclusion

Global imbalances are a key concern in the international agenda today. Although there is broad agreement that the imbalances should ultimately decline, there is no consensus on when and how this would happen. The international community agrees that that action for orderly medium-term resolution of global imbalances is a shared responsibility, and will bring greater benefit to members and the international community than actions taken individually (IMFC *Communiqué*, April 2006). There is also an agreed position on the strategy to address imbalances which include raising national saving in the United States—with measures to reduce the budget deficit and spur private saving; implementing structural reforms to sustain the growth potential and boost domestic demand in the Euro-zone, domestic demand-led growth in Japan and China, allowing greater exchange rate flexibility in a number of surplus countries in emerging Asia; and promoting efficient absorption of higher oil revenues in oil-exporting countries with strong macroeconomic policies. However, we need to recognise that the current account patterns of countries are far from homogenous. Hence, the incentives for common action are not particularly strong. Even if there are broad agreements on the strategy for an orderly unwinding, the response by different countries may be uneven in view of domestic considerations. The process of orderly unwinding would therefore be necessarily slow. But a greater recognition of the need for coordination will help.

References

Barth, Martha and Patricia Pollard (2006). "The Limits of Fiscal Policy in Current Account Adjustment", *Occasional Paper* No. 2. USA: Department of Treasury, Office of International Affairs.

Bordo, Michael (2005). "Historical Perspective on Global Imbalances", *NBER Working Paper* 11383.

Bernanke, Ben (2005). "The Global Saving Glut and the US Current Account Deficit", *Homer Jones Lecture*. St Louis, Missouri.

Bussiѐe, Matthieu, Marcel Fratzscher and Gernot J. Mіler (2005). "Productivity Shocks, Budget Deficits and the Current Account", ECB *Working Paper* 509, August.

Chinn, Menzie and Hiro Ito (2005). "Current Account Balances, Financial Development and Institutions: Assaying the World Savings Glut", *NBER Working Paper* 11761.

Cline, William R. (2005). *The United States as a Debtor Nation*. Washington DC: Institute for International Economics and Center for Global Development.

Cooper, Richard (2004). "US Deficit: It is not only Sustainable, it is Logical", *Financial Times*, October 31.

Dooley, Michael, David Folkerts-Landau and Peter Garber (2003). "An Essay on the Revived Bretton Woods System", *NBER Working Paper* 9971.

Erceg, Christopher, Luca Guerrieri and Christopher Gust (2005). "Expansionary Fiscal Shocks and the Trade Deficit", International Finance *Discussion Paper* No 825. Washington: Board of Governors of the Federal Reserve System.

Edwards, Sebastian (2005a). "Is the US Current Account Deficit Sustainable? And if not, How Costly is Adjustment Likely to be?", *NBER Working Paper* 11541.

———. (2005b). "The End of large Current Account Deficits, 1970-2002: Are There Lessons for the United States?, *NBER Working Paper* 11669.

Feldstein, Martin (2006). "The Falling Dollar Sets a Test for Asia and Europe", *Financial Times*, May 26.

Ferguson, Roger W. (2005). "US Current Account Deficit: Causes and Consequences", Speech to Economics Club of the University of North Carolina. April 20. http://www.federalreserve.gov

Forbes, Kristin J. (2005). Comments on Otmar Issing's "Addressing Global Imbalances: The Role for Macroeconomic Policy", Banque de France International Symposium on *Productivity, Competitiveness and Globalisation*.

Freund Caroline, Frank Warnock (2005). "Current Account Deficits in Industrial Countries: The Bigger they are, The Harder they Fall?", Paper Prepared for the NBER Conference G7 *Current Account Imbalances: Sustainability and Adjustment*.

Geithner, Timothy (2006a). "Policy Implications of Global Imbalances", Remarks at the Financial Imbalances Conference at Chatham House. London, January 23.

———. (2006b). "US Monetary Policy in the Global Financial Environment", Remarks at the Japan Society Corporate Luncheon. New York, March 19.

Greenspan, Alan (2003). "Current Account", Speech to 21st *Annual Monetary Policy Conference*. Washington DC: Cato Institute. November 20. http://www.federalreserve.gov/boarddocs/speeches/2003/

Gruber, Joseph, and Steven B. Kamin (2005). "Explaining the Global Pattern of Current Account Imbalances", International Finance *Discussion Papers* No. 846. Board of Governors of the Federal Reserve System.

Hausmann, Ricardo and Federico Sturzenegger (2005). "US and Global Imbalances: Can Dark matter Prevent as Big Bang". Short and long versions available at *www.utdt.edu/~fsturzen/Publications.html*

International Monetary Fund (2005a). *World Economic Outlook*. September. Washington DC.

———. (2005b). *Asia-Pacific Regional Outlook*, September, *www.imf.org*

———. (2006). *IMFC Communiqué* April. *www.imf.org*

Issing, Otmar (2005). "Addressing Global Imbalances: The Role of Macroeconomic Policy", Banque de France International Symposium on *Productivity, Competitiveness and Globalisation*.

Kumhof, Michael, Douglas Laxton, and Dirk Muir (2005). "Consequences of Fiscal Consolidation for the US Current Account: United States–Selected Issues", *IMF Staff Country Report* No. 05/258. Washington: International Monetary Fund.

Lane, Philip and Gian Maria Milesi-Ferretti (2005). "A Global Perspective on External Positions", *IMF Working Paper* 05/161. Washington: International Monetary Fund.

Mann, Catherine L. (2002). "Perspectives on the US Current Account Deficit and Sustainability", *Journal of Economic Perspectives* 16: 131-52.

Nsouli, Saleh (2006). "Petrodollar Recycling and Global Imbalances", Presentation at the CESifo's International Spring Conference. Berlin. March 23-24. International Monetary Fund, *www.imf.org*

Obstfeld, Maurice and Kenneth Rogoff (2005). "The Unsustainable US Current Account Position Revisited", *NBER Working Paper* 10869, November.

Knight, Malcolm (2006). "Notes for a Presentation at the Brussels Economic Forum", May 18Brussels BIS, Switzerland.

Rajan, Raghuram (2005). "Global Current Account Imbalances: Hard Landing or Soft landing", Talk at the Credit Suisse First Boston Conference. Hong Kong. March 15.

———. (2006). "Financial System Reform and Global Current Account Imbalances", Talk at the American Economic Association (AEA) Meetings Boston. Massachusetts. January 8.

Rato, Rodrigo (2006). "How the IMF Can Help Promote a Collaborative Solution to Global Imbalances", Remarks by Rodrigo de Rato at the Center for European Studies, Harvard Business School. Boston, April 4.

Roubini, Nouriel (2004). "The US as a Net Debtor: The Sustainability of the US External Imbalances". Roubini Global Economics. LLC. *www.rgemonitor.com*

———. (2005a). "Global Imbalances: A Contemporary Rashomon Tale with Five Interpretations...", Roubini Global Economics LLC, *www.rgemonitor.com*

———. (2005b). "Global Current Account Imbalances: Orderly or Disorderly Rebalancing?", Roubini Global Economics, LLC, *www.rgemonitor.com*

The Economist (2005). "Traffic Lights on the Blink?, *The Economist*, August 18.

Truman, Edwin M. (2005). "Postponing Global Adjustment: An Analysis of the Pending Adjustment of Global Imbalances". *Working Paper* 05-6. Washington: Institute for International Economics.

US Treasury (2006). *Report to Congress on International Economic and Exchange Rate Policies.* USA. May.

Williamson, John (2005). "What Follows the USA as the World's Growth Engine?", *India Policy Forum Public Lecture.* New Delhi: National Council of Applied Economic Research & The Brookings Institution.

The authors are grateful to Hélène Poirson, Eswar Prasad, D. Subba Rao and Saumitra Chaudhuri for their insightful comments and suggestions on an earlier draft of the article.

Money & Finance, ICRA Bulletin, January-June, 2006.

24 | Nature and Impact of Capital Flows

Capital flows across geographical frontiers have become a focus of concern particularly after the East Asian crisis. The need to reassess and understand the role of capital flows has become urgent. The importance of capital inflows to developing economies is well understood. In this context two sets of questions arise. The first set centres around whether some forms of capital flows are preferable to others. This issue has to be addressed from the angles of volatility and impact on capital formation and growth. The second set of questions relates to the extent and forms of controls that can be imposed on capital flows. In this paper these issues are addressed, drawing lessons from the East Asian and our experiences.

Capital Flows: Magnitude and Composition

Financial markets around the world are getting increasingly integrated. This process has been helped by deregulation of financial markets, advances in communication and computer technologies and the increasing role of institutional investors that are willing to invest internationally. The major benefit of this internationalisation is the more efficient allocation of global savings among countries. Developing countries are also becoming increasingly a part of this process. Large private capital flows to emerging markets are a phenomenon of the nineties. Prior to the nineties, developing countries received capital flows primarily through official aid. In 1990 official creditors accounted for 50 per cent of the total net capital flows to the emerging markets. In the eighties, they accounted for even a much larger share. Net private capital inflows to emerging markets increased from $ 31 billion in 1990 to $ 216 billion in 1996, the year preceding the East Asian crisis (Table 24.1). Half of these inflows in

1996 went to Asia. During this period net official flows came down from around $ 20 billion to almost a negligible figure in 1996. The capital outflows from the East Asian countries which began in the second half of 1997 interrupted the steady trend of increase. Since then, the overall level of net private capital inflows into emerging markets have remained positive but at levels far lower than that reached in 1996.

Table 24.1

Net Capital Flows to Emerging Markets

(Billion US dollars)

	1992	1993	1994	1995	1996	1997	1998	1999
Net Private Capital Flows	112.6	172.1	136.3	226.9	215.9	147.6	75.1	80.5
Net Direct Investment	35.4	59.4	84.0	92.6	113.2	138.6	143.3	149.8
Net Portfolio Investment	56.1	84.4	109.6	36.9	77.8	52.9	8.5	23.3
Other Net Investment	21.0	28.3	−57.3	97.4	24.9	−43.9	−76.7	−92.5
Net Official Flows	21.2	17.2	3.4	11.7	0.4	23.5	44.7	3.0
Total	133.8	189.3	139.7	238.6	216.3	171.1	119.8	83.5

Source: International Monetary Fund, *World Economic Outlook,* May 2000.

Looking at the composition of capital flows, net foreign direct investment represented the largest share of private capital flows to emerging markets. Net FDI flows increased from $ 35 billion or 31 per cent of total net private flows in 1992 to $ 113 billion (52 per cent) in 1996 and further to $ 139 billion or 94 per cent in 1997. According to World Bank estimates, the ratio of FDI to GDP in developing countries jumped from 0.8 per cent in 1991 to 2.0 per cent in 1997. Developing countries also increased their share of global FDI flows from 21 per cent in 1991 to an estimated 36 per cent in 1997. Asia and Latin American countries attracted the largest share of FDI. In fact, FDI flows to Asia was $ 53.1 billion, constituting 47 per cent of the share of flows to emerging markets in 1996.

Net portfolio investment was also an important source of finance to emerging markets, though these flows were more volatile after 1994. There was a sharp drop in portfolio flows to Latin American countries in 1995 following the onset of the Mexican crisis. The reversal of nearly $ 64 billion in Latin America in 1995 was fully reflected in the flows to emerging markets which recorded a fall by $ 73 billion. However, portfolio flows increased strongly again in 1996, as emerging markets including Mexico regained access to international capital markets. In 1997, there was a reduction of 32 per cent in portfolio flows to emerging markets as compared to the previous year, because of the Asian crisis.

Banking flows formed a major component of private flows until 1996. In addition to syndicated lending, inter-bank loans have accounted for an important share of bank lending to emerging markets, particularly Asia. These flows have also remained volatile. After strong flows up to 1993, there was a reversal in 1994, again reflecting mainly withdrawal from Latin America. The years 1995 and 1996 witnessed net inflows of $ 97 and $ 25 billion, respectively, with about 71 per cent being accounted for by Asia. In 1997, there was a net banking outflow of $ 44 billion from these countries as compared to net inflows of $ 25 billion in 1996, signifying a turnaround of $ 69 billion.

To sum-up, the nineties until 1997 marked a shift in the composition of capital flows to emerging markets, with a significant increase in net private capital inflows to emerging markets and a decline in the share of official flows. FDI was the most stable component of private flows. Both net portfolio investment and banking flows were volatile and the period witnessed major reversals in both, one following the Mexican crisis of 1994 and the other following the Asian crisis of 1997.

Capital inflows are generally welcome in a developing economy. They ease external constraints and help to achieve higher investment and growth. Such flows also serve as vehicles for the transfer of technology and management skills. However, sudden and large surges in capital flows cause several concerns. A major concern relates to the sustainability of such inflows. If capital inflows are volatile or temporary, the country will have to go through an adjustment process in both the real and financial markets, which later will have to be reversed. This reversal will not be without cost. Even when capital flows are not 'hot' or volatile, several consequences follow. Some of these concerns include excessive money supply and the consequent pressure on prices, impact on nominal and real exchange rates, increase in consumption and deterioration in the current account.

The nature of capital flows is an important factor in assessing the impact. Inflows which take the form of direct foreign investment are generally considered more permanent in character. They also have an immediate favourable impact on the real sector of the economy, including investment and output, even though not all foreign direct investment need directly increase capital formation. The concerns relating to sustainability are less when capital flows are larger in the form of direct investment. The fact that capital mobility is a 'two-way phenomenon' is best seen in the portfolio flows, which, by their very nature, are reversible in character. They are contingent upon the return available on the different asset classes and the perceived stability of a market or an economy.

Capital flows can be a response to external as well as internal factors. Thus, both push and pull factors may operate. The external factors are those which are unrelated to the policies followed by the recipient countries. A decline in the available profit opportunities, low interest rates, or the existence of recessionary conditions can cause capital to move out of a country. Some attribute the capital outflows in the early nineties from the US and other industrial countries to these factors. However, such factors alone do not explain why capital flows to one particular country or group of countries and not to others.

The internal factors are those related to the stance of domestic policies. Successful price stabilisation and structural reform programmes and the consequent acceleration, or even the prospects of acceleration, in growth can attract capital from outside. A tight monetary policy that keeps the domestic interest rate high coupled with exchange rate stability may also generate capital inflows, that is, if the domestic interest rate is higher than the external interest rate, adjusted for any expectations of devaluation and also for country risk. Added to these is the 'bandwagon effect' or 'herd mentality'. It is, however, difficult to determine the extent to which the capital flow is due to external or internal factors. Capital flows prompted purely by external factors may tend to be less sustainable than those induced by domestic factors. Even in the latter case, sustainability will rest on the continued pursuit of sound economic policies and stable economic conditions.

Both capital inflows and outflows when they are large and sudden have important implications for economies. When capital inflows are large, they can lead to an appreciation of the real exchange rate. Under such circumstances, the nominal exchange rate may remain unchanged. But because of the absorption of the inflows into reserves, money supply may expand leading to rise in prices bringing about an appreciation in real terms. Most often, it becomes difficult to sterilise the entire inflows. If the inflows, however, are not accumulated in the form of reserves, the current account deficit may widen to absorb the inflows. On the other hand, the damage that can be caused by sudden withdrawal of capital is more acute. Apart from the contraction of the economy and the collapse of the exchange rate, it can spread to other countries. Once the contagion effect takes place, the return to normalcy becomes more difficult. The problems get further compounded if there are other fundamental weaknesses in the economy.

The benefits of capital flows to an economy are clear. In fact, developing countries have been pleading for a larger flow of resources from the developed economies. However, unlike official flows, private capital flows tend to become volatile. Recent experience has clearly shown that countries need to build adequate safety mechanisms to guard against or to cushion the impact of volatility.

East Asian Crisis

The East Asian crisis burst on the world scene almost like a bolt from the blue. While some analysts had detected a few clouds of suspicion, the crisis and more so its severity took almost every one by surprise. The crisis hit hard five countries—South Korea, Malaysia, Thailand, Indonesia and the Philippines (the Asia-5)—even though its reverberations have been felt by many countries including India. The currencies of these countries came under severe pressure from the middle of 1997 which resulted in a heavy depreciation of their currencies in relation to the US dollar. The currency crisis in turn led to a severe domestic financial crisis and the two taken together plunged these countries into a severe economic depression. Most of these countries, which for several decades had experienced strong growth rates, saw a decline.

All the crisis hit countries, barring probably Indonesia, are once again on the high growth path, and private capital flows have resumed in these countries. The traumatic experience of these countries in the last three years have compelled analysts to look at various aspects of capital flows. It has also focused on what the recipient countries should be doing to avoid outflows.

In the case of Asia-5, capital inflows increased from $ 25 billion in 1990 to $ 74.2 billion in 1995 and declined slightly to $ 65.8 billion in 1996 (Table 24.2). Net direct investment increased from $ 7.3 billion in 1992 to $ 8.4 billion in 1996 while net portfolio investment increased during this period from $ 6.4 billion $ 20.3 billion. Banking flows showed the strongest rise from $ 15.3 billion to $ 37.1 billion.

Table 24.2

Net Capital Flows to Crisis Economies

(Billion US Dollars)

	1992	1993	1994	1995	1996	1997	1998	1999
Net Private Capital Flows	29.0	31.8	36.1	74.2	65.8	−20.4	−25.6	−24.6
Net direct investment	7.3	7.6	8.8	7.5	8.4	10.3	8.6	10.2
Net portfolio investment	6.4	17.2	9.9	17.4	20.3	12.9	−6.0	6.3
Other net investment	15.3	7.0	17.4	49.2	37.1	−43.6	−28.2	−41.1
Net Official Flows	2.0	0.6	0.3	0.7	−0.4	17.9	19.7	−4.7
Total	31.0	32.4	36.4	74.9	65.4	2.5	5.9	−29.3

Source: International Monetary Fund, *World Economic Outlook*, May 2000.

Reversal of private capital flows in East Asia was dramatic. According to IMF estimates, these countries experienced a turnaround of $ 86 billion in 1997, from a net inflow of $ 66 billion in 1996 to a net outflow of $ 20 billion in 1997. Figures from the Institute of International Finance indicate that the turnaround was even higher at $ 105 billion, from an inflow of $ 93 billion in 1996 to a negative $ 12 billion in 1997, accounting for more than 10 per cent of their combined GDP.

It would be interesting at this point to briefly compare the Mexican episode with the Asian crisis. Both these crises were preceded by large capital inflows. The Mexican crisis occurred because of reversal of portfolio flows, from a peak inflow of over $ 20 billion in 1993 to net outflow of $ 15 billion in 1995. In the Asian countries, the crisis was due to reversal of commercial banking flows to the extent of $ 86 billion or over 7 per cent of GDP. In respect of both the Mexican and Asian crisis, FDI inflows moderated only slightly. IMF data suggest that net portfolio flows slowed down in Asia in 1997 but remained positive.

The causes of the Asian crisis have been analysed in depth by several scholars and policy-makers. International financial institutions have also gone through a period of introspection. Questions have been raised about the way they have handled the crisis. The crisis clearly shows that when perception changes, there is a drop in confidence which may go far beyond what is justified by objective conditions. However, it is admitted that these countries despite their achieving high growth rates, for decades, had allowed several weaknesses to accumulate. Doubts have been expressed about the efficiency of these economies, since the incremental capital-output ratio remained high. The more or less pegged exchange rate in Thailand induced domestic companies to borrow from foreign markets on a short term basis to finance long term investment. Short term debt constituted around 46 per cent of the external debt of Thailand in mid-1997. In South Korea it was as high as 67 per cent. Another major factor in the crisis relates to weaknesses in the financial sector. Institutional deficiencies and distorted incentives led to an unquestioned approach to lending, resulting in speculative investment in real estate and the stock market coupled with willingness to take on mismatches. The East Asian crisis has highlighted structural and institutional challenges posed by integration with international financial markets.

While drawing lessons for the future, one aspect of the reversal of capital flows needs attention. The main cause of the crisis was not the erratic behaviour of a large number of individual or institutional portfolio investors, but the withdrawal of short term banking flows which were part of the regulated segment of the financial system. Sometimes exchange dealers and hedge funds have been blamed for the sudden withdrawal. But as Baily, *et al.* (2000) have shown, at the time when the pegged exchange rate was given up in Thailand, the Bank of Thailand had estimated that hedge funds held at most 25 per cent of the $ 28 billion in forward contract sales of the bhat. It is seen that hedge funds took their positions on the bhat after significant pressure had already built up.

The recent crisis has raised a fundamental question about the risks of capital account liberalisation. A question that is often asked now is whether the capital account is more a source of economic difficulties and risk than benefit. In retrospect, leading economists such as Krugman (1998), Bhagwati (1998) and Stiglitz (1998) are advocating some sort of capital controls. Bhagwati is of the view that full capital mobility is not a necessary condition for free trade. He argues that governments should restrict the global flow of capital even while vigorously promoting free trade in goods and services. He cautions that "any nation contemplating the embrace of free capital mobility must reckon with these costs and also consider the probability of running into a crisis". He further adds that even if one were to believe that capital flows are generally productive, there is still an important difference between embracing free portfolio capital mobility and a policy of attracting equity investment.

Krugman advocates capital controls purely as a stop-gap measure on grounds that it allows crisis hit countries to adopt more expansionary monetary and fiscal policies and hence promote a faster recovery of the real economy. Such a recovery, it is argued, can reduce the problems of insolvency and closure in the corporate sector and non-performing loans in the banking system. Krugman further argues that the controls must not be a substitute for reforms; rather they must complement reforms. In his view, controls must not in any circumstances be imposed to defend an overvalued exchange rate. At best, they should be a very temporary measure, imposed to stabilise the currency in the short-run.

Stiglitz contends that the cost of disruption due to swings in expectations is invariably high for developing countries. Thus, there exists case for more direct intervention in less sophisticated economies.

Proponents of capital account liberalisation like Stanley Fischer (1998), have been quick to point out that the benefits of liberalising the capital account outweigh the potential costs. Currency controls will impose distortions on the economy, no matter how well executed, and the longer they are in place the more serious they tend to get. In fact, in Malaysia, the regulation covering the import and export of the ringgit has already been relaxed. Fischer favours an amendment to the IMF's Articles of Agreement to ensure that capital account liberalisation is orderly and non-disruptive.

The benefits of free capital flows are well known. The Asian economies including the crisis-hit economies were important beneficiaries of capital flows. If these crisis-hit economies recover soon, as they have done already, and resume their growth path, they would still have done well in the long haul. In fact, given the weaknesses in the financial and real sectors and the political uncertainties in some of the countries, the crisis could have been triggered by other factors as well. Instead of capital outflows becoming the trigger, they could have been the consequence. Bhagwati, as noted earlier, is of the view that the case for free trade will be undermined by damage done by volatile flows in the short-term capital. While Bhagwati's view that full capital mobility is not a necessary condition for benefits of free trade is valid, one cannot afford to overlook the link between trade and capital mobility. If capital mobility can lead to better resource allocation, it becomes a contributory factor to improved output and trade. Also, a country cannot wish away capital flows in all forms other than FDI. What is needed is a clear identification of capital flows that can tend to be 'volatile' and use appropriate measures to discourage such flows. It is such a discriminative approach that will ensure the benefits of capital mobility without the harmful effects of volatility. Volatility is a phenomenon of all financial markets. It is very much so even in domestic capital markets. Nevertheless they are considered as a necessary adjunct of the real sector. International capital inflows are highly sensitive to macroeconomic policies, soundness of the financial sector and political developments. All capital receiving countries have to pay attention to these factors.

Forms of Capital Controls

Capital controls strictly defined include restrictions that affect the capital account of a country's balance of payments. Controls can be imposed on outflows and inflows. Broadly, there are three categories of capital controls, *viz.*, quantity based, price based and regulatory. Transactions that may be subjected to capital controls are numerous. They include both short and long-term transactions.

The experience of Chile in the management of capital inflows is often quoted as a successful example of a recipient country managing capital inflows through market-based prudential controls. Faced with a surge in capital inflows, Chile resolved the dilemma of maintaining tight monetary policy without hindering export competitiveness by imposing a one-year unremunerated reserved requirement on foreign loans. This was primarily designed to discourage short-term borrowing without affecting long-term foreign investments. This is analogous to the reserve requirement that RBI imposes on foreign currency non-resident deposits.

A transactions tax—the 'Tobin tax'—is another option that has been suggested. The 'Tobin tax' proposes to levy an international uniform tax on spot transactions in foreign exchange. Such a tax penalises short-term traders more and imposes less of a penalty on long-term investors since the tax is uniform across maturities. A criticism against such taxes is that they cannot be applied unilaterally, as businesses could move offshore or to other countries of equivalent risk perception, but where no tax has been imposed. There is also some scepticism regarding the administration of such taxes. Such a tax discriminates between internal and international transactions and results in new barriers. Finally, it seems inefficient to penalise all transactions rather than those that are destabilising. From the reasons of practicability, a tax on foreign exchange transactions, however, appears to be difficult.

Controls over capital flows can be imposed at source country as well. The motivation of proposals for control at source is burden-sharing between the debtor and creditor countries. A proposal has been made to introduce a risk-weighted cash reserve requirement for mutual fund/institutional investors who make cross-border investments. The cash reserve capital charge would vary with the level of countries' perceived macroeconomic risk. The objective is to make it more costly to invest in countries with weak fundamentals and prevent over concentration.

The time has also come to examine how a compulsory or semi-voluntary system of rollover or standstill or debt workout can be evolved to be applicable in times of crisis. Indiscreet lenders must pay a price. New provisions in loan contracts and IMF lending into arrears were discussed in the G-10 Report issued in the aftermath of the Mexican crisis in 1996. These recommendations were mirrored in the G-22 recommendations. The three contractual clauses outlined in the report are those that would (a) provide for collective representation of debt holders in the event of a crisis; (b) allow for qualified majority voting to after the terms and conditions of contracts; (this would prevent isolated creditors from resorting to lawsuits and other means of obstructing settlements that improve the welfare of the debtor and the vast majority of creditors); and (c) require the sharing among creditors of assets received from the debtor. Such clauses would encourage a dialogue between debtors and creditors and prevent a minority of dissident investors from holding up settlement.

The East Asian crisis holds out important lessons for developing countries, developed countries and international financial institutions. As far as regulation of capital flows is concerned, countries need to adopt a discriminatory approach. Volatile capital must be discouraged through measures which are preferably price based.

The Indian Experience

The year 1991 marks an important watershed in the post-independent economic history of the country. The approach to and content of economic policy underwent an important change. The balance of payments crisis of 1991 was converted into an occasion to introduce certain fundamental economic reforms which will lead to both stability and growth. A more open policy was adopted towards foreign trade and foreign investment. The exchange rate regime also underwent a significant change. Liberalisation of foreign trade meant a reduction in the tariff rates and dismantling of quantitative controls over imports. There has been a gradual but steady movement in these directions in the last nine years. The foreign investment regime went through a radical change. The earlier policy was restrictive. The policy initiated since 1991 has not only widened the scope of foreign investment but also allowed foreign majority participation in most of the industries. Investment in Indian stocks by foreign institutional investors has been permitted. A major change was effected in the exchange rate regime in February 1993 when after brief experience with dual exchange rates, the country adopted a unified market determined exchange rate system.

Under this system, the exchange rate was left to be determined by the market forces, while the Reserve Bank of India intervened when there was a high degree of volatility or instability in the market.

The process of liberalisation of capital account has been very gradual in India. Taking the cue from the crisis of 1991, India's policy on external sector had been cautious. In fact, the lessons drawn from the 1991 crisis were more or less similar to those flowing out of the East Asian crisis. The High Level Committee on balance of payments which was set up in 1991 had emphasised the need to maintain the current account deficit at a level which could be financed by normal capital flows. Given the background of 1991-92, the committee had recommended a current account deficit of 1.6 per cent of GDP as appropriate. It had also envisaged the need to keep down the level of short-term debt and to maintain a level of reserves which would have a relationship not only to the level of imports but also to other repayment obligations. In the post-crisis period of 1991-1999, the current account deficit of India has averaged 1.2 per cent of GDP. In a sense, the impact of the East Asian crisis on India was moderate because the capital inflows into the country in the earlier period were very modest as compared with what the countries in East Asia had received.

The cautious approach to the management of the external sector is reflected in the procedures for foreign direct investment, portfolio investment, external commercial borrowings, non-resident Indian deposit and outflows. Foreign direct investment has been recognised as a preferred form of capital inflow. Portfolio investments are restricted to foreign institutional investors. They are also subject to restrictions on investment in equity and debt. Until recently, Indian corporates were permitted to raise funds through global depository receipts and euro convertibles only after complying with a process of approval. With respect to commercial borrowing, besides monitoring the cost effectiveness and end-use, annual ceilings were being set for commitments of short-term as well as medium and long-term debt. This has worked well in terms of consolidating the country's external debt. It has also provided a measure of crisis-proofing especially in an environment where contagion effects are becoming strong. In respect of NRI deposits, controls over inflows are exercised through interest ceilings on deposits and variable reserve requirements.

Table 24.3
India's Balance of Payments

(US $ million)

	Item	1990-91	1991-92	1992-93	1993-94	1994-95	1995-96	1996-97	1997-98	1998-99	1999-2000
I	Merchandise										
	A) Exports, fob	18477	18266	18869	22683	26855	32311	34133	35680	34298	38285
	B) Imports, cif	27914	21064	24316	26739	35904	43670	48948	51187	47544	55383
	Trade balance (A-B)	-9437	-2798	-5447	-4056	-9049	-11359	-14815	-15507	-13246	-17098
II	Invisibles, net	-243	1620	1921	2898	5680	5449	10196	10007	9208	12935
III	Current account (I+II)	-9680	-1178	-3526	-1158	-3369	-5910	-4619	-5500	-4038	-4163
IV	Capital account (A to F)	7188	3777	2936	9695	9156	4689	11412	10011	8260	10565
	A) Foreign investment	103	133	557	4235	4807	4835	6153	5390	2412	5191
	B) External assistance	2210	3037	1859	1901	1526	883	1109	907	820	901
	C) Commercial borrowings, net	2248	1456	-358	607	1030	1275	2848	3999	4362	313
	D) Rupee debt service	-1193	-1240	-878	-1053	-983	-952	-727	-767	-802	-711
	E) NRI deposits, net	1536	290	2001	1205	172	1103	3350	1125	1742	2140
	F) Other capital	2284	101	-245	2800	2604	-2425	-1321	-643	-274	2731
V	Overall balance (III+IV)	-2492	2599	-590	8537	5787	-1221	6793	4511	4222	6402
VI	Monetary movements (VII+VIII+IX)	2492	-2599	590	-8537	-5787	1221	-6793	-4511	-4222	-6402
VII	Reserves (increase -, Decrease +)	1278	-3385	-698	-8724	-4644	2936	-5818	-3893	-393	-260
VIII	IMF, net	1214	786	1288	187	-1143	-1715	-975	-618	3829	-6142
IX	SDR allocation	0	0	0	0	0	0	0			

Source: Reserve Bank of India. *Handbook on Statistics on Indian Economy 1999.*

The capital account of India's balance of payments underwent a significant change in the 90s. In the 80s the current account deficit was mainly financed by three sources—external assistance, commercial borrowing and NRI deposits. The 90s saw a marked increase in non-debt creating inflows (Table 24.3). Net external assistance waned in importance with net inflows more than halving from $ 2.1 billion (1990-1995) to $ 0.9 billion (1995-2000), as disbursements declined (from $ 3.5 billion to $ 2.9 billion) coupled with increased amortisation (from $ 1.4 billion to $ 2.0 billion). Net external commercial borrowings during the second half of the 90s averaged $2.6 billion per annum. Inflows under NRI deposits averaged $ 1.8 billion during the second half of the 90s. All these three sources taken together accounted for a much lower share of the capital flows during the 90s and more particularly in the second half. The contribution of FDI inflows to total capital flows increased from an average of only 7 per cent during the first half of the 90s to around 33 per cent during 1995-2000. Portfolio inflows increased from 18 per cent to 28 per cent over the same period. Thus the share of the non-debt creating inflows comprising of direct investment and portfolio investment in the total capital inflows increased to 61 per cent during 1995-2000.

The key change in India's capital account in the 90s is in relation to foreign investment inflows (Table 24.4). These inflows were negligible until 1992-93. Since then they have increased from $ 0.5 billion in 1992-93 to $ 5.2 billion in 1999-2000. Direct investment increased from 0.3 billion to $ 2.1 billion in 1999-2000. Foreign direct investment has shown a steady increase. Even in the aftermath of East Asian crisis, there has been no decline. The major sectors in which such investments have been made are chemical and allied products, engineering and electronics and electrical equipment. These three sectors taken together account for more than 50 per cent of the total foreign direct investment. In that sense, the sectors which have attracted foreign direct investment are those which are relevant from the point of view of the growth of the economy.

Portfolio investment is a new phenomenon that came to occupy a place in the capital account only after 1992-93. In 1993-94 and 1994-95 there was a substantial inflow of portfolio investment of the order of $ 3.5 billion and $ 3.8 billion respectively. Half of this amount came in the form of GDRs and ADRs while the other half was investment in the stocks by foreign institutional investors. In the wake of the East Asian crisis, portfolio investment came down very sharply in 1997-98. Investment by FIIs fell down by about a billion dollar from the level reached in the previous year. In 1998-99 investment by FIIs turned negative to the extent of $ 390 million. This is once again as a consequence of the worldwide reaction to the events in the east Asian countries. However, portfolio investment picked up in 1999-2000 and stood at the level of $ 3 billion with investment by FIIs reaching $ 2.1 billion. Looking at the trends in foreign direct investment and in portfolio investment, it comes out clearly that while the flow in the form of direct investment was steady, portfolio investment had been somewhat volatile.

Table 24.4

Foreign Investment Inflows of India

(US $ million)

	1990-91	1991-92	1992-93	1993-94	1994-95	1995-96	1996-97	1997-98	1998-99	1999-2000
A Direct investment	97	129	315	586	1314	2144	2821	3557	2462	2155
a. Government (SIA/FIPB)	-	66	222	280	701	1249	1922	2754	1821	1410
b. RBI	-	-	42	89	171	169	135	202	179	171
c. NRI	-	63	51	217	442	715	639	241	62	84
d. Acquisition of shares	-	-	-	-	-	11	125	360	400	490
B Portfolio investment	6	4	244	3567	3824	2748	3312	1828	-61	3026
a. GDRs/ADRs	-	-	240	1520	2082	683	1366	645	270	768
b. FIIs	-	-	1	1665	1503	2009	1926	979	-390	2135
c. Offshore funds and others	6	4	3	382	239	56	20	204	59	123
Total (A+B)	103	133	559	4153	5138	4892	6133	5385	2401	5181

Source: RBI Bulletin, October 2000.

Foreign direct investment has always been preferred by countries because of its long-term commitment. It also generally adds to the productive capacity of the capital receiving countries. Foreign direct investment set a new record in 1999 when global inflows touched $ 865 billion. FDI flows to developing countries reached a level of $ 208 billion. This was an increase of 16 per cent over 1998. The *World Investment Report* 2000 mentions that over the period 1991-1999, 94 per cent of the 1,035 changes worldwide in the laws governing foreign direct investment created a more favourable framework for FDI. The driving force behind FDI flows among industrial countries is mergers and acquisitions (M&As). Such acquisitions account for a substantial share of total flows. Certain concerns have been expressed about cross border, M&As. It is felt that entry through the takeover of domestic firms is less beneficial for economic development. At the heart of these concerns is that foreign acquisitions do not add to the productive capacity but simply transfer ownership and control from domestic to foreign hands. It is also feared that such acquisitions may reduce competition in domestic markets. A concern from the political angle is that such acquisitions can lead to strategic firms or even entire industries falling under foreign control. The argument that M&As do not add to the productive capacity applies only at the initial stage, cross border M&As are often followed by consequential investments by the foreign acquirers. Therefore, over the long term M&As can lead to enhanced investment in production just as greenfield FDI does. Also even initially when the domestic firms are acquired by the foreign firms, it releases funds in the hands of domestic firms which may utilise these funds for further investment elsewhere. This possibility must also be taken into account while looking at the impact on the enhancement of productive capacity. In fact, the impact of FDI on the capital receiving country is not easy to distinguish by mode of entry, once the initial period is passed. In looking at this problem from the Indian angle, available data indicate that acquisition of shares as part of direct investment has been a negligible proportion of the total. In the five-year period beginning 1995-1996, the total direct investment in the country amounted to $ 13.1 billion. Of this, the acquisition of shares amounted to $ 1.3 billion which is roughly 10 per cent of the total. While in some individual industries the share of foreign firms might have increased because of acquisition, by and large most of the foreign direct investment to India has been green field investment. In this context it is also interesting to note that FDI inflow into India is very small as compared with many other countries. While the total foreign direct investment over the entire 90s in India has been of the order of $ 15 billion, the inflow into China in 1994 alone has been $ 33.8 billion

(Table 24.5). During 1994-1999, China received $ 238 billion of direct investment. In comparison, the inflow into India pales into insignificance. Malaysia received during this period $ 30.4 billion. Thailand, Korea and Indonesia have received $ 22.9 billion, $ 23.3 billion and $ 13.6 billion respectively. As mentioned earlier, the foreign direct investment that has come to India has gone into areas which are of critical significance to India. Given the worldwide situation, there is

Table 24.5

FDI Inflows to Asia

(US $ million)

Region/Economy	1994	1995	1996	1997	1998	1999
South, East and South-East Asia	65954	71654	87952	93518	87158	96148
Of which						
Bangladesh	11	2	14	141	308	150
Brunei Darussalam	6	13	11	5	4	5
Cambodia	69	151	294	168	121	135
China	33787	35849	40180	44236	43751	40400
Hong Kong, China	7828	6213	10460	11368	14776	23068
India	973	2144	2426	3577	2635	2168
Indonesia	2109	4346	6194	4677	-356	-3270
Korea, Republic of	991	1357	2308	3088	5215	10340
Lao Peoples Democratic Republic	59	88	128	86	45	79
Macau, China	4	2	6	3	-	1
Malaysia	4581	5816	7296	6513	2700	3532
Maldives	9	7	9	11	12	10
Mongolia	7	10	16	25	19	30
Myanmar	126	277	310	387	315	300
Nepal	7	8	19	23	12	132
Pakistan	419	719	918	713	507	531
The Philippines	1591	1459	1520	1249	1752	737
Singapore	8550	7206	8984	8085	5493	6984
Sri Lanka	166	65	133	435	206	202
Taiwan	1375	1559	1864	2248	222	2926
Thailand	1343	2000	2405	3732	7449	6078
Vietnam	1936	2349	2455	2745	1972	1609

Source: World Investment Report, 2000.

no reason to be apologetic about encouraging the flow of foreign direct investment. While some inflows may go into inessential areas, by and large given an appropriate policy environment, foreign direct investment can be channelled to supplement Indian capital in sectors which coincide with national priorities.

The nineties witnessed large private capital flows to emerging markets. Some countries have gained immensely by capital inflows which have helped them to grow faster. It should not be forgotten that the five countries caught in the East Asian crisis had benefited greatly for almost a decade by large capital inflows. At the peak, net private capital inflows accounted for as much as 17.4 per cent of the GDP in Malaysia in 1993 and 12.5 per cent of the GDP in Thailand in 1995. While foreign direct investment has remained steady, portfolio investment and banking inflows have fluctuated. In the east Asian situation, even after the advent of the crisis, direct investment and portfolio investment remained positive. It was only banking flows which turned negative. They continue to remain negative even now. Opening up of capital account need not preclude the imposition of moderate controls, either price-based or regulatory, of capital flows. Controls should be selective, designed to achieve the specific objective of containing speculative flows. Controls should not be disruptive or dislocate genuine trade related activities. The Asian crisis is not an argument against capital account liberalisation. Capital account liberalisation is not a discrete event. It is a process and should be done in stages. The scope for raising resources and investing can be steadily expanded. An important lesson to draw from the recent events in Asia and elsewhere is that capital account liberalisation and reform of the financial system should move in tandem. The Indian system already operates with a number of capital controls. If anything, we should move towards a more liberalised regime, even as the regulatory system of the financial sector keeps improving. India as a country must take full advantage of the global changes in capital flows and attract not only more but also high quality investment which has strong links to the domestic economy, export orientation and advanced technology.

References

Baily, Martin N. et al., (2000). "The Colour of Hot Money", *Foreign Affairs*, March/April.

Bhagwati, J. (1998). "The Capital Myth: The Difference between Trade in Widgets and Dollars", *Foreign Affairs* 77: 7-12.

Camdessus, Michel (1998). "The IMF's Role in Today's Globalised World", Address to the IMF-Bundesbank Symposium. Frankfurt, Germany. July 2.

Commonwealth Secretariat (1998). *Protecting against Volatile Capital Flows*. A report of the Commonwealth Expert Group on Protecting Countries against the Destabilising Effects of Volatile capital flows. London, UK.

Fischer, Stanley (1998). "The Asian Crisis: A View from the IMF", address at the Midwinter Conference of the Bankers' Association for Foreign Trade. Washington DC, January 22.

Institute of International Finance (2000). *Capital Flows to Emerging Market Economies*. September.

International Monetary Fund (2000). *World Economic Outlook*. Washington DC: International Monetary Fund. May.

Krugman, Paul (1994). "The Myth of Asia's Miracle", *Foreign Affairs*, November/December.

—— (1998). "Saving Asia: It's Time to Get Radical", *Fortune*: 33-38, September 7.

Nukul Commission Report (1998). *Analysis and Evaluation of Facts behind Thailand's Economic Crisis*.

Rangarajan, C. (1994). "Capital Flows and Developing Countries: The Indian Experience", Keynote address at the *Global Asset Management Conference*. Hong Kong, October 27. Included in C. Rangarajan (1998). *Indian Economy: Essays on Money and Finance*. New Delhi: UBSPD.

Rangarajan, C. and A. Prasad (1999). "Capital Account Liberalisation and Controls: Lessons from the East Asian Crisis", ICRA Bulletin, *Money & Finance* 9, April-June, included in C. Rangarajan (2000). *Perspectives on Indian Economy*. New Delhi: UBSPD.

Reddy, Y.V. (1998). "Asian Crisis: Asking the Right Questions", Speech delivered at India International Centre, New Delhi.

Stiglitz, J. (1998). "The Role of International Financial Institutions in the Current Global Economy", Address to the Chicago Council on Foreign Relations. Chicago. February 27.

UNCTAD (2000). *Trade and Development Report, 2000*. New York and Geneva: United Nations.

United Nations (2000). *World Investment Report: Cross Border Mergers and Acquisitions and Development*. New York and Geneva.

World Bank (1998). *Global Development Finance*. Washington DC.

This paper is the text of the Sir Purshotamdas Thakurdas Memorial Lecture delivered by the author in November 2000. The author is thankful to A. Prasad and K.U.B. Rao for their help in the writing of the paper.

Economic and Political Weekly, December 9-15, 2000.

25 | The Financial Crisis and its Fallout

The new year is opening on a sombre mood. The world is passing through a difficult time. More so, the developed world. The industrially advanced countries are now officially in recession, having had two consecutive quarters of negative growth. It is not known at this stage how long will this recession last and how deep will it be. This will be perhaps the deepest recession in the post-Second World War Period.

The impact of the financial crisis is felt by the developing economies as well. Growth is slowing down in all these countries. India's growth rate in the current year will be around 7 per cent as compared to 9 per cent in the previous year. Prospects for 2009-10 do not appear to be better than that for this year. While in the current year, the first half escaped the impact of global recession, in the next year the impact will be felt throughout the year. Globalisation spreads both prosperity and distress. The contagion works both ways.

Evolution of the Crisis

The international financial crisis originated in the sub-prime mortgage crisis which surfaced nearly two years ago in the US With interest rates rising and home prices falling, there was a sharp jump in defaults and foreclosures. However, this would have remained as a purely mortgage market crisis but for the fact that these sub-prime mortgages were securitised and packaged into products that were rated as investments grade. Once doubts about these assets arose they turned illiquid; it also became very hard to price them. As a result, it started affecting a host of institutions which had invested in these products. These institutions were not confined to the US alone. Financial institutions in Europe and to a much lesser extent in East Asia had such assets on their books. With the failure of a few leading institutions and most notably Lehman Brothers, the entire financial system was enveloped into an acute crisis. There was mutual distrust among the financial institutions which led to freezing up of several markets including the overnight inter-bank market. Many think today that letting the Lehman Brothers to fail was a great mistake. The crisis in the financial system has now moved to affect the real sector in a significant way.

Regulatory Failure

What stands out glaringly in the current episode is the regulatory failure. The regulatory failure was three-fold. First, the regulation was soft and unfocused on segments of the market which should have been closely regulated. Second, some parts of the financial system were either loosely regulated or were not regulated at all, a factor which led to "regulatory arbitrage" with funds moving more towards the unregulated segments.

The third failure lies in the imperfect understanding of the implications of various derivative products. In one sense, derivative products are a natural corollary of financial development. They meet a felt need. However, if the derivative products become too complex to discern where the risk lies, they become a major source of concern. Rating agencies in the present episode were irresponsible in creating a booming market in suspect derivative products. Quite clearly, there was a mismatch between financial innovation and the ability of the regulators to monitor them. It is ironic that such a regulatory failure should have occurred at a time when intense discussions were being held in Basel and elsewhere to put in place a sound regulatory framework.

Immediate Tasks

The immediate tasks before the authorities in the developed world are two-fold. One is to fix the financial system and the other is to maintain the aggregate demand at a high enough level to stimulate the real sector. Since it is the tail of the financial system that is wagging the dog of the economy, the first priority is to take care of the financial system and this is being done in a number of ways. Liquidity is being provided to key institutions which are locked into assets that cannot be easily realised. In the US, the Federal Reserve has lowered the policy rate to near zero. It has also injected liquidity in an abundant measure. Consequently, the balance sheet of the Federal Reserve has expanded from $900 billion to $2.2 trillion. The recovery package of $700 billion approved by the US Congress is being utilised to inject more capital into banks and other institutions. Whether the package will be used to buy distressed assets is not clear at the moment. Some think that buying the assets is important because this will lead to revival of markets such as housing. To stimulate the economy, a massive revival package is being thought of in the U.S. This is a straightforward application of the Keynesian prescription. It is expected that Mr. Obama will unveil such a package after his assumption as President.

Medium Term Concerns

Even as these immediate tasks are addressed, there are medium term concerns. Many of the weaknesses of the financial system were developed in an environment of very low interest rates. Pushing interest rates below a level that is not sustainable can also have its consequences. The U.S. has been incurring heavy current account deficits year after year for a decade or so. While analysts have been pointing out to the danger of such a situation, the authorities have been brushing aside these concerns by saying that the U.S. was the desired destination for the investors. But the danger of such a situation is that once there is loss of confidence, it can have serious consequences. The U.S. must address this issue. Closely related to this is the issue of leverage. Almost every segment of the U.S. society including households is a net borrower. Many of the institutions that have fallen into trouble in the current episode are those which were highly leveraged. The net savings rate of the household sector stands negative. It is true that in a globalised system a country's investment rate is not solely determined by its savings rate. Nevertheless, the extent of leverage is an issue which regulators and policy makers must pay attention, if financial stability is to be achieved.

Impact on India

The Indian financial system is not directly exposed to the 'toxic' or 'distressed' assets of the developed world. This is not surprising since Indian banks have very few branches abroad. However, the indirect impact on the economy because of the recession abroad is very much there. The 'decoupling' theory does not hold good.

The indirect impact is felt both through trade and capital flows. The fall in international commodity prices and more particularly crude oil will reduce the import bill from previous estimates. The import growth rate this year may be around 20 per cent. The recession abroad will have an adverse effect on our exports of goods and services. The overall effect will be to take the current account deficit in 2008-09 to around 2.5 per cent of GDP. The decline in growth rate in exports will affect strongly some sectors where exports constitute a significant proportion of the total production. In contrast, to the strong inflow of over $100 billion last year, this year may not see any net increase in capital flows. Portfolio capital has already turned negative, with a significant impact on the stock market. Indian firms may also experience difficulties in raising money abroad. All this will impact the exchange rate. However, draw down of reserves would moderate the impact.

Monetary and Fiscal Actions

The Indian financial system has not been affected in the same way the financial system abroad has been affected for reasons already explained. However, there is the impact of the drying up of liquidity because of the fall in reserves. The inability of Indian firms to raise funds abroad, including trade credit, puts pressure on the domestic banking system for more credit. It is, in this context, one must view the actions of the Reserve Bank in expanding liquidity. Reduction of the CRR and repo and reverse repo rates are steps in the right direction. It is necessary for the RBI to watch the liquidity situation and take such actions as are necessary. It is being pointed out that the actions of the RBI have not percolated to the ground level. People point to the slow growth in credit. Is this a case of "taking the horse to the pond but cannot compel it to drink?". The role of the Reserve Bank of India is to create an environment in which additional credit can be made available.

Our fiscal actions to stimulate the economy have taken two forms. One is to cut excise duty and the second is to enlarge government expenditure. Both should lead to stimulating aggregate demand. It depends finally on whether the additional expenditures planned are actually incurred. Also we need to look at the composition of expenditure and effectiveness of expenditures. "Digging holes and filling them up" is not a right prescription. Expenditures should be biased towards investment so that capacities can be created which can facilitate growth later. That public spending should remain at a high level in a situation like the present one is not a matter for dispute. With the two Supplementary Grants approved by the Parliament, perhaps the fiscal deficit in the current year will exceed 5 per cent of GDP, at least 2 percentage points above the FRBM target. While it is correct to argue that the fiscal deficit target should be an average over the cycle, we need to remember that even in boom years we have not been able to hold the deficit at the target level. Keeping the target as a cyclical average is a good guidance in the medium term.

It is contended by some that India "escaped" from a serious impact of the financial crisis because financial sector reforms were not pushed forward. This is a false assertion. The financial sector reforms in India are intended to improve the efficiency of the financial system. Had we pushed hard in this direction, it would not have had any adverse effect. The shock waves produced by the financial crisis will have their own effect on the structure of capitalism. Acceptable capitalism would require more regulation. Run-a-way financial innovations that are dysfunctional do more harm than good.

Index

A

Abel, Andrew B.N. 115
accountability 188, 190
  fiduciary 219
  question of 221
Achilles heel of the crisis 232
administrative machinery 244
Administrative Reforms Commission 223
Administrative Statistical System 253
advantage, comparative 237, 349
Africa/African 185, 194, 355
  Sub-Saharan 185
    chronic poverty in 170
Aggarwal, A. 286
Agricultural and Livestock Censuses 248
agricultural/agriculture 167, 203, 211, 273, 358
  and allied sectors, elasticity for 207
  growth
    accelerating 173
    in employment, share of 199
    rate 207
      deceleration in 288
    stepping up 169
  productivity, low 325
  sector 166
All-India Council of Technical Education 257
All-India Educational Survey 257

American Depository Receipts 281
Andhra Pradesh 182
Andhra Pradesh Electricity Reform Act 329
Annual Survey of Industries 249
Arif, R.R. 40, 43
Asia/Asian 185
  chronic poverty in Sub-Saharan South 170
  countries, experience of the East 231
  crisis 390, 402
    causes of the 391
  economies, meltdown in the East 232
  South 185
asset/s
  creation 222
  prices 80
  liability management 232
  non-performing 318
auction system 36
Australia 126
Austrian school 227
autonomy
  provincial 124
  sub-national 124

B

backlash effects 233
backward linkages 167
Balakrishnan, Pulapre 286

balance of payments 35
   capital account of India's 398
   crisis 35
     of 1991 234, 395
   meltdown 164
   statistics 262
Bank of International Settlements 69
Bank of Japan 93
Bank of Thailand 391
bank/banking
   crises 62
   flows 387
   nationalisation in 1969 34, 317
   profitability levels 301
   rate 37
   sector reform 81, 306
   SHG linkage programme 314
   vulnerability of 64
Barro, Robert 39
Barth, Martha 376
Basel Capital Accord 67, 406
   Basel-I 67, 303
   Basel-II 68, 70, 303
   new 69
Berger, Allen N. 63
Bergsten, C. Fred 287, 362
Bernanke, Ben 369, 373
Bhagwati, J. 392, 393
Bihar 182
Blair, Tony 236
Blue Box 361
Borio, Claudio 63
borrowers, small 309
borrowings, small 309
Budget documents 104
budgetary support, gross 85
budgeting
   demand based 223
   outcome 190, 191
   output 191

Bundesbank 38
business
   correspondent model 325
   cycle 354
   facilitator model 325

C

CAG Report on
   Union Government 104
   Union Finances 106
Canada 126
capacity building 219
capital
   account
     liberalisation 46, 402
       process of 396
       risks of 392
   adequacy 298, 303
     ratio 35, 66, 67, 74, 317
   controls 89, 90, 393
   economies, private 230
   expenditure/s 91
     relative to GDP 135
   flows 349, 385, 386, 388, 408
     benefits of 389
     composition of 387
     controls over 394
     role of 385
     to emerging market 402
   formation 267
   inflows 36, 388
   issues 264
   market 351
   mobility 349, 388
     free 354
   movement of 346
   nature of 387
   outflows 51
   output ratio 234

capital *(...contd...)*
  physical 185
  portfolio 408
capitalism 229
  acceptable 409
  structure of 409
Caruana, Jaime 68
cash reserve ratio 35, 112, 317
Census Commissioner of India 256
Central Bank/s 80
  autonomy of 48
Central Board of Direct Taxes 262
Central Electricity Regulatory Commission Act 328
Central Processor Unit 312
Central Regulatory body 328
Central Statistical Organisation (CSO) 148, 243, 256, 258, 260, 261, 269
centralisation 124
certificate of deposits 261
Chakravarty, Sukhamoy 35, 39, 228
Chakravarty Committee 41, 42
Chile 393
China 360, 362, 370, 401
Chinn, Menzie 373, 374, 376
commercial banks 33, 260, 305, 308, 323, 325
commercial papers 261
Committee on Financial Inclusion 309, 313, 314
commodity prices, international 408
communication technologies 362
Communist Party 233
communist system 232
community participation 181
competition, perfect 229
competition law 188
competitiveness, international 165
Compulsory Provident Fund Cum Pension Scheme 340, 341

Consolidated Banking Statistics 260
Constitution 126, 133
  73rd Amendments 127, 190, 254
  74th Amendments 127, 190, 254
  80th Amendment 127
Consumer Price Index 263
consumption externalities 227
controls
  quantitative 357
    dismantling of 395
Cooper, Richard 368
coordination, vertical 243, 269
Corporate Index Number 264
corporate sector, private 267
corruption 191, 192, 194
  combating 188, 194
  incidence of 193
  opportunities for 193, 194
credit
  allocation of 36
  delivery of 307
  delivery system 308
  provision of 304
crisis
  management 78
  prevention 78
Crockett, Andrew 47, 62
crop
  area forecasts 248
  statistics 246
current account 357
  convertibility 46
  deficit 95, 349, 358, 378
    in the US 367, 370, 372
    of India 396

D

data
  collection 241
  gaps 242

debt
  accumulation of 99, 115
    process, intra-year variability in the 110
  ceiling 91
  change in outstanding 102
  crisis in Latin America 185
  dynamics 95, 109
  GDP ratio 88, 97, 99, 107-109, 115, 116, 120, 121, 152
    central 112
    combined 152
    rising 138
  instruments 63
  relative to GDP, growth of 100
  service obligations 91
  servicing 90
    burden 89
  sustainability 97
decentralisation 123, 124, 129, 190, 191
  democratic 254
decoupling theory 408
deficit/s
  appropriate level of fiscal 94, 137
  burgeoning fiscal 93
  cumulated primary 99, 107, 115
  derived fiscal 105, 106
  derived primary 107
  excessive fiscal 168
  financing, role of 34
  GDP ratio, primary 116
  level, advisable fiscal 89
  monetisation of the 36
    fiscal 35
  primary 96, 107, 136
  right level of fiscal 136
  quality of fiscal 135
  share of revenue deficit in fiscal 88
  sustainable levels of fiscal 136
  target, zero revenue 96

deficit/s (...contd...)
  unrestrained fiscal 95
  year-on-year 88
  zero revenue 91
delivery systems 219
demand
  aggregate 93
  diversified 232
demographic changes 339
Department of Agricultural Research and Education 257
Department of Company Affairs 261
Department of Health 257
Department of Industrial Policy and Promotion (DIPP) 250
deregulation 165
  of financial markets 258, 385
  of interest rates 317
developed
  countries 273
  world 406
developing
  countries 33, 37, 77, 333, 346, 351, 360, 362
    aggregate world output of 355
    share of 354
  economies/economy 175, 273, 405
development 175, 183
  aim of 227
  balanced regional 175
  challenge of 183
  economics 33
  social 178
  strategy of 183
  sustainable 175
devolution formulae 151
digital divide 352
Directorates of Economic and Statistics 267
distribution, equitable 175
diversification 75, 335

Doha 361
Dooley, Michael 368
Dreze, J. 228
dualism 124
Duisenberg, Willem F. 38

E

e-commerce 251
e-governance systems 193
East Asia/Asian 170, 185
   crisis 37, 46, 62, 350, 351, 385, 389, 391, 395, 396, 399
East India Company Syndrome 350
economic/economy 178
   commanding heights of the 235
   crisis in 1991 35
   development 225
      socio 306
   disparities 163
   globalised 353
   globalisation 349
   growth 41, 163, 164, 170, 171, 178, 182, 185, 285, 334
      accelerated 182
      evolution of thought on 175
      indicators of 176
      issue of 231
      process of 33, 175, 233
   integration 345
   of the west, market-based 230
   open 280
   planning 124, 230
      Approach Paper to the Eleventh Plan 85
      Eighth Plan 234, 276
      First Plan 34, 233
      Second Five Year Plan 273
   policy
      environment 131
      new 179, 276
      objectives of 39

economic/economy (...contd...)
   reform/s 92, 165, 187, 225
      agenda 165
      implementation of 193
      process of our 166
   world 367
economies, success story of the command 230
economies, third world 229
Edwards, Sebastian 369
education, universal elementary 231
efficiency, comparative 238
elasticity, aggregate 209
electricity
   generation 327
   sector 328
employment
   elasticities/elasticity 198, 202, 204, 205, 207
      of the service sector 287
      sectoral 207
   exchanges, role of 257
   full 227, 229
   growth 197, 207, 212
      rate 209
   opportunities 163
   scenario 212
   self 200
   share of the manufacturing sector in 200
   organised 201
   quality of 173, 201, 212
Employment Guarantee Scheme (EGS) 215, 219, 220
   implementation of the 222
environment/environmental
   conservation of 258
   controlled 193
   degradation 175
   statistics 258

equalisation 126, 139
  approach 151, 157
equity 138
  and growth 179
  concerns, inter-temporal 90
  issues 128, 148
  markets 65
Euroarea 378
European Central Bank 38, 48
European Union 354, 367
  countries 358
Evans, Owen 73
exchange
  controls 264
  rate
    crises 62
    dollar 372
    dual 395
    management 45, 47, 77, 303
    nominal 389
    of the rupee 358
    regime 395
      flexible 353
    system
      market determined 46
expenditure
  effect of public 231
  ratio, human 180
export/s
  pessimism 164
  promotion 231, 232
  world 354
external sector statistics 259, 262
Extra Budgetary Resources 262

F

facilitator 236
  role 235
family welfare statistics 255

farm households 307
farmers
  marginal 325
  sub-marginal 309, 325
federal
  fiscal systems 133, 155
  reserve 407
  structure 241
federalism 123, 124, 129
  centralising 124
  competitive 129
  cooperative 124
  creative 124
  evolution of 124
  rationale of 124
Feldstein, Martin 379
Fifth Central Pay Commission 86, 156
FIIs 399
Finance Commission/s 127, 128 133, 139, 146, 155
  Eleventh Finance Commission 127, 133, 136, 152, 157
  Ninth Finance Commission 134, 146
  Seventh Finance Commission 139, 146
  Sixth Finance Commissions 146
  Tenth Finance Commission 135, 146, 156
  Twelfth Finance Commission 85, 95, 127, 133, 154, 155, 157, 158, 168, 181
financial
  assets 137
  crises/crisis 61, 62, 258, 409
    contagion of 351
    impact of the 405
    international 405
  derivatives 63
  entities 300

financial (...contd...)
  flows 63, 351
    cross-border 259
  inclusion 307, 315
  infrastructure 79
  innovation/s 258, 406
  instability 61
  institutions 33, 63, 64, 66, 69, 79, 80, 81, 260, 333, 335
    regulation of 75
  intermediaries 300
  intermediation 31, 295, 297
    theory 374
  liberalisation 300
  markets 232, 259, 385
  products 167
  repression 61, 296
  sector 232
    competitive 317
    developmental role of the 61
    growth of 61
    informal 260
    reform/s 35, 37, 295, 297, 299, 300, 317, 409
      programme, ongoing 317
    weaknesses in the 232
  services 75, 307
  stability 47, 51, 61, 64, 76, 79, 81, 258, 358, 407
  statistics 260
    harmonisation of 259
  strategy, global 304
  system/s 62, 295
    functioning of the 77
    organised 308
    performance of the 301
    stable 79
    streamlining 219
    weaknesses of the 407
firms, exit of 231

fiscal
  adjustment 90, 168
  autonomy 354
  consolidation 85, 155, 168, 169
  contraction 85, 91
  deficit/s 36, 77, 85, 87-91, 93, 94, 96, 97, 102, 106, 135, 137, 138, 159
    Centre and states, combined 137
    combined 86, 95
    continued 90
    target 409
  expansion 85, 90, 91
    argument 93
  federalism 125, 126, 131
    in India, roots of 127
  imprudence 129, 139
  policies/policy 153, 377
    counter-cyclical 96
    expansionary 90
  prudence 158
  reforms 121
  resources 341
  responsibility 96
    legislations 159
  restraint 85, 90
  sustainability 138
  transfers 128, 138, 139, 146
    to the states 146
  trends, overall 134
Fiscal Responsibility and Budget Management 48, 52, 85, 153, 299
Fischer, Stanley 392
Folkerts-Landau, David 368
food
  grains 273
  processing industry 167
  security 358
  shortages, chronic 166
forces of globalisation 123

foreign direct investment (FDI) 350, 399
  entry 350
  inflows 281
  net 386
foreign
  exchange 36
    market/s 62, 65, 77, 79, 351
      volatility in the 351
    rate 77
    reserves 36, 46, 163, 358
  investment 356
    approach to 357
    policy 165, 357
    regime 395
  trade regime/s 45, 51
formal sector 340
Frankel, Jeffrey A. 346, 349, 351
FRBM Act 85, 95, 168, 409
FRBM target/s 86, 88, 90, 97
Freedom Movement 124
Friedman, Milton 32

G

G-22 recommendations 395
Garber, Peter 368
GDP
  annual growth rate in 176
  growth rate 100
  Index 182
    real 182
  non-tax revenue relative to 134
  ratio/s
    of debt to 95
    of revenue deficit to 135
Geithner, Timothy 369, 370
gender statistics 258
geography, end of 363
Gladwell, Malcolm 193
Global Depository Receipts 281

globalisation 169, 236, 306, 345, 346, 353, 362, 363
  benefits of 345
  challenges of 130, 364
  concerns about 347
  downside to 354
  era of 125
  gains and losses from 349
  growing 360
  impact of 123, 352
    on Indian industries 358
  implications of 345
  issue of 169
  managing 169
  pace of 346
gold standard mechanism 380
Goodhart, Charles A.E. 47, 76
Gorbachev, M. 232
governance 164
  characteristics of good 188
  process 123
  global 354
  good 170, 173, 185, 186, 195
government
  borrowing 90
  expenditure 180
  failure 232
  final consumption expenditure 267
  finances, restructuring 159
  intervention in production 231
  securities 35, 36
  non-democratic forms of 228
  quasi 303
  role of the 123, 187
  structure of 124
Government of India Acts of 1919 and 1935 127
Gram Panchayats 216, 219, 220
Gram Sabhas 219

Great Depression of the 1930s 93, 227
Green Box 361
Greenspan, Alan 368
growth 32, 405
   accelerating 85
   and equity 183
   dynamics of 176
   global 375
   interest rate differential 102, 107, 108, 109, 136
   jobless 198
   phase, high 295
   rate/s 136, 137
      industrial production 250
      developing countries 355
      labour force 205, 207
      nominal 110
      real 99, 115
      service sector 281
      volatility 110
   sources of output 285
   trickle down effect of 227

H

Haryana 182
Hausmann, Ricardo 369
Hayek, Fredrich 227
Health Management Information System 255
herd mentality 388
Hoggarth, Glenn 61
Hong Kong 358
human
   development 176, 178, 183
      countries, medium 182
      Index 177, 182
         global 182
         indicators 179
      process of 257

human *(contd...)*
   resource development 231, 235
   skills, specialised 352

I

IDBI 262
IMF 370
imbalance/s
   adjusting global 378
   correction in the 374
   global 367, 372, 378, 381
   horizontal 126, 133, 154, 155, 157
   vertical 126, 133, 155, 156
import
   licensing 264
   substitution 274, 275, 356
      approach 234
      industrialisation regime 347
income
   developing countries, per capita 356
   inequitous distribution of 353
   transfers 179
   per capita 163
Independence struggle 124
Index of Industrial Production 250
India/Indian 126, 180
   agriculture 360
   Constitution 127, 133, 155
   economic
      policy towards foreign trade 274, 356
      reforms 165
   economy 234, 358
      performance of the 176
      post-independence 177
   growth rate 358, 405
   federal structure 130
   financial system 296, 306, 408
   statistical system 242-244, 269
   stock markets 358

Indian Public Finance Statistics 104
Indian Statistical Service 245
Indian System of Medicines and
  Homeopathy 255
indicators, social 163, 177
Indonesia 401
industrial
  agriculture relationship 273
  countries 38
  growth 273
  licensing 264, 275
  organisation 347
  production 241
Industrial Development and
  Regulation Act 250
Industrial Development Bank of India
  (IDBI) 260
Industrial Investments Bank of India
  104
industrial
  licencing, abolition of 92
  production
    decelerating trend in 288
    growth in 281
Industrial Policy of 1992 277
industrialisation 273, 274
  inward looking 274
  process 274, 275, 281
industrially advanced countries 333,
  358, 405
industries
  dereservation of 92
  heavy 273
inequality 352
infant mortality rate 242
inflation 43, 77, 91, 163
  control of 377
  rate/s 43, 341, 90
  expectations 44
  near-term 81
  pressures 33, 370

inflation (...contd...)
  stabilising 39
  threshold level of 41
informal sector 212
information
  public access to 191
  right to 190
  technology 243, 284
    role of 246
infrastructure 173
  deficit 167
  definition of 252
  development 169
  physical 89, 90
  sector 252
  social 90, 168, 236
institutional
  framework 37
  infrastructure 259
  mechanisms 189
  reforms 298
insurance 334
  contract 333
  industry 336
  market 335
  sector 260, 261
Insurance Regulatory and Development Authority (IRDA) 260, 261,
  262, 335, 336, 342
intellectual property rights 361
inter-governmental
  flows 139
  transfers 126
interest
  effective 109
  payments 135
  rate/s 90, 91
    fluctuations 77
    in the US, low 374
    level of 44, 377

interest (...contd...)
    market determined 37
    nominal 109, 110, 138
    real 44, 45, 99, 112, 115
    structure
        administered 36, 37, 61, 300
        dismantling of the administered 50
        effective 115
        falling nominal 136
        global 92
intermediaries, auditing of 300
internal rating based approach (IRB) 69
International Standard Classification of Education 258
intervention, intensity of 238
intervention, quality of public 235
investment
    allocation of 231
    climate 163
    direct 238
    lumpy 231
    portfolio 350, 398, 399
    position, international 262
    rate, aggregate 159
Issing, Otmar 375, 377
Ito, Hiro 373, 376

J

Jalan, Bimal 46
Japan 367
Jeemol, Unni 198
Joshi, Himansu 43

K

Kamin, Steven 42
Kathuria, Vinish 285
Kautilya's Arthashastra 192
Kerala 182

Keynes/Keynesian 32, 227, 229
    doctrine 229
    effect 93
    macroeconomics 229
    paradigm 137
    prescription 137, 407
    world view 93
Khan, Mohsin S. 39
Knight, Frank 334
Knight, Malcolm 374
knowledge
    economy 163, 169
    intensive 352
Korea 401
    South 44, 231, 362
Krishna, Raj 193
Krugman, Paul 392
Kudremukh Iron Ore Project 104
Kumar, Nagesh 286

L

labour
    acts 257
    force 197, 212
        female participation in the 205
        growth rate 209
        total 207
    participation rate 197
Lahiri, A. 115
Laker, J.F. 80
land
    records 264
    use statistics 247
Lane, Philip 369
law, rule of 188, 189
Lehman Brothers 406
lender of last resort 78
Lerner, Abba P. 230
liabilities/liability, outstanding 102, 104, 106, 107

liberalisation 115, 165, 187
   financial sector 112
   period, post 281
   rationale for 190
licence-control regime 193
licensing
   machinery 234
   rationalisation of branch 317
life expectancy 163, 178, 182
   at birth 177
life insurance 333
Life Insurance Corporation 303
linkages, forward 167
liquidity 407
   adjustment facility 37
   excess 35
literacy
   rates 178
   female 177
Livestock Census, results of 16th 242
loan/s
   non-performing 301
   portfolio 62
Locational Banking Statistics 260
London

M

macroeconomic 258
   policies/policy 258
      environment 284
   principles 229
   stabilisation/stability 48, 86, 133, 136, 152, 187, 351
   variables 74
Maharashtra experience 221
Maizels, Alfred 346
Malaysia 358, 401
Mann, Catherine L. 368

market/markets 62, 123, 165
   access 360
   benefits of a large 124
   crisis, mortgage 405
   economies 187
   efficiency of 228
   emerging 387
   failure/s 187, 228, 231, 232
      instrumentalities for correcting 228
      nature of 228
   forces 227
   integration 46, 347
   interdependence of 62
   liquidity 37
   role of 123
   regulation of 232
   structure of 228, 229
Mastricht Treaty 94, 95
mergers and acquisitions, cross border 350
Mexican
   crisis in 1996 394
   episode 390
micro-finance 324
   institutions 313
Milesi-Ferretti, Gian Maria 369
Ministry of Agriculture 241
Ministry of Environment and Forests 258
Ministry of Finance 159, 260, 262
Ministry of Human Resource Development 257
Ministry of Labour 256
Ministry of Statistics and Programme Implementation 243, 244
Mises, Ludwig von 227
Mishkin, Frederic S. 42
monetary
   action 81

monetary (...contd...)
  aggregates 32, 43
  challenges for 31
  controls, indirect 37
  policy 35-37, 47
    actions, effectiveness of 79
    effectiveness of 79
    environment 36
    objectives of 31, 38, 39, 50
    role of 377
    tight 35
  statistics 260
  system, international 380
  targeting 32
money
  demand function for 32, 43
  reserve 34
monopolies, natural 188
mortgage crisis, sub-prime 405
Multi-Fibre Agreement 361
multiplier effect 93

N

Nachane, D.M. 67, 69
Nag, Ashok K. 43
nagarpalikas 254, 256
national accounts 241, 242
National Accounts Statistics (NAS) 254, 256, 264
  credibility of 265
National Advisory Board on Statistics 244
National Bank for Agriculture and Rural Development (NABARD) 260-262, 309, 310, 314, 324
National Commission on Statistics 244, 269
National Council of Teacher Education 257
National Industrial Classification 252, 260

National Rural Employment Guarantee Act 215
National Rural Financial Inclusion Plan 314
National Sample Survey/s 197, 242
National Sample Survey Organisation 256, 305
National Small Savings Fund 103
National Statistical Commission 268
National Statistical Organisation 245, 251
natural resources, distribution of 352
needs, basic 175, 176, 183, 227
Negotiable Instruments 299
Negotiable Instruments Act 2002 299
non-banking finance companies (NBFCs) 260, 261, 313
NSS surveys 217
  55th Round 198
  60th Round 198
  61st Round 197
NSSO data 207, 307

O

Obama, B. 407
Obstfeld, Maurice 369
OECD area 109
OECD countries 109
oil
  bonds 88
  crude 408
  prices 370
  producing countries 378
Oil Pool Account, winding up of the 104
openness, indicator of 358
organised sector 201
Osborne, David 188
Oscar Lange 230

Outcome Budget 181
outflows 388
overheating 171, 172
   disguised 80

P

panchayati raj institutions 216, 219
panchayats 127, 254, 255, 256
parliament 217
patronage 193
patwari agency 247
payment and settlement mechanism 76
payment crisis, external 164
performance parameters, social 176
pension/s 135
   funds 342
      management of 342
   scheme 339-341
people, migration of 346
PFCE 267
Phelps, Edmund S. 32
Phelps' golden rule 44
planning, micro level 242
Planning Commission 127, 139, 153, 159
polices/policy
   interventions 231
   pro-poor 179
   public 351
political
   federalism 125
   interference 189
   leadership, role of the 193
   structure 229
Pollard, Patricia 376
Population Census 254
portfolio investment, net 386
poverty
   alleviation programmes 178

poverty *(contd...)*
   eradication of 175
   line 178
   programmes, anti 186
   ratio 356
   reducing growth 163
   reduction 170, 185
power 253, 327
Prasad, A. 41
Prevention of Money Laundering Act 299
price
   discrimination 330
   indices 80, 241
   mechanism 32
   stabilisation/price stability 32, 33, 38, 39, 40, 41, 388
priority sector 33, 34, 36
private sector 123
production base 349
production or consumption externalities 230
productivity 163
   shocks 374
projects, planning of inter-sectoral 223
protectionism, rise in 370
Provident Fund 340
   Scheme 341
prudential indicators, macro 73, 74
prudential norms 35, 67
   adoption of 317
prudential regulation/s 75, 232, 300
Public Account of India 104
public expenditures 86
public finance/s 61, 86
   literature 94
   restructuring 133, 152
Public Provident Fund Scheme 341

public sector
    enterprises, proliferation of 164
    intervention 79
    investment 85

Q
Quantity Theory of Money 31

R
Rajan, Raghuram 373
Rangarajan, C. 33, 37, 39-41, 48, 49, 199, 204, 260
rank corelation coefficient 182
    with GDP Index 182
Rato, Rodrigo 376
Ravindran, G. 198, 207
real estate 80
real sector 77
rebalance, orderly global 375
Receipts Budget 103, 106, 107
    Central Government 102
recession 405
Reddy, Y.V. 351
reform facility, medium term 151, 154
Regional Rural Banks (RRBs) 261, 311, 314
Registrar General of India 255, 256
regulator 235, 236
regulatory 238
    failure 406
    framework 328
    role of the government 236
    system 342
Regulatory Commissions 331
rent seeking 193
research and development 286
Reserve Bank of India (RBI) 33, 34, 38, 72, 159, 242, 259, 262, 312, 408
    role of the 409

resource/s
    allocation of 124, 349
    availability 238
    endowments 171
    intensive 352
    optimal allocation of scarce 234
revenue
    account 135
        balance 135, 152
        non-plan 135
        plan 135
    deficit/s 86, 87, 90, 96
        combined 86
Reynolds, P. 116
Ricardian Equivalence 137
risk management 303, 304
    system 72
road transport 252
ROCs 264
Rogoff, Kenneth 369
Roubini, Nouriel 373, 375, 368, 369
rupee, devaluation of the 35, 45
rural
    branches 309
    credit 324, 325
        market 323
    development 180
    lending 309, 323
Russia 370
    collapse of communism in 232

S
safety nets 78, 79
Saggar, Mridul 43
Samantaraya, A. 41
Saporta, Victoria 61
Sarel, Michael 39
Saudi Arabia 370

saving/s 267
  by the household sector, gross 137
  collapse
    global 370
    glut, global 373
  household sector 137
  instruments 333
  over its investments, excess 95
  rate 234
    aggregate 159
    small 104
Schroder, Gerhard 233
Scotland 123
SEBs 328, 331
secondary sector 211
Securities and Exchange Board of India (SEBI) 260-262
Securitisation Act 298
security, internal 124
self-help groups 261
Sen, A. 228
Senhadji, A.S. 39
service sector 281
sharing, vertical 146
SHG-Bank linkage programme 310, 318
Shigehara, K. 109
Singapore 358
smart card 312
Smith, Adam 225, 226
social safety nets 341
  programmes 215
services, social 138
socialist
  economies 230
  regimes of the USSR and eastern Europe 229
software exports 251
Soviet bloc countries 347
Special Data Dissemination Standards 259

Sri Lanka 180
Srinivasan, Gopal 284
stability, macro 47
State Directorates of Economics and Statistics 242
State Electricity Boards (SEBs) 327
state
  and market, respective roles of 225, 232, 233, 237
  intervention 235, 238
    direct 227
    importance of 227
  level organisations 241
  minimalism 227
  nature of the 228
  ownership of means of production 164
  plan 153
  role of 123, 231, 236
  statistical systems 245
  terrorism 228
  versus market 225
statistical
  inference 241
  standards 242
  system 241
    national 254
statutory liquidity ratio (SLR) 34, 35, 112, 317
Stiglitz, Joseph E. 64, 66, 392
stock market 80
Streeten, Paul 237, 346
structural
  adjustment 165, 225
  constraints on growth 173
  imbalance 33
  reform/s 276, 378
    programmes 388
Sturzenegger, Federico 369
subsidies 231, 330
Sundaram, K. 199, 204, 207

T

T&D losses 329
tariff/s
  appropriate fixation of 331
  barriers 360
  fixation of 329
  rates 292, 357
    reduction in 292
    weighted average 358
    stability in 292
tax/taxes
  buoyancy 91
  devolution 133, 146, 151, 157
  GDP ratio 134, 156, 160
  indirect 134
  value added 130
Taylor, John B. 39
  rule 44
technological/technology 286
  changes 211, 363
  forces 346
  phenomenon 363
  modernisation 287
Thailand 401
Tobin tax 394
total factor productivity 212, 285
trade
  barriers to flow of 346
  borderless 236
  flows 46, 346
  international 349, 352
  liberalisation 92
  policy, inward looking 164
  practices, unfair 283
trading
  arrangements, international 364
  system
    global 283
    new 361

transfers
  horizontal 157
  vertical 139
transmission mechanism 32
  of monetary policy 76
transparency, degree of 193
Transparency International 193
treasury bills 36, 48
  ad hoc 51
Trivedi, Pushpa 285
Truman, Edwin M. 373, 377, 368, 369
trust laws, anti 236

U

Udell, Gregory F. 63
UNDP's Human Development Index 163
unemployment 205
  allowance 217, 219
UNESCO 258
United Kingdom 123
United States (US) 126, 354, 358, 362, 369, 407
  assets 370
  current account deficit 369, 371, 372, 373, 374, 376
  Federal Reserve 93
  fiscal deficit 375
  interest rates 367
Unni, Jeemol 207
UP 182
Upadhyay, G. 43
urbanisation 167
UTI 104

V

Vasudevan, A. 41
voluntary organisations, role of 237

W

wage
  bill 340
  goods 273
  rate
    minimum 215
    under the EGS 215
ways and means advances 36, 48
welfare
  economics 226
  function 138
  provider 235
wholesale price index 263

work on demand 223
workforce 205, 212
  activity status distribution 200
World Bank 359
World Trade Organisation 283, 360
  arrangements on Indian
  agriculture, impact of present 360
World War I, pre 346
World War II 346
  post 32, 346, 405

Z

Zyuganov, Gennady 233